My apologies to anyone who is worried about me. I'm still alive. I've also managed to lose 8 kg! Yay! Here's *World Trigger* volume 18.

—**Daisuke Ashihara, 2017**

Daisuke Ashihara began his manga career at the age of 27 when his manga *Room 303* won second place in the 75th Tezuka Awards. His first series, *Super Dog Rilienthal*, began serialization in *Weekly Shonen Jump* in 2009. *World Trigger* is his second serialized work in *Weekly Shonen Jump*. He is also the author of several shorter works, including the one-shots *Super Dog Rilienthal*, *Trigger Keeper* and *Elite Agent Jin*.

W RLD TRIGGER

WORLD TRIGGER VOL. 18
SHONEN JUMP Manga Edition

STORY AND ART BY DAISUKE ASHIHARA

Translation/Toshikazu Aizawa
Touch-Up Art & Lettering/Annaliese Christman
Design/Julian [JR] Robinson
Editor/Marlene First

Printed in the U.S.A.

Published by VIZ Media, LLC
P.O. Box 77010
San Francisco, CA 94107

10 9 8 7 6 5 4 3 2 1
First printing, January 2018

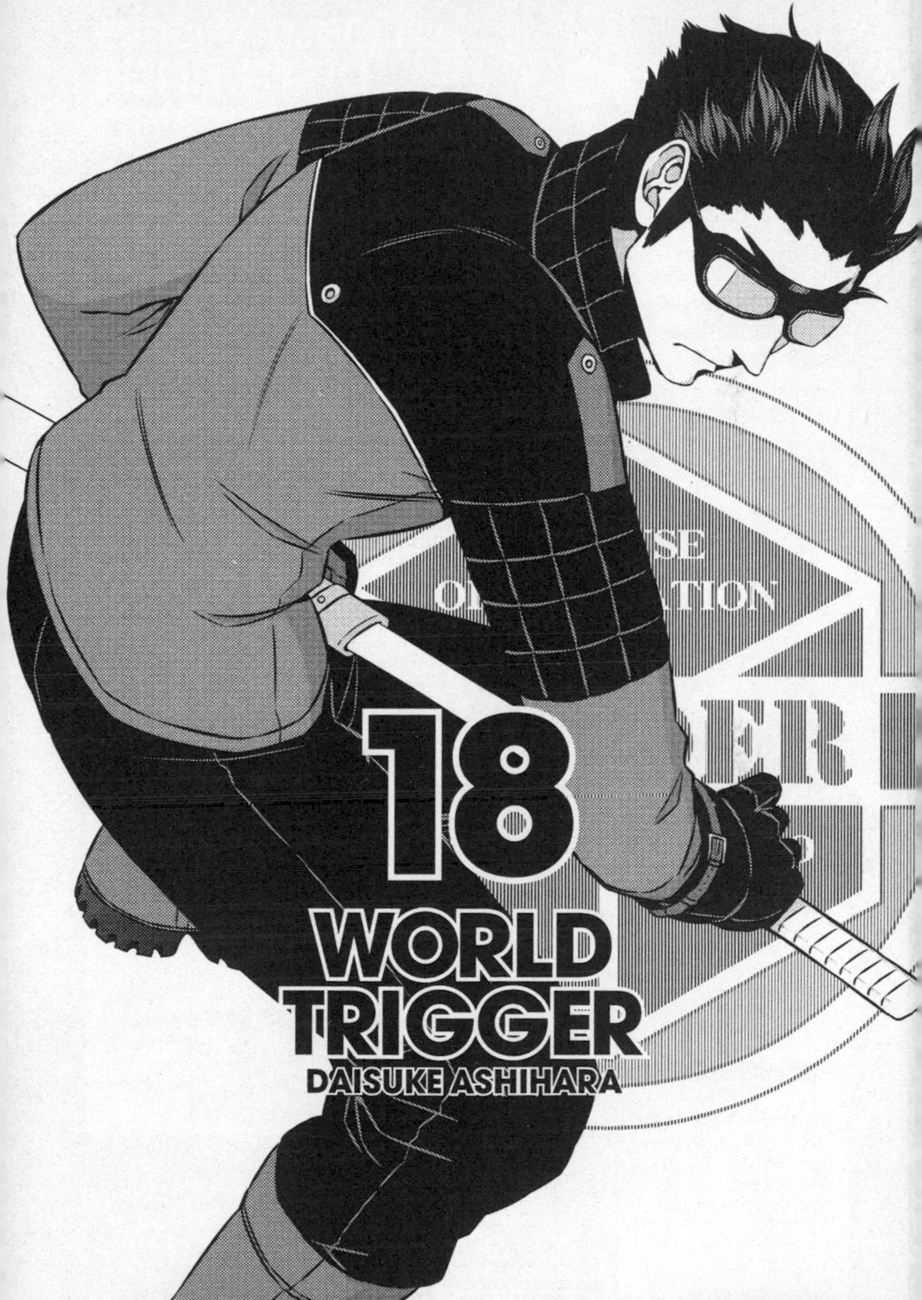

18

WORLD TRIGGER

DAISUKE ASHIHARA

SHONEN JUMP MANGA EDITION

WORLD TRIGGER DATA BASE

BORDER

An agency founded to protect the city's peace from Neighbors.

S-Rank Black Trigger Users (i.e. Tsukihiko Amo)

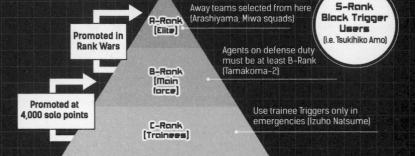

A-Rank [Elite] — Away teams selected from here (Arashiyama, Miwa squads)

Promoted in Rank Wars

B-Rank [Main force] — Agents on defense duty must be at least B-Rank (Tamakoma-2)

Promoted at 4,000 solo points

C-Rank [Trainees] — Use trainee Triggers only in emergencies (Izuho Natsume)

TRIGGER...
ON!!

TRIGGER

A technology created by Neighbors to manipulate Trion. Used mainly as weapons, Triggers come in various types.

ARE YOU INSANE?
ANYTHING BIGGER THAN THAT WOULD REQUIRE TOO MUCH TRION TO LAUNCH!
AWW.

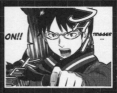

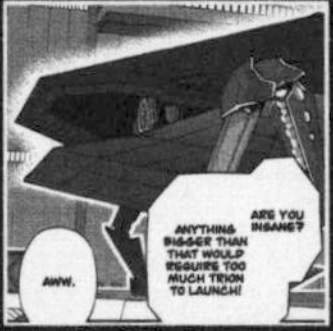

◀ Away mission ships also run on Trion.

POSITIONS

Border classifies them into three groups: Attacker, Gunner and Sniper.

Attacker

Close-range attacks. Weapons include: close-range Scorpions that are good for surprise attacks, the balanced Kogetsu sword, and the defense-heavy Raygust.

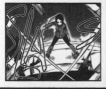

Gunner

Shoots from mid-range. There are several types of bullets, including multipurpose Asteroids, twisting Vipers, exploding Meteors, and tracking Hounds. People who don't use gun-shaped Triggers are called Shooters.

ASTEROID.

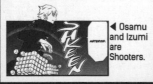

◀ Osamu and Izumi are Shooters.

Sniper

Fires from a long distance. There are three sniping rifles: the well-balanced Egret, the light and easy Lightning, and the powerful but unwieldy Ibis.

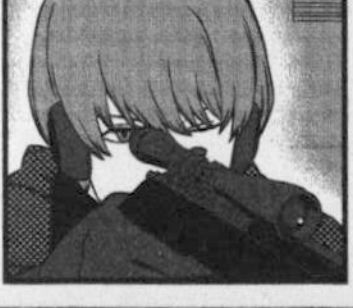

Operator

Supports combatants by relaying information such as enemy positions and abilities.

RANK WARS

Practice matches between Border agents. Promotions in Border are based on good results in the Rank Wars and defense duty achievements.

B-Rank agents are split into top, middle, and bottom groups. Three to four teams fight in a melee battle. Defeating an opposing squad member earns you one point and surviving to the end nets two points. Top teams from the previous season get a bonus.

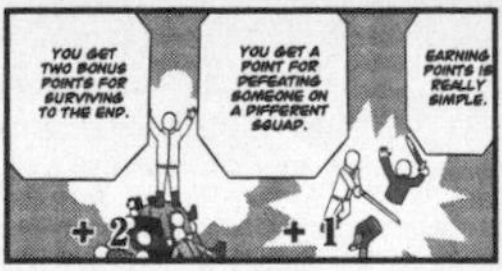
EARNING POINTS IS REALLY SIMPLE.
YOU GET A POINT FOR DEFEATING SOMEONE ON A DIFFERENT SQUAD.
YOU GET TWO BONUS POINTS FOR SURVIVING TO THE END.
+1
+2

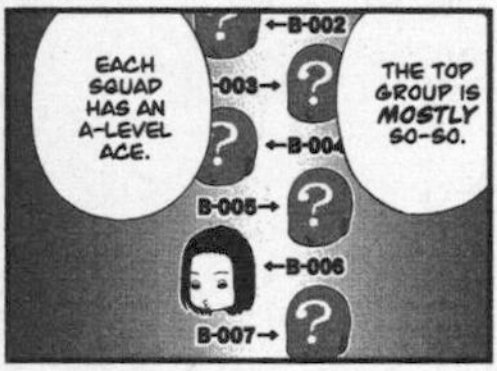
THE TOP GROUP IS MOSTLY SO-SO.
EACH SQUAD HAS AN A-LEVEL ACE.
←B-002
-003→
←B-004
B-005→
←B-006
B-007→

B-Rank middle groups have set strategies. Top groups all have an A-Rank level ace.

The lowest-ranked team in each match gets to pick the stage.

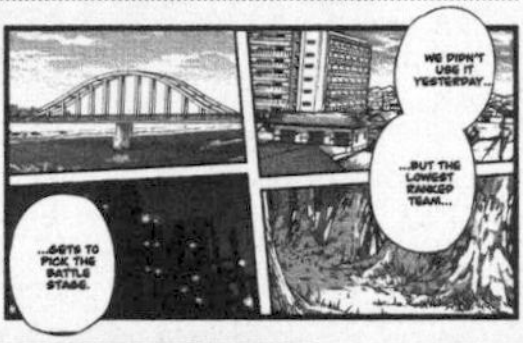
WE DIDN'T USE IT YESTERDAY...
...BUT THE LOWEST RANKED TEAM...
...GETS TO PICK THE BATTLE STAGE.

A-Rank

Top two B-Rank squads get to challenge A-Rank.

B-Rank

Agents ▶ (B-Rank and above) can't fight trainees (C-Rank) for points.

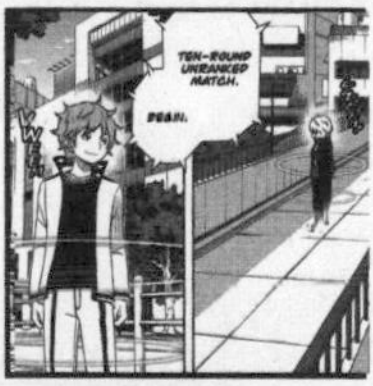
TEN-ROUND UNRANKED MATCH.
BEGIN.

C-Rank Wars are fought through solo matches. Beating someone with more points than you gets you a lot of points. On the other hand, beating someone with fewer points doesn't get you as many.

C-Rank

STORY

About four years ago, a Gate connecting to another dimension opened in Mikado City, leading to the appearance of invaders called Neighbors. After the establishment of the Border Defense Agency, people were able to return to their normal lives.

Osamu Mikumo is a junior high student who meets Yuma Kuga, a Neighbor. Yuma is targeted for capture by Border, but Tamakoma branch agent Yuichi Jin steps in to help. He convinces Yuma to join Border instead, then gives his Black Trigger to HQ in exchange for Yuma's enlistment. Now Osamu, Yuma and Osamu's friend Chika work toward making A-Rank together.

Aftokrator, the largest military nation in the Neighborhood, begins another large-scale invasion!! Border succeeds in driving them back, but over 30 C-Rank trainees are kidnapped in the process. Border implements more plans for away missions to retrieve the missing Agents.

Osamu's squad, Tamakoma-2, enters the Rank Wars for a chance to be chosen for away missions. The fifth round was about to begin when Border HQ came under attack by Galopoula, Aftokrator's subordinate nation. As the battle was coming to a close, Hyuse meets up with Reghindetz and defeats him. The Rank Wars Round 5 also comes to an end with Tamakoma-2 coming out on top. He also managed to convince the higher-ups at Border to allow Hyuse on his squad. And now, Round 6 is about to begin... and Tamakoma-2 faces off against Kakizaki and Katori Squads using a brand new wire technique!

WORLD TRIGGER CHARACTERS

TAMAKOMA BRANCH

Understanding toward Neighbors. Considered divergent from Border's main philosophy.

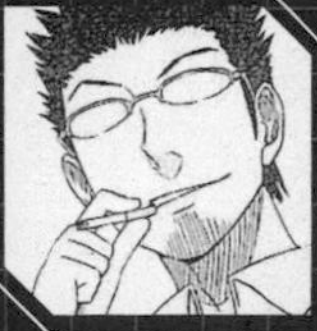

TAKUMI RINDO

Tamakoma Branch Director.

TAMAKOMA-2

Tamakoma's B-Rank squad, aiming to get promoted to A-Rank.

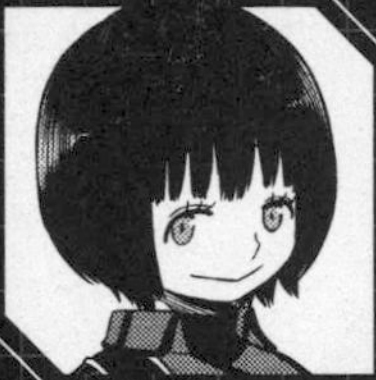

CHIKA AMATORI

Osamu's childhood friend. She has high Trion levels.

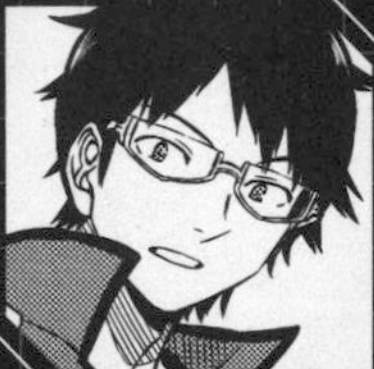

OSAMU MIKUMO

Ninth-grader who's compelled to help those in trouble. Captain of Tamakoma-2 (Mikumo squad).

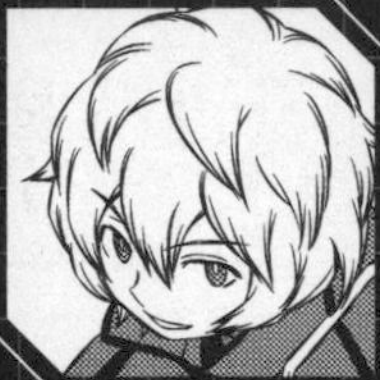

YUMA KUGA

A Neighbor who carries a Black Trigger.

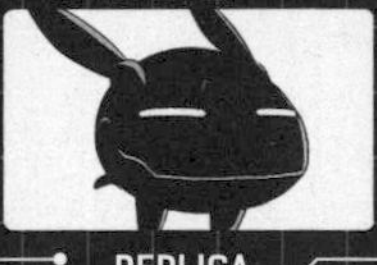

REPLICA

Yuma's chaperone. Missing after recent invasion.

TAMAKOMA-1

Tamakoma's A-Rank squad.

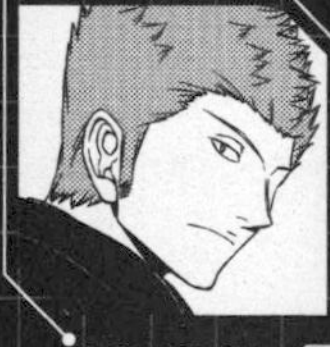

REIJI KIZAKI

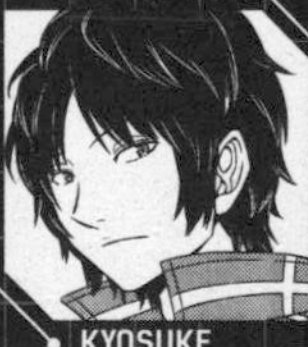

KYOSUKE KARASUMA

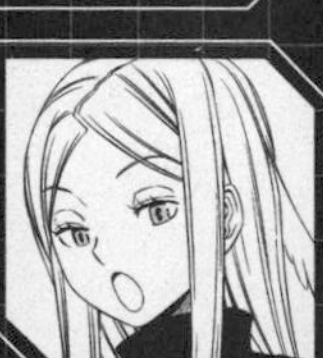

KIRIE KONAMI

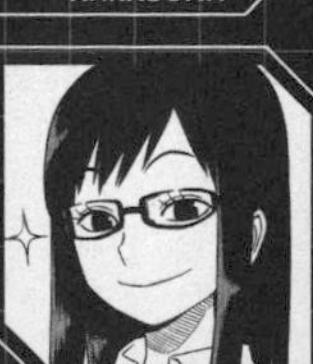

SHIORI USAMI

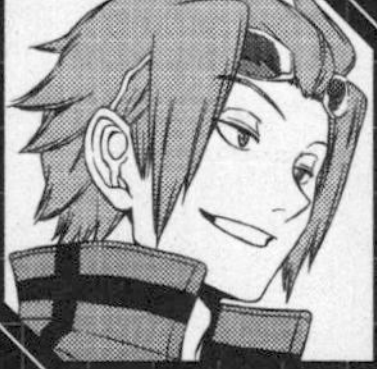

YUICHI JIN

Former S-Rank Black Trigger user. His Side Effect lets him see the future.

OJI SQUAD

Border HQ B-Rank #5.

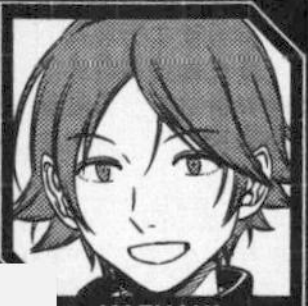

KAZUAKI OJI

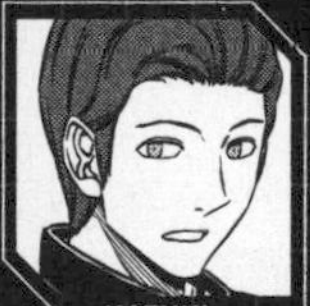

KAZUKI KURAUCHI

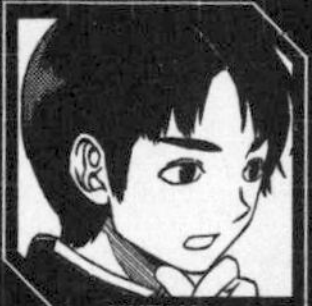

YUTAKA KASHIO

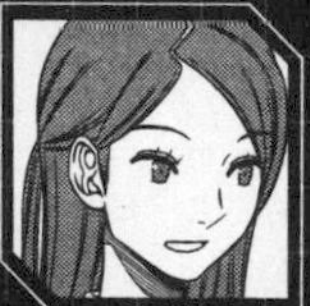

HAYA KITTAKA

IKOMA SQUAD

Border HQ B Rank #3 Squad with five agents.

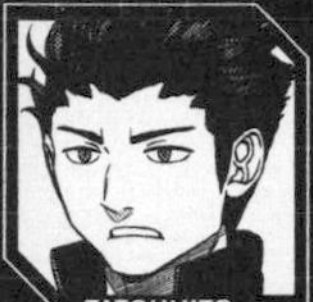

TATSUHITO IKOMA

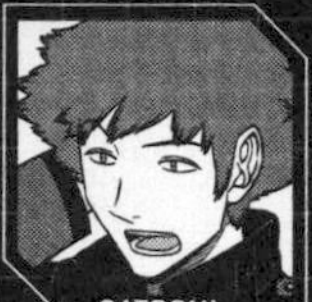

SATOSHI MIZUKAMI

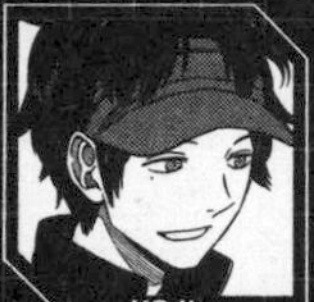

KOJI OKI

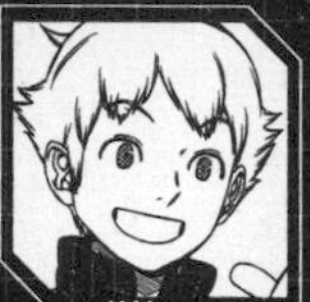

KAI MINAMISAWA

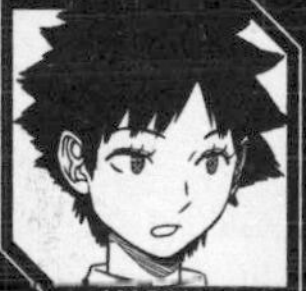

MAORI HOSOI

A-RANK AGENTS

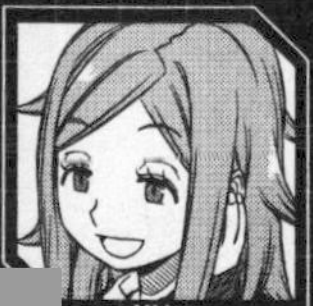

YU KUNICHIKA

Agent from A-Rank #1 Tachikawa Squad.

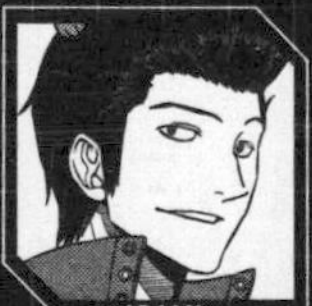

ISAMI TOMA

Sniper from A-Rank #2 Fuyushima Squad.

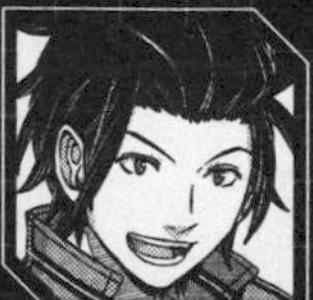

JUN ARASHIYAMA

Captain of A-Rank #5 Arashiyama Squad.

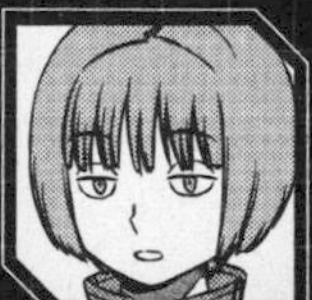

MITSURU TOKIEDA

All-Rounder from A-Rank #5 Arashiyama Squad.

B-RANK AGENTS

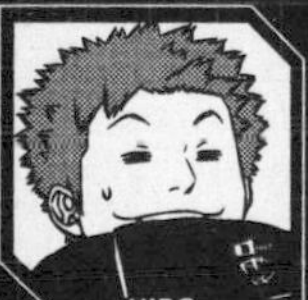

HIRO KITAZOE

Gunner from B-Rank #2 Kageura Squad.

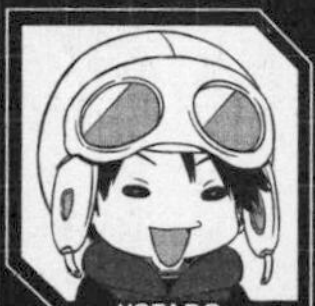

YOTARO RINDO

Tamakoma Branch kid.

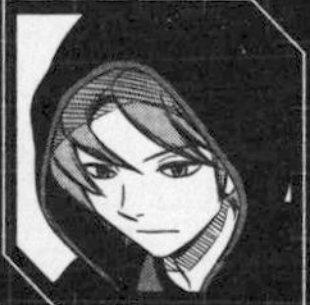

HYUSE

A Neighbor from Aftokrator abandoned during the large-scale invasion.

WORLD TRIGGER
CONTENTS

Chapter 152: Tamakoma-2: Part 17 • 9

Chapter 153: Tatsuhito Ikoma • 29

Chapter 154: Tatsuhito Ikoma: Part 2 • 49

Chapter 155: Oji Squad • 69

Chapter 156: Kazuaki Oji • 89

Chapter 157: Tamakoma-2: Part 18 • 109

Chapter 158: Tamakoma-2: Part 19 • 129

Chapter 159: Hyuse: Part 3 • 149

Chapter 160: Hyuse: Part 4 • 169

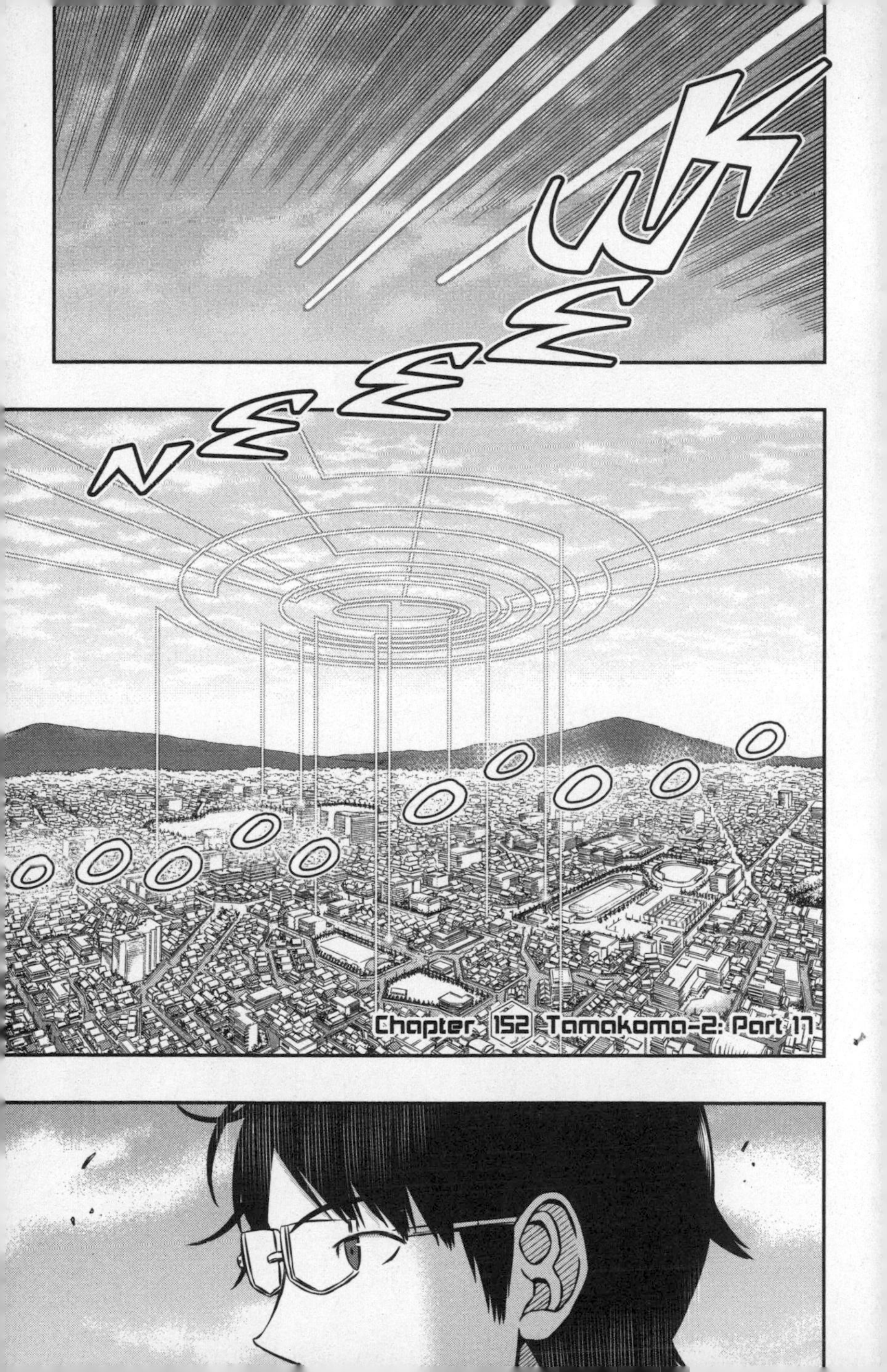
WHNEEEEEEN
OOOOOOOOOOOOO
Chapter 152 Tamakoma-2: Part 11

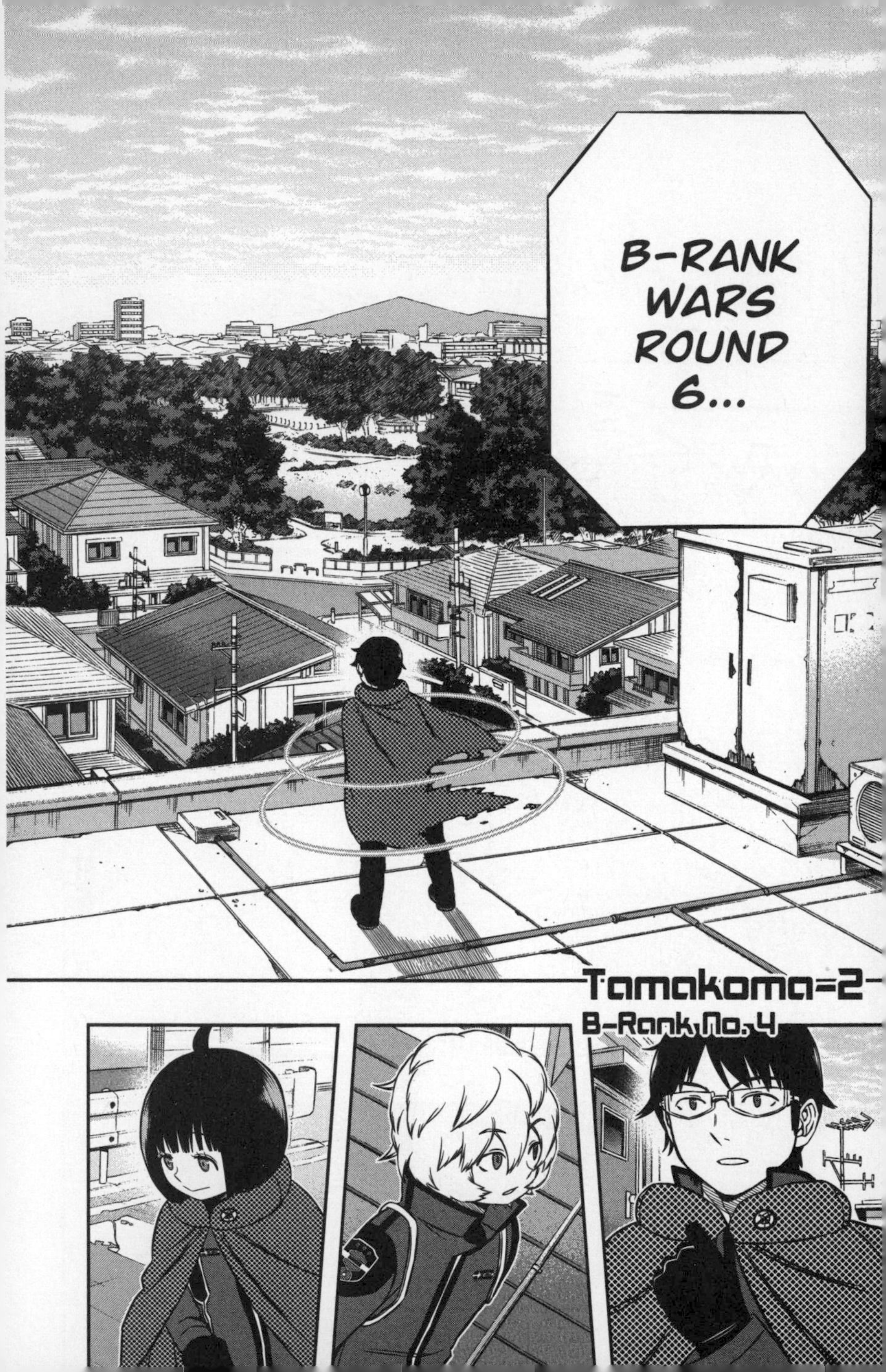
B-RANK WARS ROUND 6...
Tamakoma-2
B-Rank No. 4

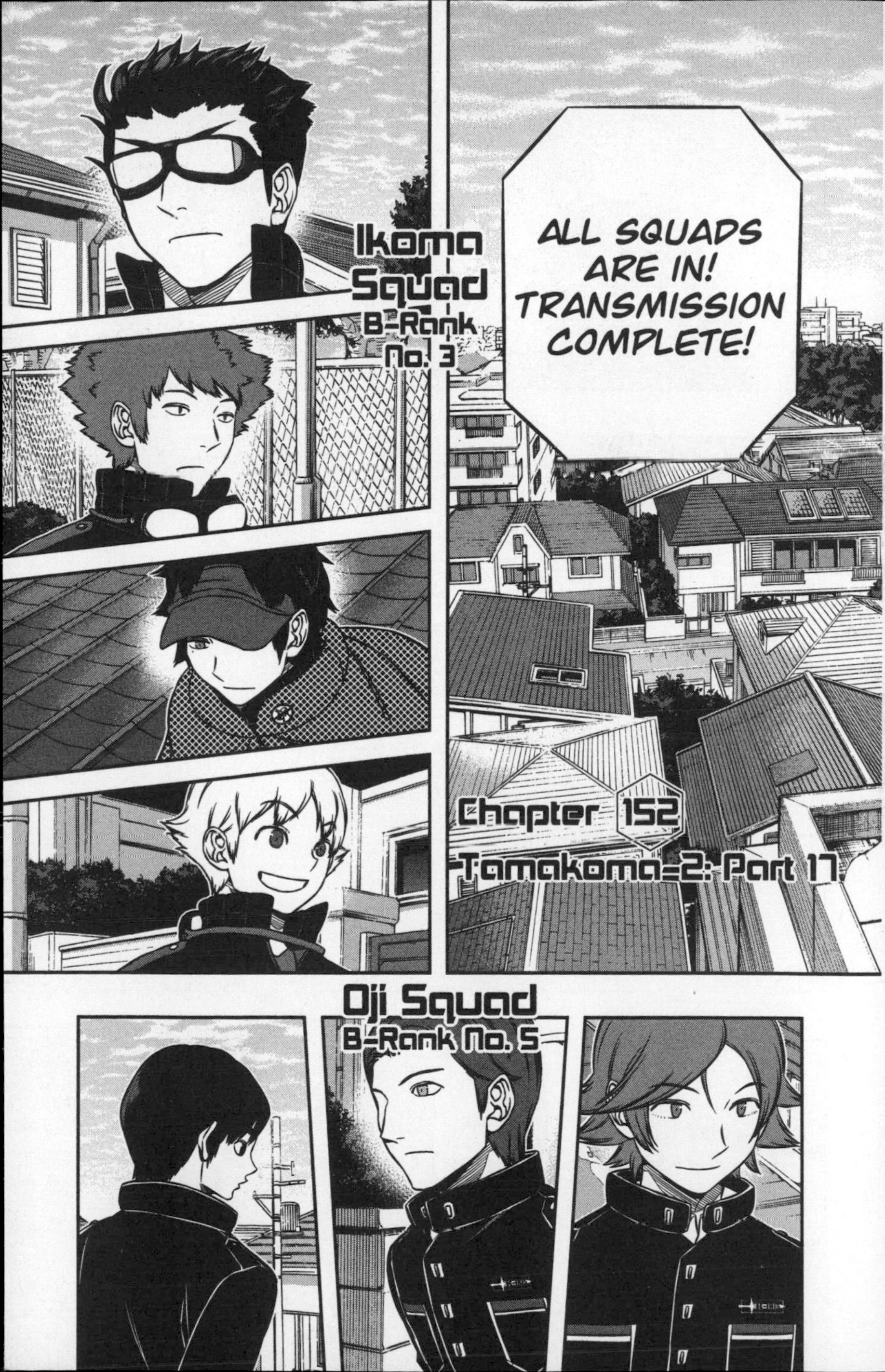
ALL SQUADS ARE IN! TRANSMISSION COMPLETE!
Chapter 152
Tamakoma-2: Part 17
Ikoma Squad
B-Rank No. 3
Oji Squad
B-Rank No. 5

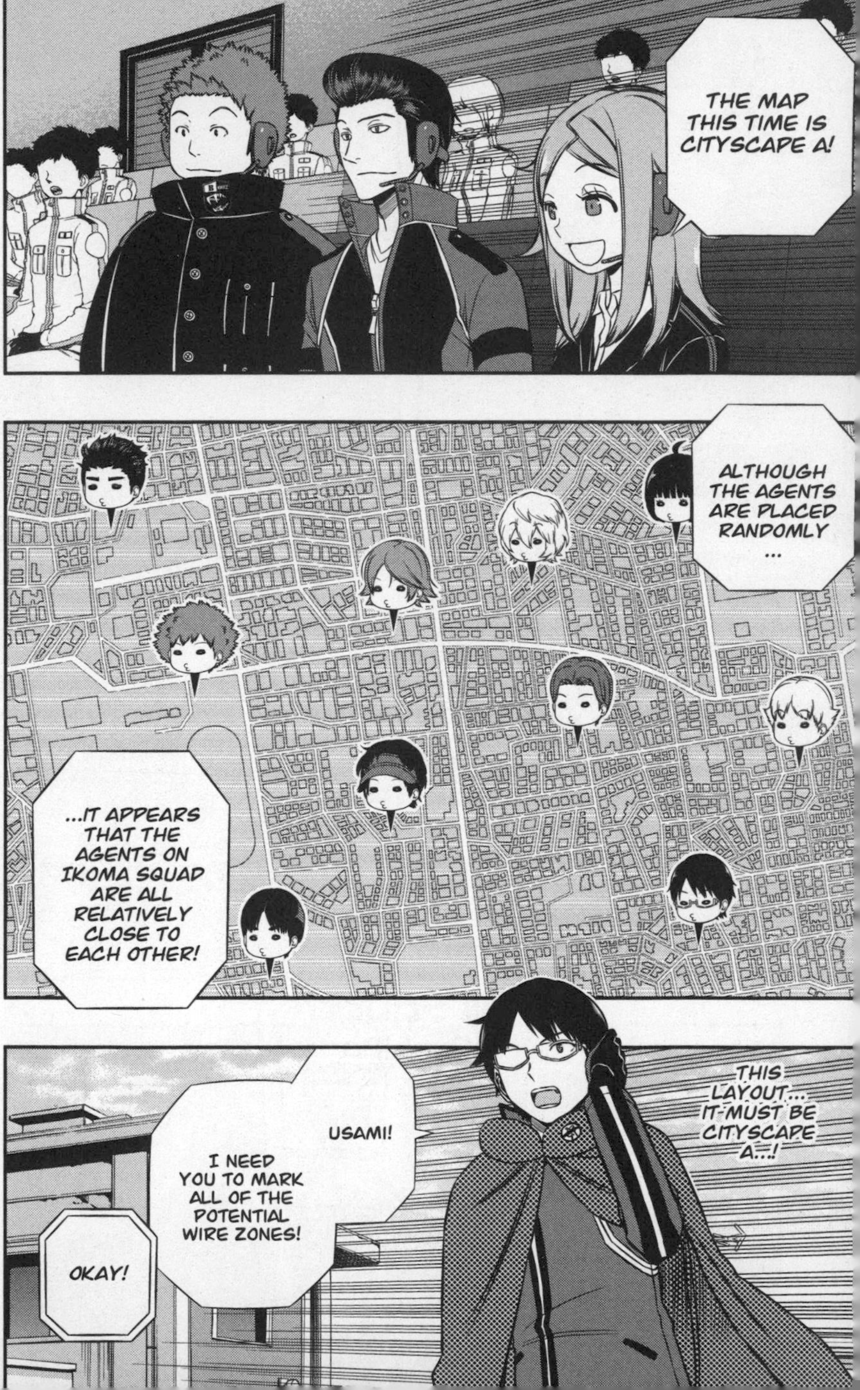
THE MAP THIS TIME IS CITYSCAPE A!
ALTHOUGH THE AGENTS ARE PLACED RANDOMLY ...
...IT APPEARS THAT THE AGENTS ON IKOMA SQUAD ARE ALL RELATIVELY CLOSE TO EACH OTHER!
THIS LAYOUT... IT MUST BE CITYSCAPE A...!
USAMI!
I NEED YOU TO MARK ALL OF THE POTENTIAL WIRE ZONES!
OKAY!

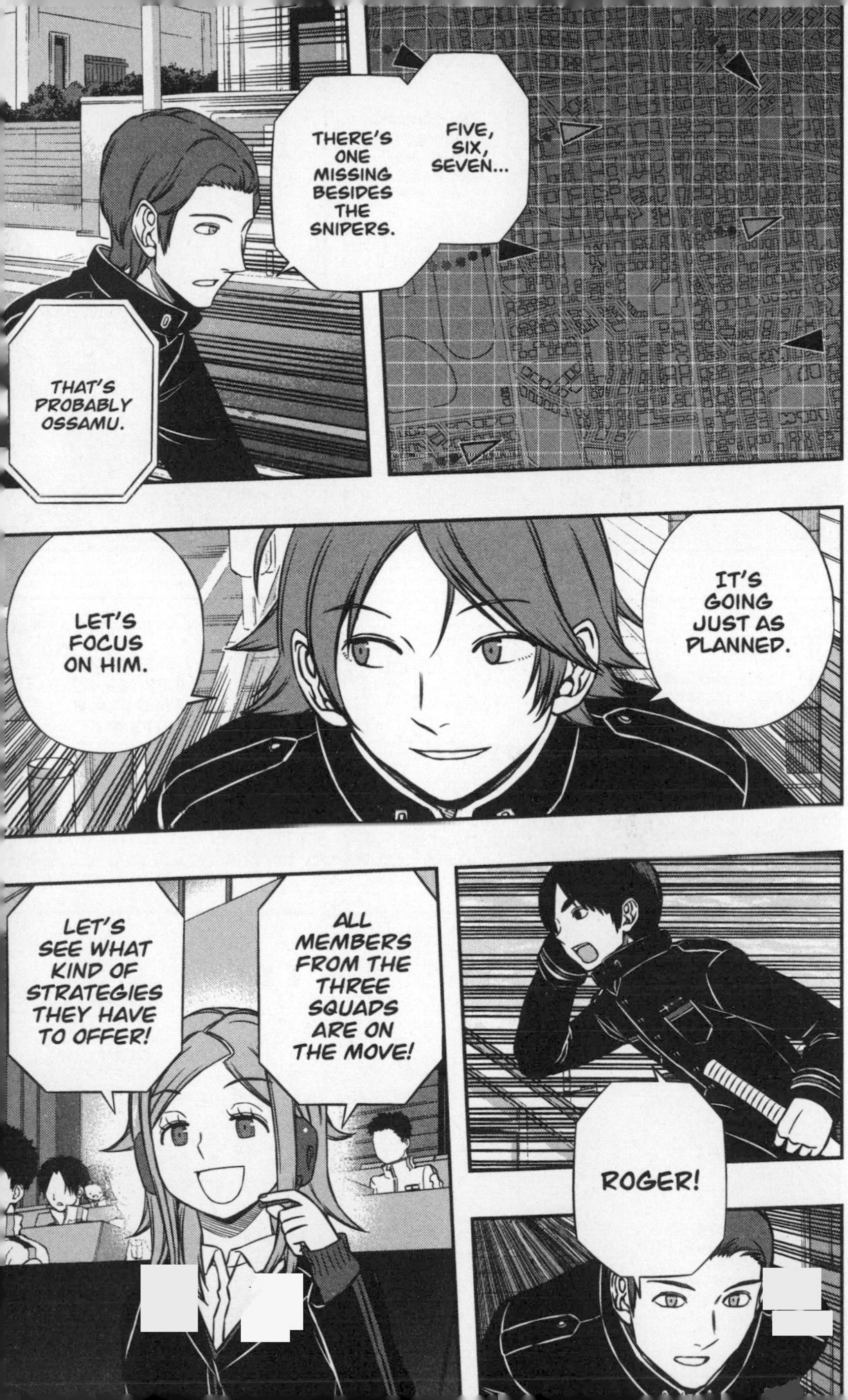
FIVE, SIX, SEVEN...
THERE'S ONE MISSING BESIDES THE SNIPERS.
THAT'S PROBABLY OSSAMU.
IT'S GOING JUST AS PLANNED.
LET'S FOCUS ON HIM.
ROGER!
ALL MEMBERS FROM THE THREE SQUADS ARE ON THE MOVE!
LET'S SEE WHAT KIND OF STRATEGIES THEY HAVE TO OFFER!

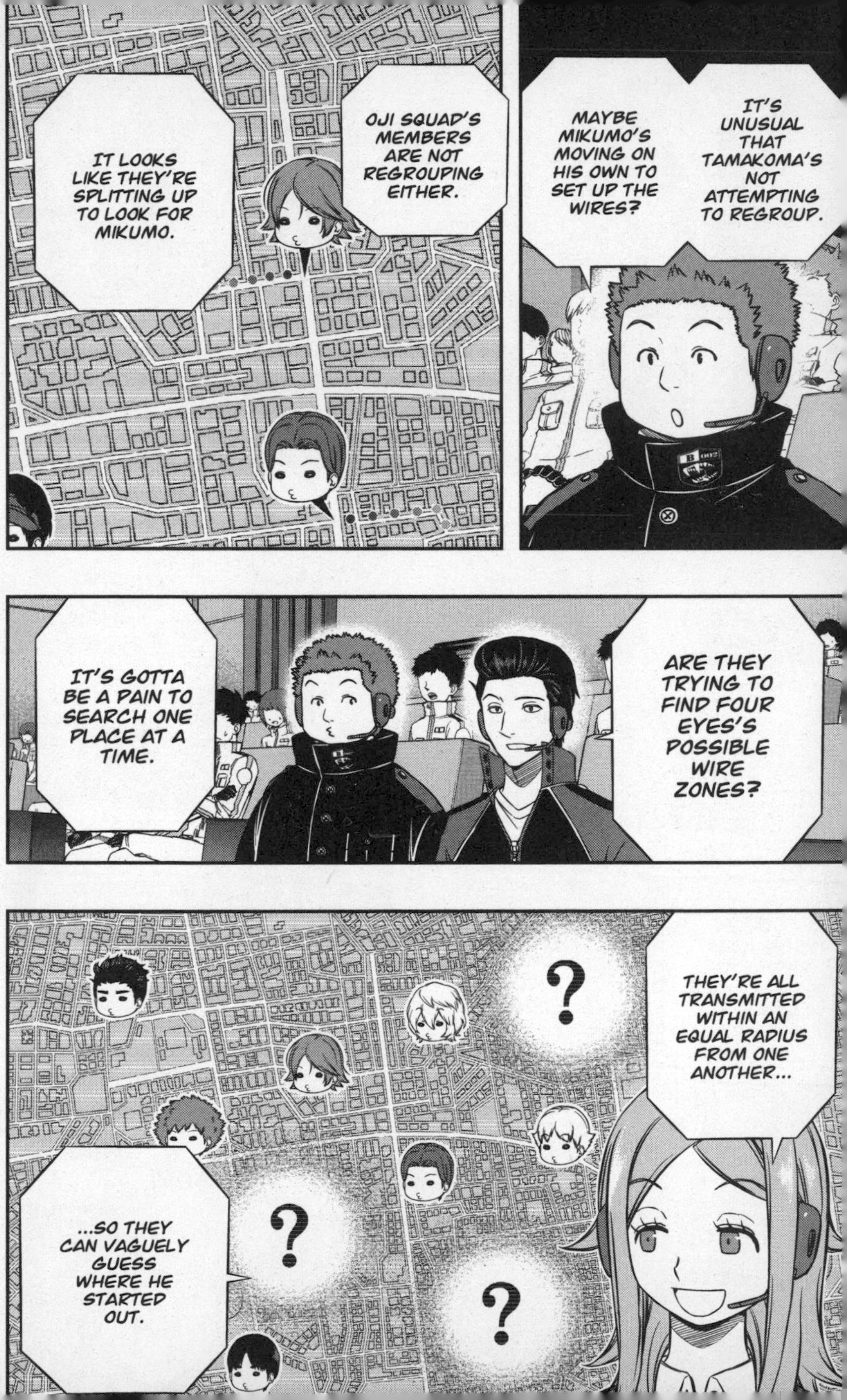
IT'S UNUSUAL THAT TAMAKOMA'S NOT ATTEMPTING TO REGROUP.
MAYBE MIKUMO'S MOVING ON HIS OWN TO SET UP THE WIRES?
OJI SQUAD'S MEMBERS ARE NOT REGROUPING EITHER.
IT LOOKS LIKE THEY'RE SPLITTING UP TO LOOK FOR MIKUMO.
ARE THEY TRYING TO FIND FOUR EYES'S POSSIBLE WIRE ZONES?
IT'S GOTTA BE A PAIN TO SEARCH ONE PLACE AT A TIME.
THEY'RE ALL TRANSMITTED WITHIN AN EQUAL RADIUS FROM ONE ANOTHER...
...SO THEY CAN VAGUELY GUESS WHERE HE STARTED OUT.

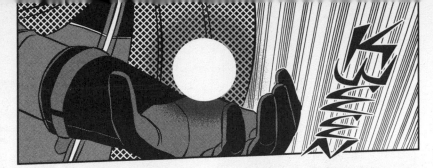

SNIPER IN POSITION.

TMP

SNIPER IN POSITION.

CAREFUL.

ONE HOSTILE'S APPROACHING FROM THE RIGHT.

POP

POP

POP

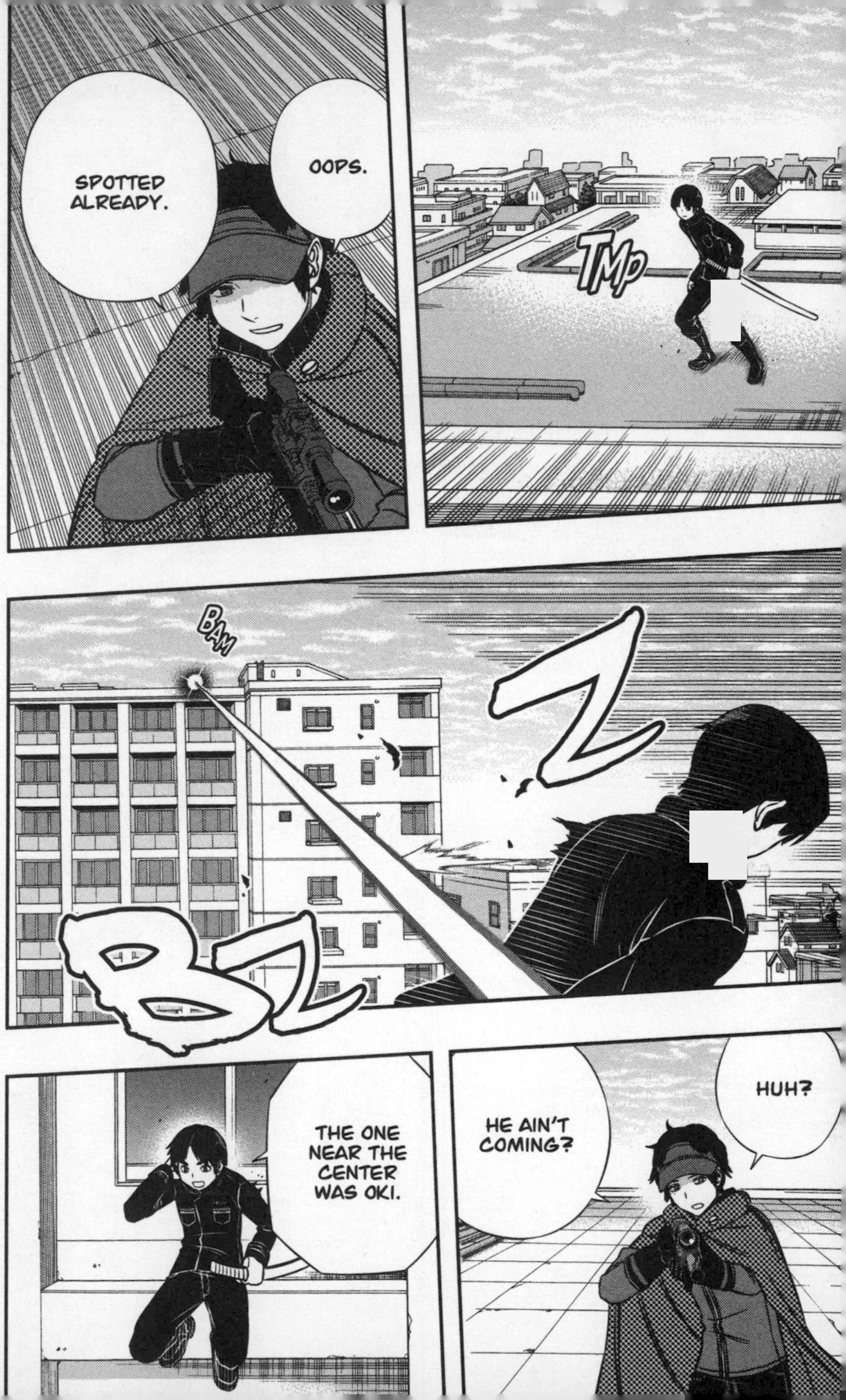
TMP
OOPS.
SPOTTED ALREADY.
BAM
Z
BZ
HUH?
HE AIN'T COMING?
THE ONE NEAR THE CENTER WAS OKI.

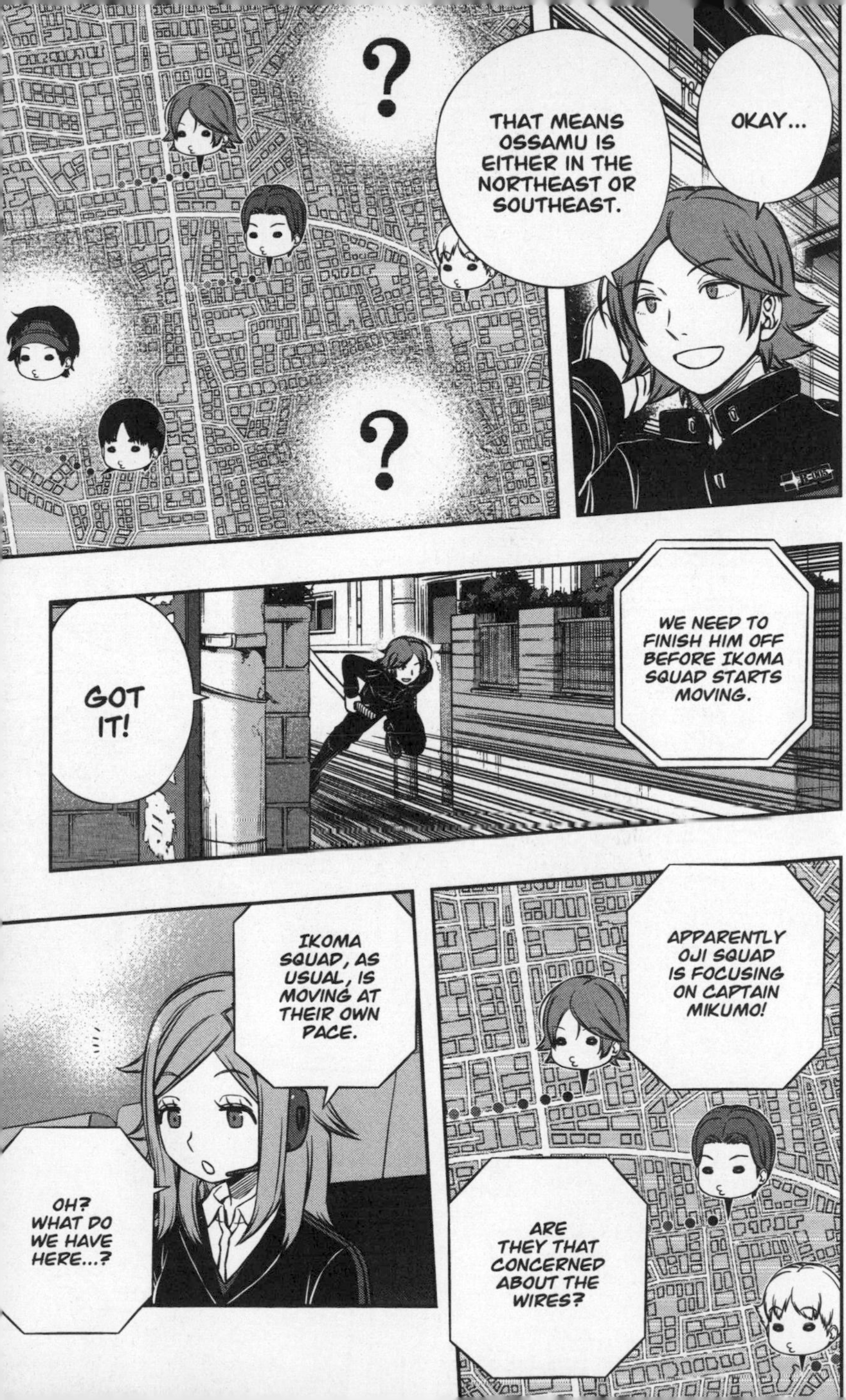
?
?
OKAY...
THAT MEANS OSSAMU IS EITHER IN THE NORTHEAST OR SOUTHEAST.
WE NEED TO FINISH HIM OFF BEFORE IKOMA SQUAD STARTS MOVING.
GOT IT!
APPARENTLY OJI SQUAD IS FOCUSING ON CAPTAIN MIKUMO!
ARE THEY THAT CONCERNED ABOUT THE WIRES?
IKOMA SQUAD, AS USUAL, IS MOVING AT THEIR OWN PACE.
OH? WHAT DO WE HAVE HERE...?

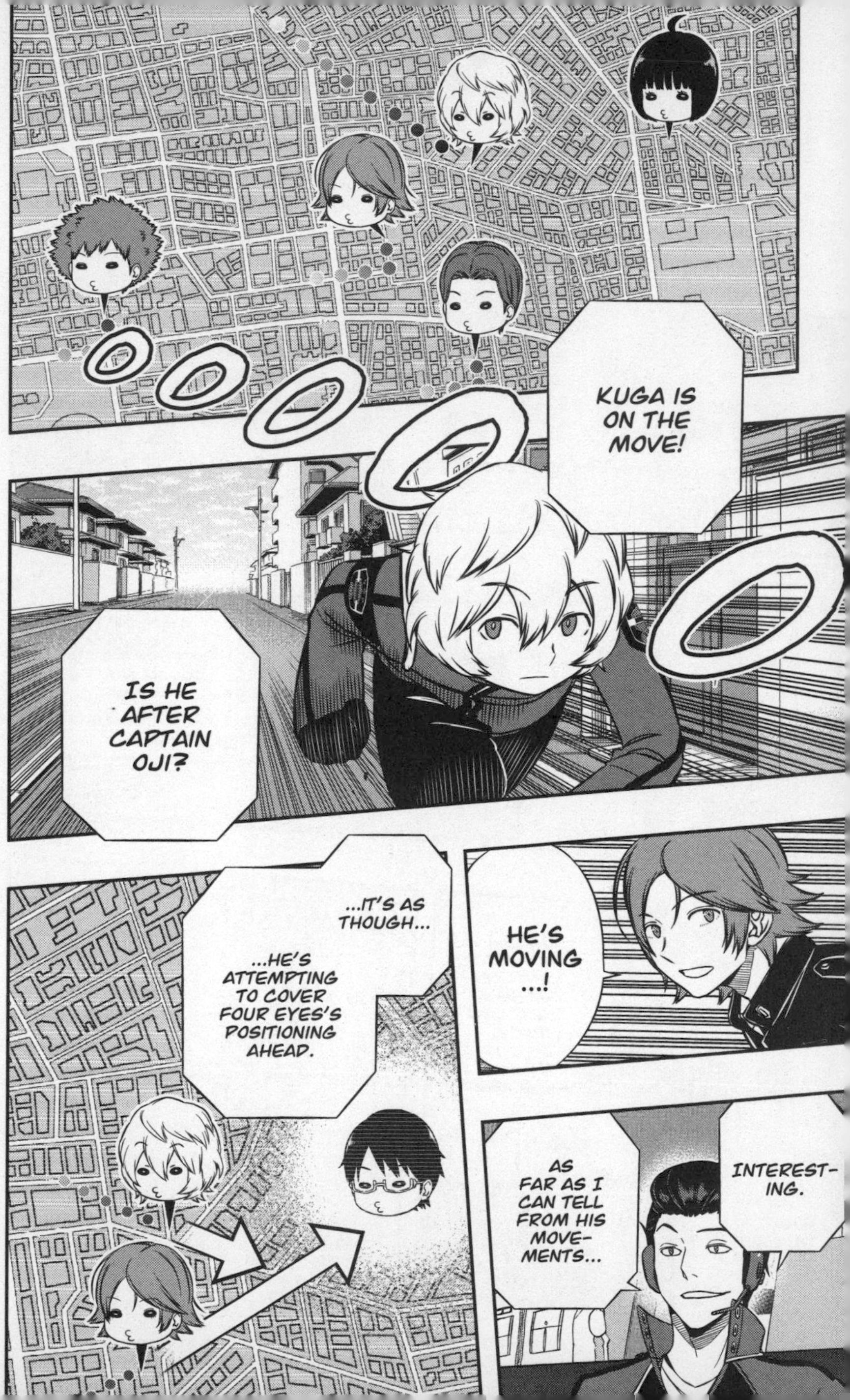
KUGA IS ON THE MOVE!
IS HE AFTER CAPTAIN OJI?
HE'S MOVING ...!
INTERESTING.
AS FAR AS I CAN TELL FROM HIS MOVEMENTS...
...IT'S AS THOUGH...
...HE'S ATTEMPTING TO COVER FOUR EYES'S POSITIONING AHEAD.

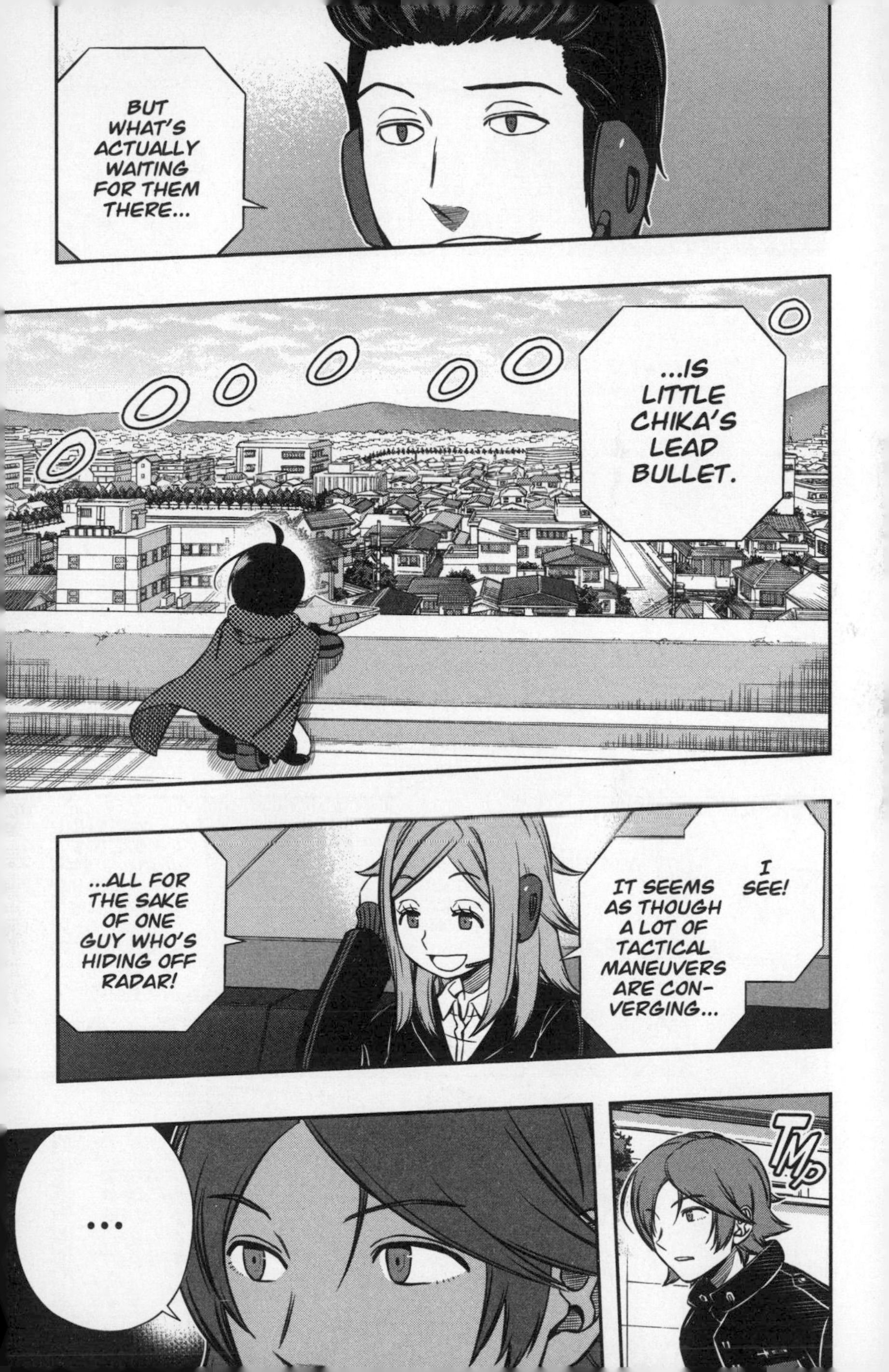
BUT WHAT'S ACTUALLY WAITING FOR THEM THERE...
...IS LITTLE CHIKA'S LEAD BULLET.
I SEE!
IT SEEMS AS THOUGH A LOT OF TACTICAL MANEUVERS ARE CON-VERGING...
...ALL FOR THE SAKE OF ONE GUY WHO'S HIDING OFF RADAR!
TMP
...

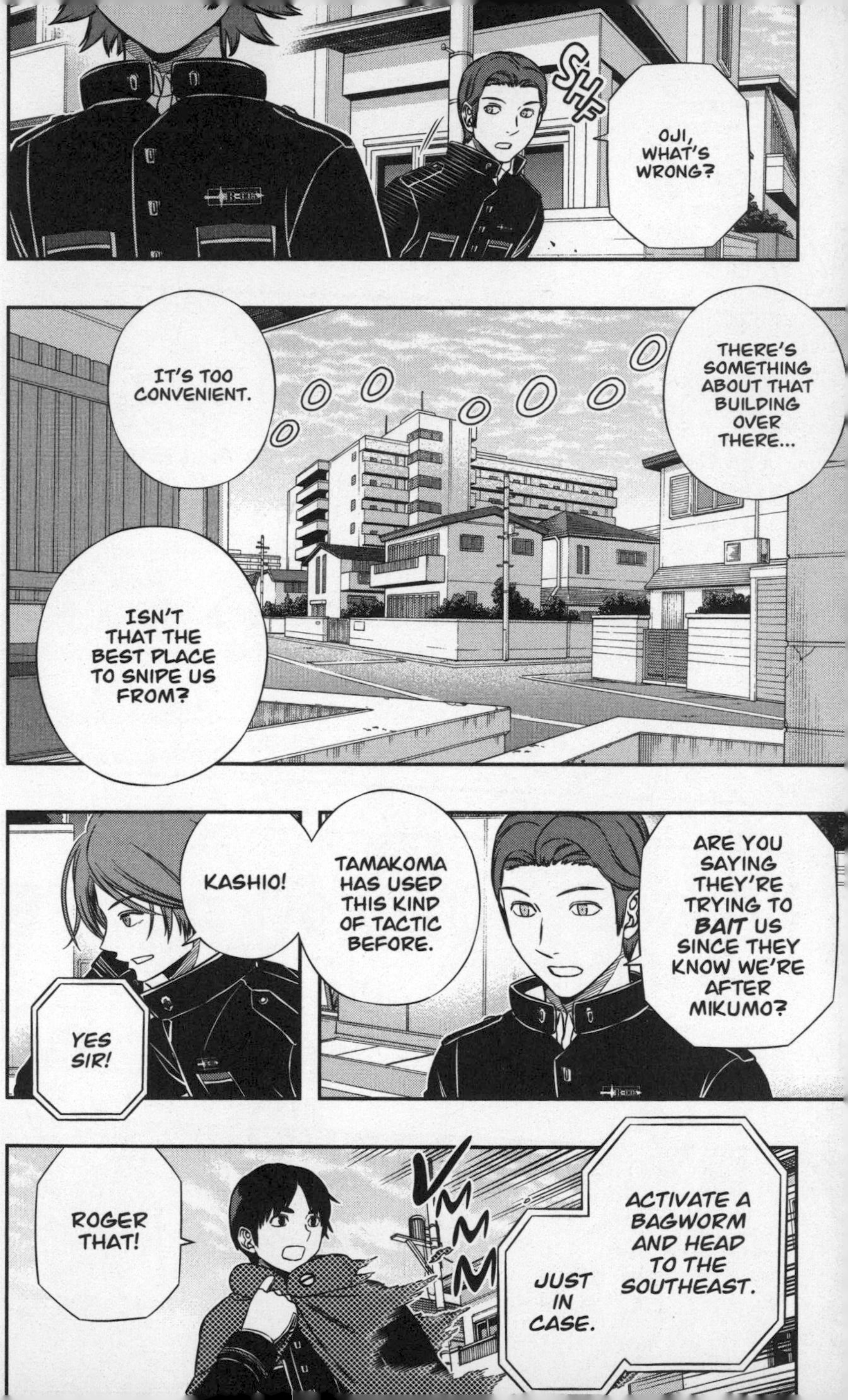
SHF
OJI, WHAT'S WRONG?
THERE'S SOMETHING ABOUT THAT BUILDING OVER THERE...
IT'S TOO CONVENIENT.
ISN'T THAT THE BEST PLACE TO SNIPE US FROM?
ARE YOU SAYING THEY'RE TRYING TO BAIT US SINCE THEY KNOW WE'RE AFTER MIKUMO?
TAMAKOMA HAS USED THIS KIND OF TACTIC BEFORE.
KASHIO!
YES SIR!
ACTIVATE A BAGWORM AND HEAD TO THE SOUTHEAST.
JUST IN CASE.
VMMM
ROGER THAT!

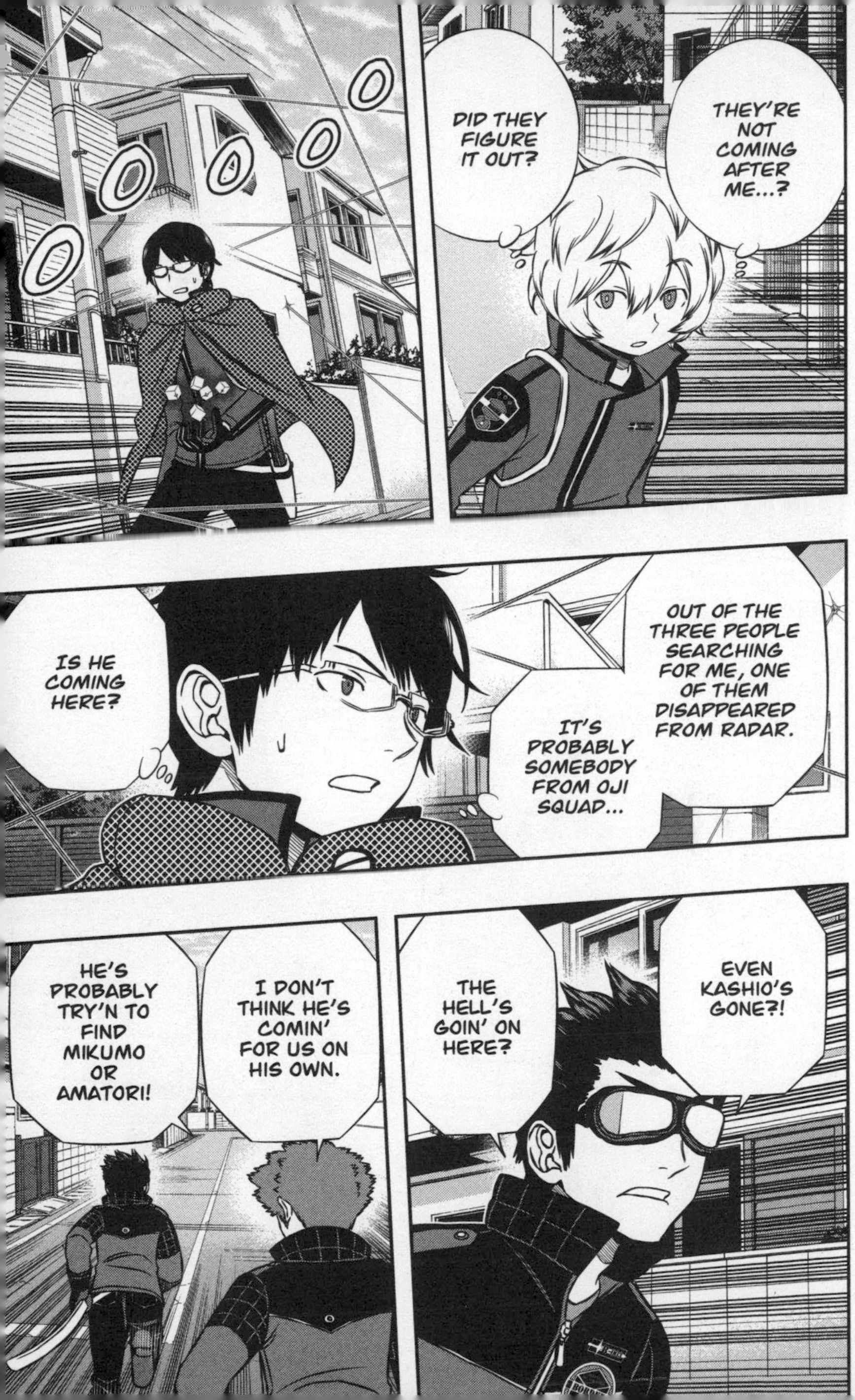
THEY'RE NOT COMING AFTER ME...?
DID THEY FIGURE IT OUT?
OUT OF THE THREE PEOPLE SEARCHING FOR ME, ONE OF THEM DISAPPEARED FROM RADAR.
IT'S PROBABLY SOMEBODY FROM OJI SQUAD...
IS HE COMING HERE?
EVEN KASHIO'S GONE?!
THE HELL'S GOIN' ON HERE?
I DON'T THINK HE'S COMIN' FOR US ON HIS OWN.
HE'S PROBABLY TRY'N TO FIND MIKUMO OR AMATORI!

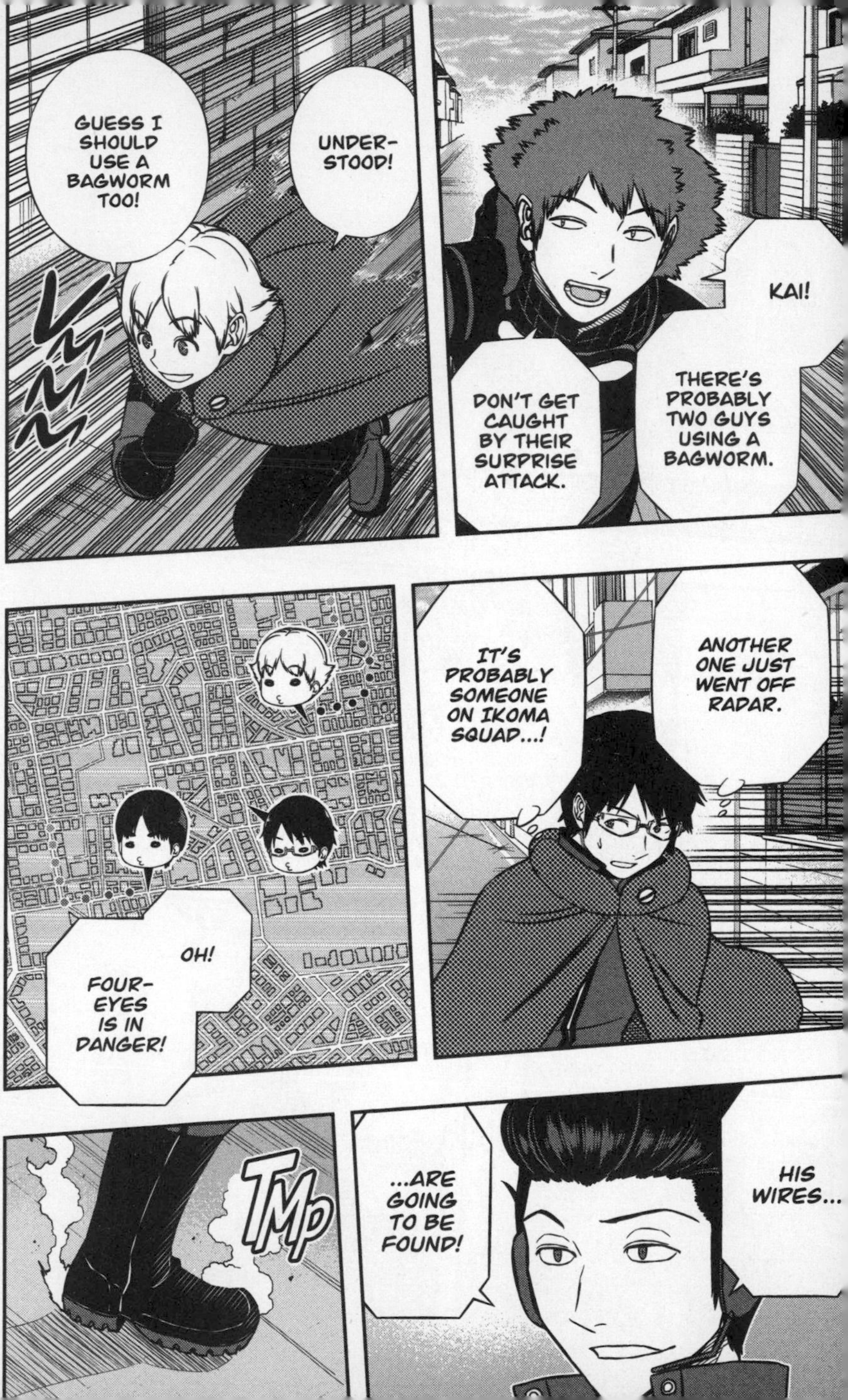
KAI!
THERE'S PROBABLY TWO GUYS USING A BAGWORM.
DON'T GET CAUGHT BY THEIR SURPRISE ATTACK.
UNDER-STOOD!
GUESS I SHOULD USE A BAGWORM TOO!
ANOTHER ONE JUST WENT OFF RADAR.
IT'S PROBABLY SOMEONE ON IKOMA SQUAD...!
OH!
FOUR-EYES IS IN DANGER!
HIS WIRES...
...ARE GOING TO BE FOUND!
TMP

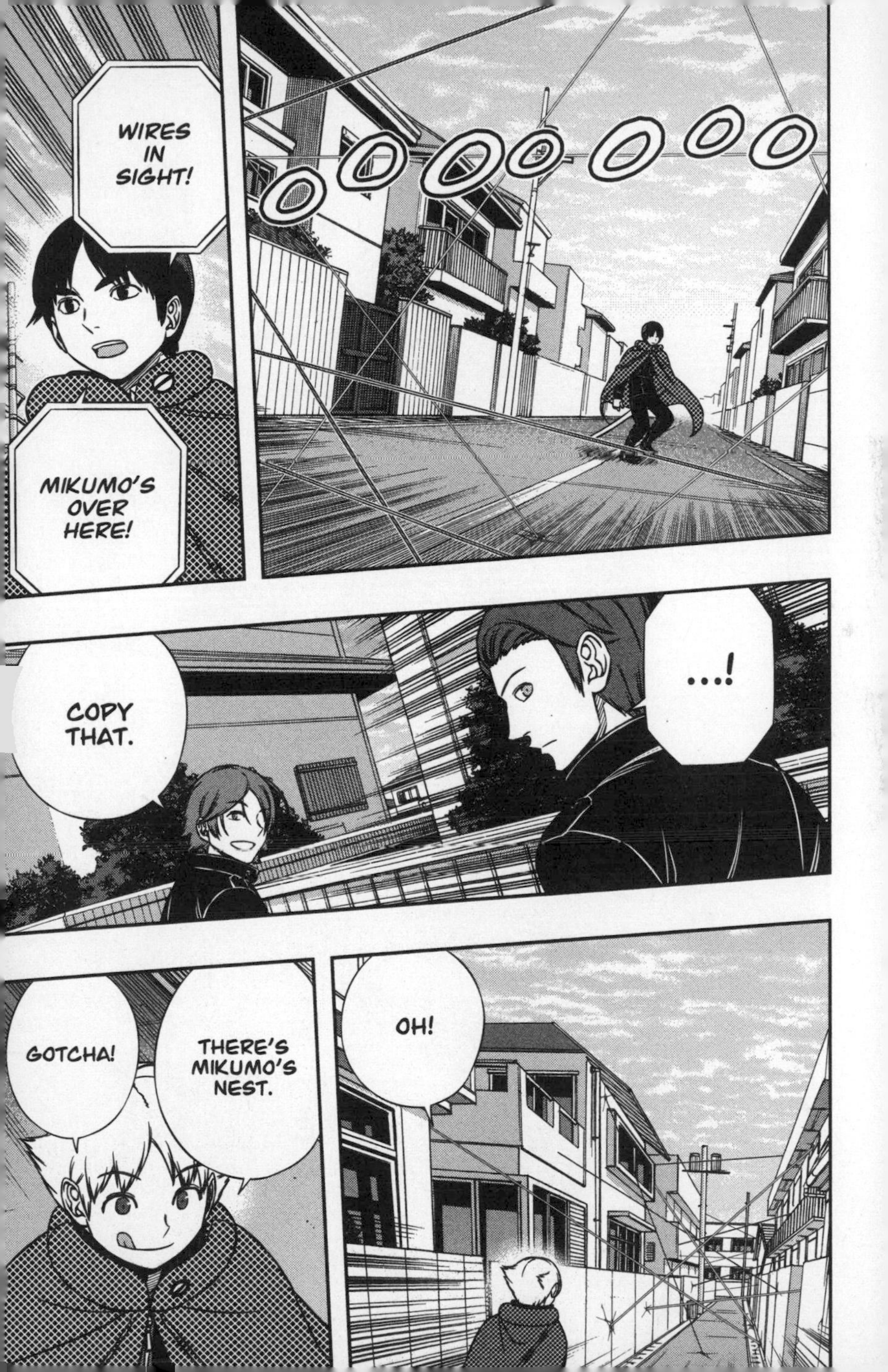
WIRES IN SIGHT!
MIKUMO'S OVER HERE!
...!
COPY THAT.
OH!
THERE'S MIKUMO'S NEST.
GOTCHA!

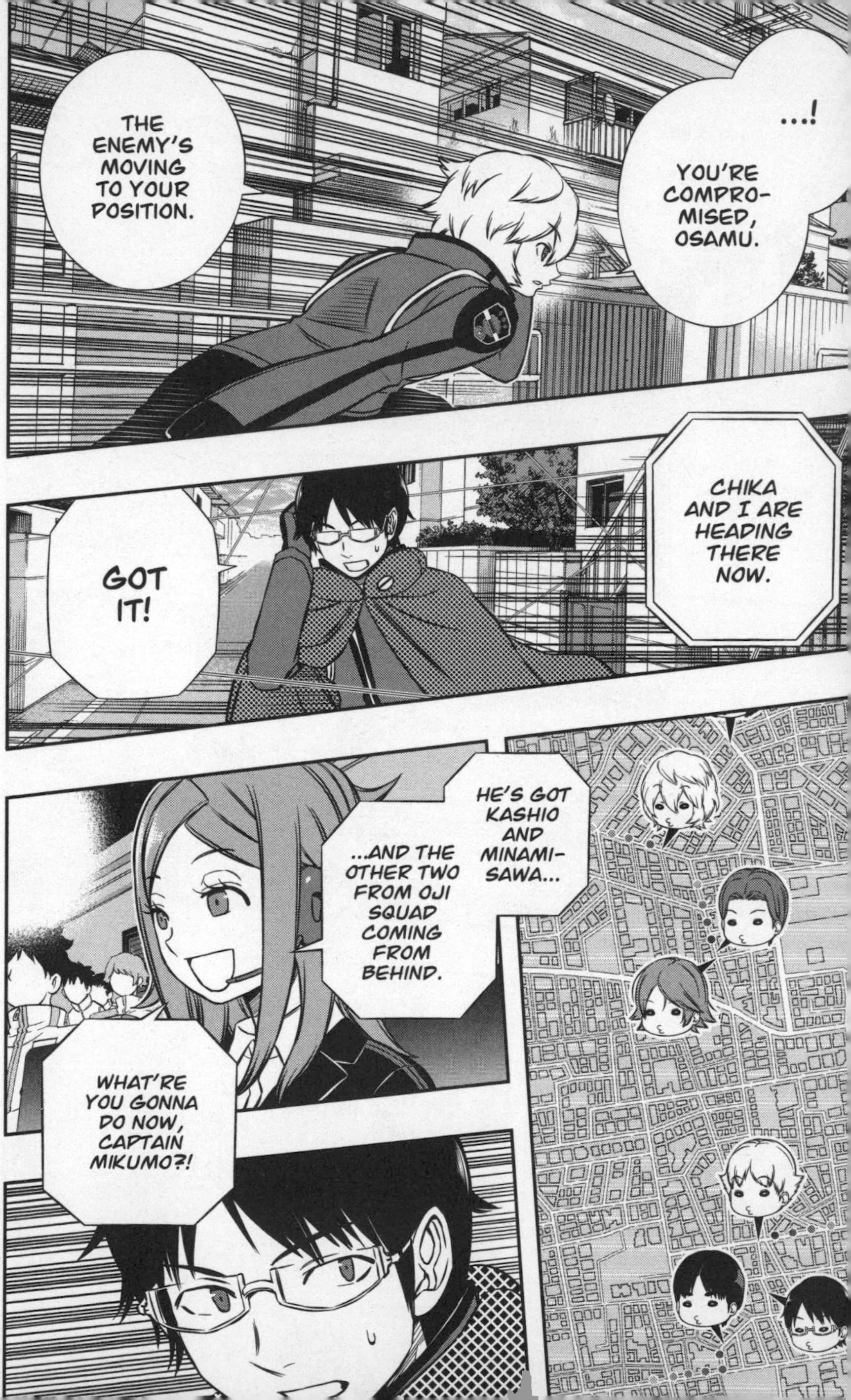
...!
YOU'RE COMPROMISED, OSAMU.
THE ENEMY'S MOVING TO YOUR POSITION.
CHIKA AND I ARE HEADING THERE NOW.
GOT IT!
HE'S GOT KASHIO AND MINAMI-SAWA...
...AND THE OTHER TWO FROM OJI SQUAD COMING FROM BEHIND.
WHAT'RE YOU GONNA DO NOW, CAPTAIN MIKUMO?!

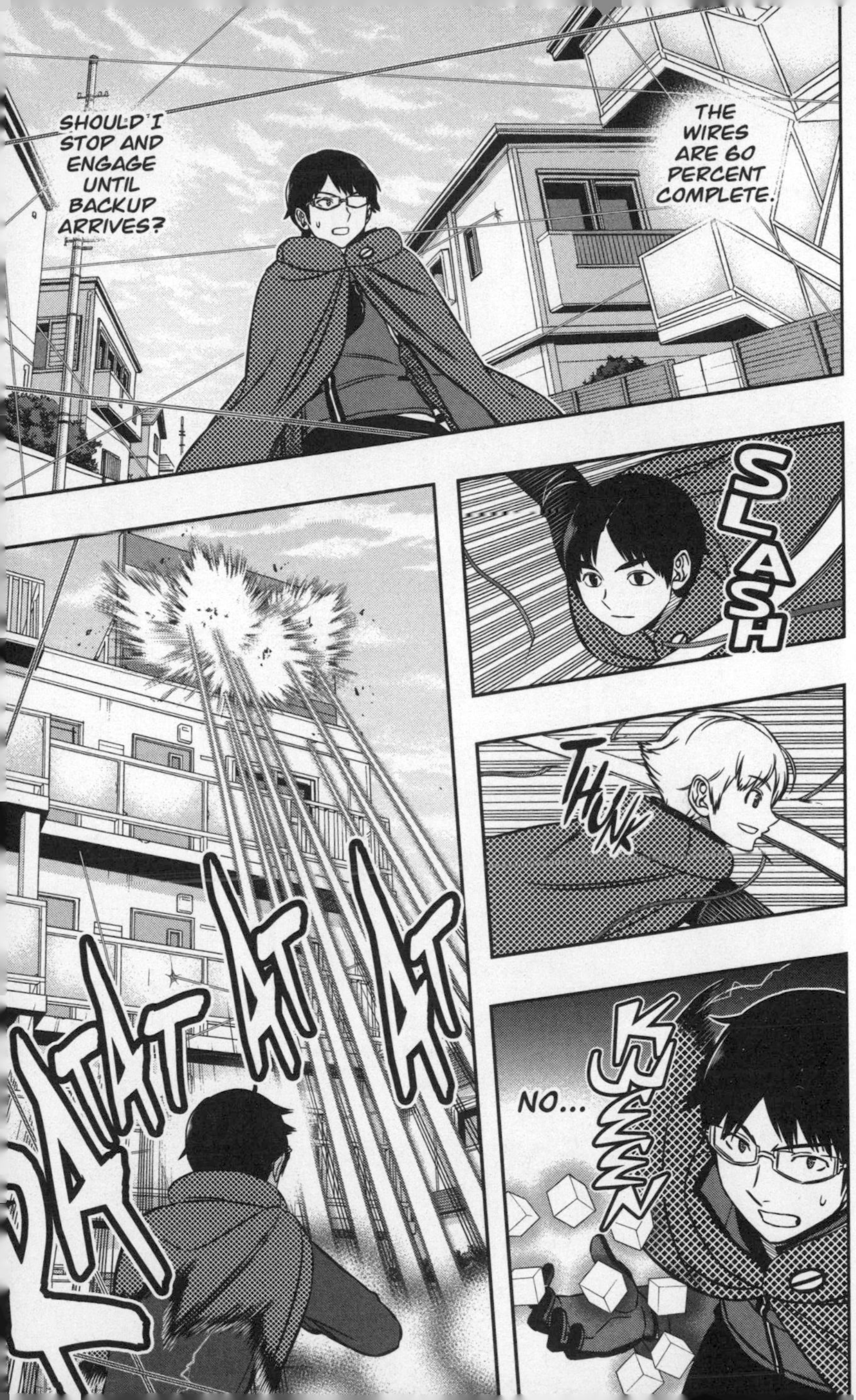
THE WIRES ARE 60 PERCENT COMPLETE.
SHOULD I STOP AND ENGAGE UNTIL BACKUP ARRIVES?
SLASH
THUNK
KYUEEEN
NO...
ATATATAT

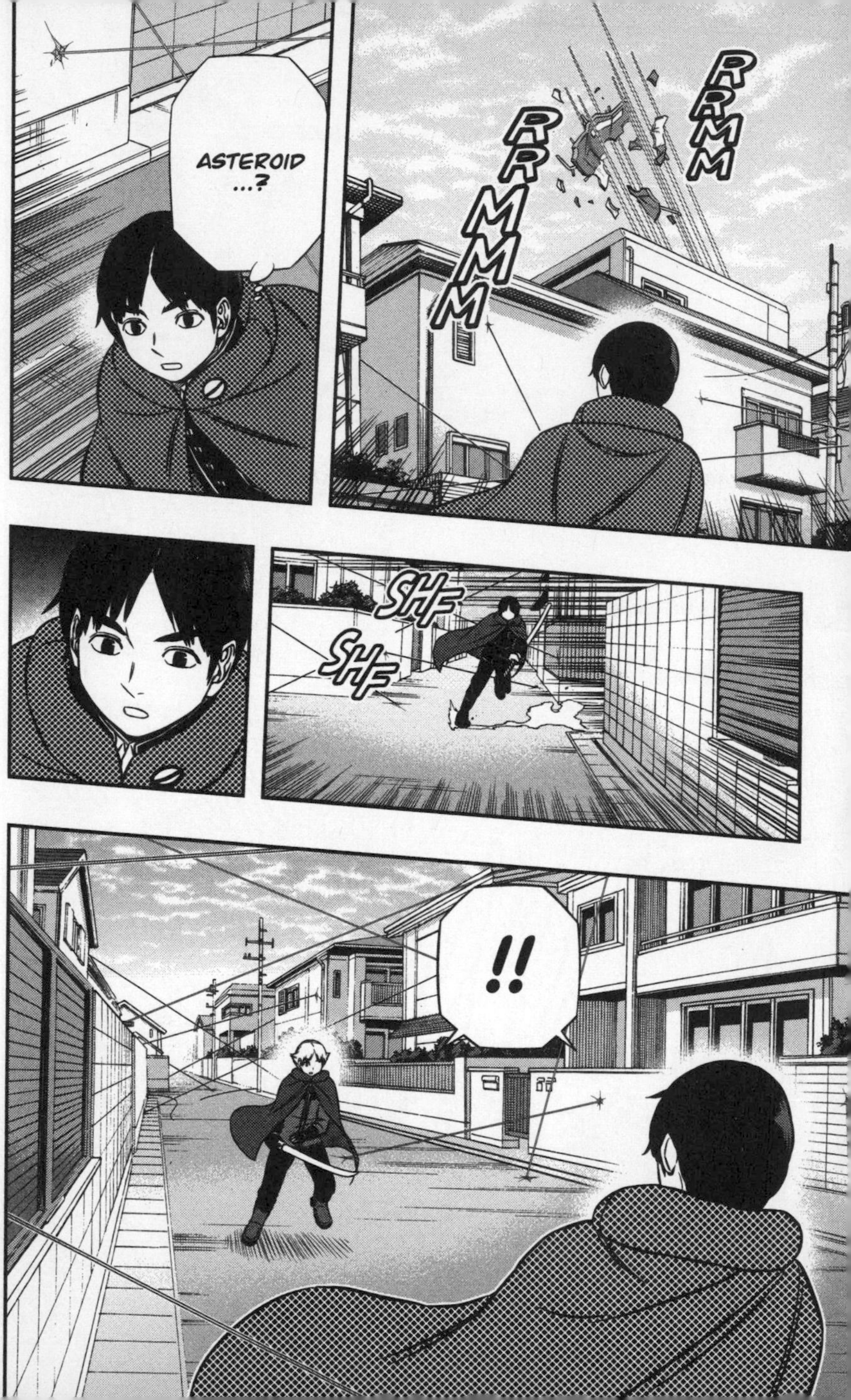
RRMM
RRMMMM
ASTEROID ...?
SHF
SHF
!!

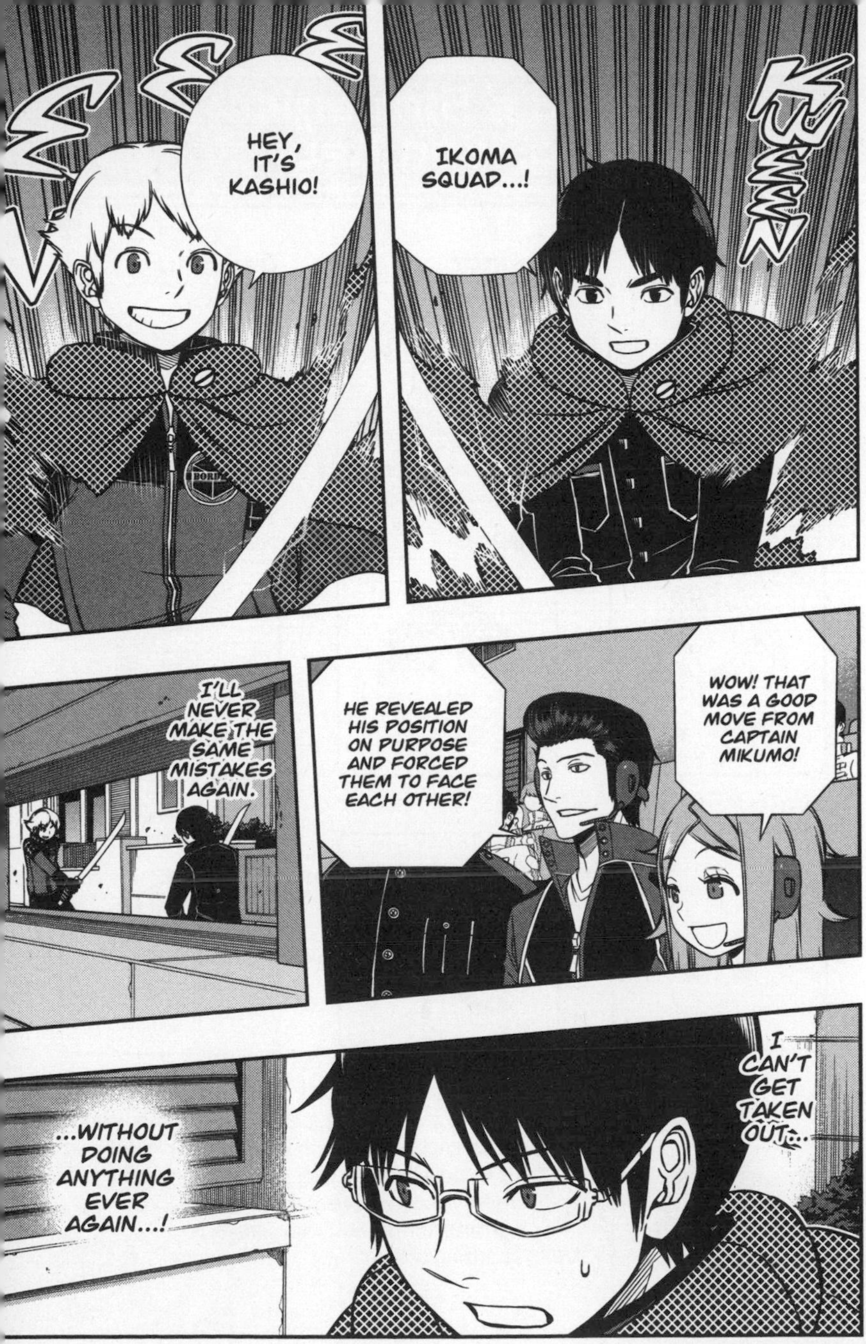
IKOMA SQUAD...!
HEY, IT'S KASHIO!
WOW! THAT WAS A GOOD MOVE FROM CAPTAIN MIKUMO!
HE REVEALED HIS POSITION ON PURPOSE AND FORCED THEM TO FACE EACH OTHER!
I'LL NEVER MAKE THE SAME MISTAKES AGAIN.
I CAN'T GET TAKEN OUT...
...WITHOUT DOING ANYTHING EVER AGAIN...!

Oji Squad's Strategic Meeting: Icon Key

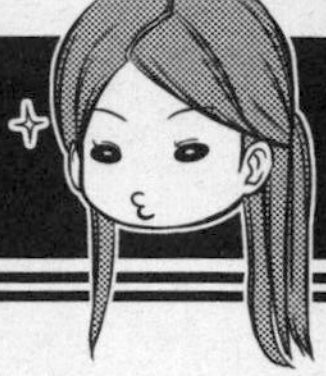

Amatriciana

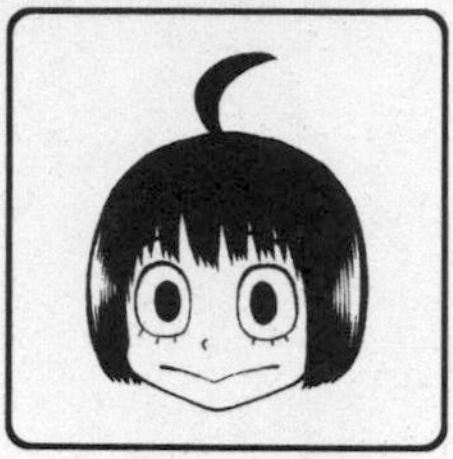

Cougar

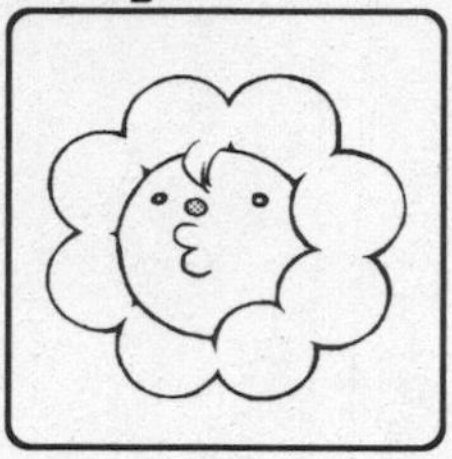

Ossamu

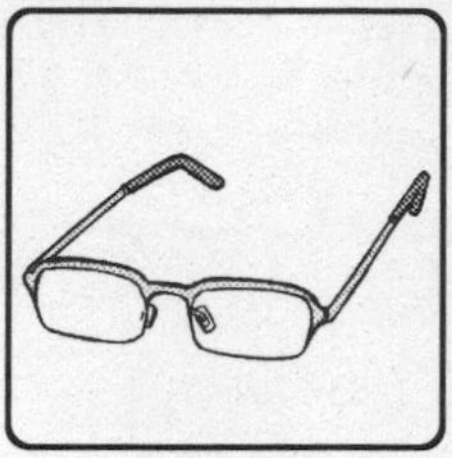

Oji

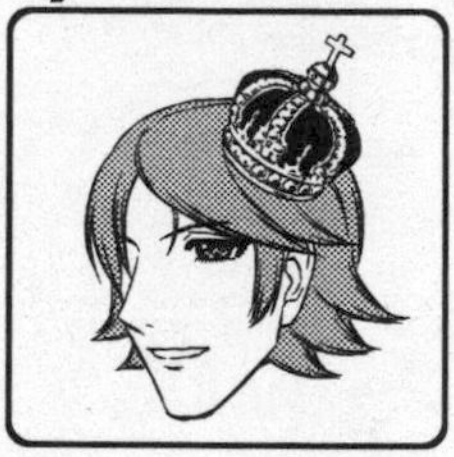

Kashio

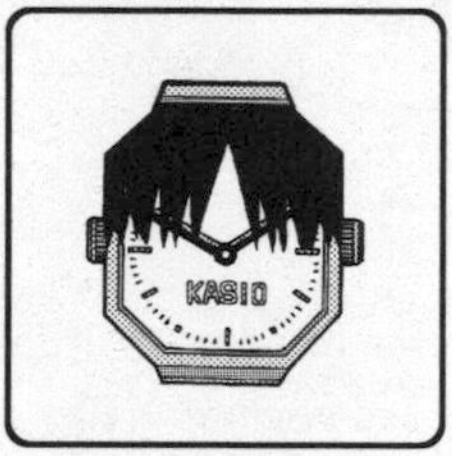
KASIO

Kurauchi

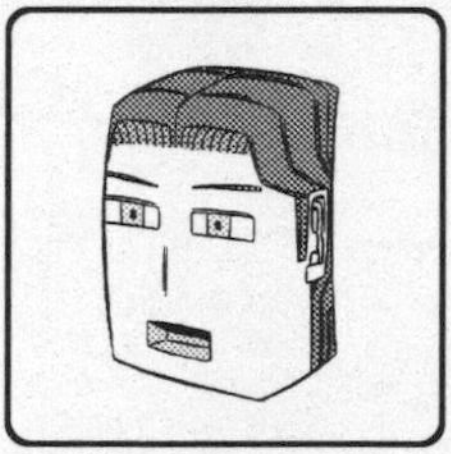

Kai

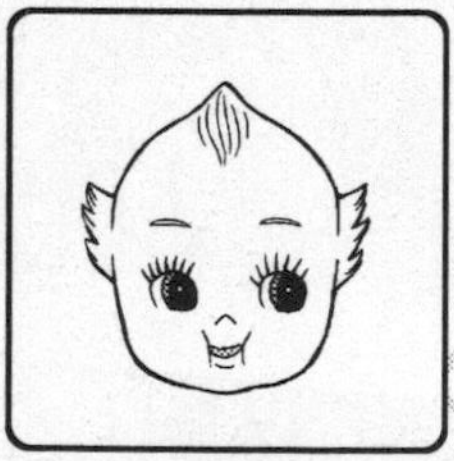

Okki

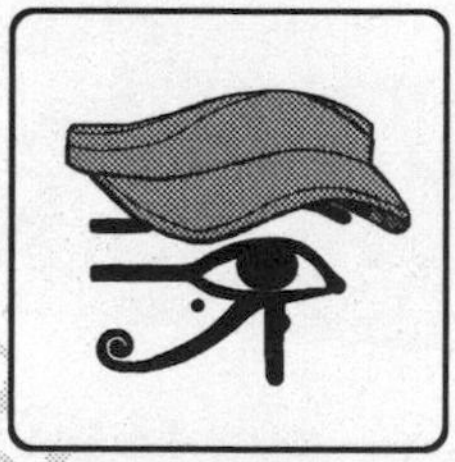

Mizucoming

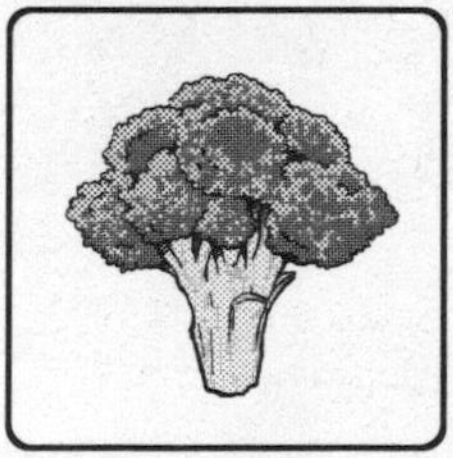

Iko

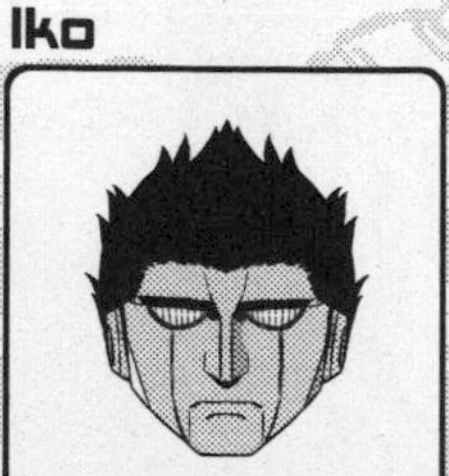

The weird icons used by Oji Squad were all designed by Haya at Oji's request. He personally requested that his own icon look like that, which probably shows that Oji is most likely an idiot. Amatriciana is based on Tsuyu from "*My Hero Academia*" (without permission), but Horikoshi Sensei later approved of it.

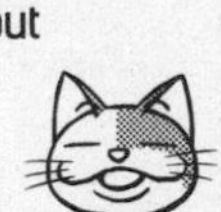

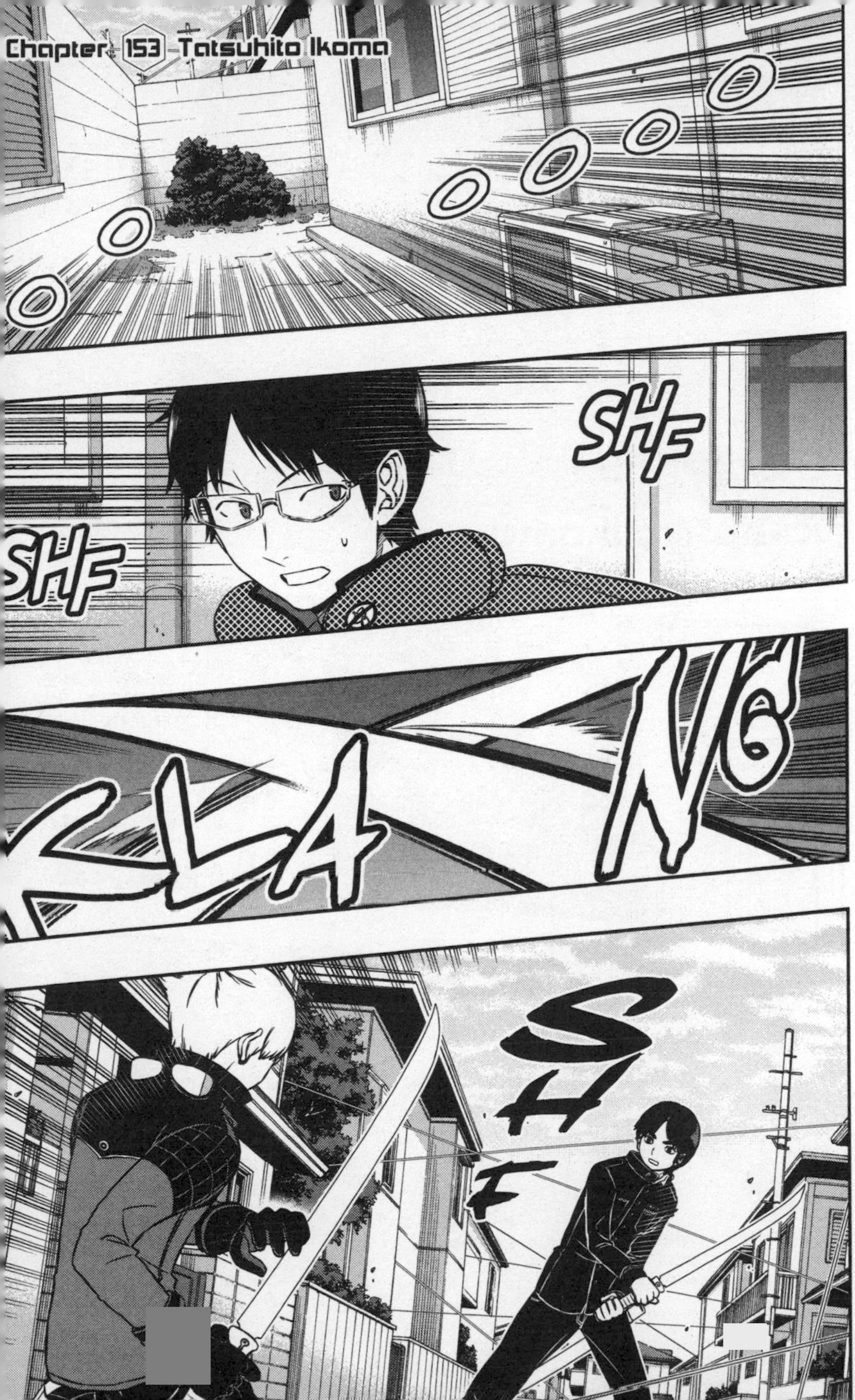
Chapter 153 Tatsuhito Ikoma
OOOOOOOO
SHF
SHF
LANG
SHF

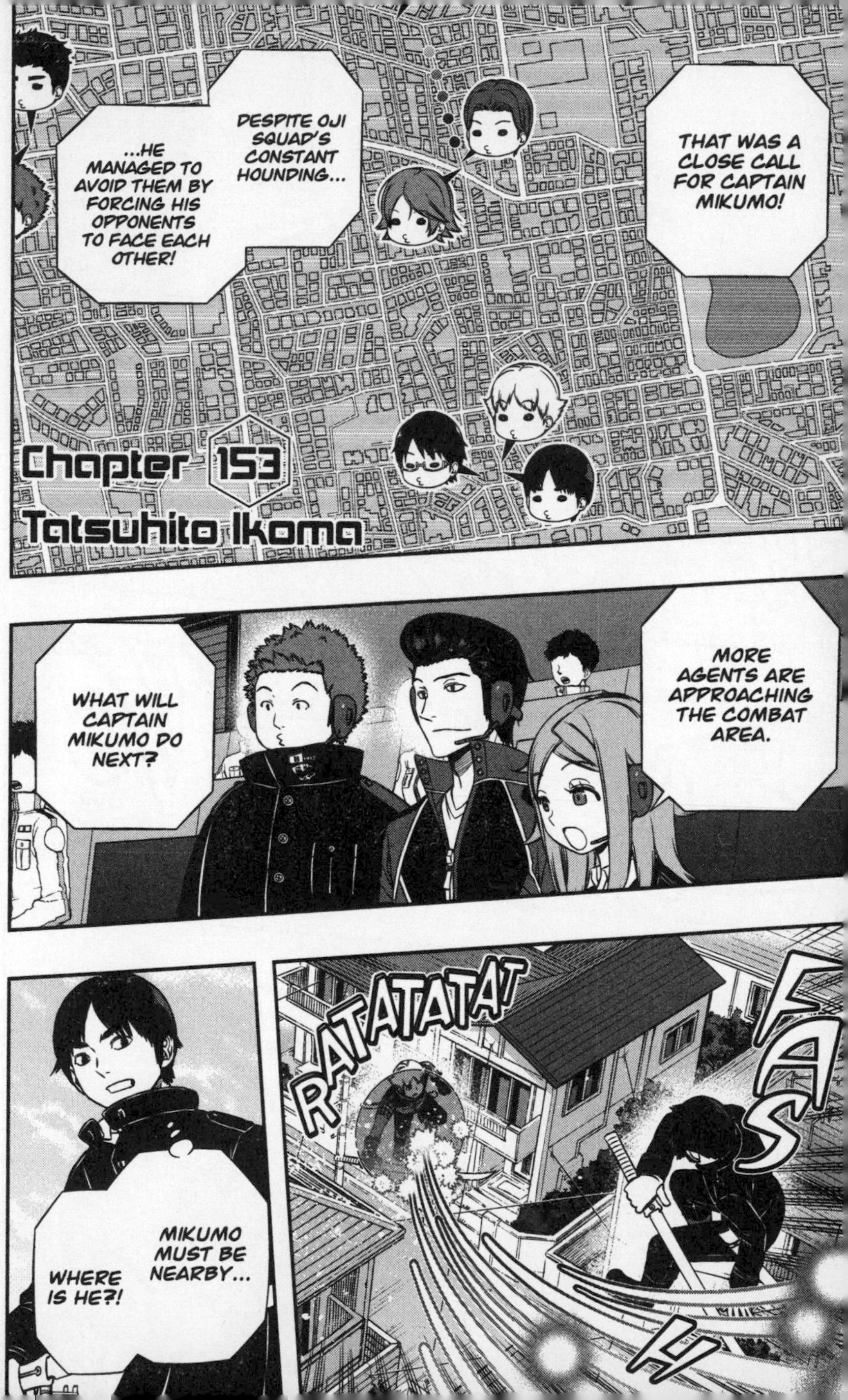
THAT WAS A CLOSE CALL FOR CAPTAIN MIKUMO!
DESPITE OJI SQUAD'S CONSTANT HOUNDING...
...HE MANAGED TO AVOID THEM BY FORCING HIS OPPONENTS TO FACE EACH OTHER!
Chapter 153
Tatsuhito Ikoma
MORE AGENTS ARE APPROACHING THE COMBAT AREA.
WHAT WILL CAPTAIN MIKUMO DO NEXT?
FASH
RATATATAT
MIKUMO MUST BE NEARBY...
WHERE IS HE?!

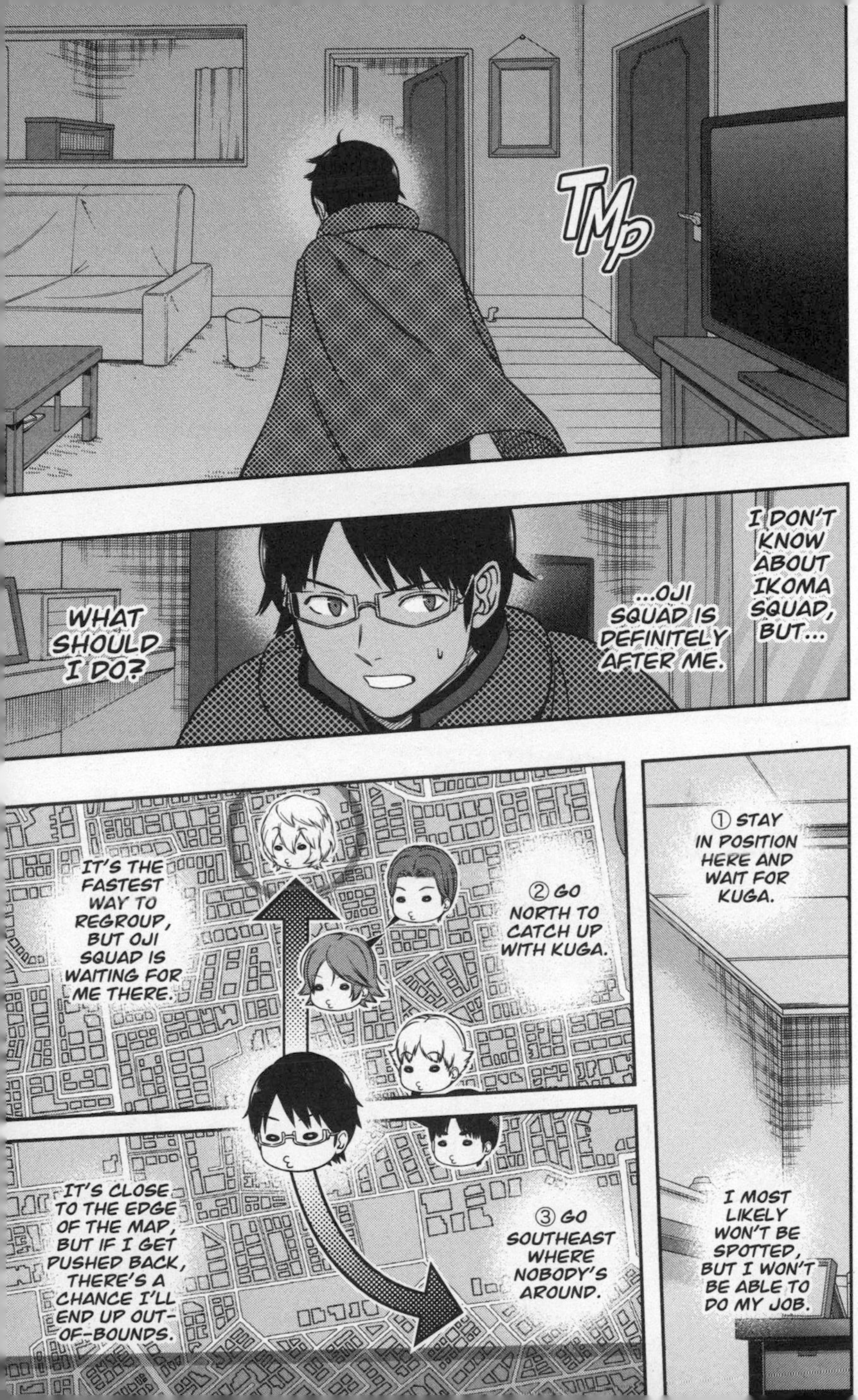
TMP
I DON'T KNOW ABOUT IKOMA SQUAD, BUT...
...OJI SQUAD IS DEFINITELY AFTER ME.
WHAT SHOULD I DO?
① STAY IN POSITION HERE AND WAIT FOR KUGA.
I MOST LIKELY WON'T BE SPOTTED, BUT I WON'T BE ABLE TO DO MY JOB.
② GO NORTH TO CATCH UP WITH KUGA.
IT'S THE FASTEST WAY TO REGROUP, BUT OJI SQUAD IS WAITING FOR ME THERE.
③ GO SOUTHEAST WHERE NOBODY'S AROUND.
IT'S CLOSE TO THE EDGE OF THE MAP, BUT IF I GET PUSHED BACK, THERE'S A CHANCE I'LL END UP OUT-OF-BOUNDS.

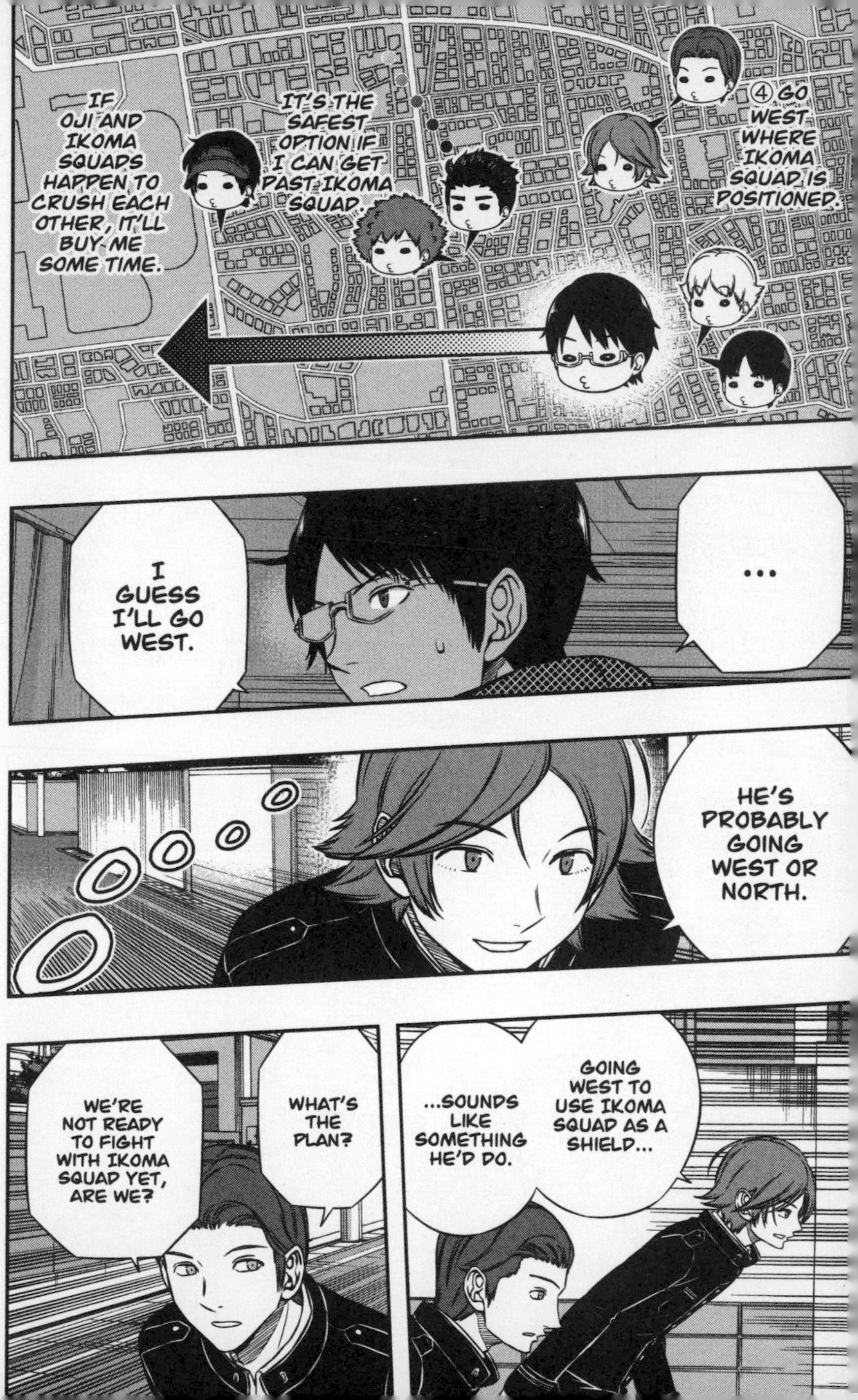
④ GO WEST WHERE IKOMA SQUAD IS POSITIONED.
IT'S THE SAFEST OPTION IF I CAN GET PAST IKOMA SQUAD.
IF OJI AND IKOMA SQUADS HAPPEN TO CRUSH EACH OTHER, IT'LL BUY ME SOME TIME.
...
I GUESS I'LL GO WEST.
HE'S PROBABLY GOING WEST OR NORTH.
GOING WEST TO USE IKOMA SQUAD AS A SHIELD...
...SOUNDS LIKE SOMETHING HE'D DO.
WHAT'S THE PLAN?
WE'RE NOT READY TO FIGHT WITH IKOMA SQUAD YET, ARE WE?

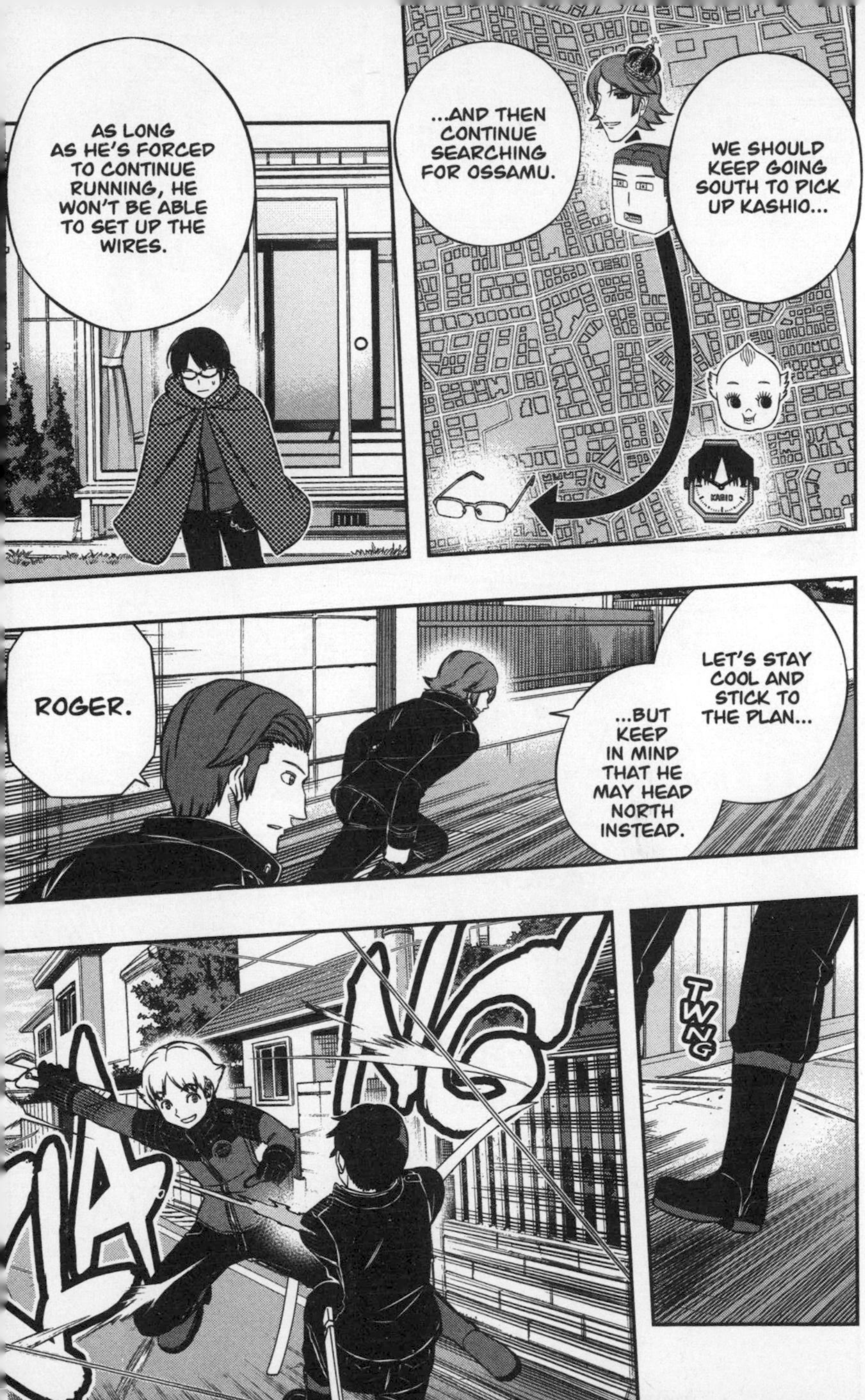
WE SHOULD KEEP GOING SOUTH TO PICK UP KASHIO...
...AND THEN CONTINUE SEARCHING FOR OSSAMU.
AS LONG AS HE'S FORCED TO CONTINUE RUNNING, HE WON'T BE ABLE TO SET UP THE WIRES.
LET'S STAY COOL AND STICK TO THE PLAN...
...BUT KEEP IN MIND THAT HE MAY HEAD NORTH INSTEAD.
ROGER.
TWNG

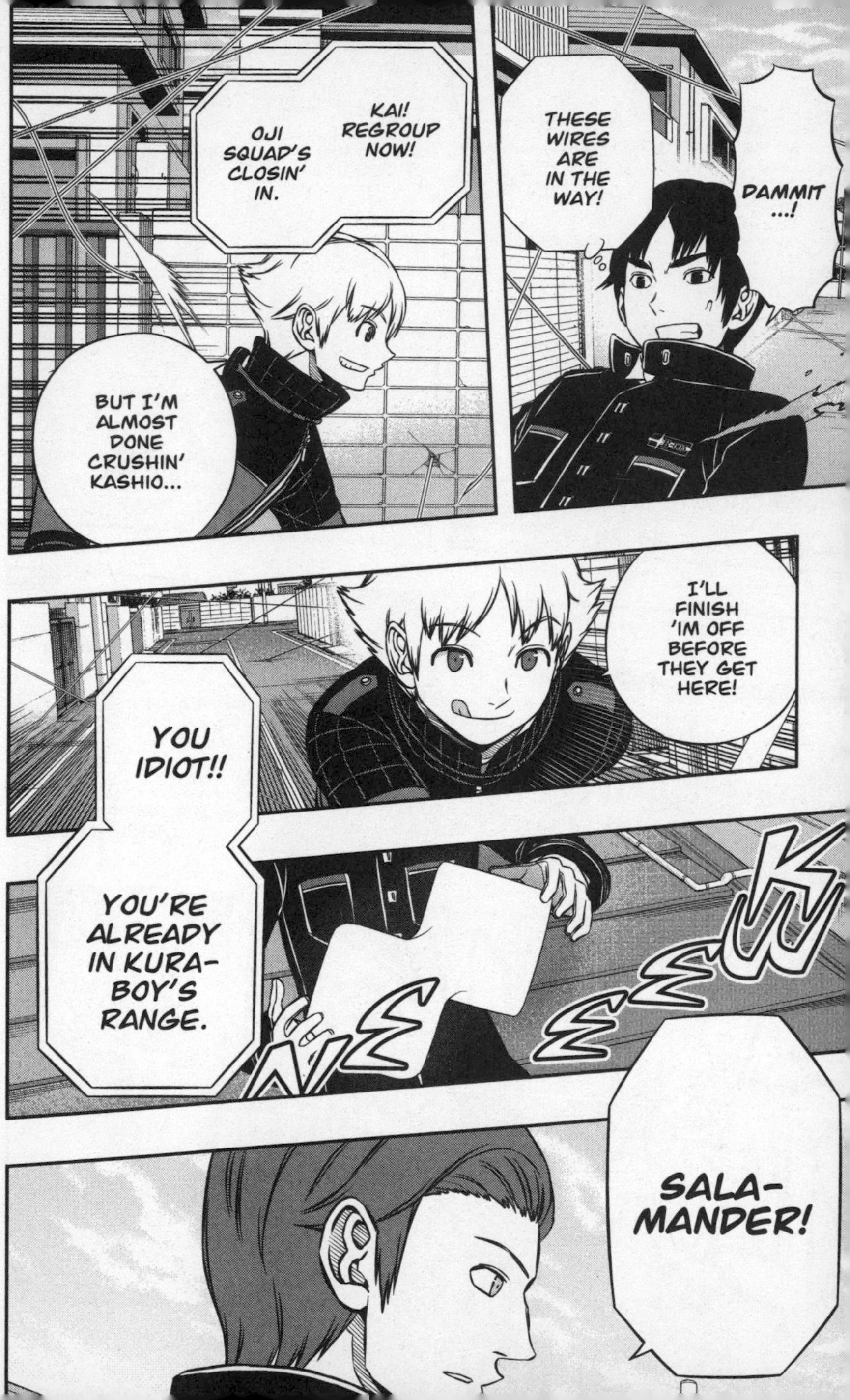
DAMMIT...!
THESE WIRES ARE IN THE WAY!
KAI! REGROUP NOW!
OJI SQUAD'S CLOSIN' IN.
BUT I'M ALMOST DONE CRUSHIN' KASHIO...
I'LL FINISH 'IM OFF BEFORE THEY GET HERE!
YOU IDIOT!!
YOU'RE ALREADY IN KURA-BOY'S RANGE.
KWEEEN
SALA-MANDER!

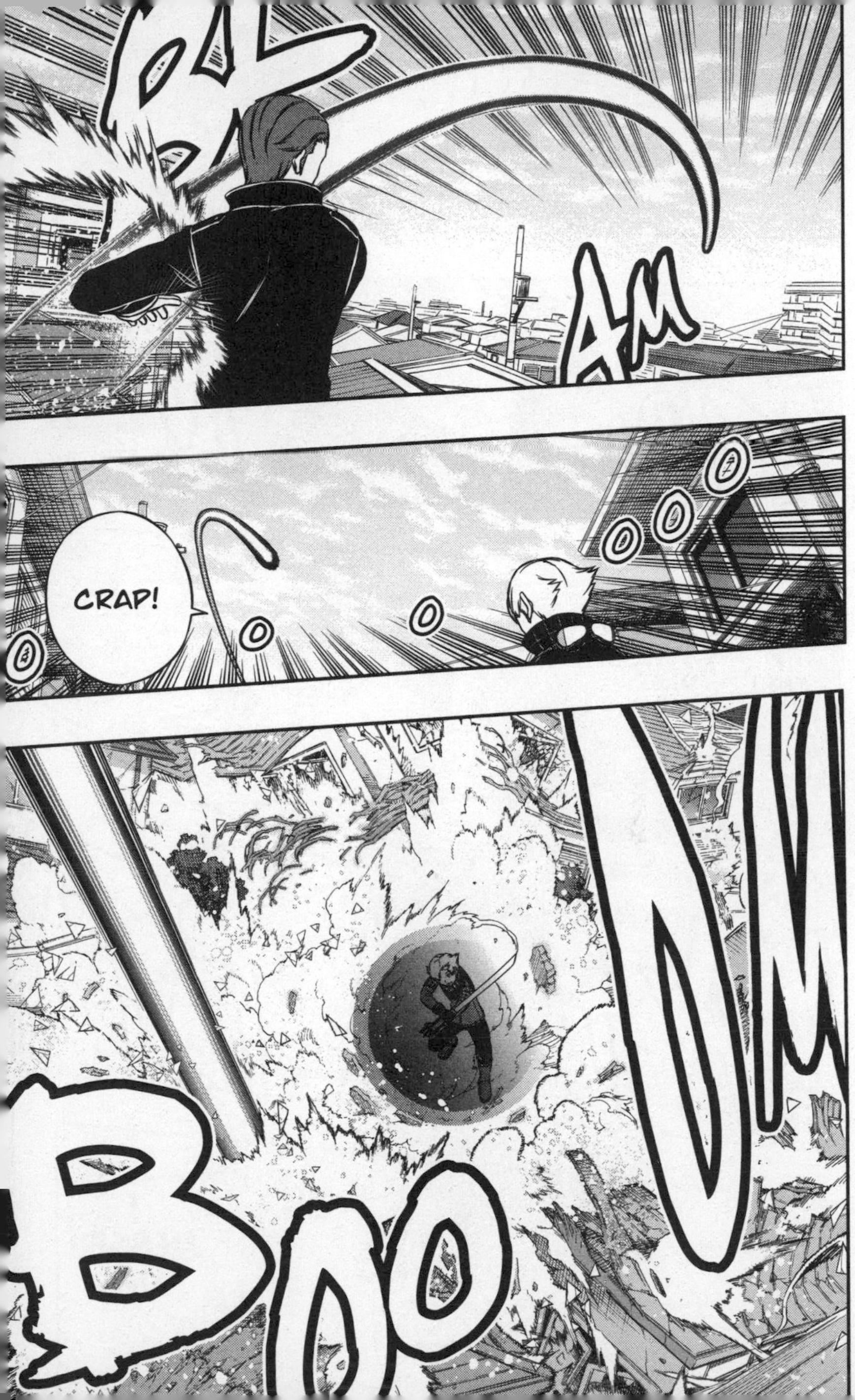
CRAP!
BOOOM

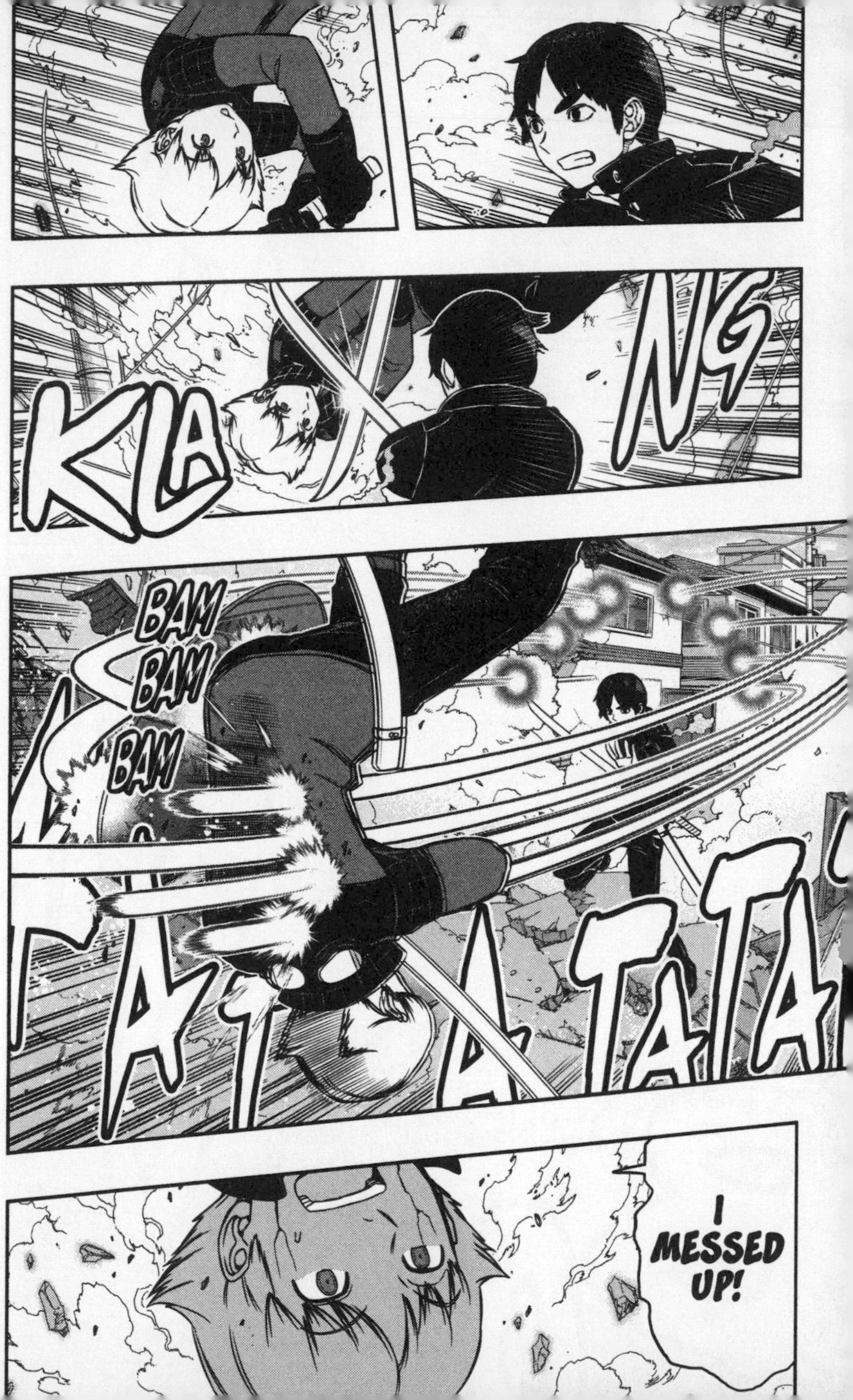
KLANG
BAM
BAM
BAM
TATATATA
I MESSED UP!

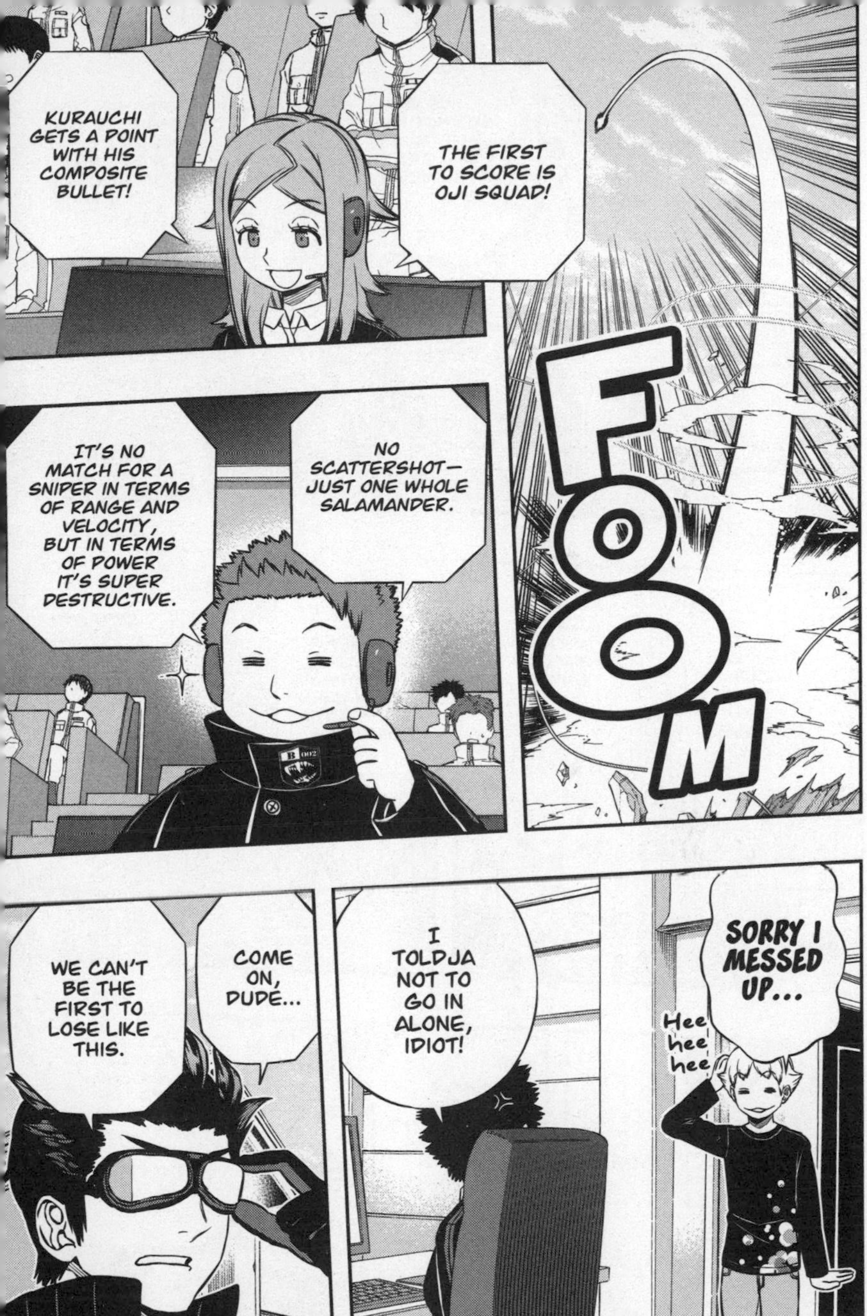
FOOM
THE FIRST TO SCORE IS OJI SQUAD!
KURAUCHI GETS A POINT WITH HIS COMPOSITE BULLET!
NO SCATTERSHOT— JUST ONE WHOLE SALAMANDER.
IT'S NO MATCH FOR A SNIPER IN TERMS OF RANGE AND VELOCITY, BUT IN TERMS OF POWER IT'S SUPER DESTRUCTIVE.
SORRY I MESSED UP...
Hee hee hee
I TOLDJA NOT TO GO IN ALONE, IDIOT!
COME ON, DUDE...
WE CAN'T BE THE FIRST TO LOSE LIKE THIS.

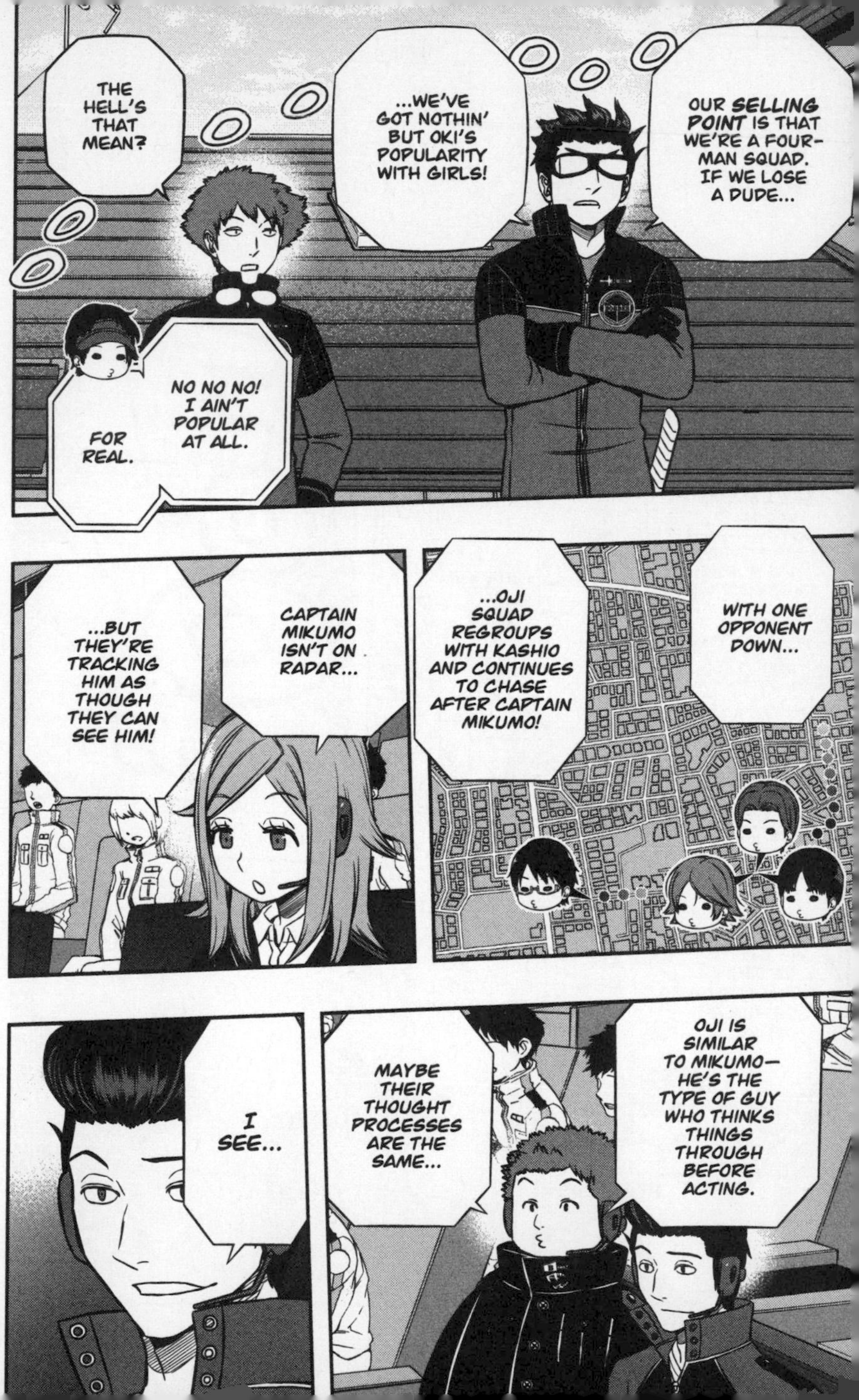
OUR SELLING POINT IS THAT WE'RE A FOUR-MAN SQUAD. IF WE LOSE A DUDE...
...WE'VE GOT NOTHIN' BUT OKI'S POPULARITY WITH GIRLS!
THE HELL'S THAT MEAN?
NO NO NO! I AIN'T POPULAR AT ALL.
FOR REAL.
WITH ONE OPPONENT DOWN...
...OJI SQUAD REGROUPS WITH KASHIO AND CONTINUES TO CHASE AFTER CAPTAIN MIKUMO!
CAPTAIN MIKUMO ISN'T ON RADAR...
...BUT THEY'RE TRACKING HIM AS THOUGH THEY CAN SEE HIM!
OJI IS SIMILAR TO MIKUMO—HE'S THE TYPE OF GUY WHO THINKS THINGS THROUGH BEFORE ACTING.
MAYBE THEIR THOUGHT PROCESSES ARE THE SAME...
I SEE...

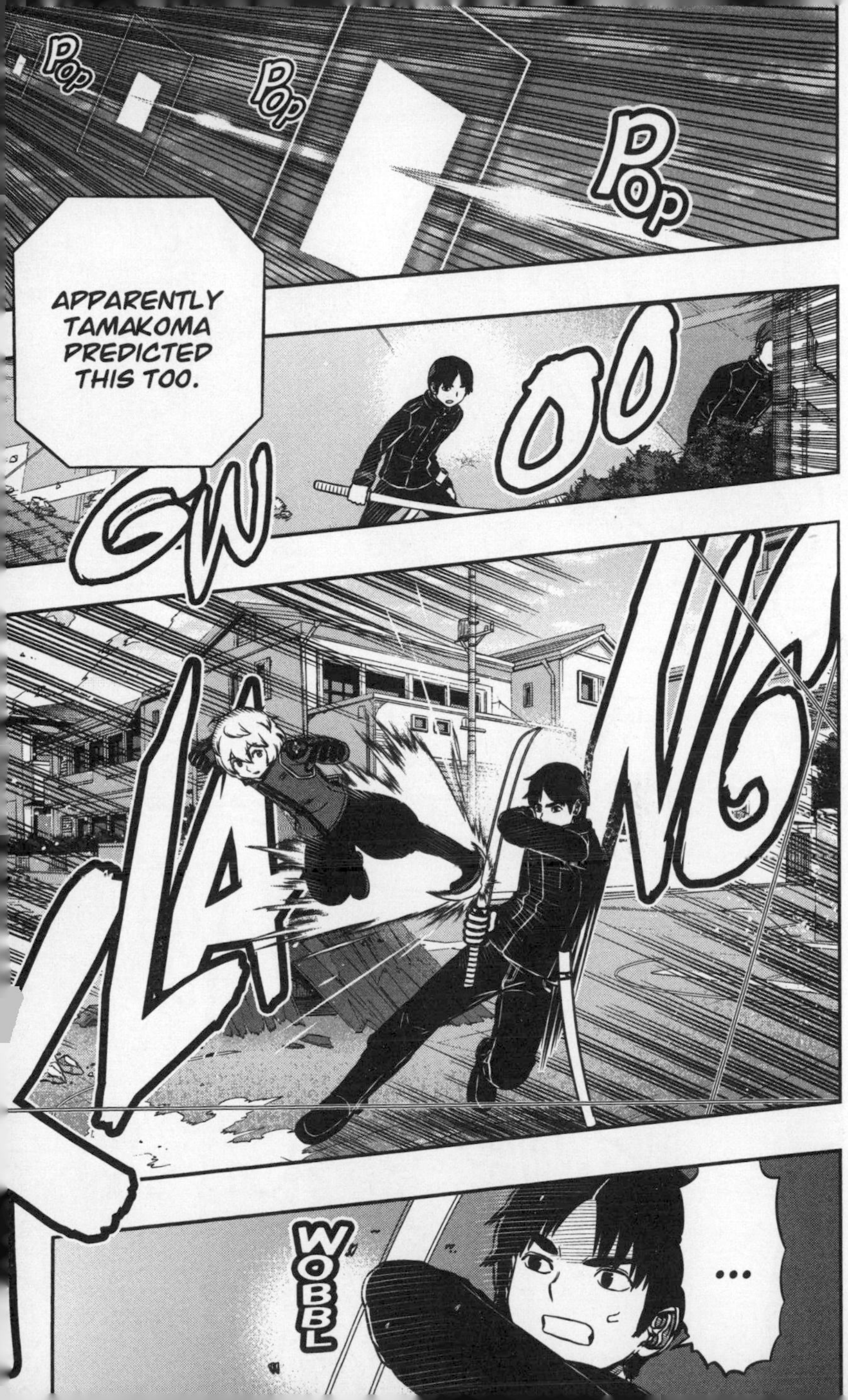
Pop
Pop
Pop
APPARENTLY TAMAKOMA PREDICTED THIS TOO.
GWOO
ZANG
...
WOBBL

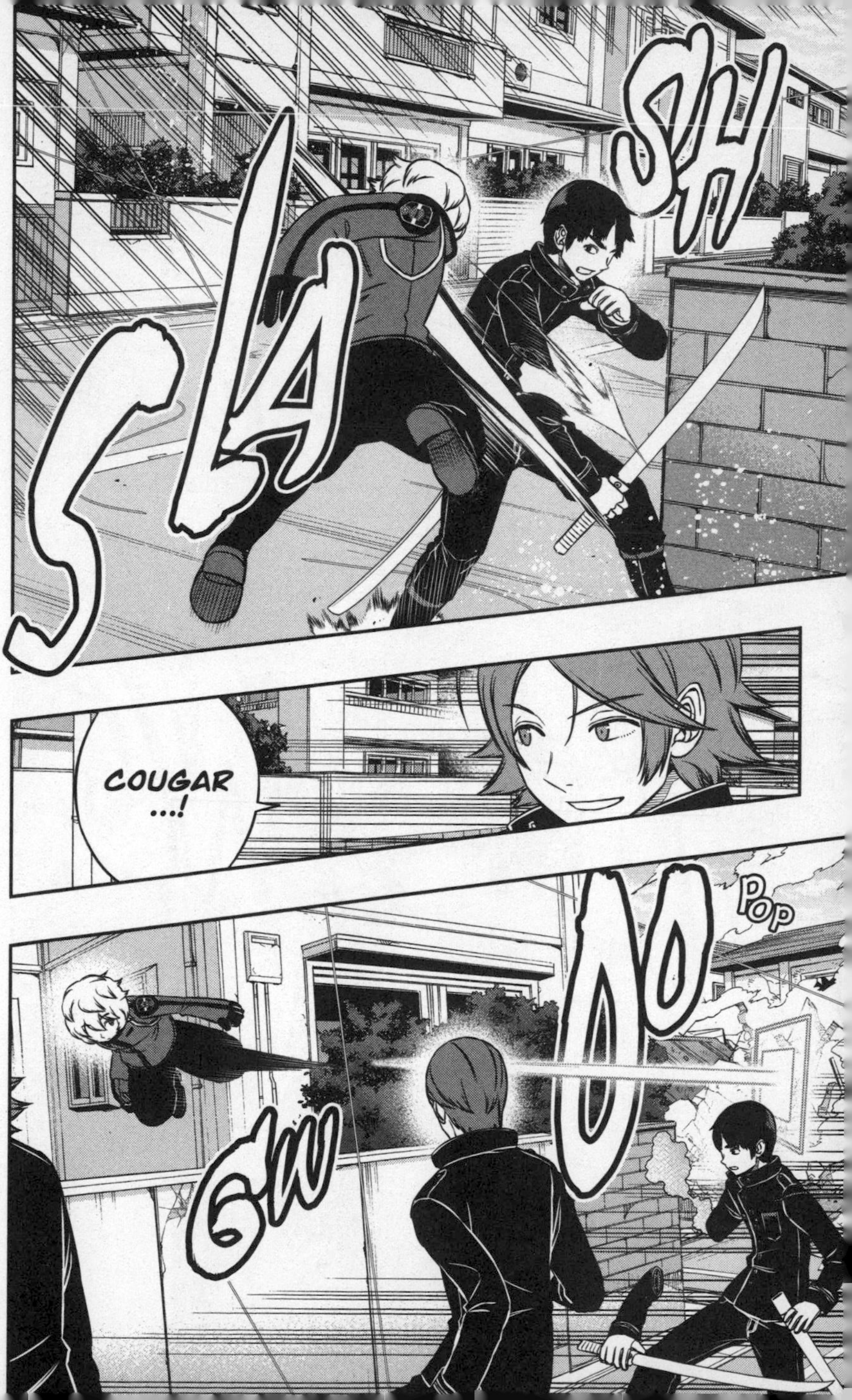
SLASH
COUGAR ...!
POP
GW

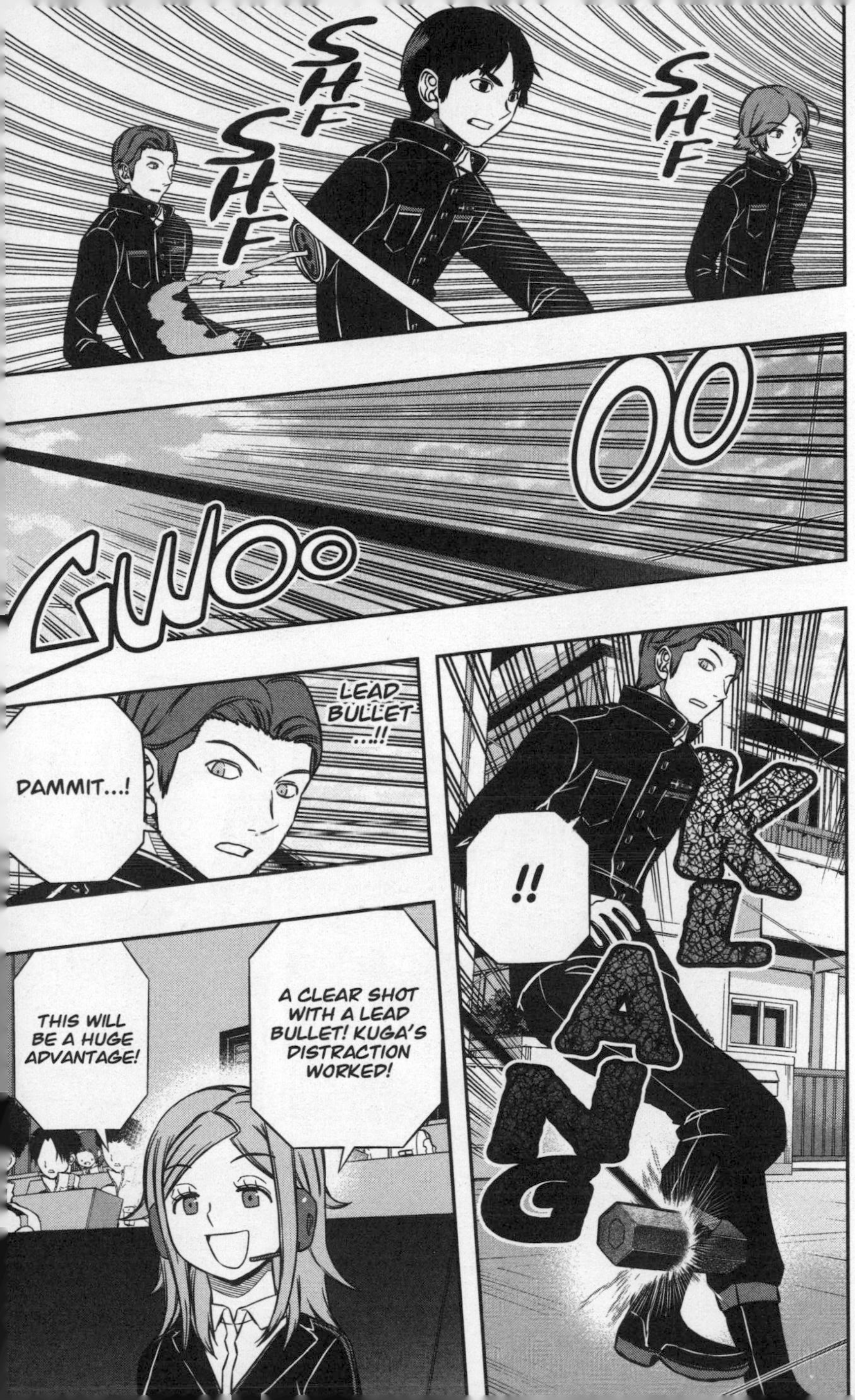
SHF
SHF SHF
GUOOOO
!!
KLANG
LEAD BULLET ...!!
DAMMIT...!
A CLEAR SHOT WITH A LEAD BULLET! KUGA'S DISTRACTION WORKED!
THIS WILL BE A HUGE ADVANTAGE!

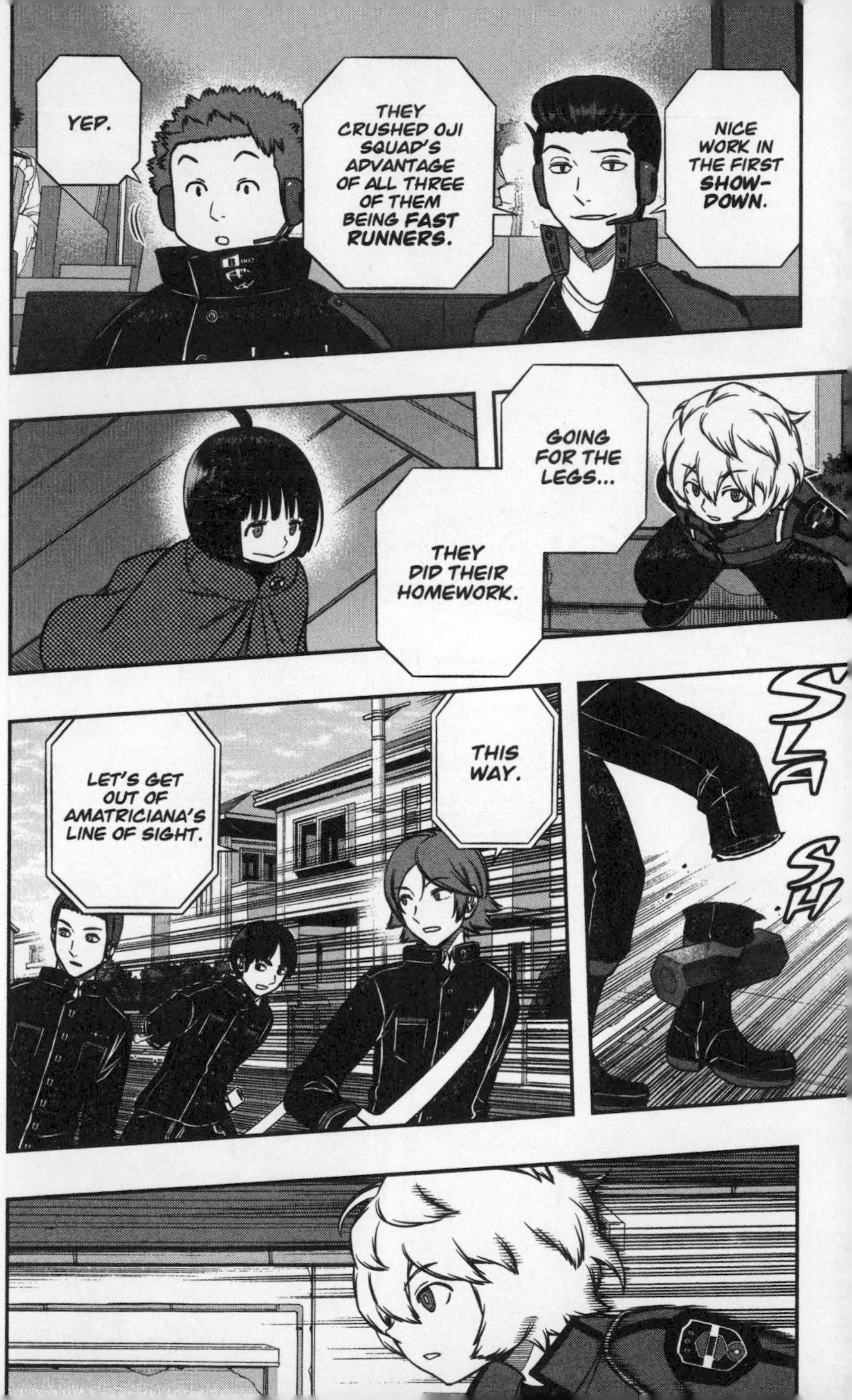
NICE WORK IN THE FIRST SHOW-DOWN.
THEY CRUSHED OJI SQUAD'S ADVANTAGE OF ALL THREE OF THEM BEING FAST RUNNERS.
YEP.
GOING FOR THE LEGS...
THEY DID THEIR HOMEWORK.
SLASH
THIS WAY.
LET'S GET OUT OF AMATRICIANA'S LINE OF SIGHT.

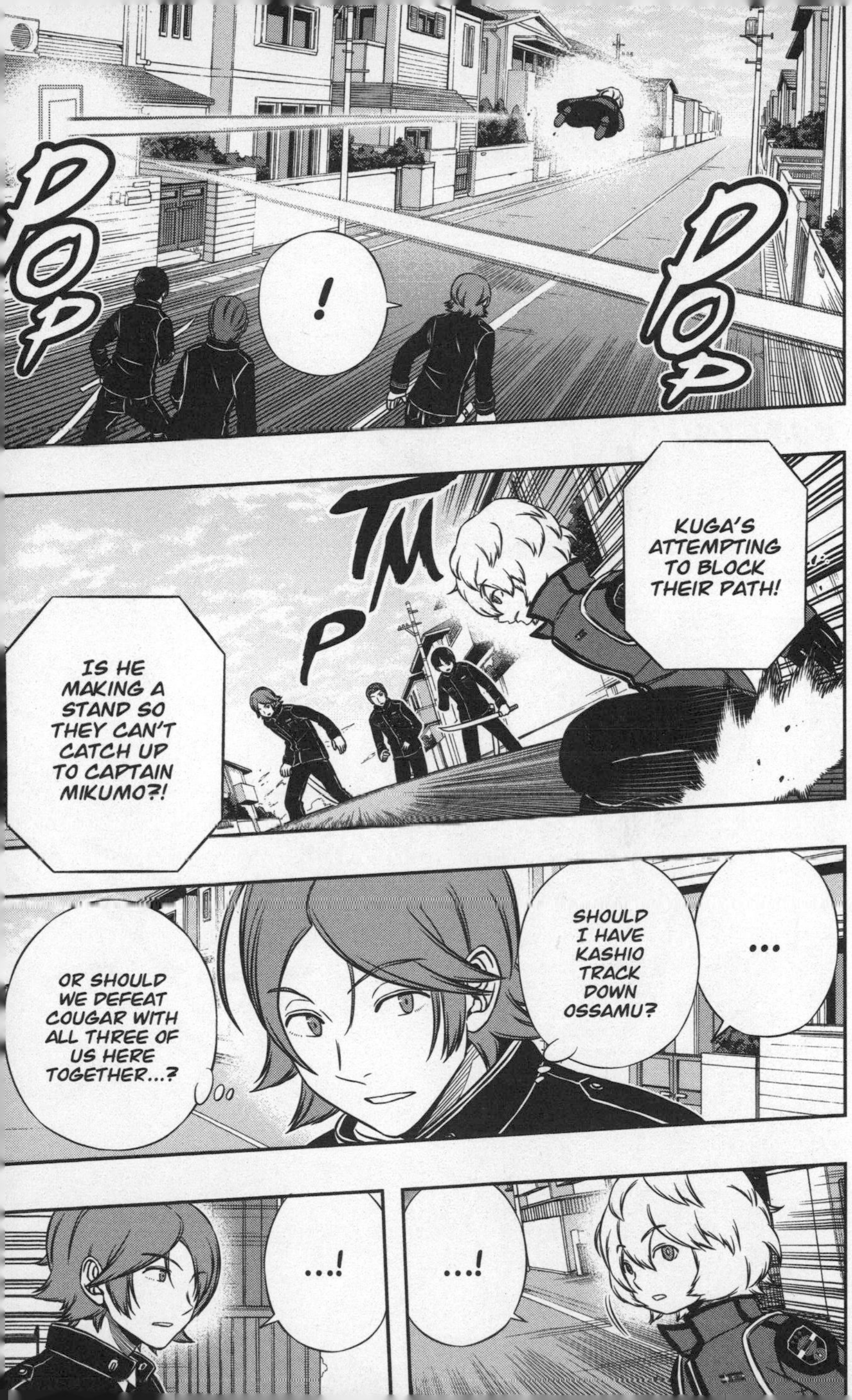
POP
!
POP
KUGA'S ATTEMPTING TO BLOCK THEIR PATH!
TMP
IS HE MAKING A STAND SO THEY CAN'T CATCH UP TO CAPTAIN MIKUMO?!
...
SHOULD I HAVE KASHIO TRACK DOWN OSSAMU?
OR SHOULD WE DEFEAT COUGAR WITH ALL THREE OF US HERE TOGETHER...?
...!
...!

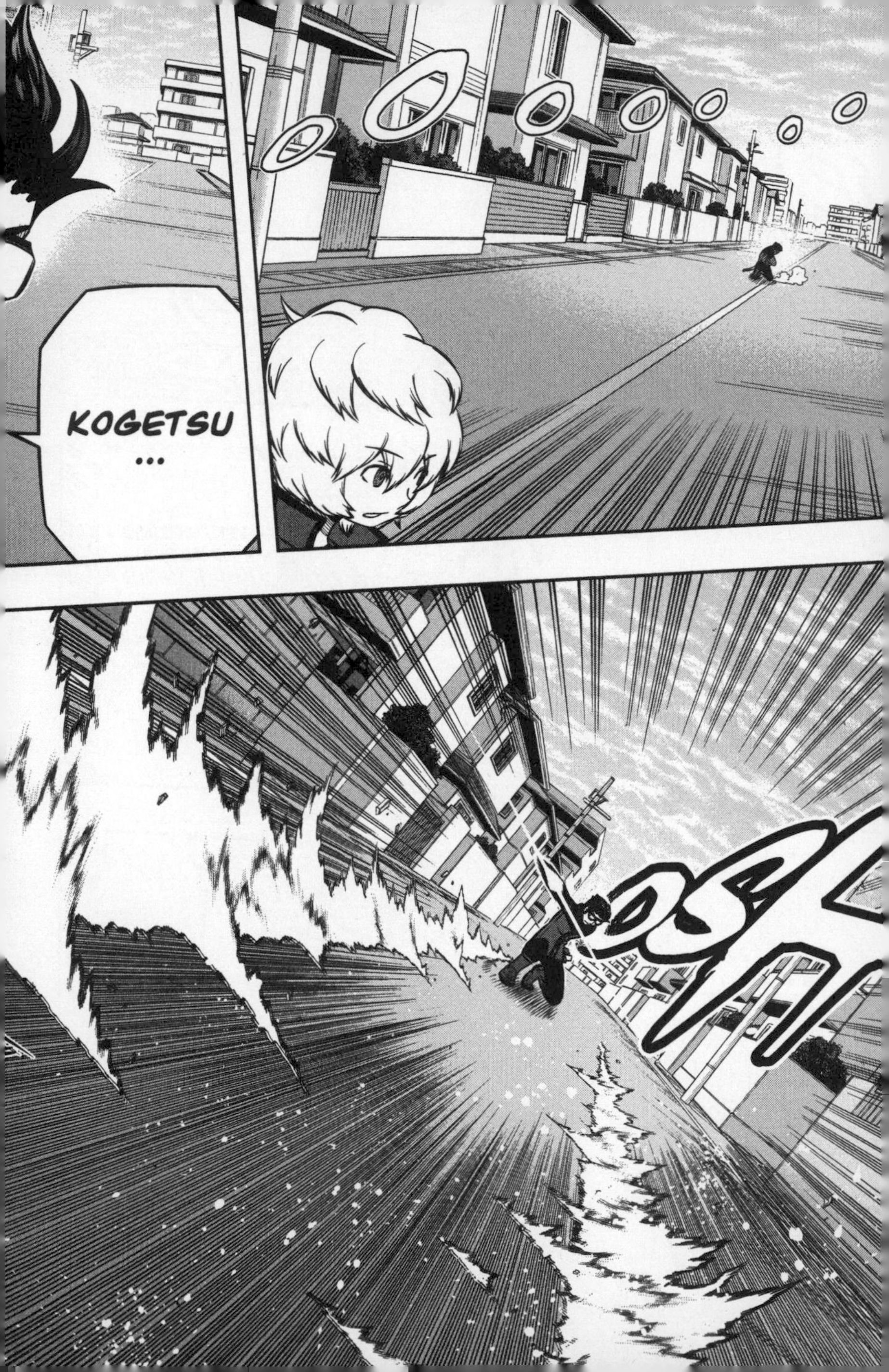
KOGETSU ...

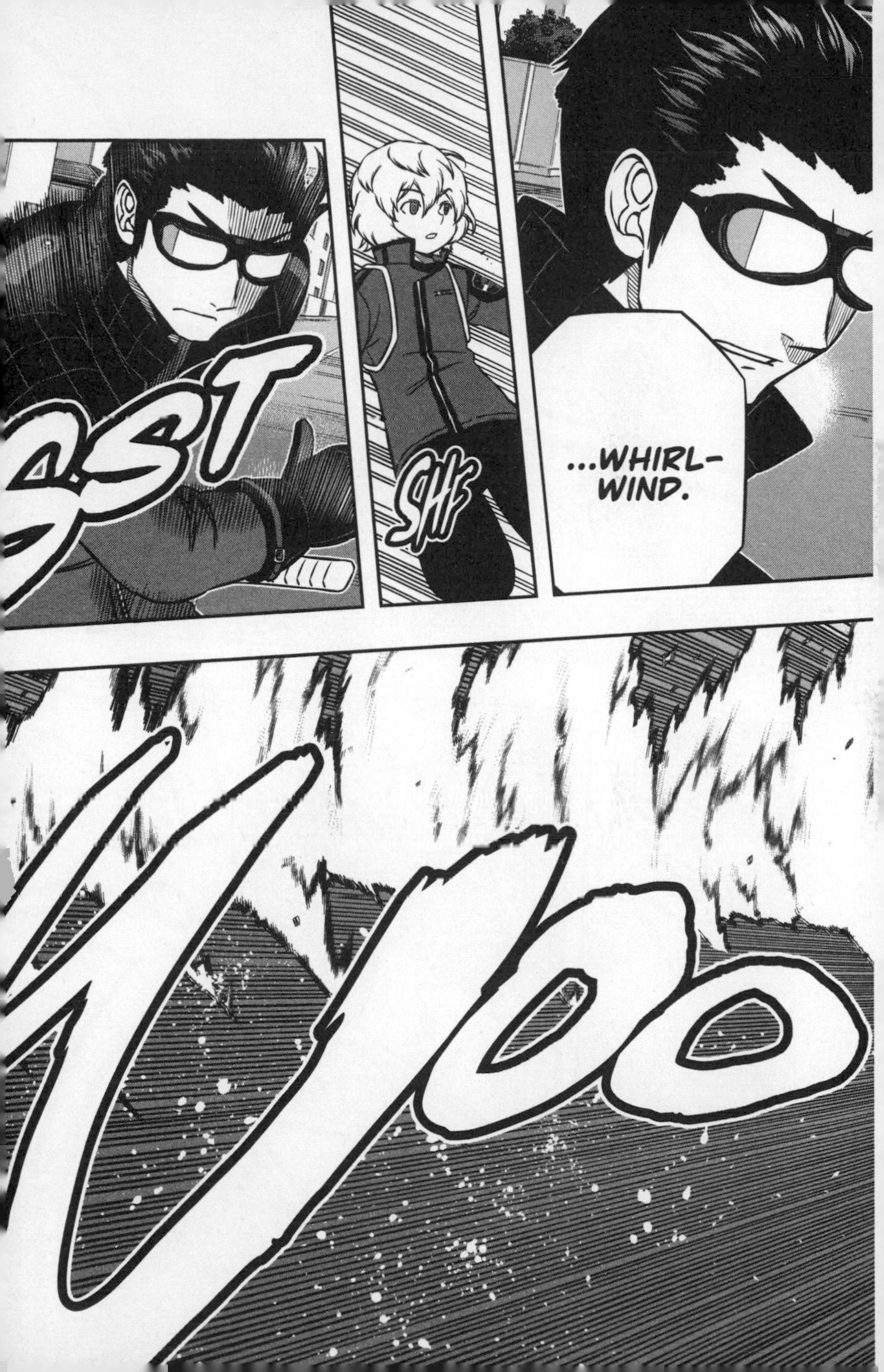
...WHIRL-WIND.
SHF

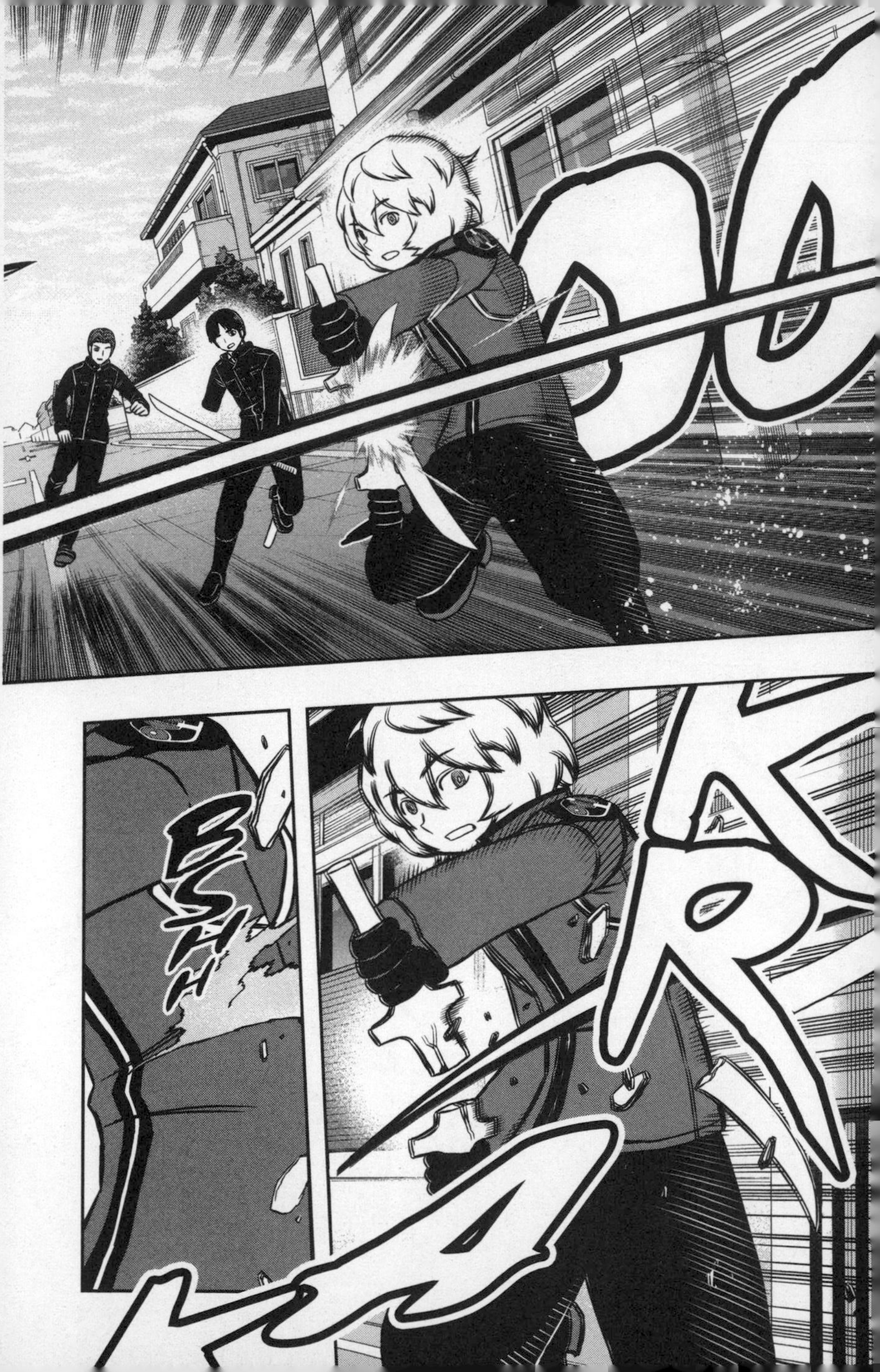
SSHH

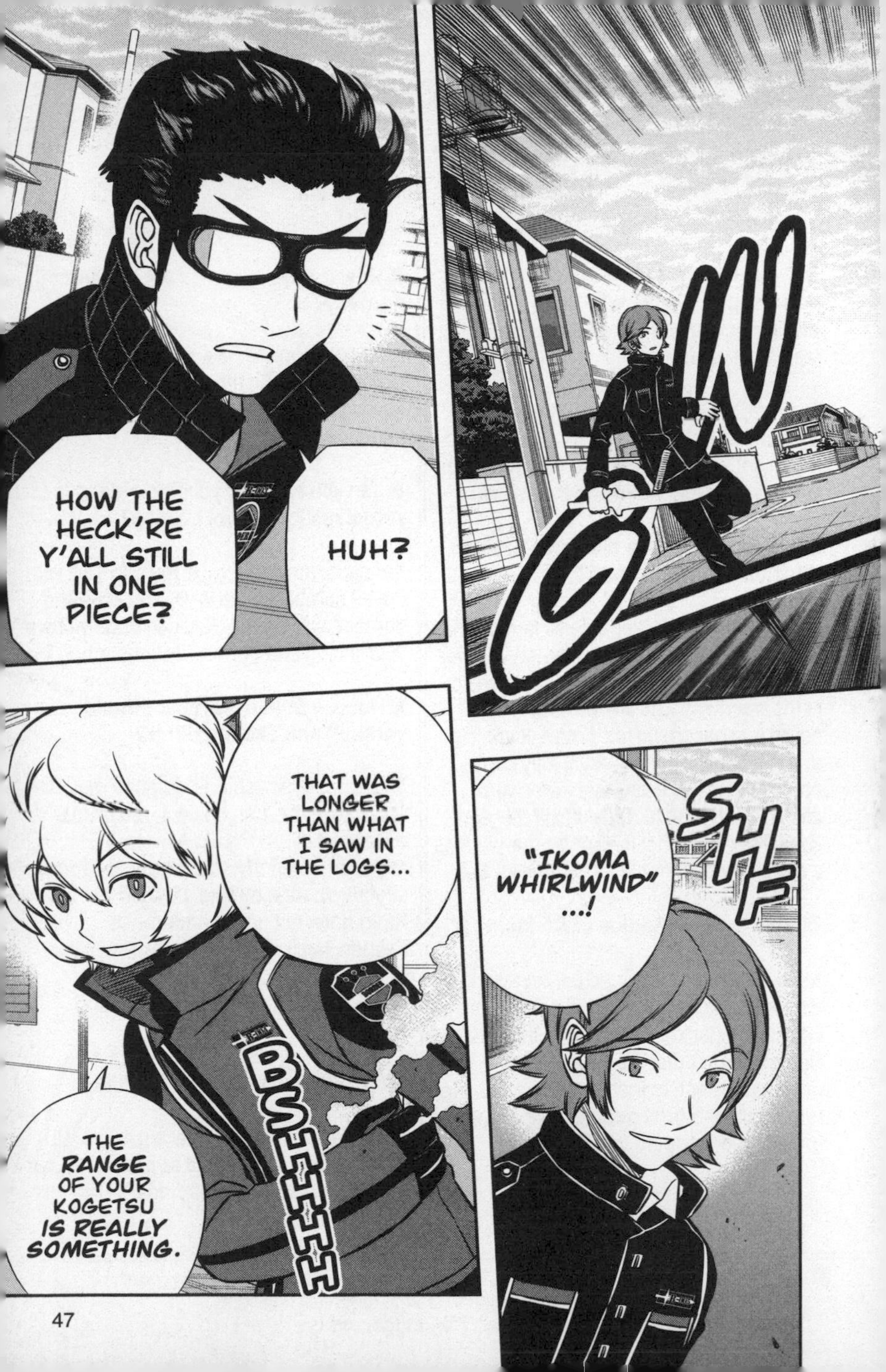
HUH?
HOW THE HECK'RE Y'ALL STILL IN ONE PIECE?
SHF
"IKOMA WHIRLWIND" ...!
THAT WAS LONGER THAN WHAT I SAW IN THE LOGS...
BSHHHHH
THE RANGE OF YOUR KOGETSU IS REALLY SOMETHING.

Q&A: Part 11

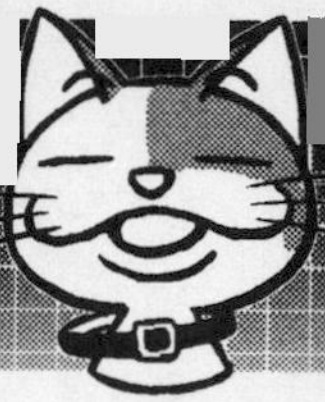

Questions that I forgot about...

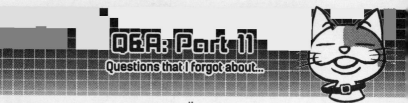

■C-Rank agents are supposed to have one weapon Trigger. Why does Chika equip Bagworm during Tamakoma's training session?

That one was a Tamakoma exclusive Trigger that Reiji prepared for Chika to teach her sniper basics. The Trigger comes with three sniper rifles and Bagworm.

■Are there any other branches besides Tamakoma and Suzunari?

Border has six branches in total: Tamakoma, Suzunari, Watayu, Yumitemachi, Hayanuma and Kuma. These branches are comprised of the members who are too busy to commit to becoming full-time A-Rank due to work and school, since they can't participate in two Rank Wars every week. Each branch is on the outskirts of the alert zone. They all, except for Tamakoma, work as a contact window for local citizens as well.

■What is the definition of All-Rounder?

An All-Rounder is defined as "an agent who has reached over 6,000 solo points with both Attacker and Gunner Triggers." Due to the fact that the overall level among Border has increased in quality in recent times, some people have argued to raise the standard to 8,000 points.

■How do you come up with character names?

I first come up with last names that are easy to pronounce and don't stand out too much. As for first names, I try to think about the parents who named their kids.

■Can you exercise your Trion gland in virtual reality combat training?

You can't. The only things you can train with the VR combat mode is your reflexes and combat experiences. You can only improve your Trion gland by actually consuming Trion.

■How do Shield, Raygust (Shield version) and Escudo differ?

Shield: Transformable. Endurance may change by size. Can be deployed from a distance.
Raygust: Transformable. Endurance may slightly change by size. Holding it in your hand does not affect endurance.
Escudo: Not transformable. Not movable. High endurance. Requires advance positioning in various places (ground, wall, etc.).

■Can Escudo block Lead Bullets?

Yes, because Escudo materializes Trion. It works in the same regard as protecting yourself behind walls and buildings.

■ Sometimes we answer the questions asked in fan letters on Twitter. Having more and more followers will help our person in charge to go visit New York.
World Trigger Official Twitter Account: @W_Trigger_off

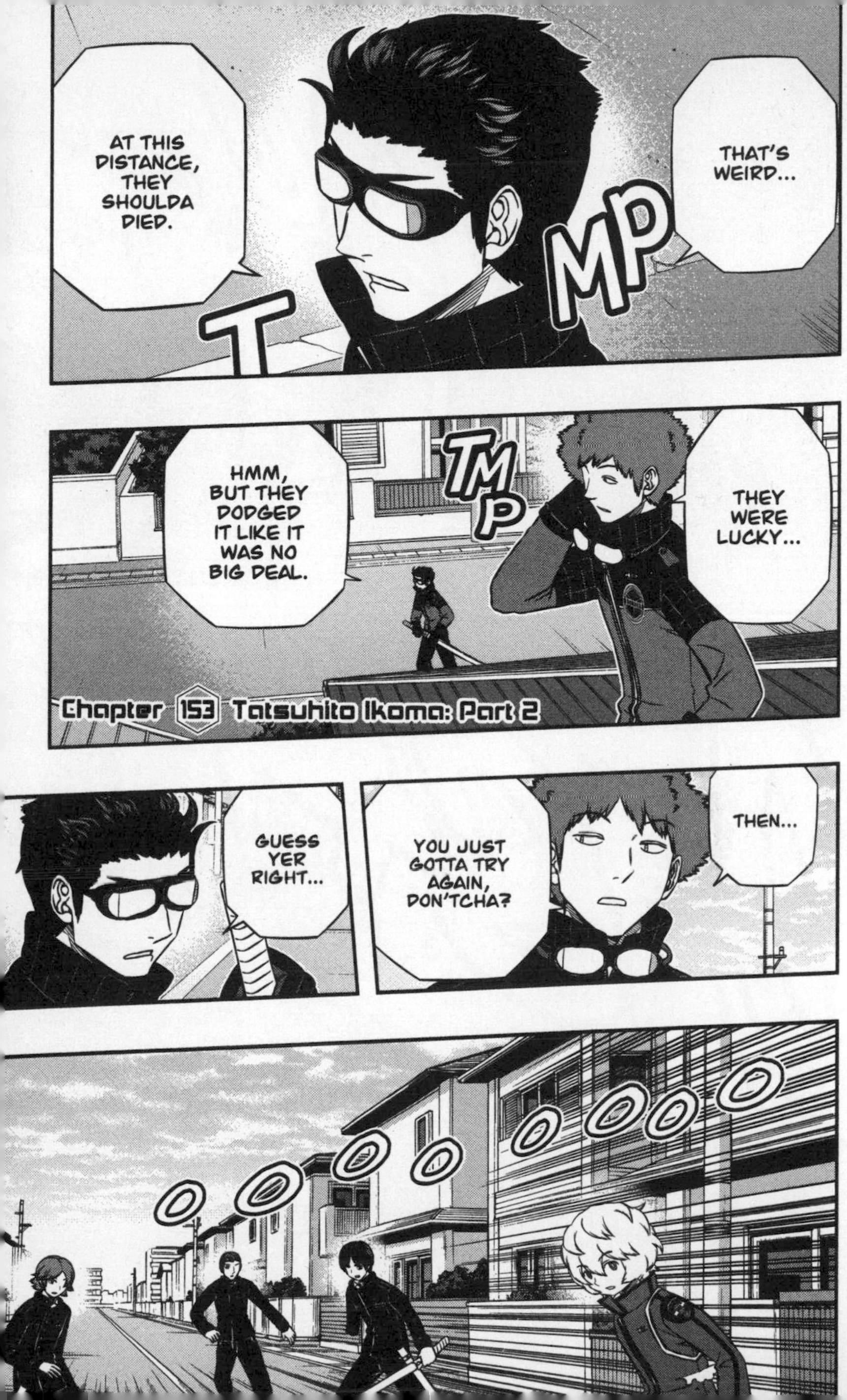
THAT'S WEIRD...
TMP
AT THIS DISTANCE, THEY SHOULDA DIED.
THEY WERE LUCKY...
TMP
HMM, BUT THEY DODGED IT LIKE IT WAS NO BIG DEAL.
Chapter 153 Tatsuhito Ikoma: Part 2
THEN...
YOU JUST GOTTA TRY AGAIN, DON'TCHA?
GUESS YER RIGHT...
OOOOOOOOO

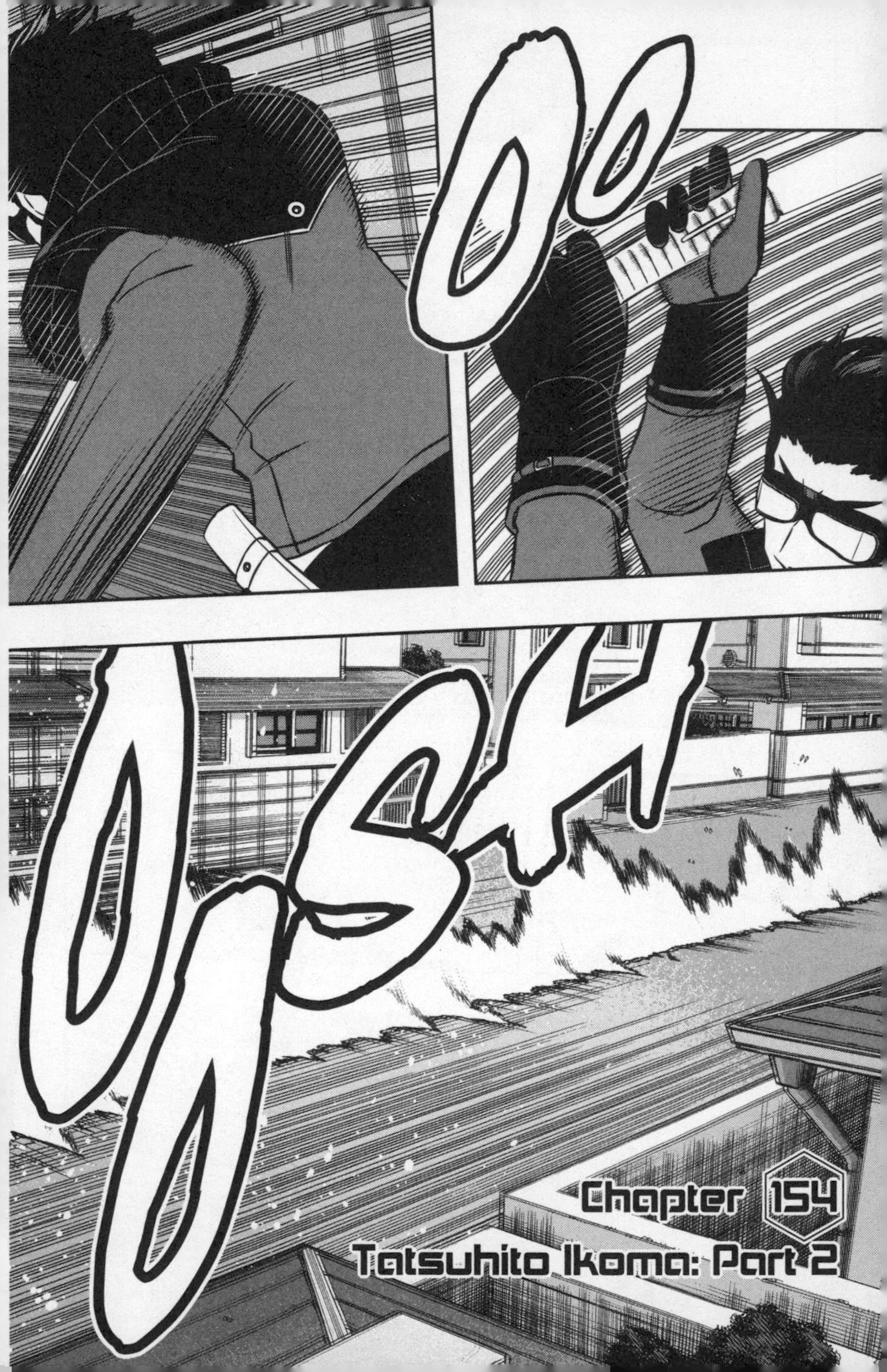
Chapter 154
Tatsuhito Ikoma: Part 2

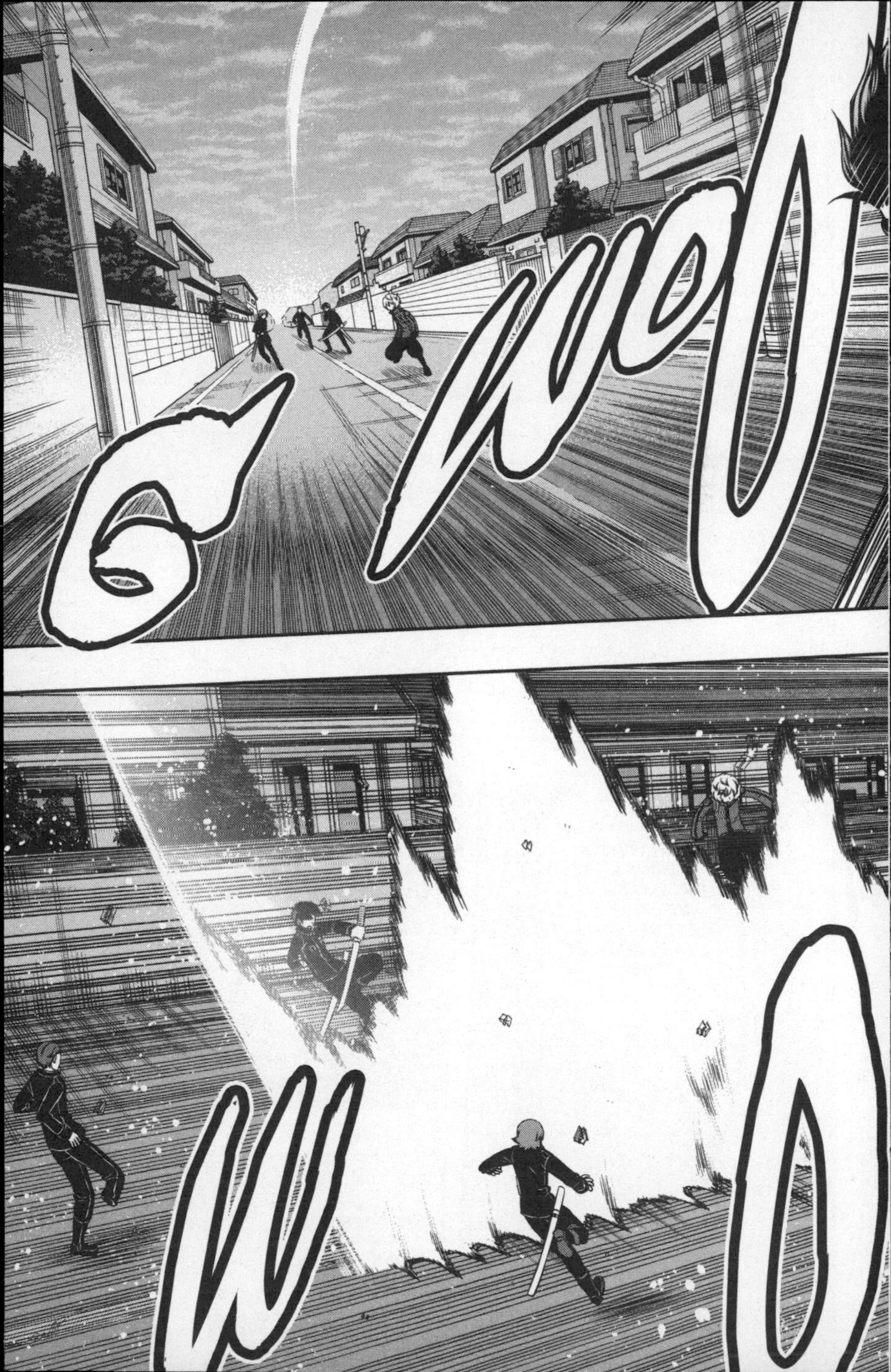

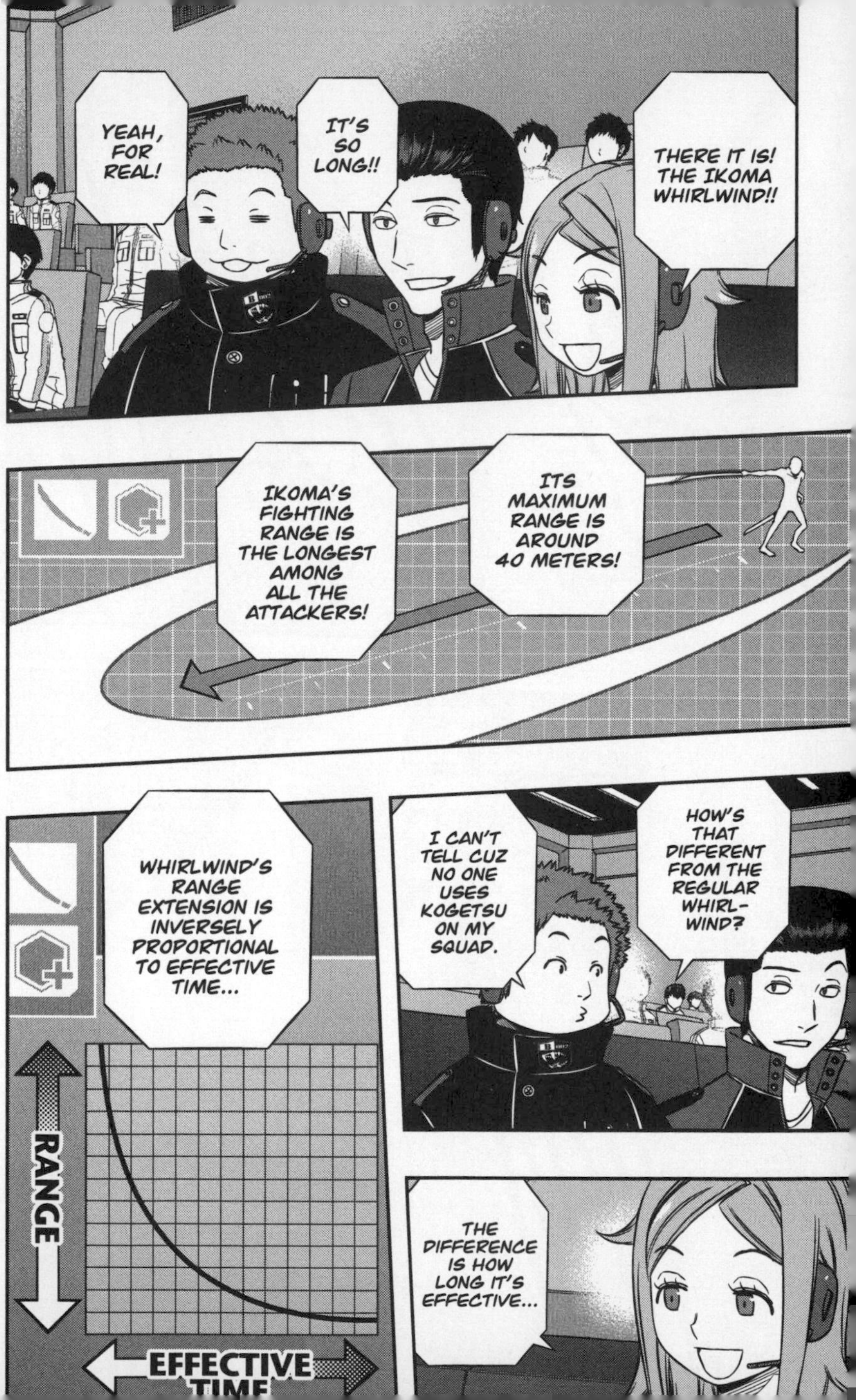
THERE IT IS! THE IKOMA WHIRLWIND!!
IT'S SO LONG!!
YEAH, FOR REAL!
ITS MAXIMUM RANGE IS AROUND 40 METERS!
IKOMA'S FIGHTING RANGE IS THE LONGEST AMONG ALL THE ATTACKERS!
HOW'S THAT DIFFERENT FROM THE REGULAR WHIRL-WIND?
I CAN'T TELL CUZ NO ONE USES KOGETSU ON MY SQUAD.
THE DIFFERENCE IS HOW LONG IT'S EFFECTIVE...
WHIRLWIND'S RANGE EXTENSION IS INVERSELY PROPORTIONAL TO EFFECTIVE TIME...
RANGE
EFFECTIVE TIME

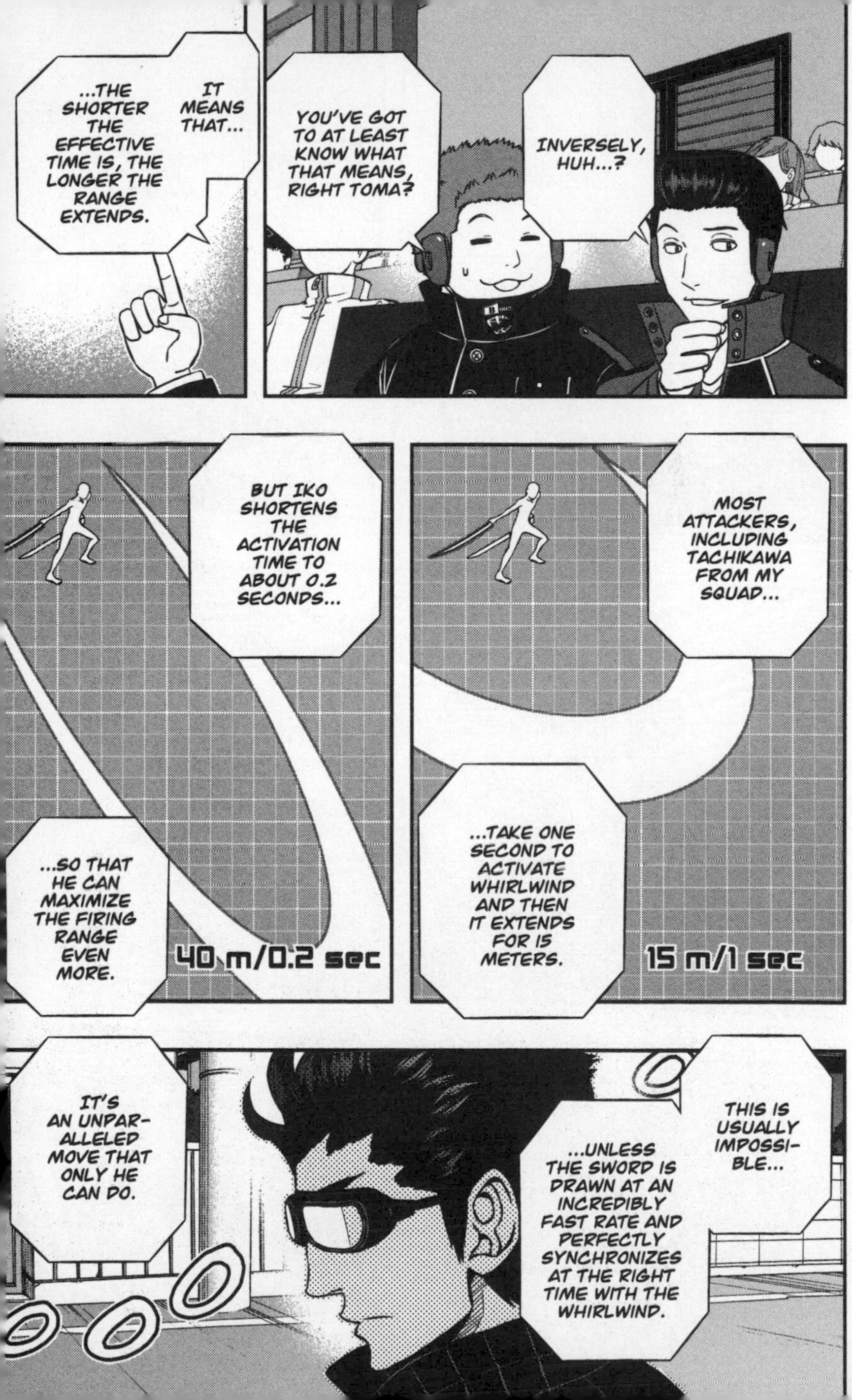
INVERSELY, HUH...?
YOU'VE GOT TO AT LEAST KNOW WHAT THAT MEANS, RIGHT TOMA?
IT MEANS THAT...
...THE SHORTER THE EFFECTIVE TIME IS, THE LONGER THE RANGE EXTENDS.
MOST ATTACKERS, INCLUDING TACHIKAWA FROM MY SQUAD...
...TAKE ONE SECOND TO ACTIVATE WHIRLWIND AND THEN IT EXTENDS FOR 15 METERS.
15 m/1 sec
BUT IKO SHORTENS THE ACTIVATION TIME TO ABOUT 0.2 SECONDS...
...SO THAT HE CAN MAXIMIZE THE FIRING RANGE EVEN MORE.
40 m/0.2 sec
THIS IS USUALLY IMPOSSI-BLE...
...UNLESS THE SWORD IS DRAWN AT AN INCREDIBLY FAST RATE AND PERFECTLY SYNCHRONIZES AT THE RIGHT TIME WITH THE WHIRLWIND.
IT'S AN UNPAR-ALLELED MOVE THAT ONLY HE CAN DO.

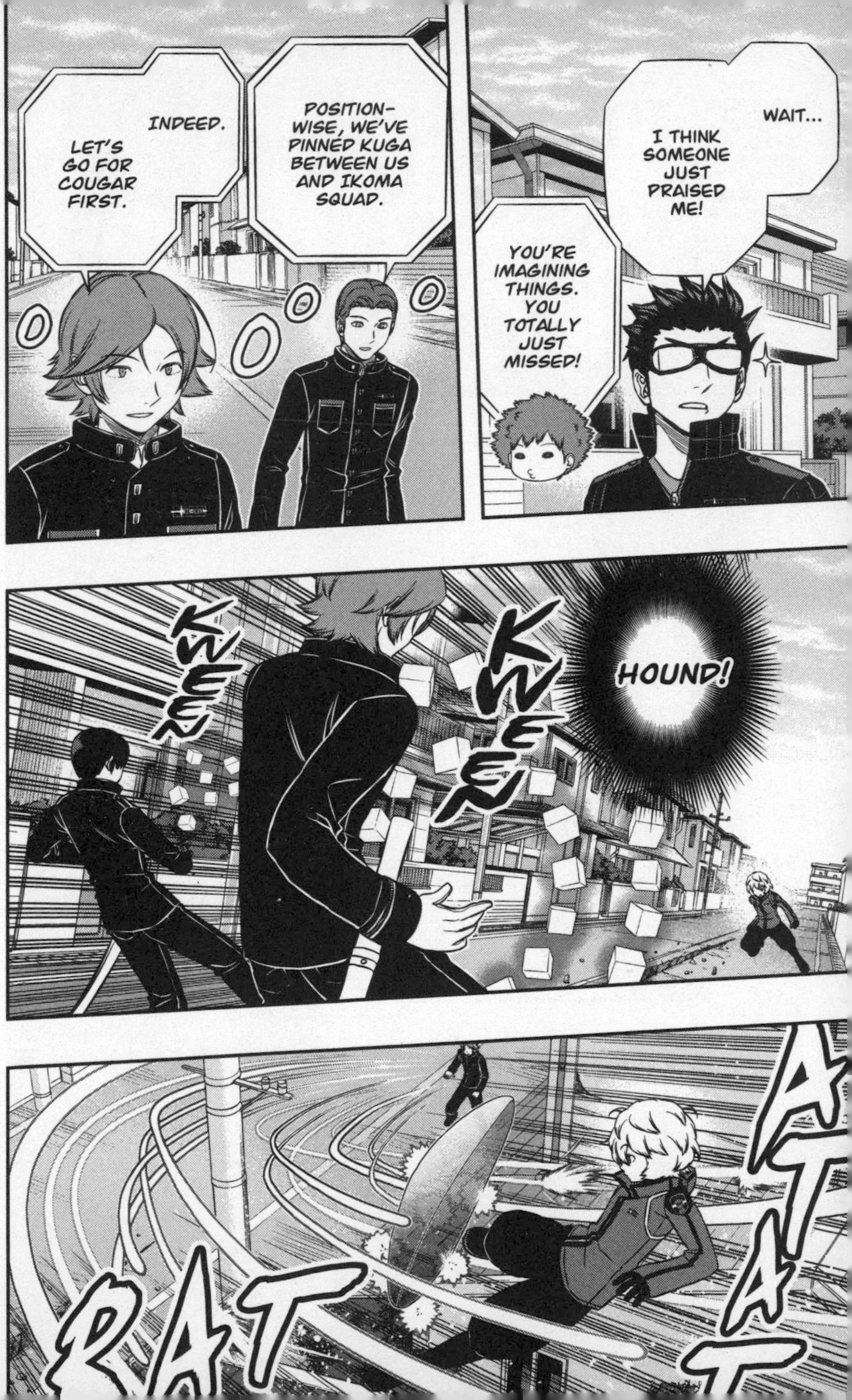
WAIT...
I THINK SOMEONE JUST PRAISED ME!
YOU'RE IMAGINING THINGS. YOU TOTALLY JUST MISSED!
POSITION-WISE, WE'VE PINNED KUGA BETWEEN US AND IKOMA SQUAD.
INDEED.
LET'S GO FOR COUGAR FIRST.
HOUND!
KWEEN
KWEEN
ATAT
RAT

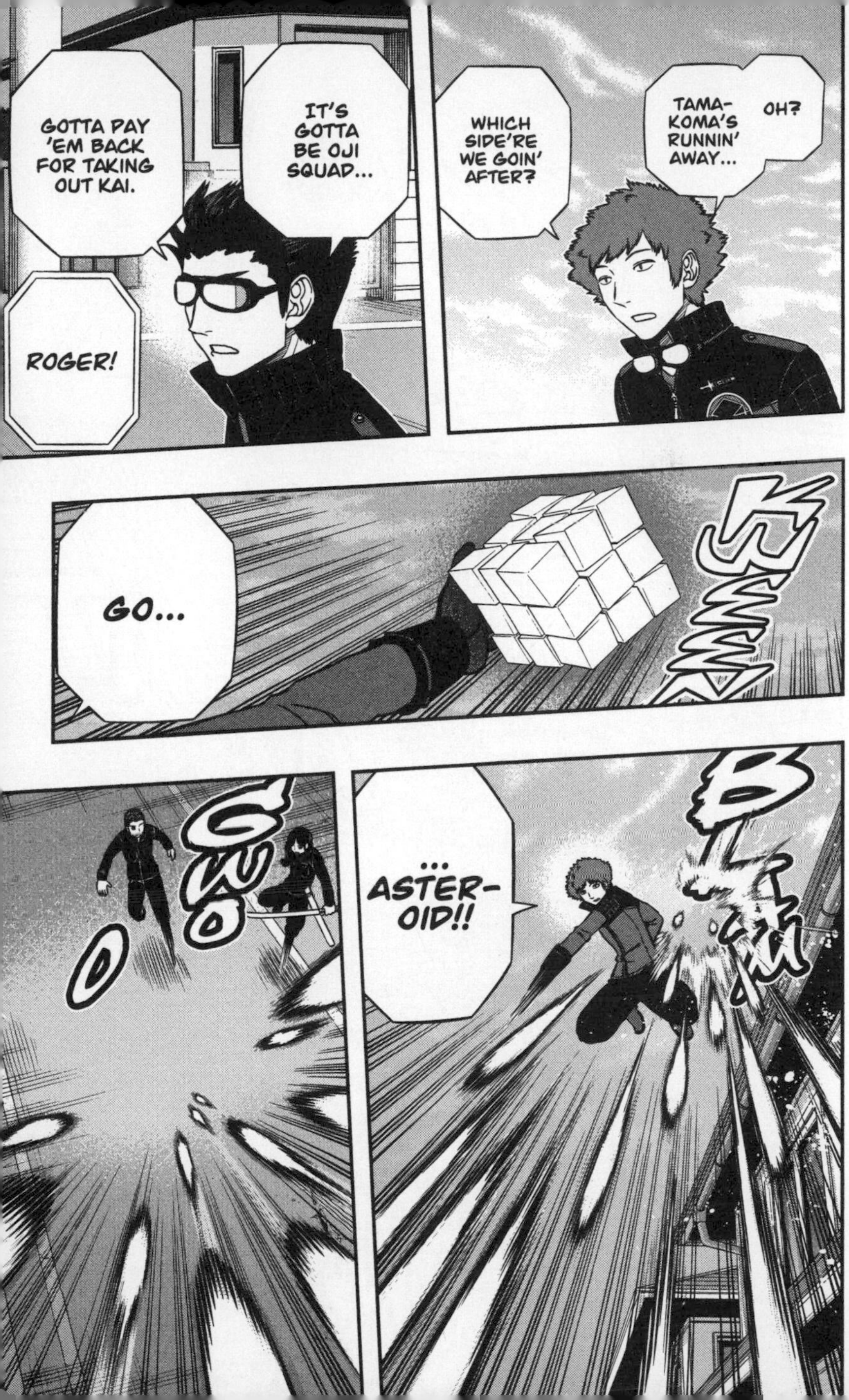
OH?
TAMA-KOMA'S RUNNIN' AWAY...
WHICH SIDE'RE WE GOIN' AFTER?
IT'S GOTTA BE OJI SQUAD...
GOTTA PAY 'EM BACK FOR TAKING OUT KAI.
ROGER!
GO...
...ASTER-OID!!

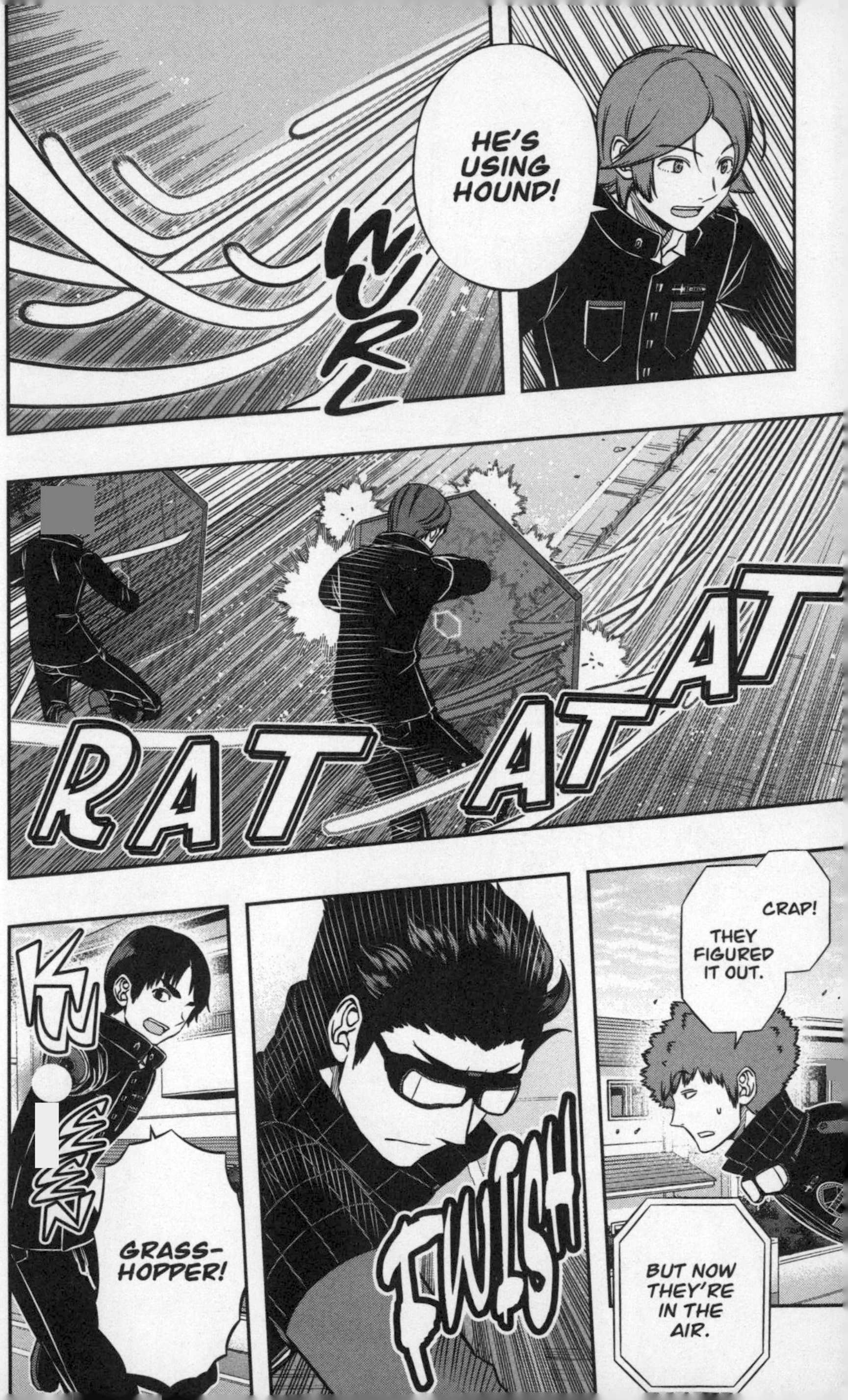
HE'S USING HOUND!
WURL
RAT AT AT
CRAP!
THEY FIGURED IT OUT.
BUT NOW THEY'RE IN THE AIR.
TWISH
GRASS-HOPPER!

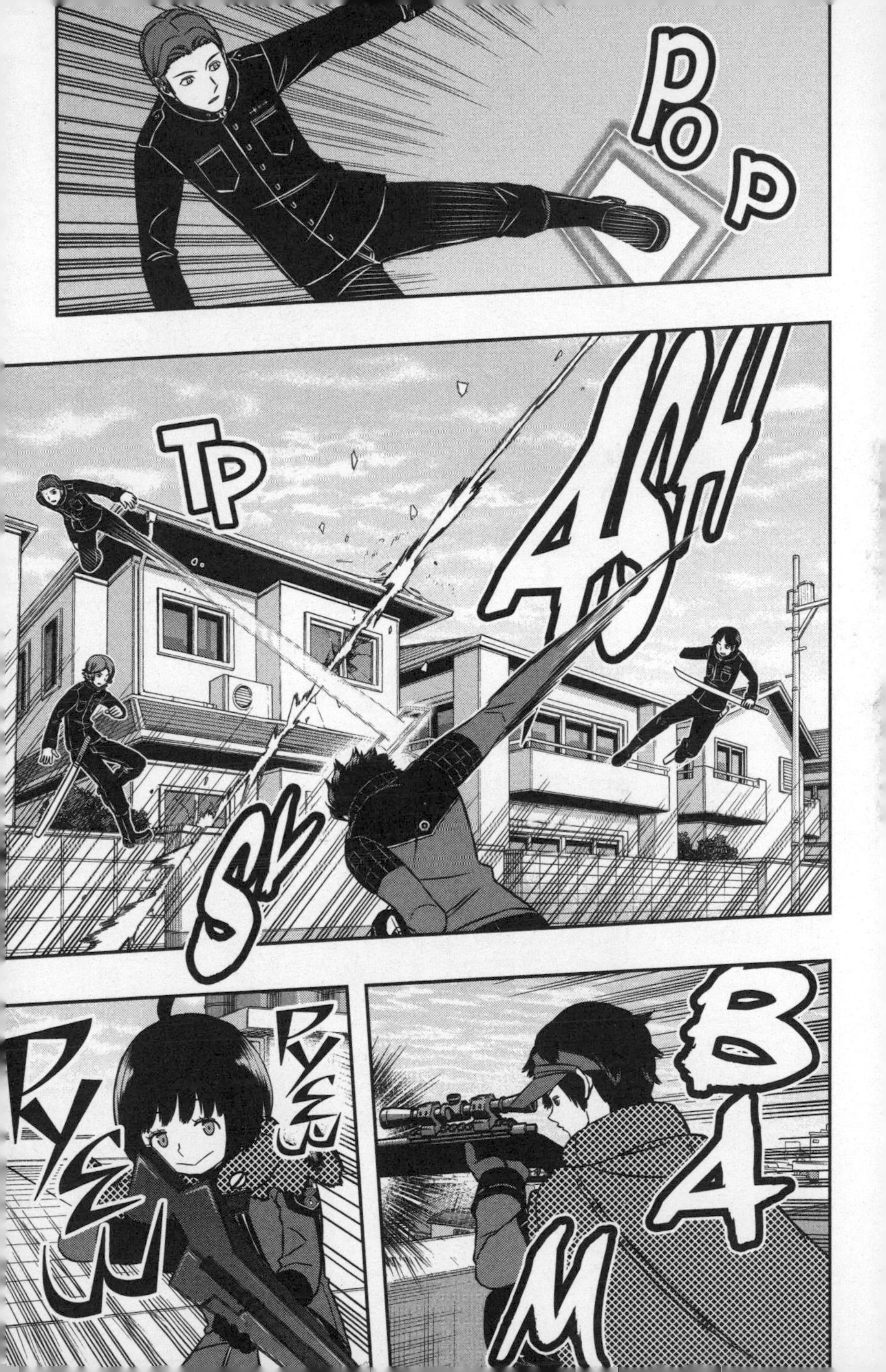
POP
TP
BAM
PYEW
PYEW

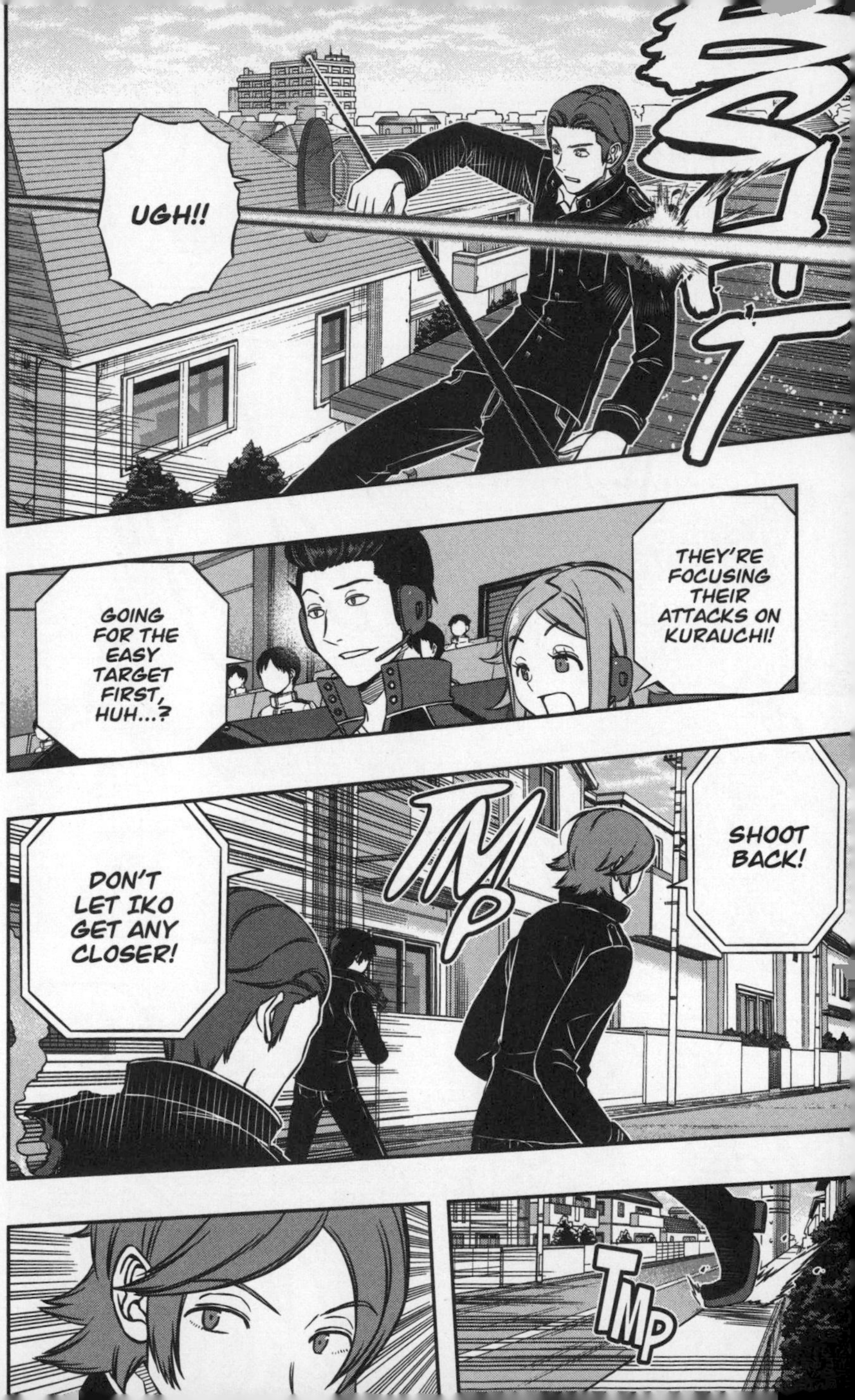
UGH!!
THEY'RE FOCUSING THEIR ATTACKS ON KURAUCHI!
GOING FOR THE EASY TARGET FIRST, HUH...?
SHOOT BACK!
TMP
DON'T LET IKO GET ANY CLOSER!
TMP

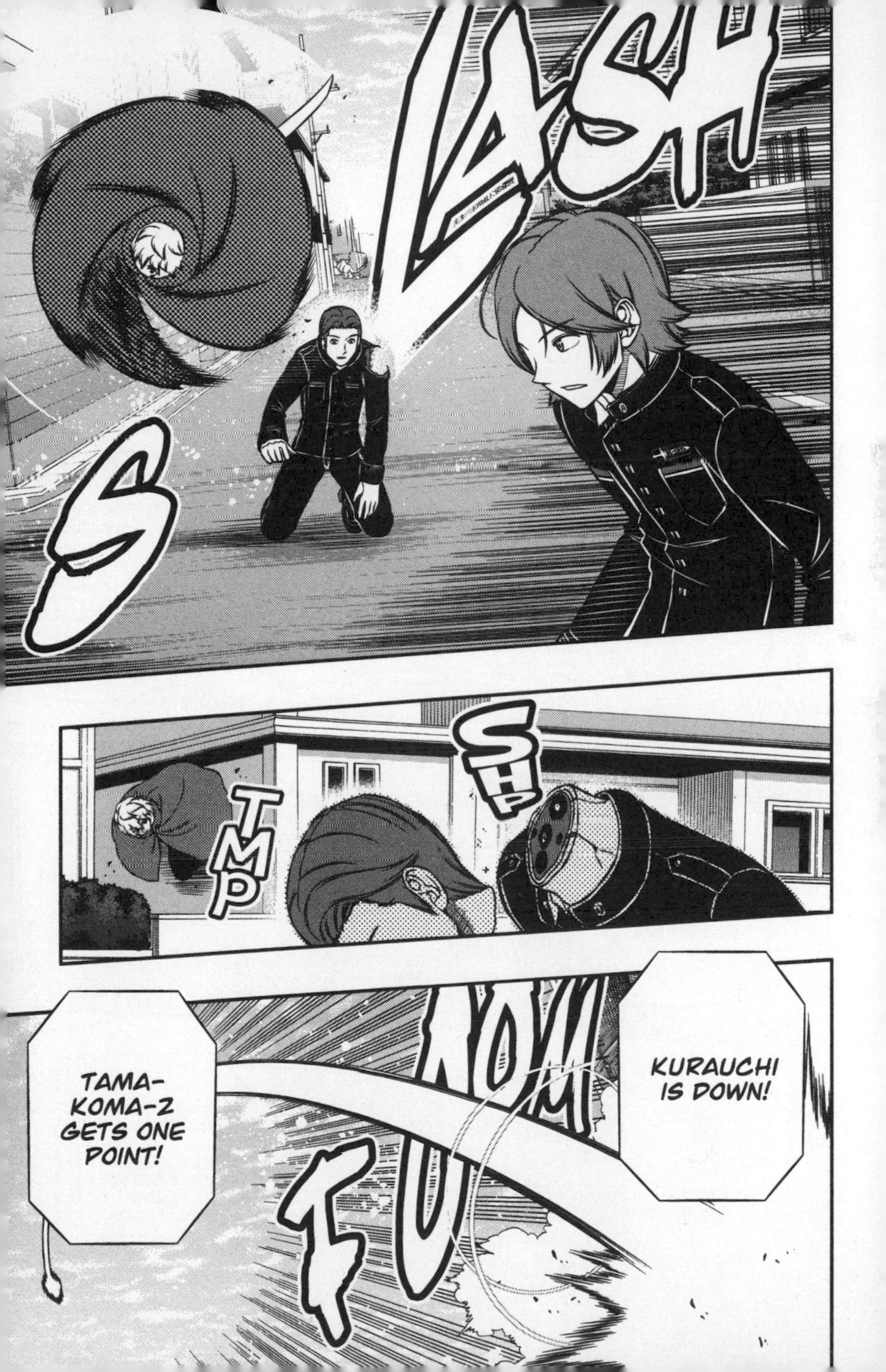
LASH
S
SHP
TMP
KURAUCHI IS DOWN!
TAMA-KOMA-2 GETS ONE POINT!

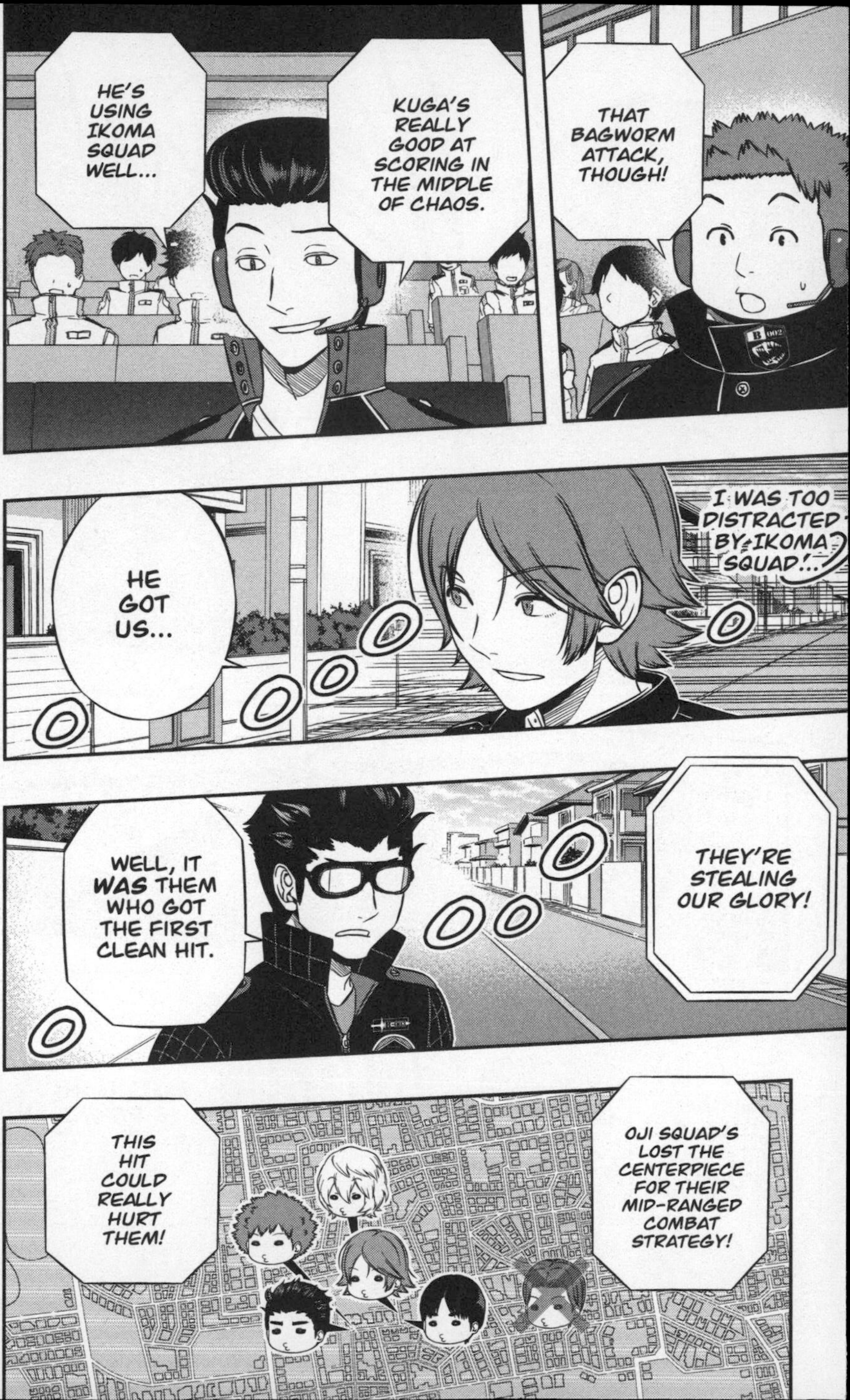
THAT BAGWORM ATTACK, THOUGH!
KUGA'S REALLY GOOD AT SCORING IN THE MIDDLE OF CHAOS.
HE'S USING IKOMA SQUAD WELL...
I WAS TOO DISTRACTED BY IKOMA SQUAD...
HE GOT US...
THEY'RE STEALING OUR GLORY!
WELL, IT **WAS** THEM WHO GOT THE FIRST CLEAN HIT.
OJI SQUAD'S LOST THE CENTERPIECE FOR THEIR MID-RANGED COMBAT STRATEGY!
THIS HIT COULD REALLY HURT THEM!

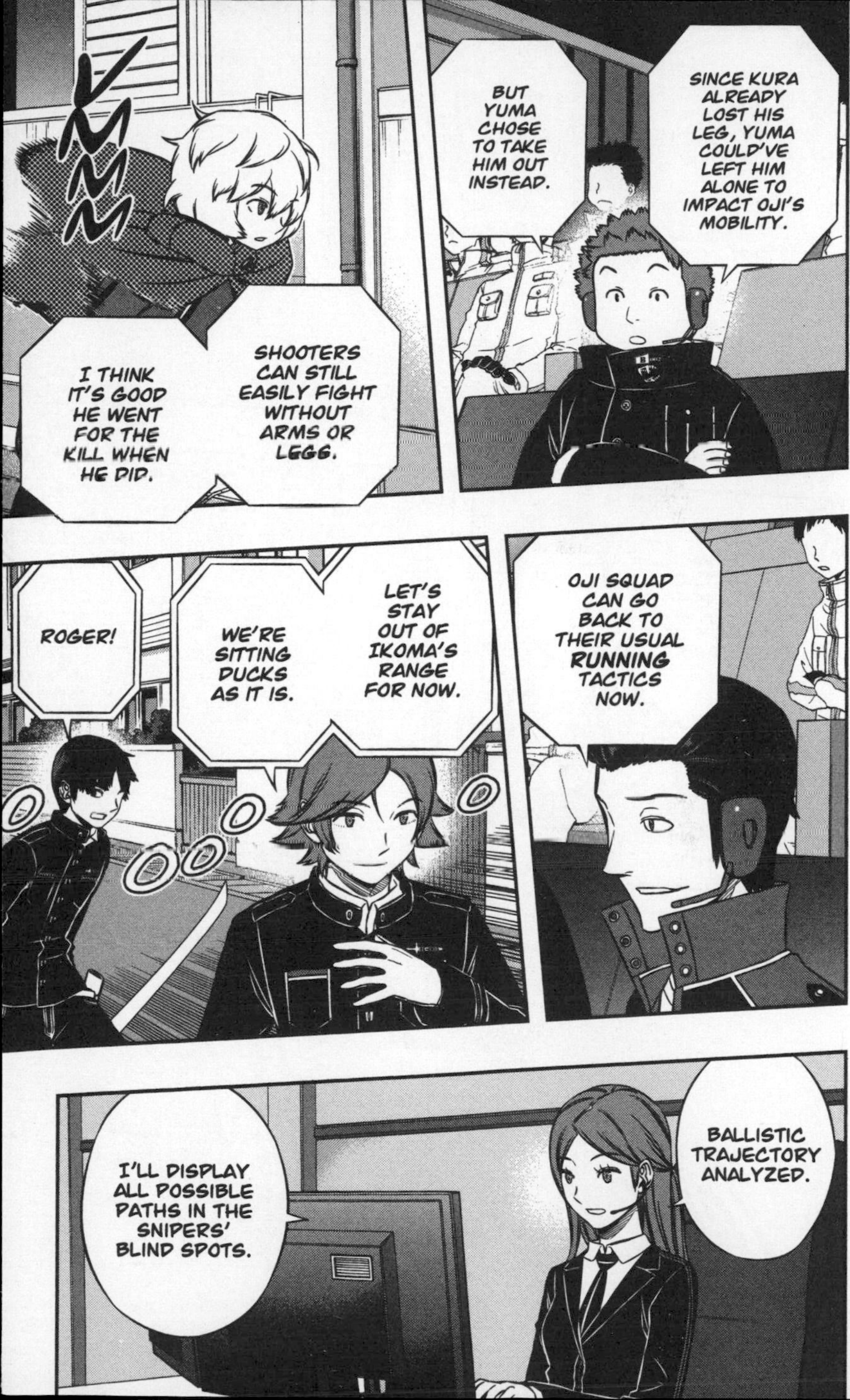
SINCE KURA ALREADY LOST HIS LEG, YUMA COULD'VE LEFT HIM ALONE TO IMPACT OJI'S MOBILITY.
BUT YUMA CHOSE TO TAKE HIM OUT INSTEAD.
SHOOTERS CAN STILL EASILY FIGHT WITHOUT ARMS OR LEGS.
I THINK IT'S GOOD HE WENT FOR THE KILL WHEN HE DID.
OJI SQUAD CAN GO BACK TO THEIR USUAL RUNNING TACTICS NOW.
LET'S STAY OUT OF IKOMA'S RANGE FOR NOW.
WE'RE SITTING DUCKS AS IT IS.
ROGER!
BALLISTIC TRAJECTORY ANALYZED.
I'LL DISPLAY ALL POSSIBLE PATHS IN THE SNIPERS' BLIND SPOTS.

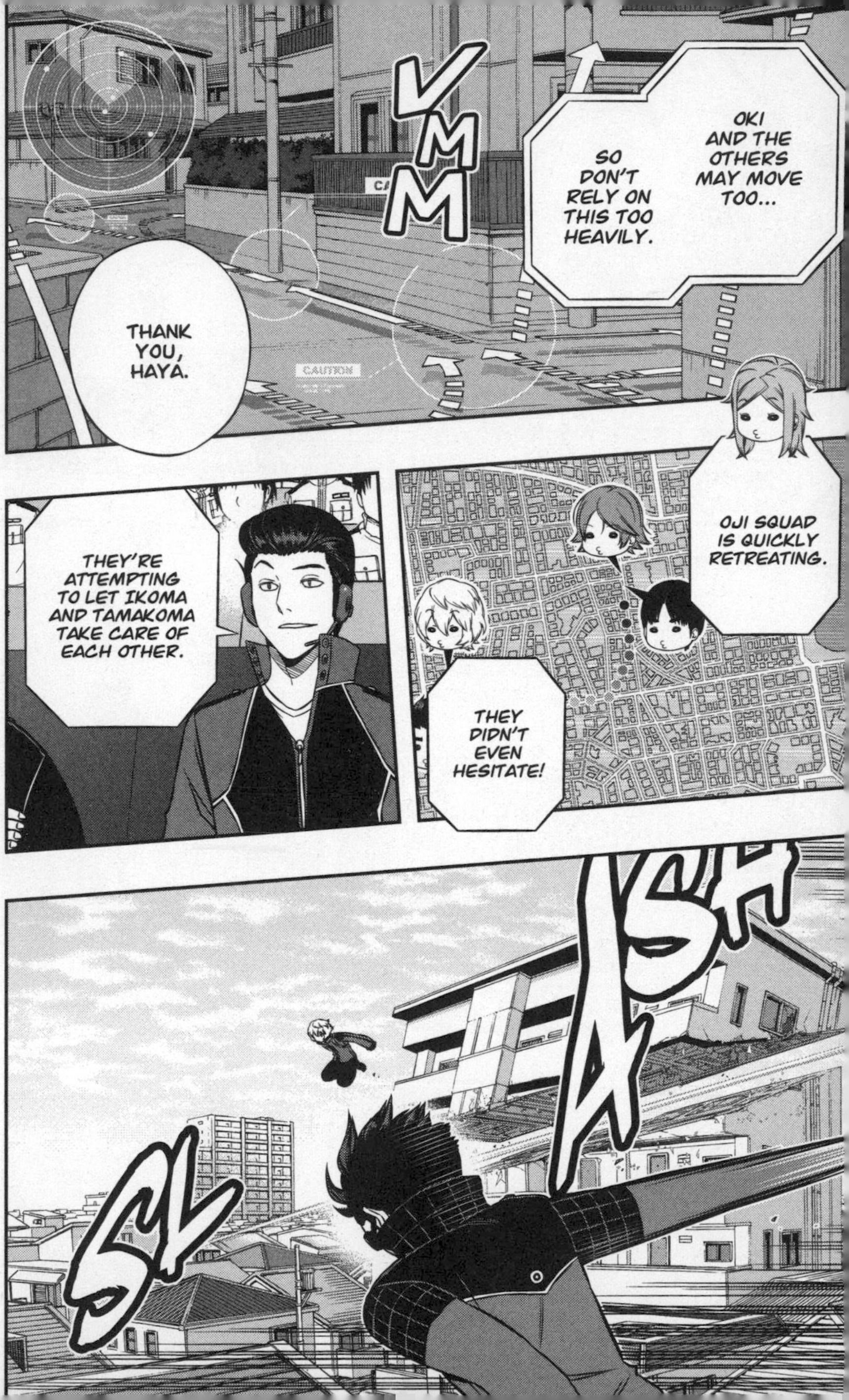
OKI AND THE OTHERS MAY MOVE TOO...
SO DON'T RELY ON THIS TOO HEAVILY.
VMM
CAUTION
THANK YOU, HAYA.
OJI SQUAD IS QUICKLY RETREATING.
THEY DIDN'T EVEN HESITATE!
THEY'RE ATTEMPTING TO LET IKOMA AND TAMAKOMA TAKE CARE OF EACH OTHER.

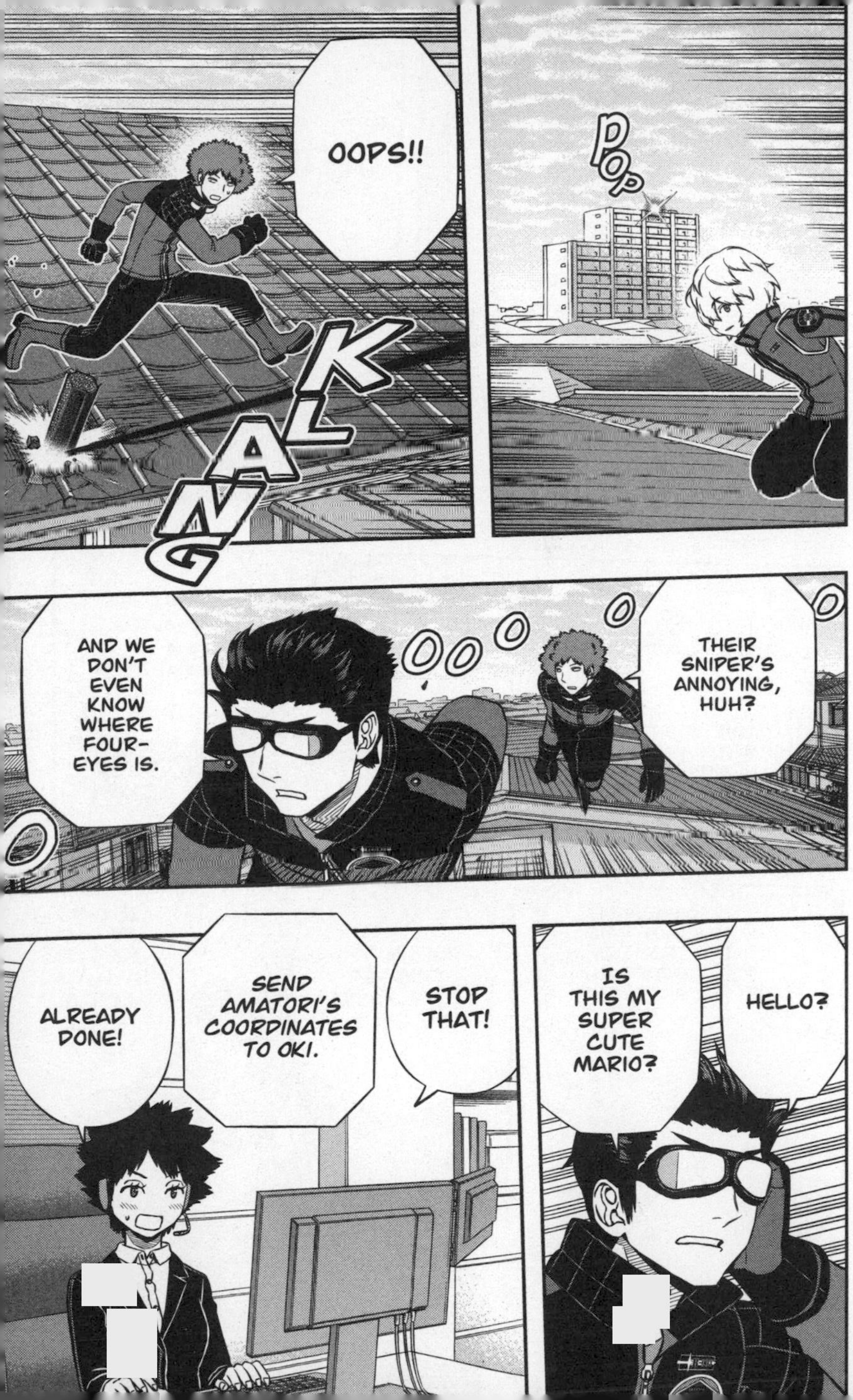
POP
POP
OOPS!!
KLANG
THEIR SNIPER'S ANNOYING, HUH?
AND WE DON'T EVEN KNOW WHERE FOUR-EYES IS.
HELLO?
IS THIS MY SUPER CUTE MARIO?
STOP THAT!
SEND AMATORI'S COORDINATES TO OKI.
ALREADY DONE!

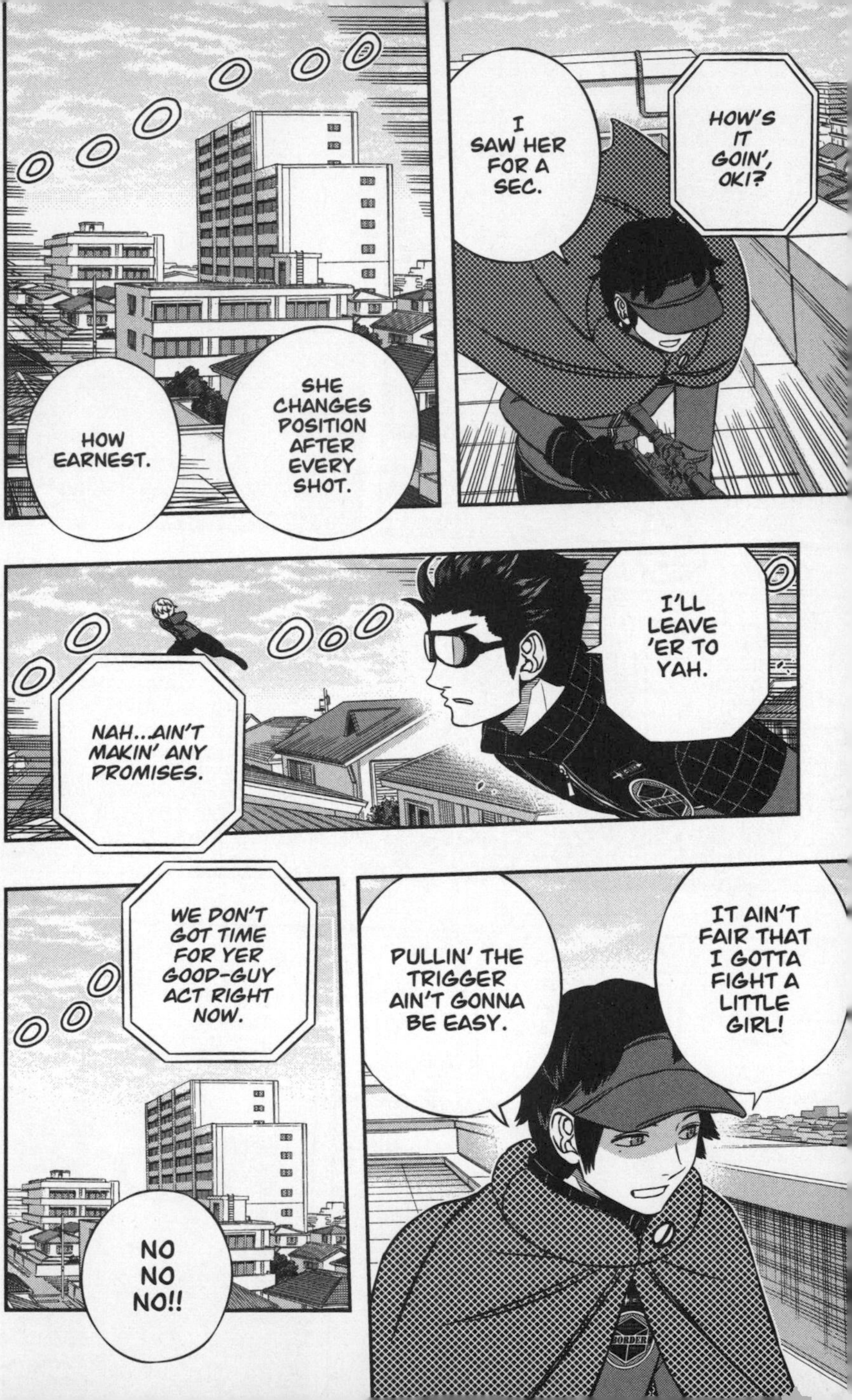
HOW'S IT GOIN', OKI?
I SAW HER FOR A SEC.
SHE CHANGES POSITION AFTER EVERY SHOT.
HOW EARNEST.
I'LL LEAVE 'ER TO YAH.
NAH...AIN'T MAKIN' ANY PROMISES.
IT AIN'T FAIR THAT I GOTTA FIGHT A LITTLE GIRL!
PULLIN' THE TRIGGER AIN'T GONNA BE EASY.
WE DON'T GOT TIME FOR YER GOOD-GUY ACT RIGHT NOW.
NO NO NO!!

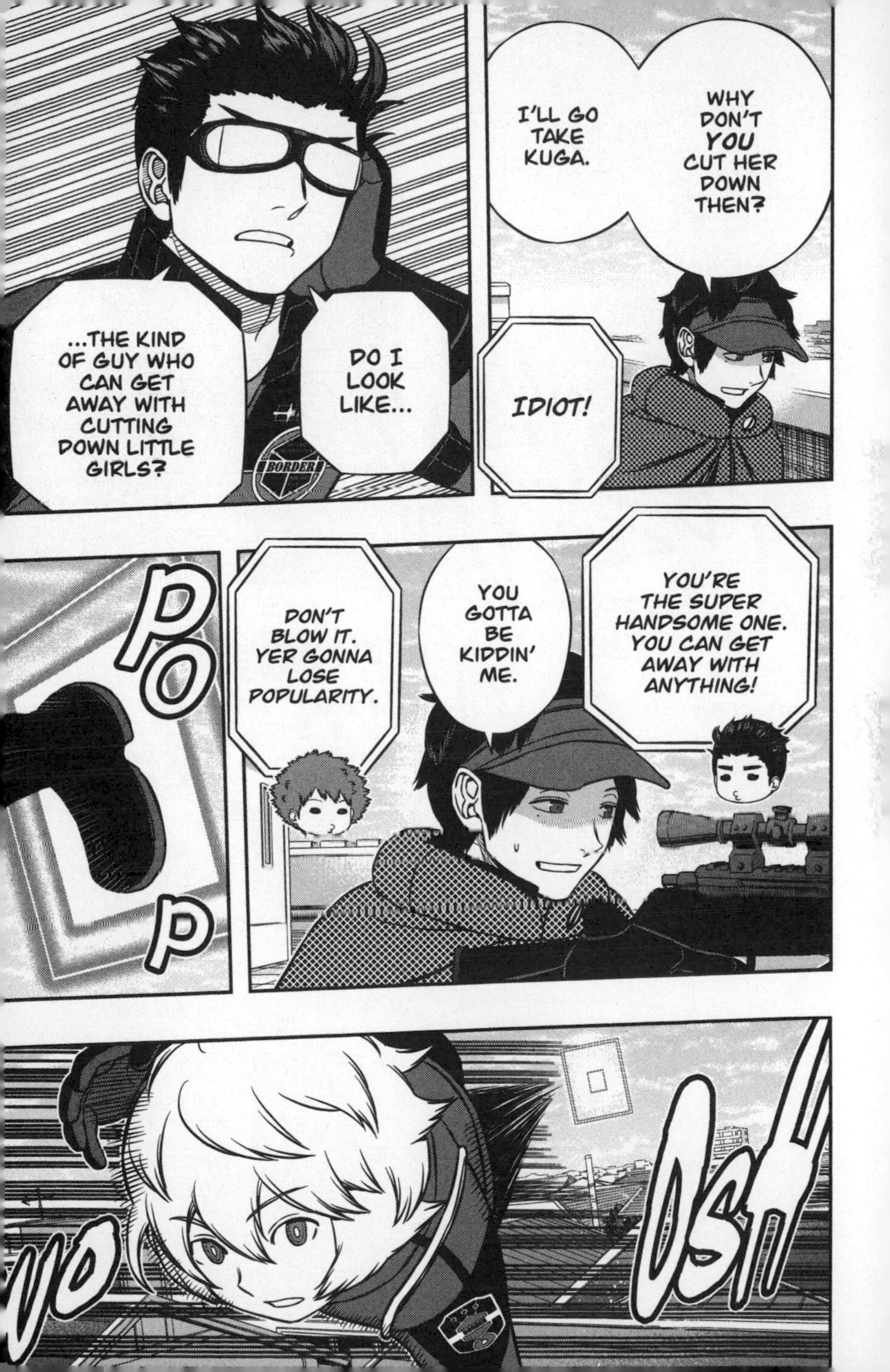
WHY DON'T YOU CUT HER DOWN THEN?
I'LL GO TAKE KUGA.
IDIOT!
DO I LOOK LIKE...
...THE KIND OF GUY WHO CAN GET AWAY WITH CUTTING DOWN LITTLE GIRLS?
YOU'RE THE SUPER HANDSOME ONE. YOU CAN GET AWAY WITH ANYTHING!
YOU GOTTA BE KIDDIN' ME.
DON'T BLOW IT. YER GONNA LOSE POPULARITY.
POP
WOOSH!

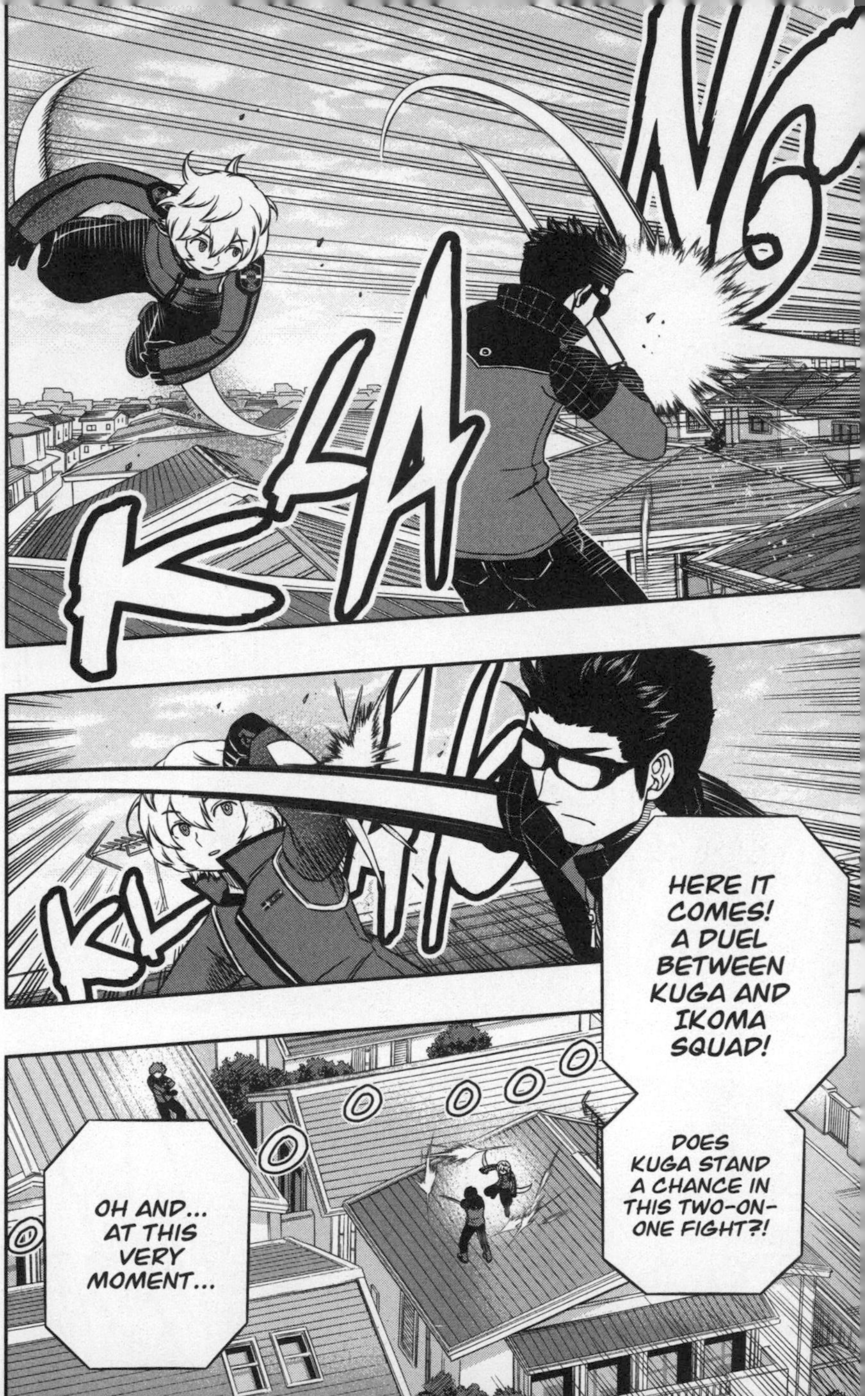

NG
KLANG
KL
HERE IT COMES! A DUEL BETWEEN KUGA AND IKOMA SQUAD!
DOES KUGA STAND A CHANCE IN THIS TWO-ON-ONE FIGHT?!
OH AND... AT THIS VERY MOMENT...

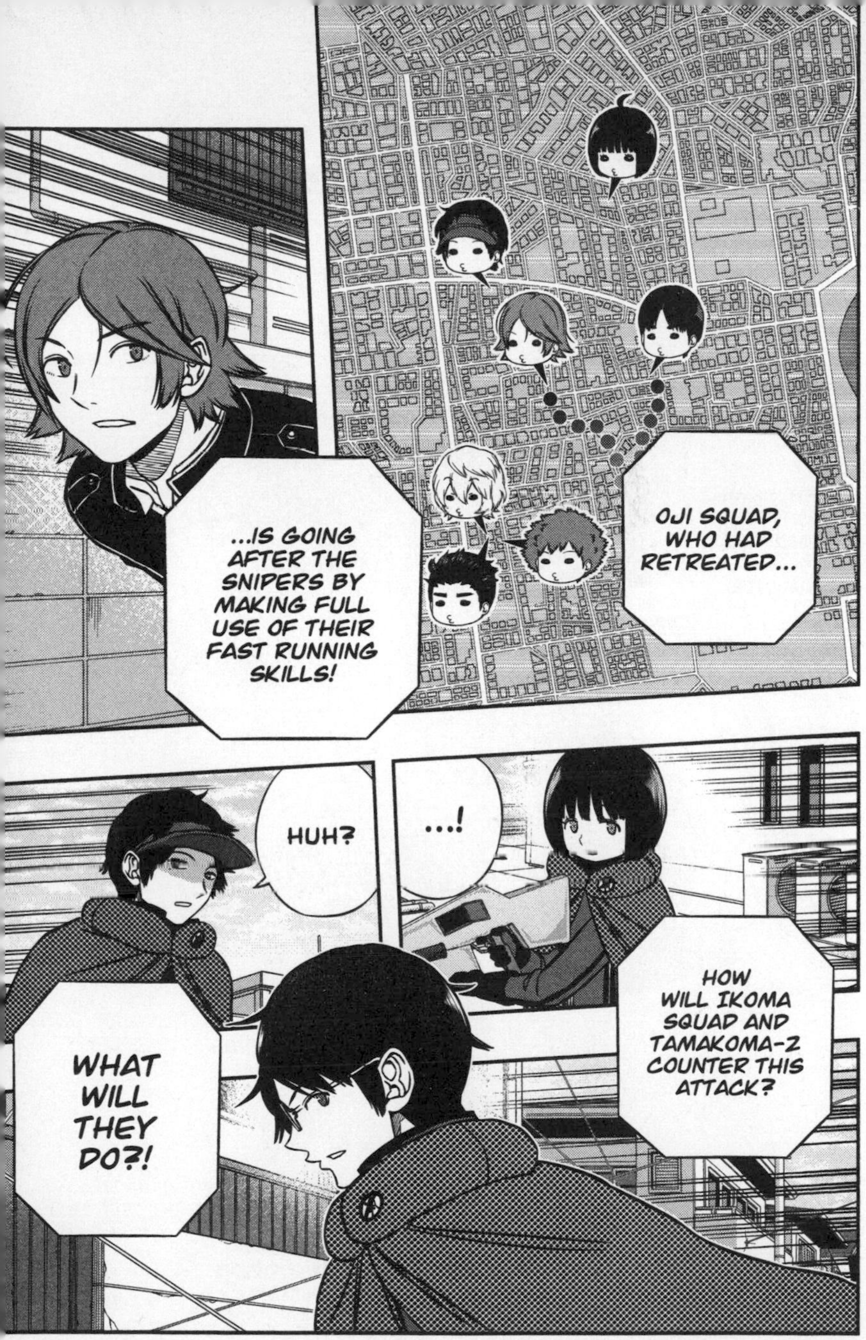
OJI SQUAD, WHO HAD RETREATED...
...IS GOING AFTER THE SNIPERS BY MAKING FULL USE OF THEIR FAST RUNNING SKILLS!
...!
HUH?
HOW WILL IKOMA SQUAD AND TAMAKOMA-2 COUNTER THIS ATTACK?
WHAT WILL THEY DO?!

Oji Squad Strategy Room

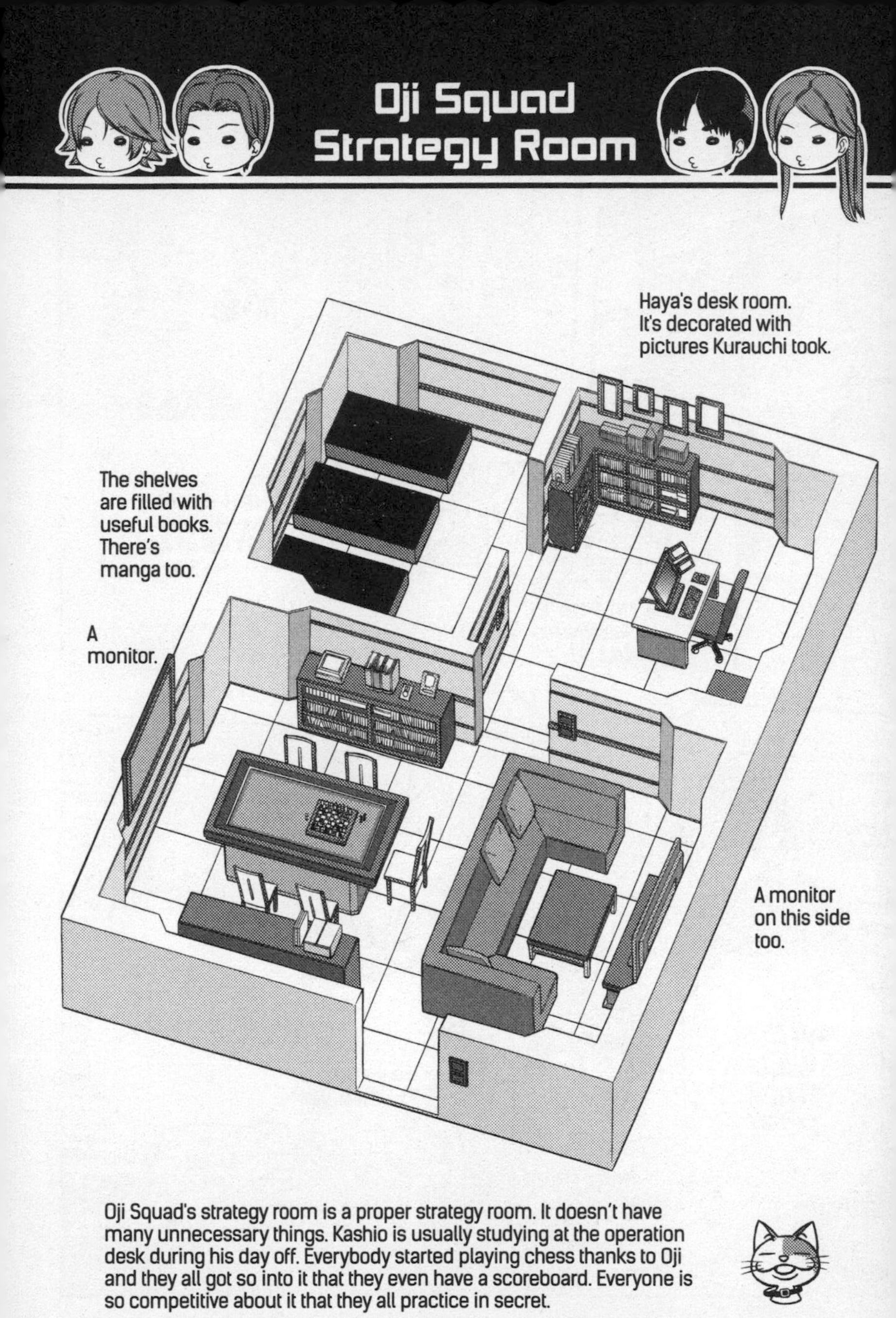
Haya's desk room. It's decorated with pictures Kurauchi took.
The shelves are filled with useful books. There's manga too.
A monitor.
A monitor on this side too.

Oji Squad's strategy room is a proper strategy room. It doesn't have many unnecessary things. Kashio is usually studying at the operation desk during his day off. Everybody started playing chess thanks to Oji and they all got so into it that they even have a scoreboard. Everyone is so competitive about it that they all practice in secret.

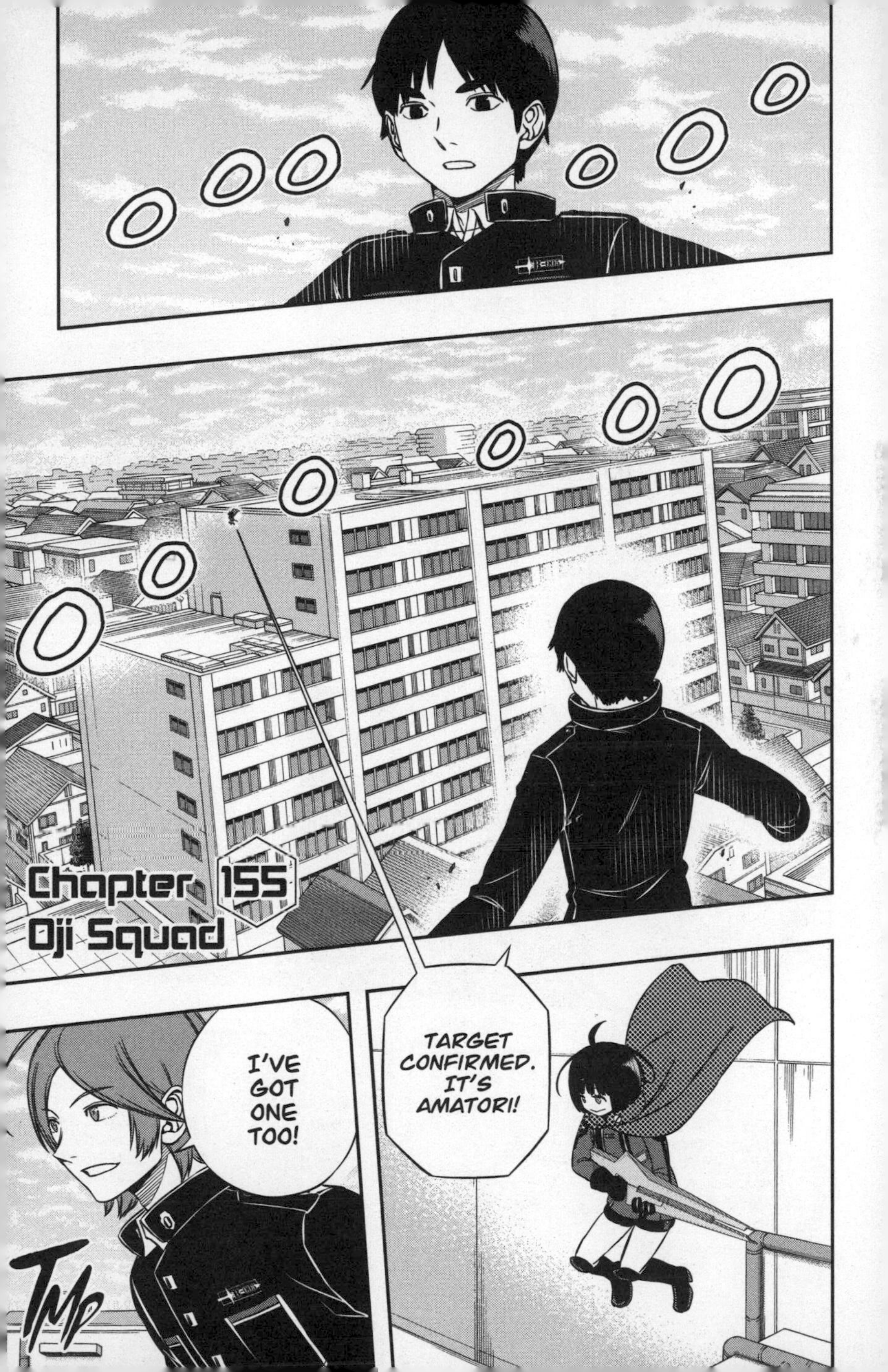
Chapter 155
Oji Squad
TARGET CONFIRMED. IT'S AMATORI!
I'VE GOT ONE TOO!

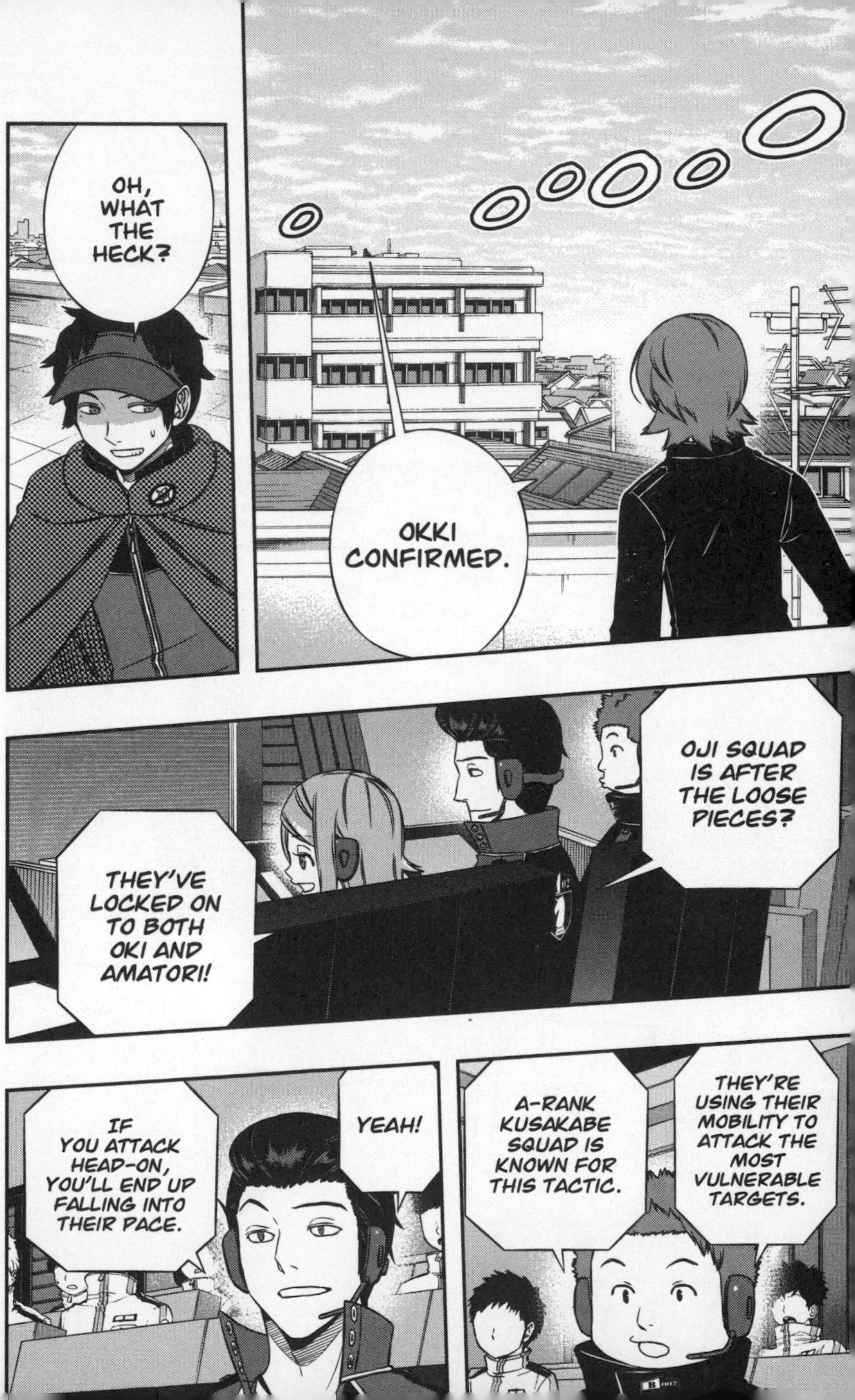
OKKI CONFIRMED.
OH, WHAT THE HECK?
OJI SQUAD IS AFTER THE LOOSE PIECES?
THEY'VE LOCKED ON TO BOTH OKI AND AMATORI!
THEY'RE USING THEIR MOBILITY TO ATTACK THE MOST VULNERABLE TARGETS.
A-RANK KUSAKABE SQUAD IS KNOWN FOR THIS TACTIC.
YEAH!
IF YOU ATTACK HEAD-ON, YOU'LL END UP FALLING INTO THEIR PACE.

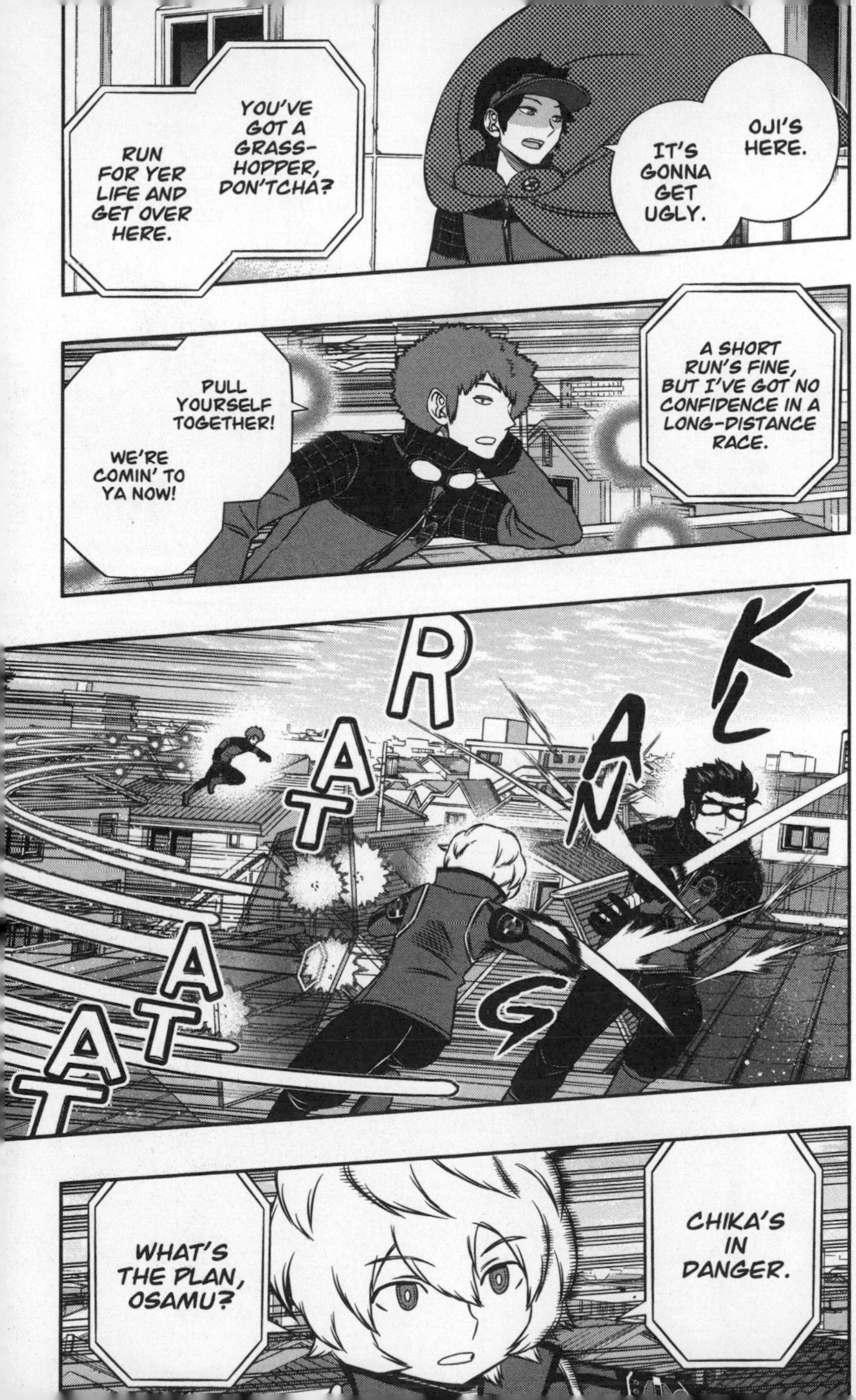
OJI'S HERE.
IT'S GONNA GET UGLY.
YOU'VE GOT A GRASS-HOPPER, DON'TCHA?
RUN FOR YER LIFE AND GET OVER HERE.
A SHORT RUN'S FINE, BUT I'VE GOT NO CONFIDENCE IN A LONG-DISTANCE RACE.
PULL YOURSELF TOGETHER!
WE'RE COMIN' TO YA NOW!
KLANG
RATATAT
CHIKA'S IN DANGER.
WHAT'S THE PLAN, OSAMU?

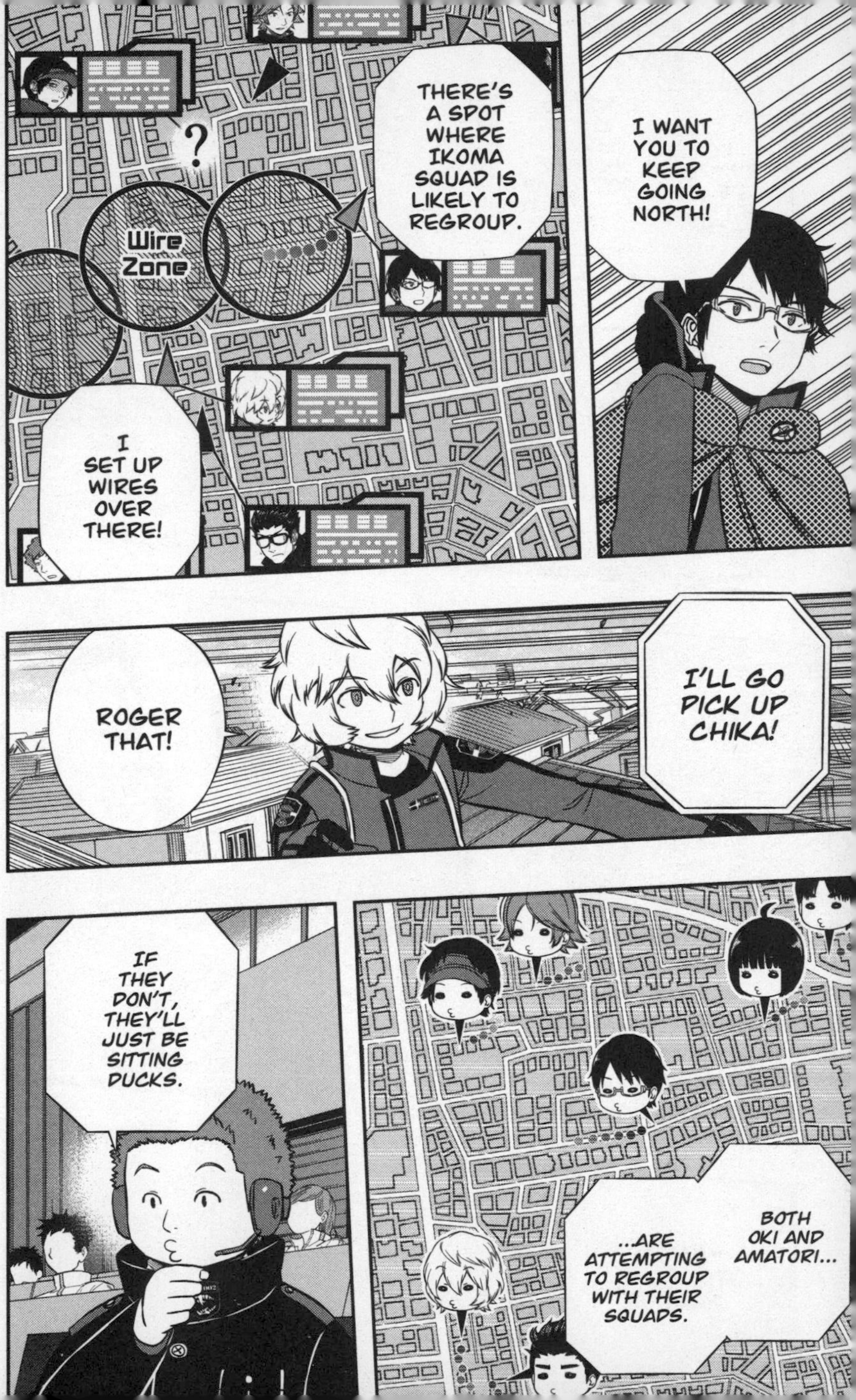
I WANT YOU TO KEEP GOING NORTH!
THERE'S A SPOT WHERE IKOMA SQUAD IS LIKELY TO REGROUP.
?
Wire Zone
I SET UP WIRES OVER THERE!
I'LL GO PICK UP CHIKA!
ROGER THAT!
BOTH OKI AND AMATORI...
...ARE ATTEMPTING TO REGROUP WITH THEIR SQUADS.
IF THEY DON'T, THEY'LL JUST BE SITTING DUCKS.

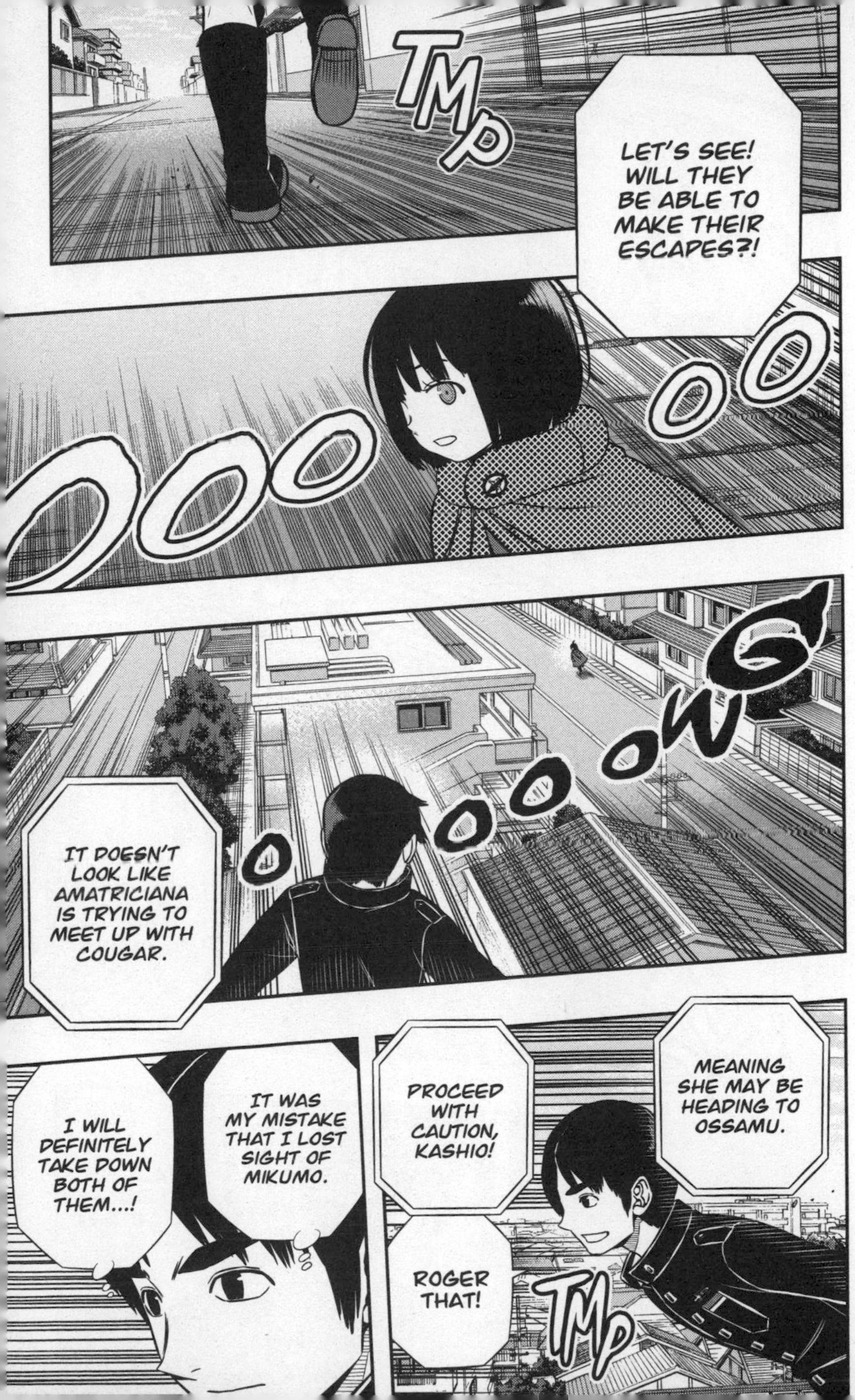
LET'S SEE! WILL THEY BE ABLE TO MAKE THEIR ESCAPES?!
TMP
IT DOESN'T LOOK LIKE AMATRICIANA IS TRYING TO MEET UP WITH COUGAR.
MEANING SHE MAY BE HEADING TO OSSAMU.
PROCEED WITH CAUTION, KASHIO!
ROGER THAT!
TMP
IT WAS MY MISTAKE THAT I LOST SIGHT OF MIKUMO.
I WILL DEFINITELY TAKE DOWN BOTH OF THEM...!

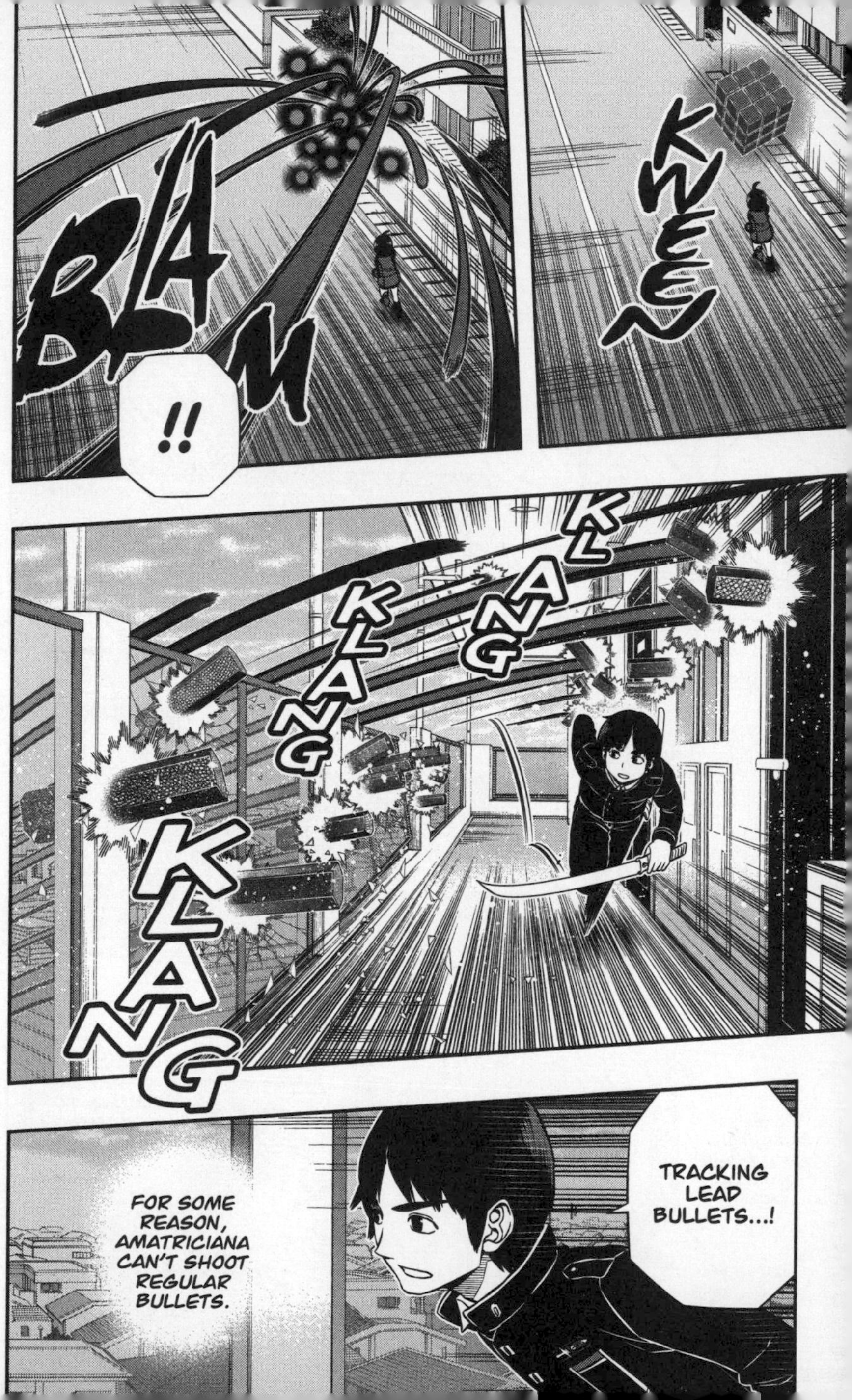
KWEEN
BLAM
!!
KLANG
KLANG
KLANG
TRACKING LEAD BULLETS...!
FOR SOME REASON, AMATRICIANA CAN'T SHOOT REGULAR BULLETS.

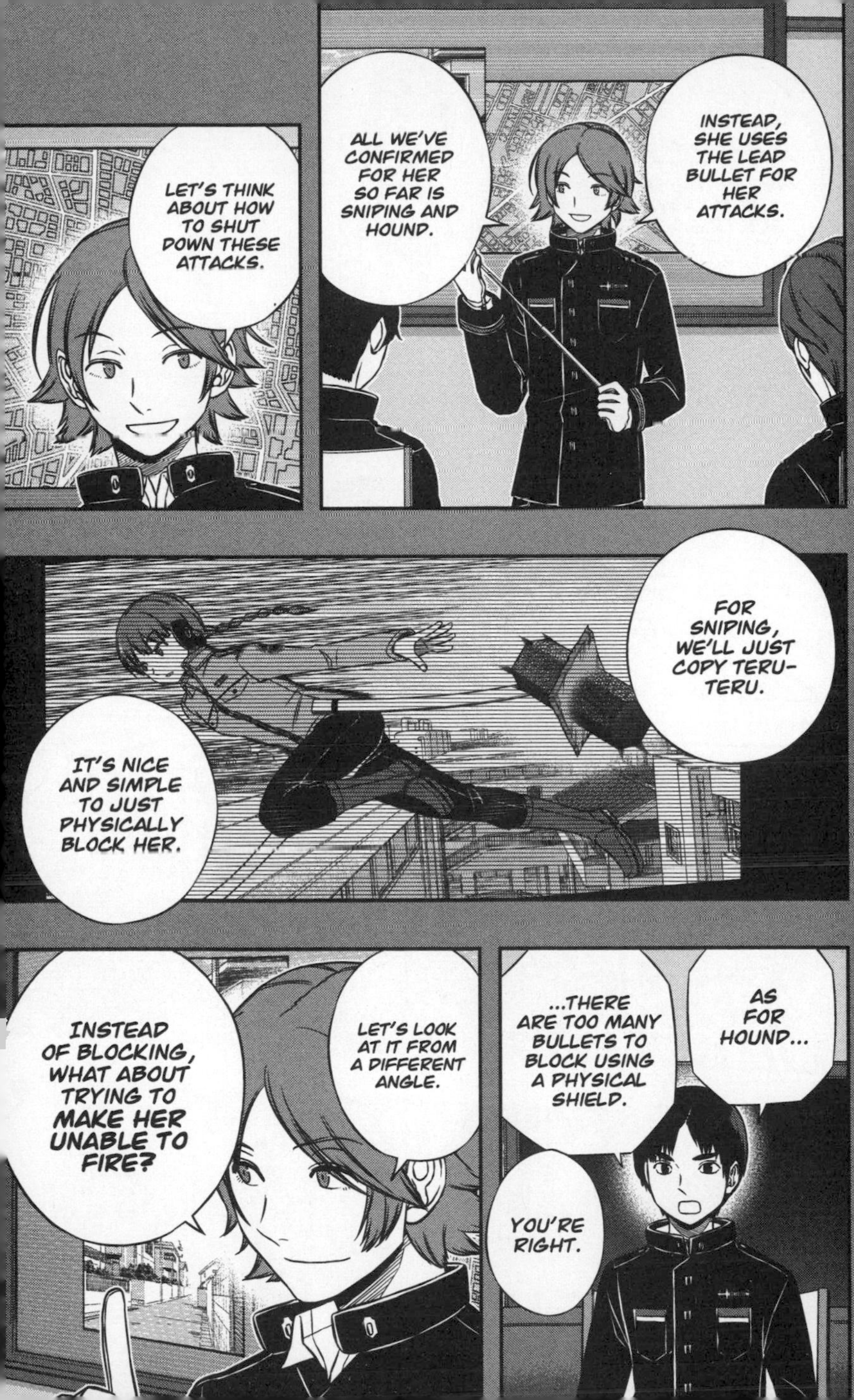
INSTEAD, SHE USES THE LEAD BULLET FOR HER ATTACKS.
ALL WE'VE CONFIRMED FOR HER SO FAR IS SNIPING AND HOUND.
LET'S THINK ABOUT HOW TO SHUT DOWN THESE ATTACKS.
FOR SNIPING, WE'LL JUST COPY TERU-TERU.
IT'S NICE AND SIMPLE TO JUST PHYSICALLY BLOCK HER.
AS FOR HOUND...
...THERE ARE TOO MANY BULLETS TO BLOCK USING A PHYSICAL SHIELD.
YOU'RE RIGHT.
LET'S LOOK AT IT FROM A DIFFERENT ANGLE.
INSTEAD OF BLOCKING, WHAT ABOUT TRYING TO MAKE HER UNABLE TO FIRE?

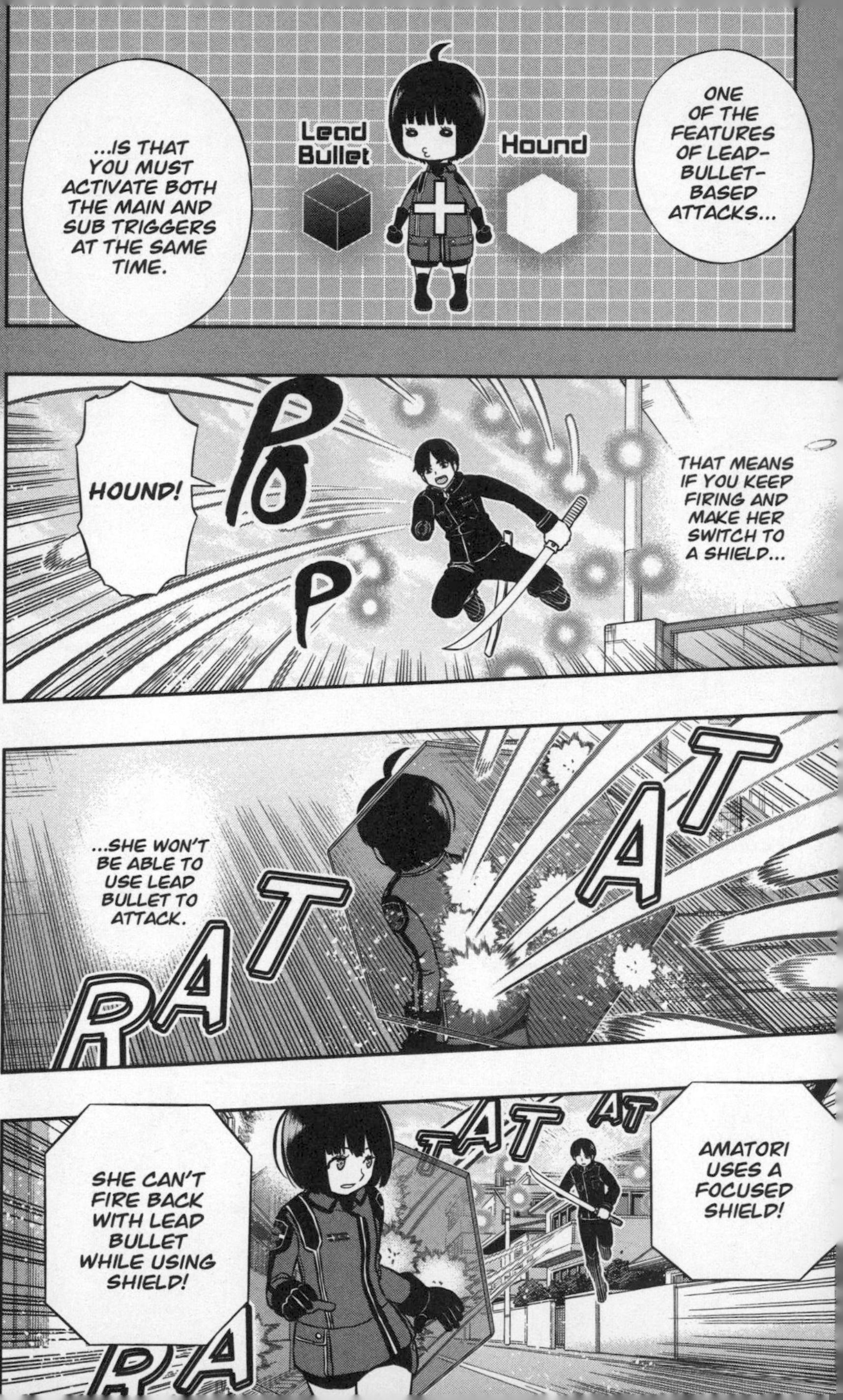
ONE OF THE FEATURES OF LEAD-BULLET-BASED ATTACKS...
Lead Bullet
Hound
...IS THAT YOU MUST ACTIVATE BOTH THE MAIN AND SUB TRIGGERS AT THE SAME TIME.
THAT MEANS IF YOU KEEP FIRING AND MAKE HER SWITCH TO A SHIELD...
POP
HOUND!
RATAT
...SHE WON'T BE ABLE TO USE LEAD BULLET TO ATTACK.
AMATORI USES A FOCUSED SHIELD!
TATAT
SHE CAN'T FIRE BACK WITH LEAD BULLET WHILE USING SHIELD!
RA

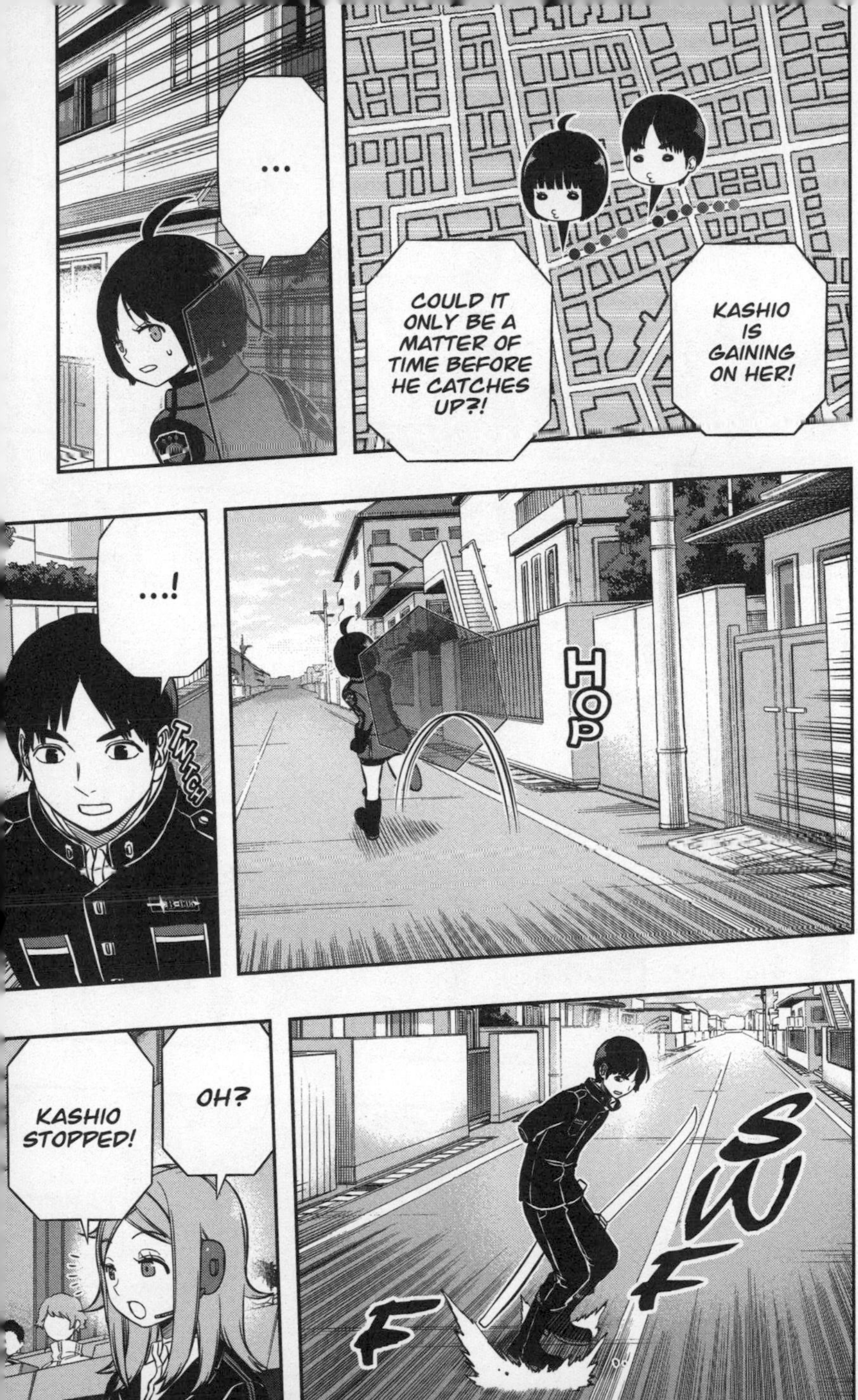
KASHIO IS GAINING ON HER!
COULD IT ONLY BE A MATTER OF TIME BEFORE HE CATCHES UP?!
...
HOP
...!
TWITCH
SWF
F
OH?
KASHIO STOPPED!

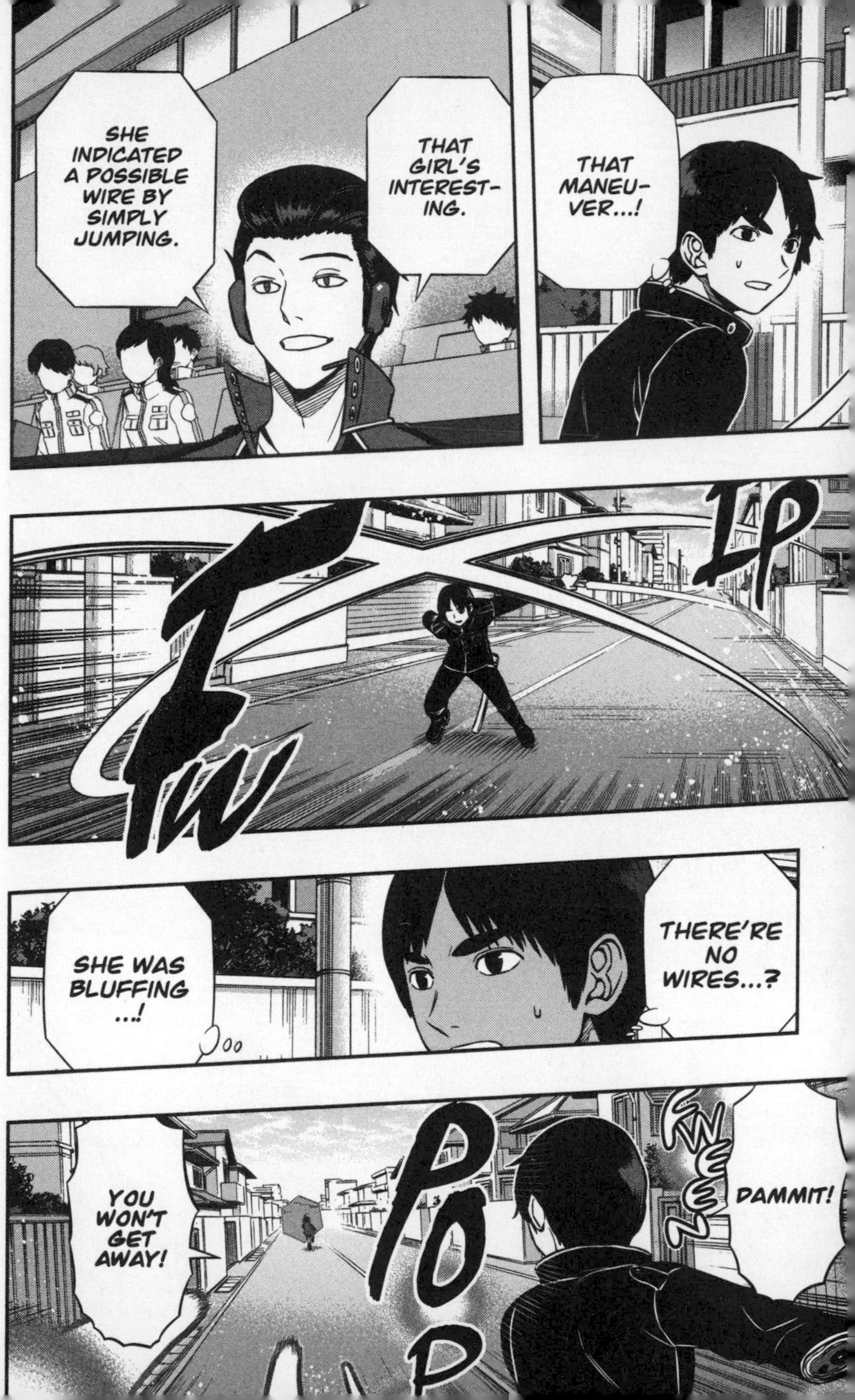
THAT MANEU-VER...!
THAT GIRL'S INTEREST-ING.
SHE INDICATED A POSSIBLE WIRE BY SIMPLY JUMPING.
TWIP
THERE'RE NO WIRES...?
SHE WAS BLUFFING ...!
DAMMIT!
POP
YOU WON'T GET AWAY!

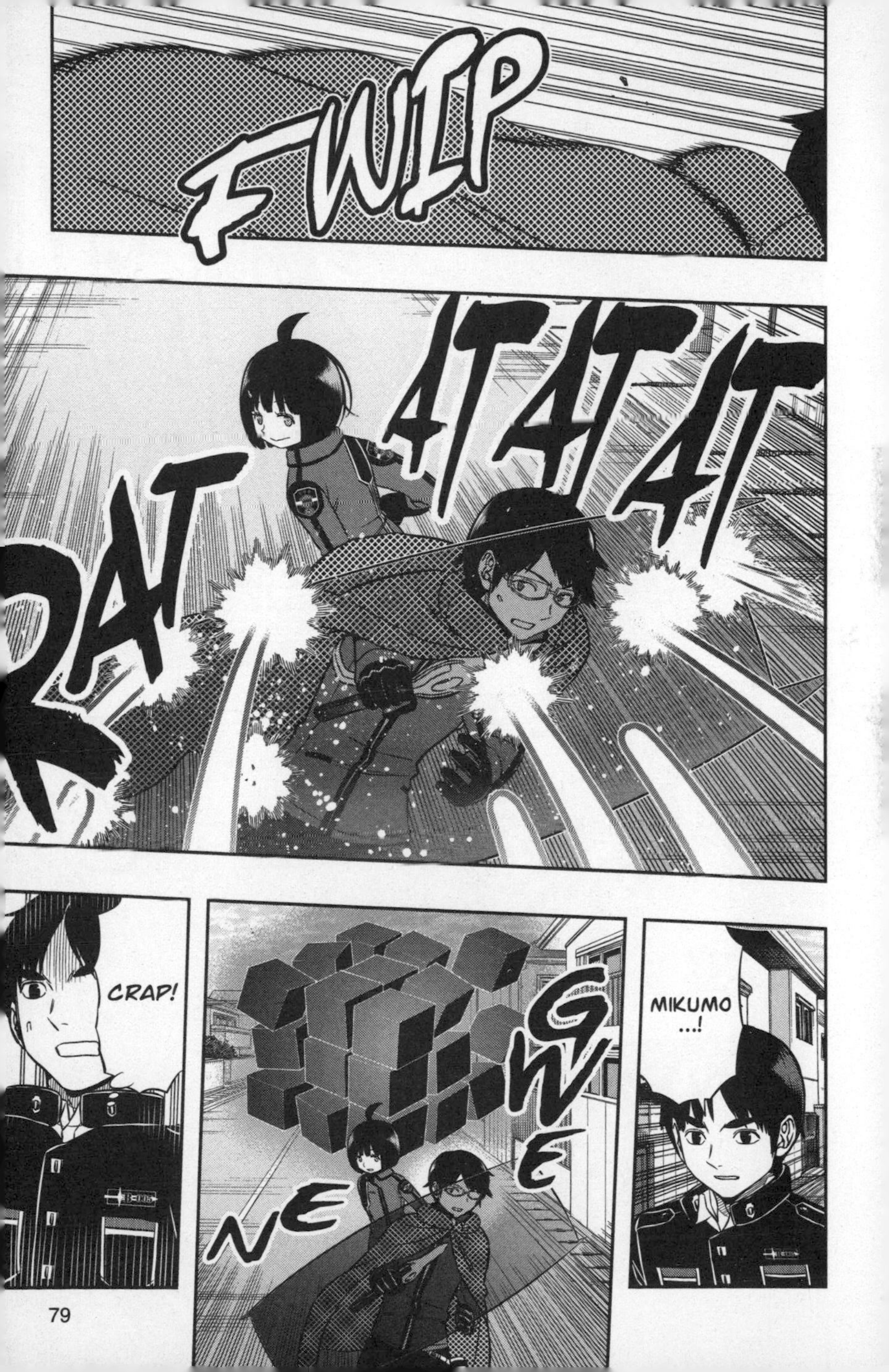
FWIP
RATATATAT
MIKUMO ...!
CRAP!

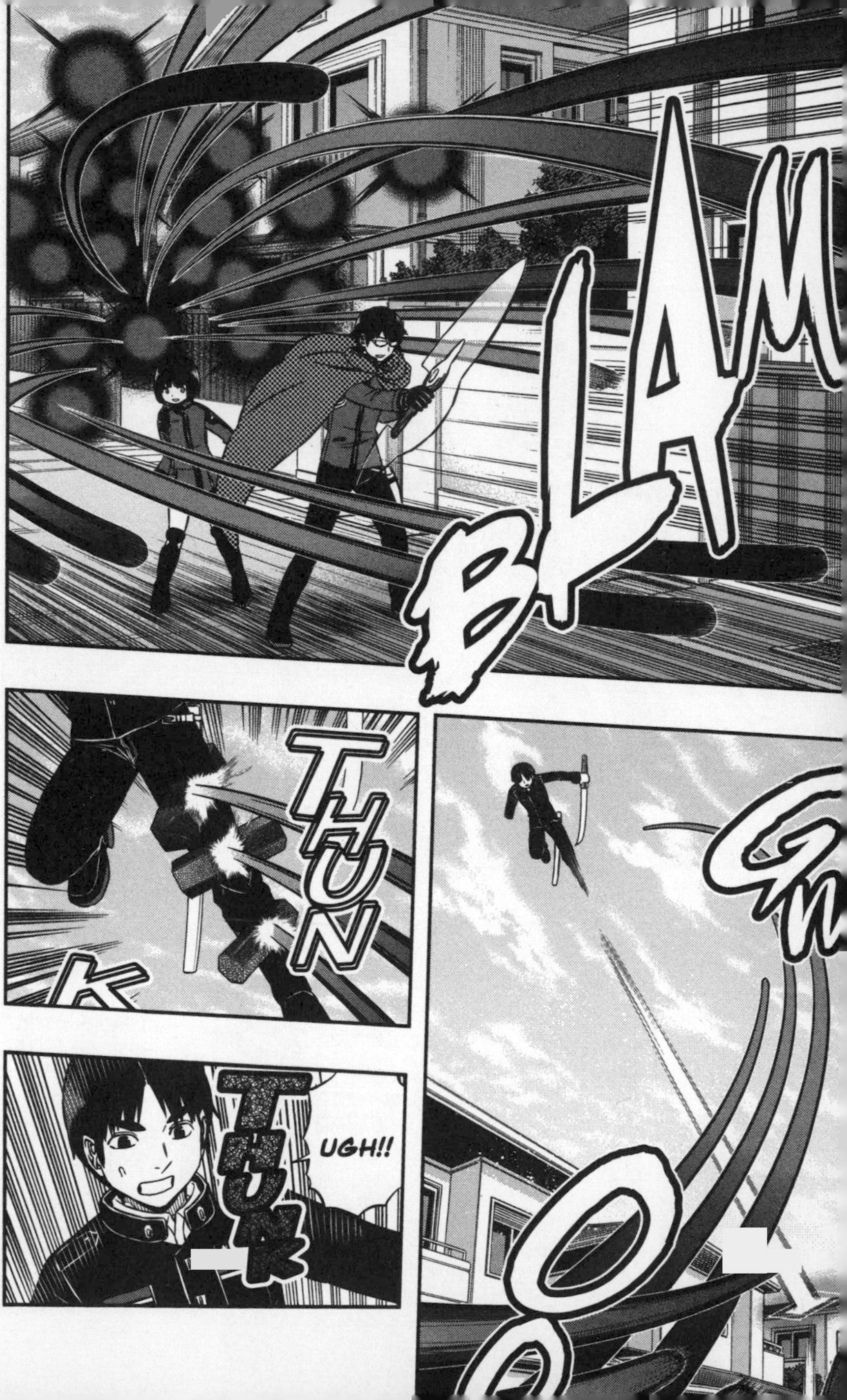
BLAM
THUNK
THUNK
UGH!!

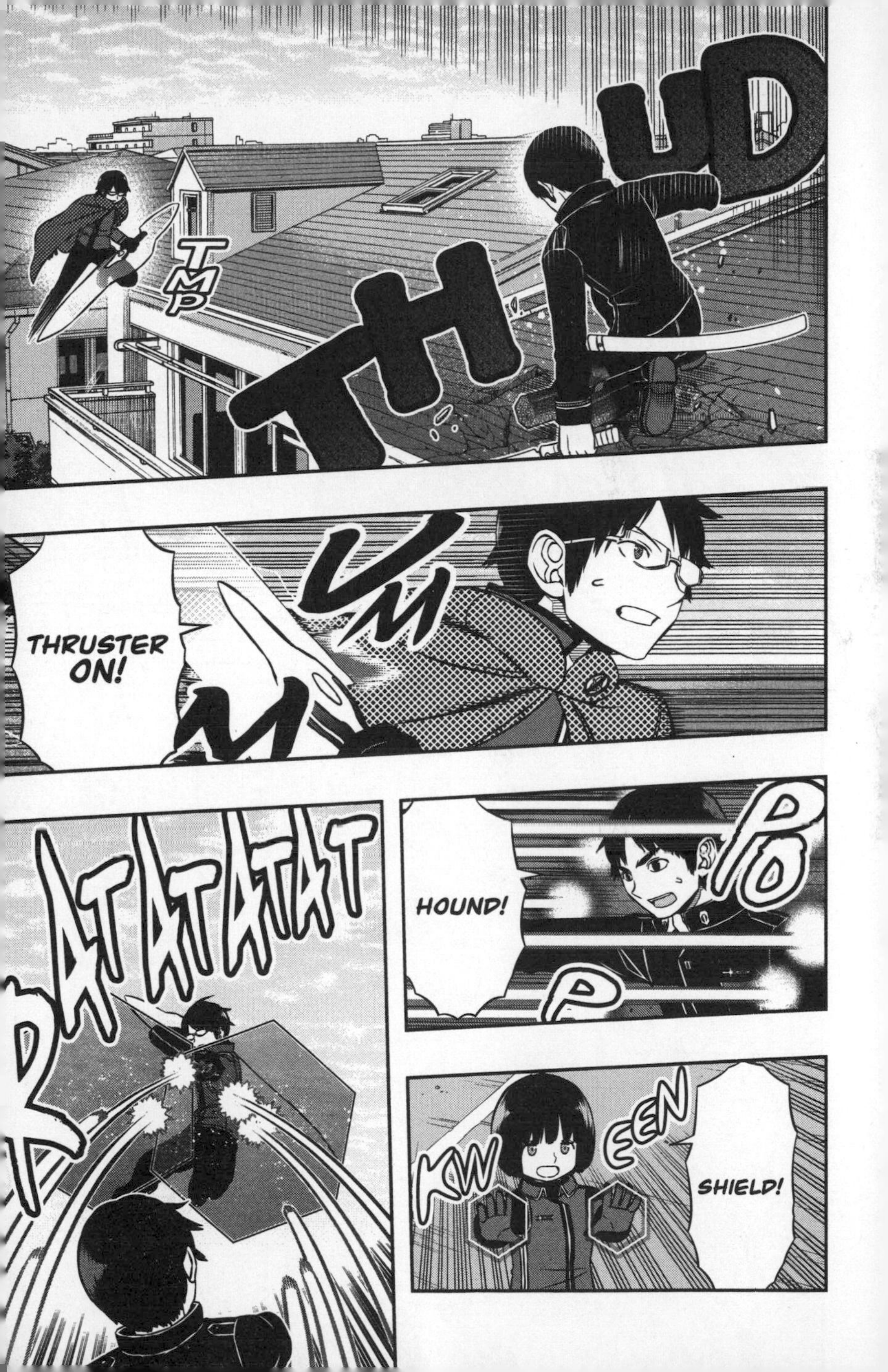

THUD
TMP
VMM
THRUSTER ON!
POP
HOUND!
KWEEN
SHIELD!
BATATATAT

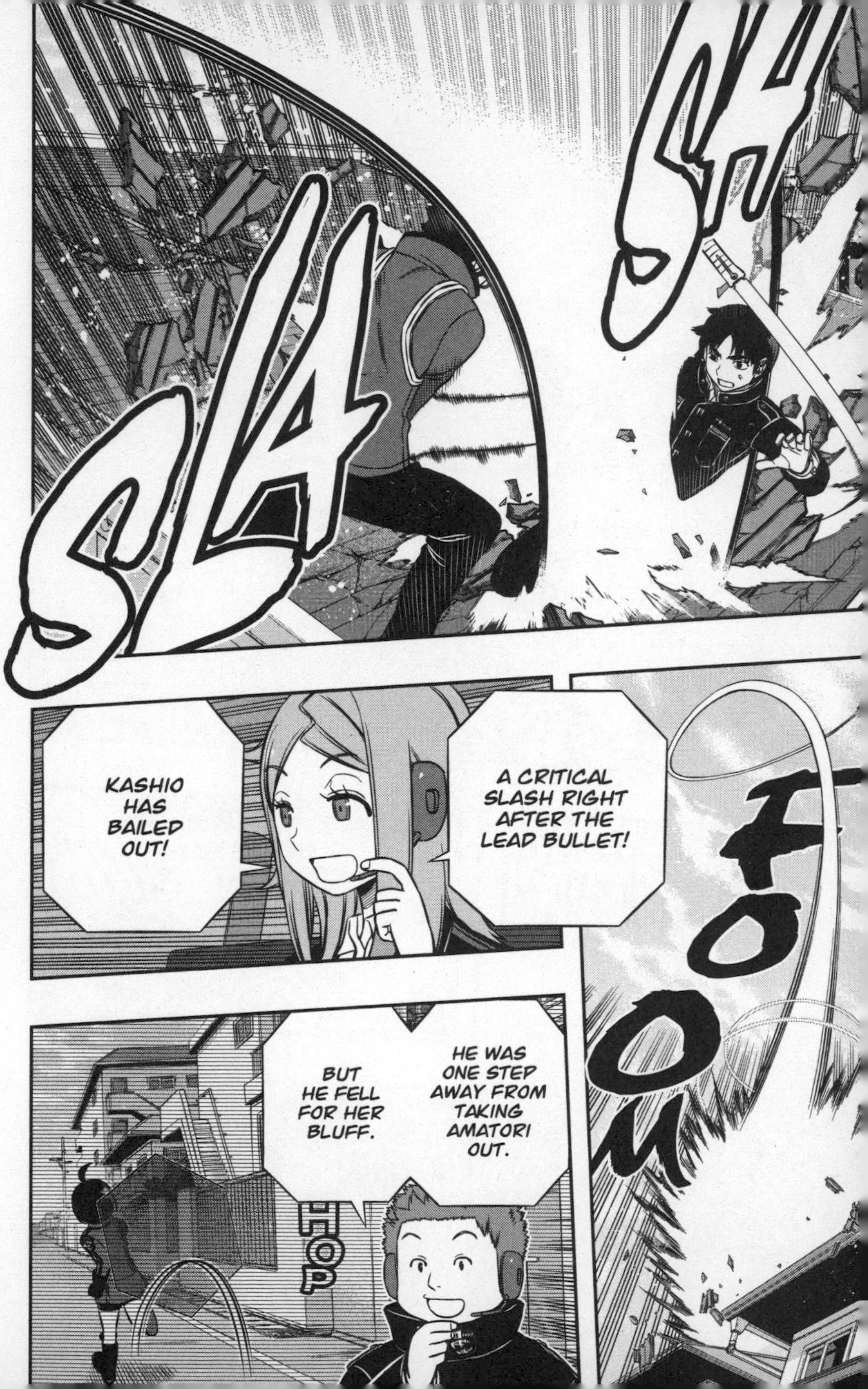
SH
SLA
FOOM
A CRITICAL SLASH RIGHT AFTER THE LEAD BULLET!
KASHIO HAS BAILED OUT!
HE WAS ONE STEP AWAY FROM TAKING AMATORI OUT.
BUT HE FELL FOR HER BLUFF.
HOP

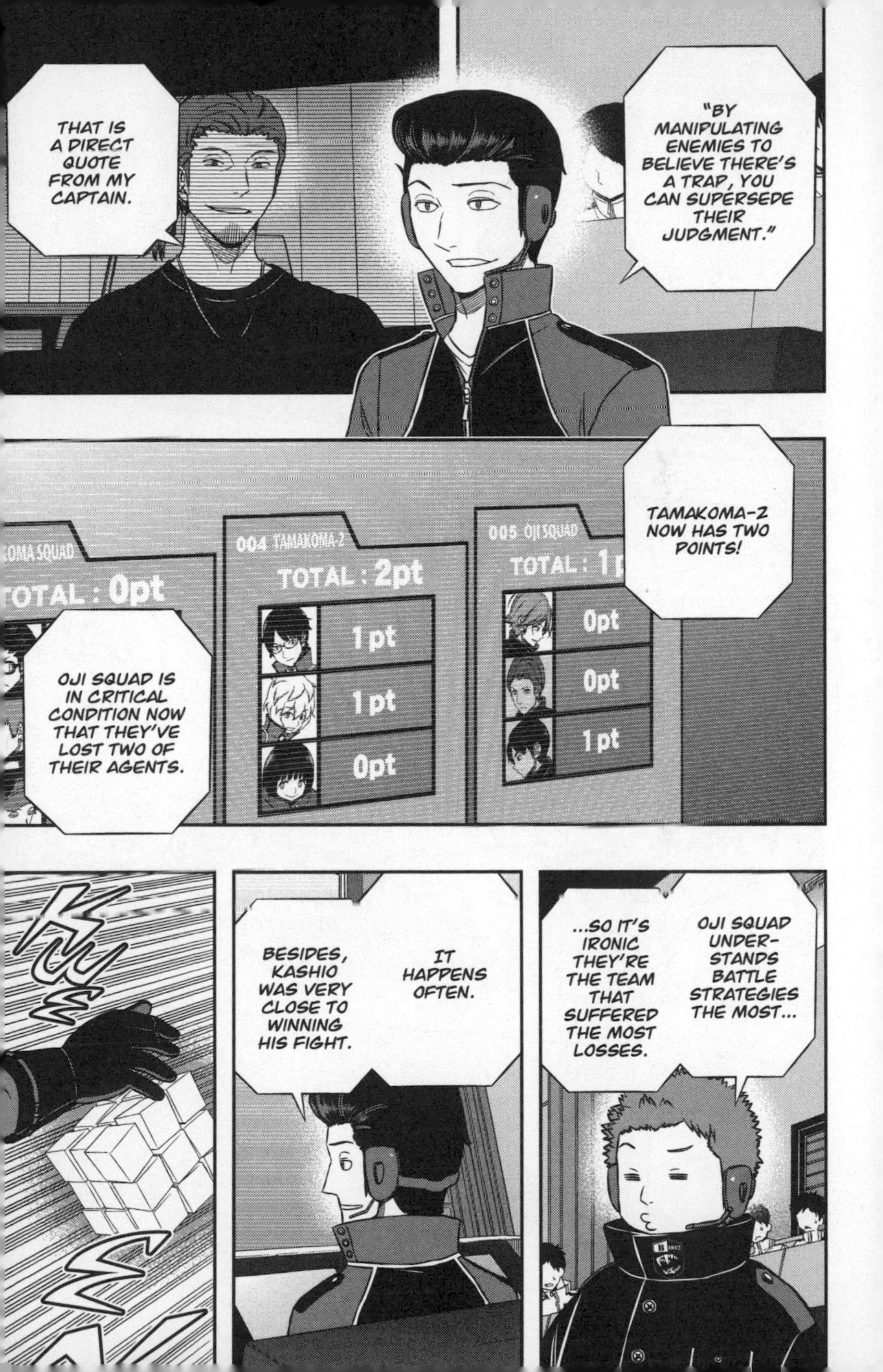
"BY MANIPULATING ENEMIES TO BELIEVE THERE'S A TRAP, YOU CAN SUPERSEDE THEIR JUDGMENT."
THAT IS A DIRECT QUOTE FROM MY CAPTAIN.
TAMAKOMA-2 NOW HAS TWO POINTS!
005 OJI SQUAD
0pt
0pt
1pt
004 TAMAKOMA-2
TOTAL : 2pt
1pt
1pt
0pt
TOTAL : 0pt
OJI SQUAD IS IN CRITICAL CONDITION NOW THAT THEY'VE LOST TWO OF THEIR AGENTS.
OJI SQUAD UNDERSTANDS BATTLE STRATEGIES THE MOST...
...SO IT'S IRONIC THEY'RE THE TEAM THAT SUFFERED THE MOST LOSSES.
IT HAPPENS OFTEN.
BESIDES, KASHIO WAS VERY CLOSE TO WINNING HIS FIGHT.

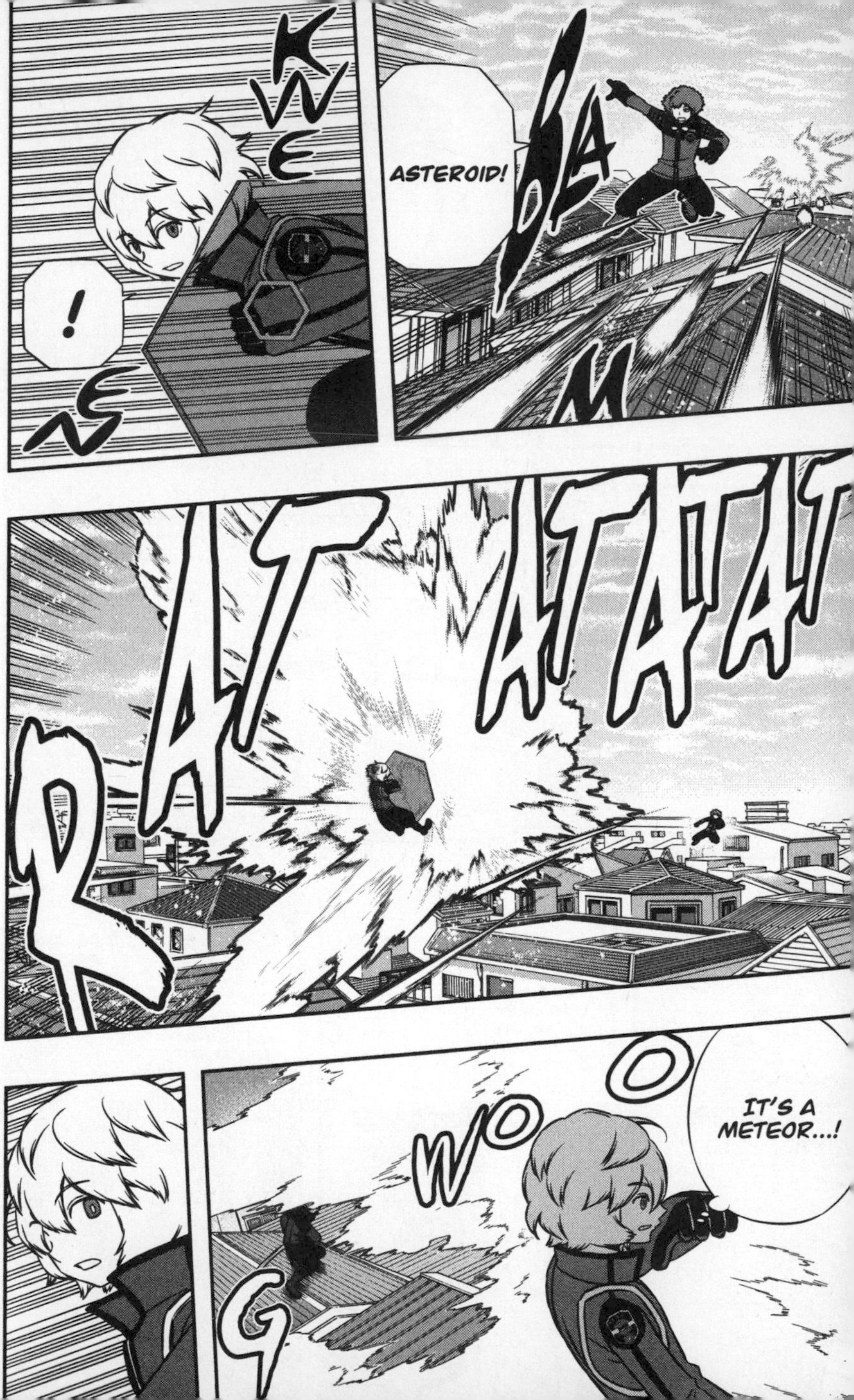
ASTEROID!
BAM
!
KWEEN
RATATATAT
IT'S A METEOR...!
GWOO

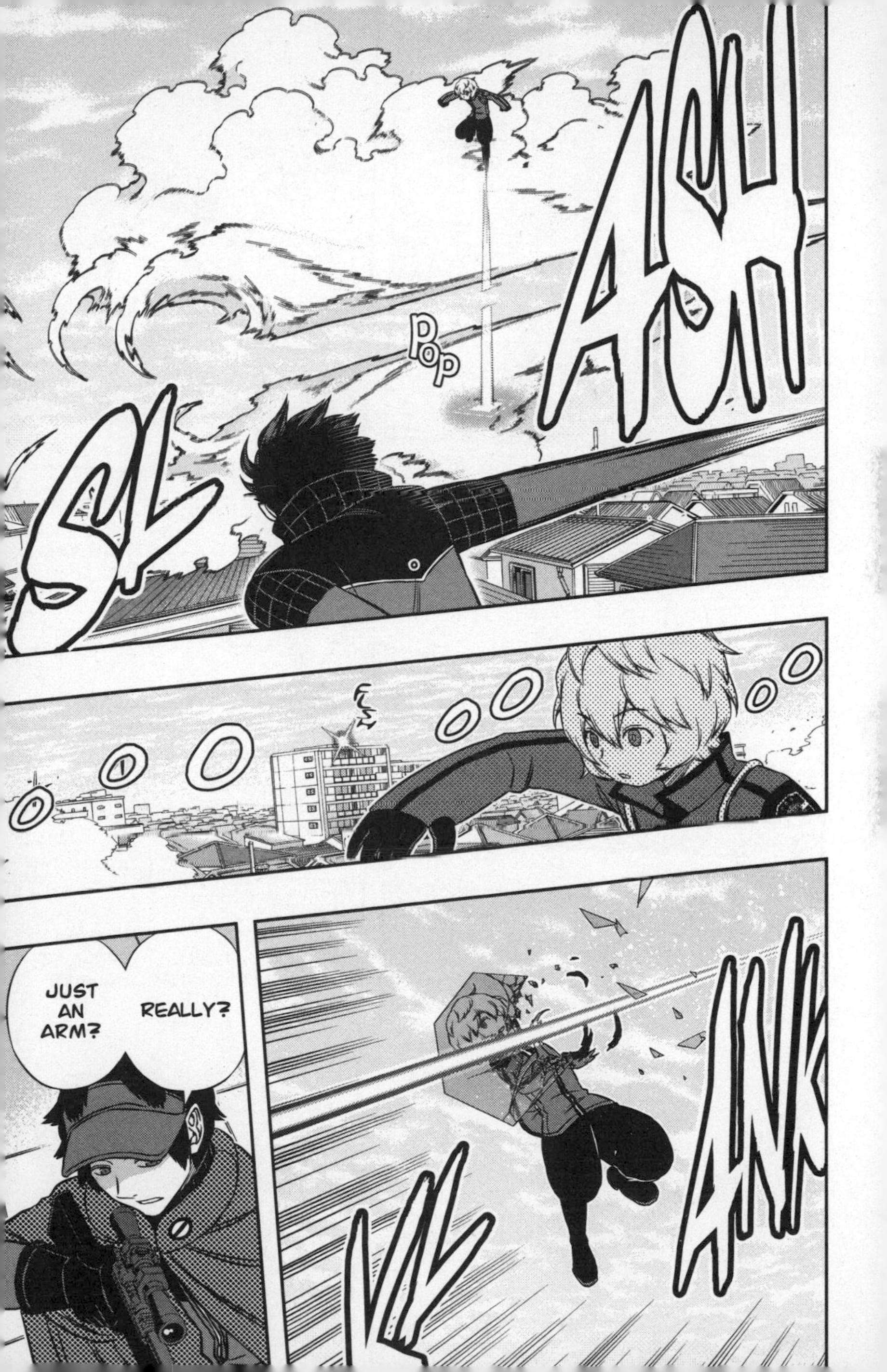
POP
REALLY?
JUST AN ARM?

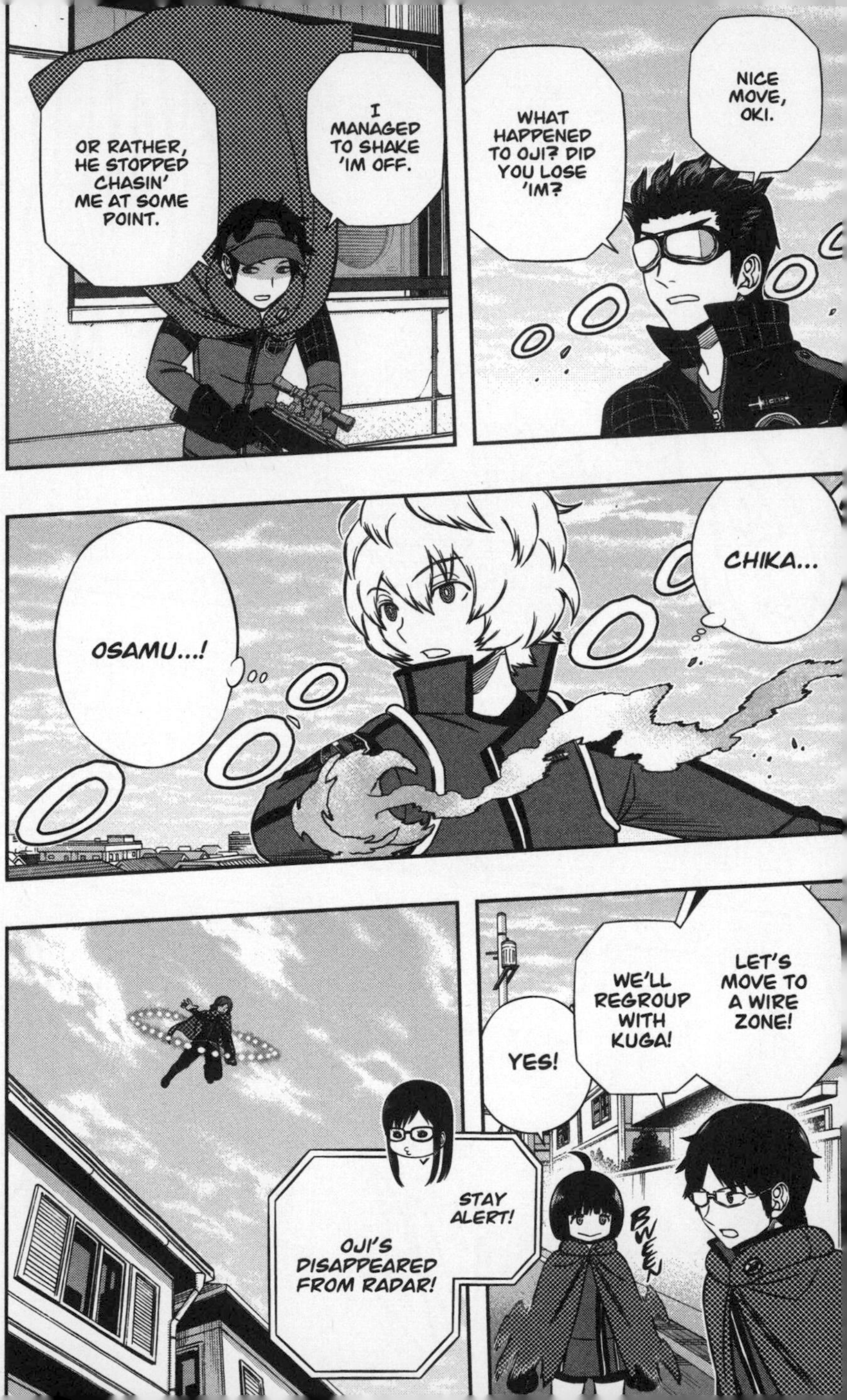
NICE MOVE, OKI.
WHAT HAPPENED TO OJI? DID YOU LOSE 'IM?
I MANAGED TO SHAKE 'IM OFF.
OR RATHER, HE STOPPED CHASIN' ME AT SOME POINT.
CHIKA...
OSAMU...!
LET'S MOVE TO A WIRE ZONE!
WE'LL REGROUP WITH KUGA!
YES!
BWEEN
STAY ALERT!
OJI'S DISAPPEARED FROM RADAR!

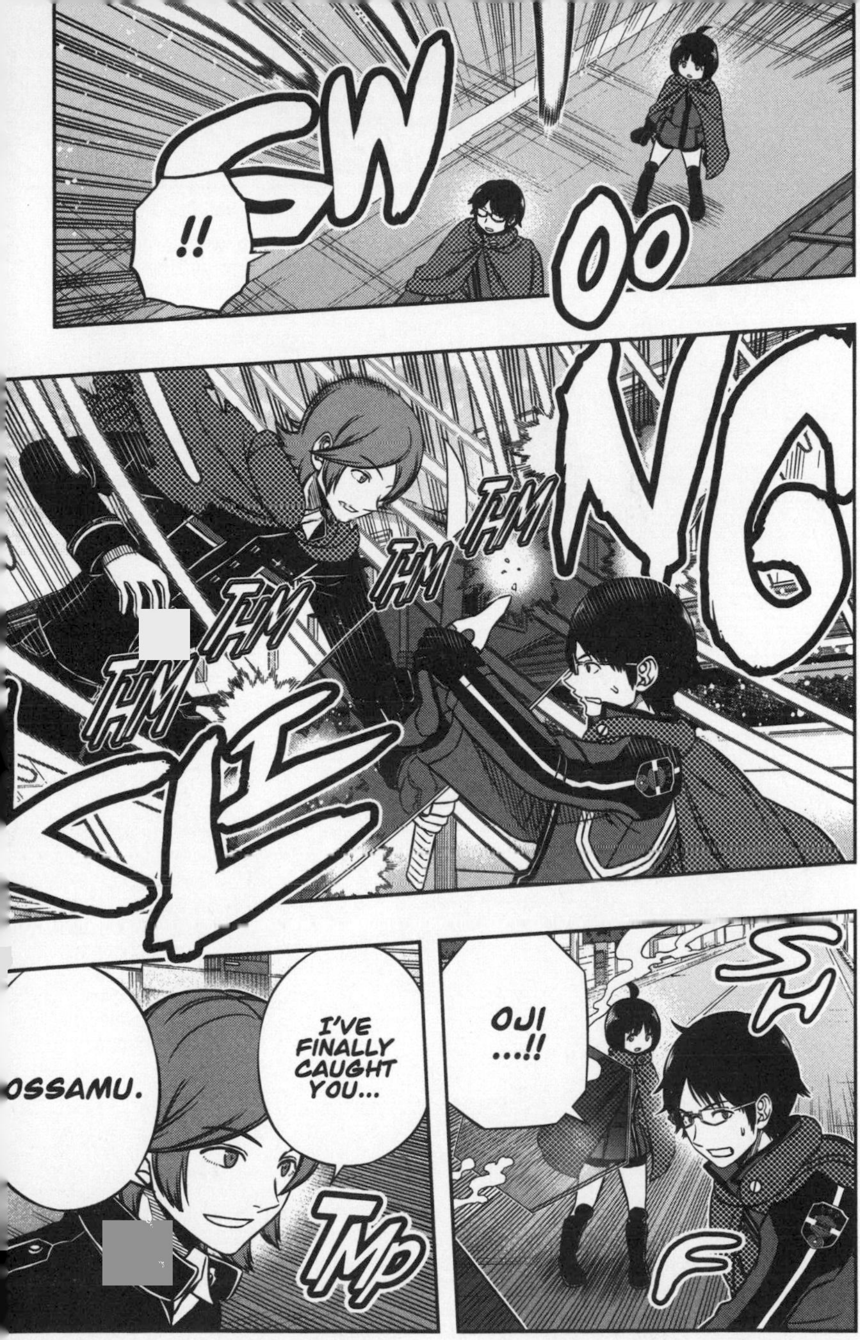
SWOO
!!
THM
THM
THM
THM
OJI ...!!
SH
F
I'VE FINALLY CAUGHT YOU...
OSSAMU.
TMP

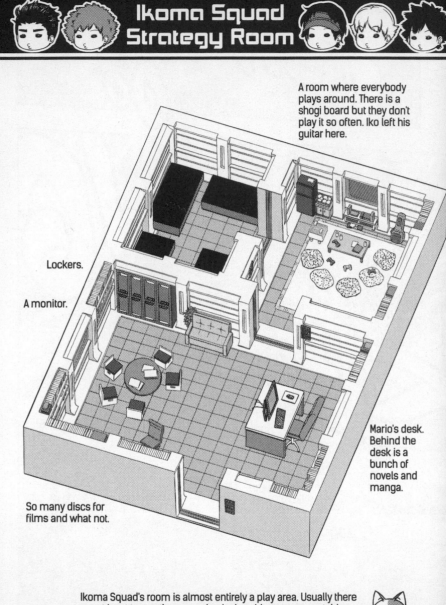

Ikoma Squad Strategy Room

A room where everybody plays around. There is a shogi board but they don't play it so often. Iko left his guitar here.

Lockers.

A monitor.

Mario's desk. Behind the desk is a bunch of novels and manga.

So many discs for films and what not.

Ikoma Squad's room is almost entirely a play area. Usually there are at least two or three people playing video games, watching films and/or chatting. The room is not that messy since the squad members like to keep things somewhat clean.

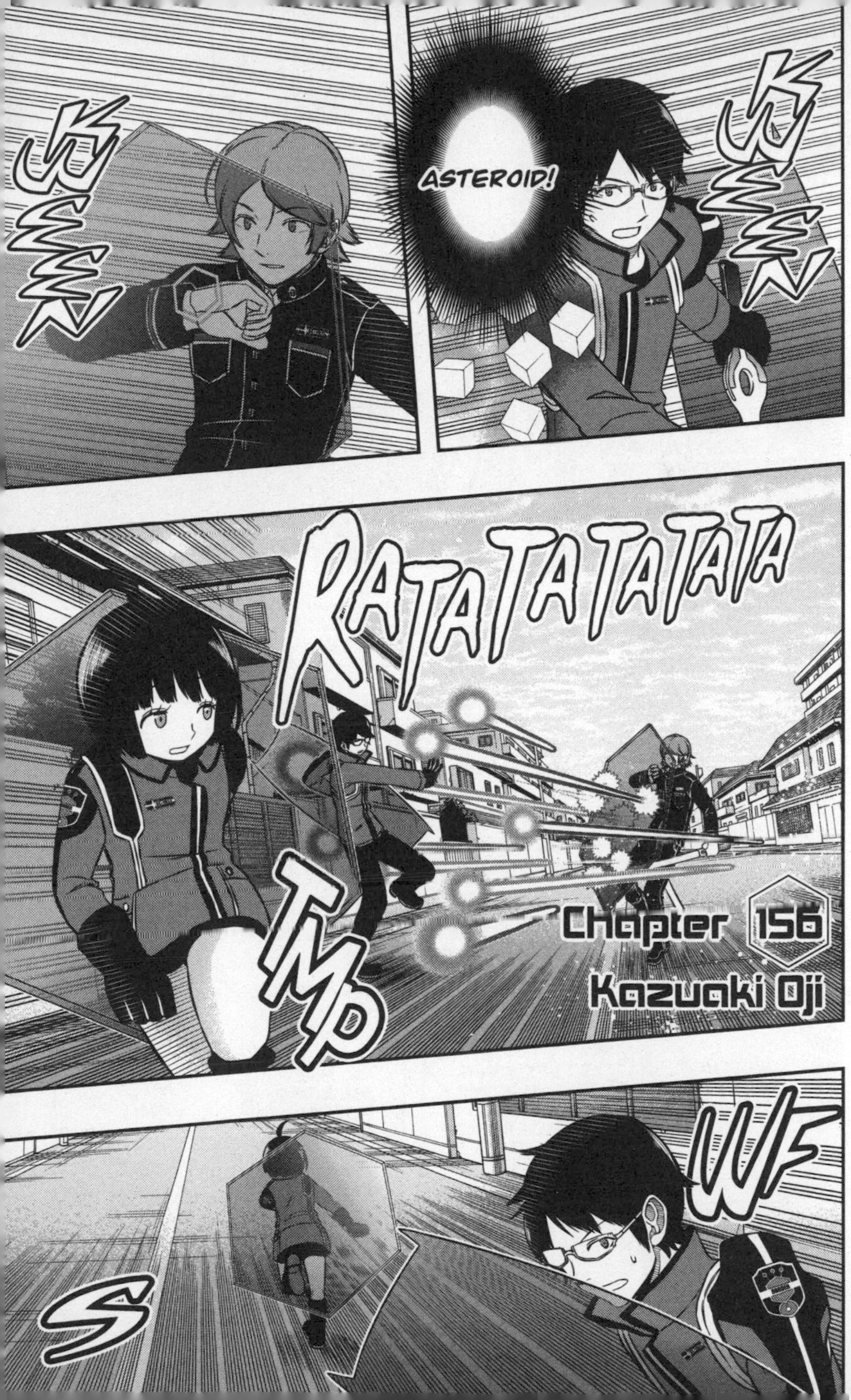
KYEEN
ASTEROID!
KYEEN
RATATATATATA
TMP
Chapter 156
Kazuaki Oji
WF
S

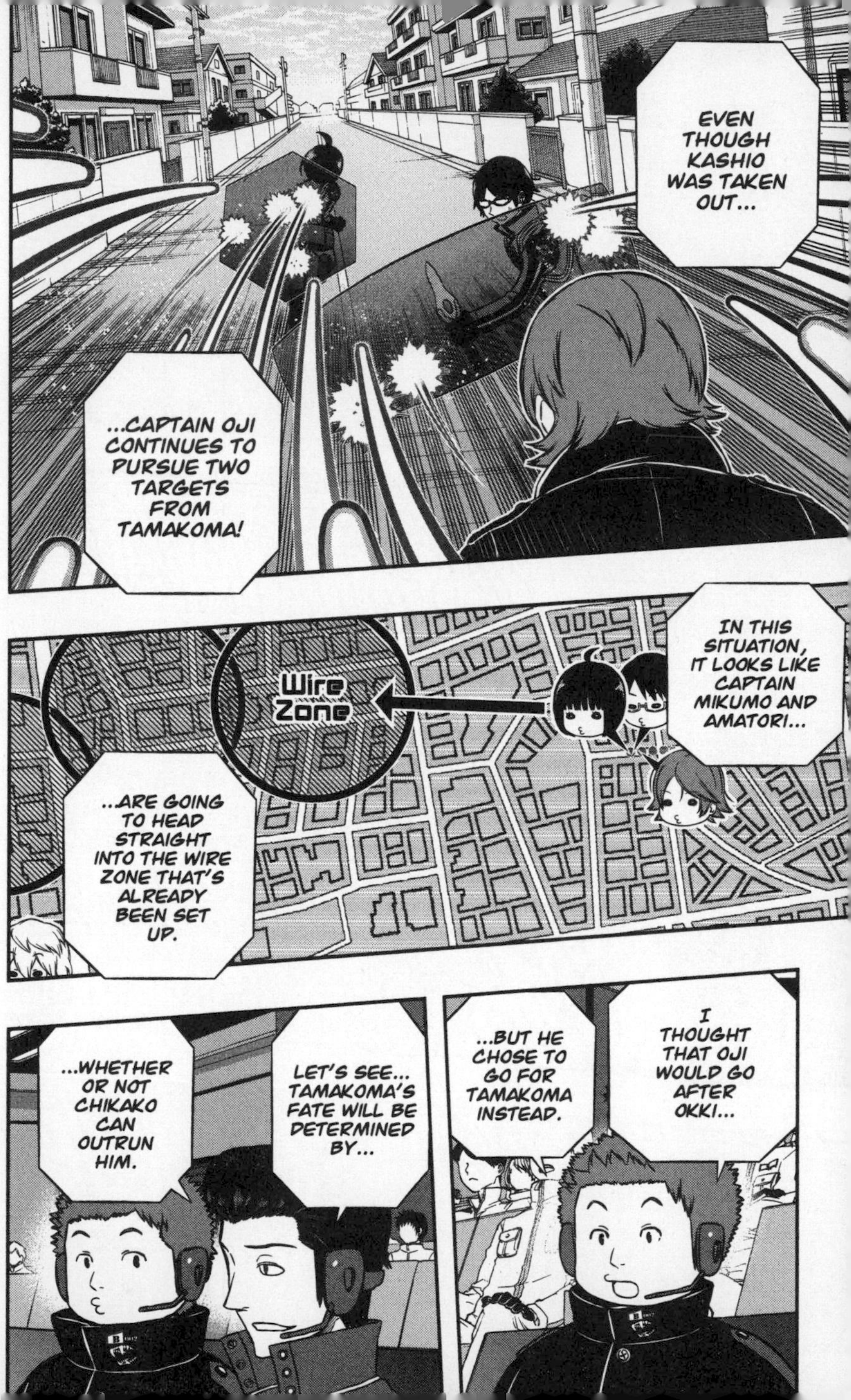
EVEN THOUGH KASHIO WAS TAKEN OUT...
...CAPTAIN OJI CONTINUES TO PURSUE TWO TARGETS FROM TAMAKOMA!
IN THIS SITUATION, IT LOOKS LIKE CAPTAIN MIKUMO AND AMATORI...
Wire Zone
...ARE GOING TO HEAD STRAIGHT INTO THE WIRE ZONE THAT'S ALREADY BEEN SET UP.
I THOUGHT THAT OJI WOULD GO AFTER OKKI...
...BUT HE CHOSE TO GO FOR TAMAKOMA INSTEAD.
LET'S SEE... TAMAKOMA'S FATE WILL BE DETERMINED BY...
...WHETHER OR NOT CHIKAKO CAN OUTRUN HIM.

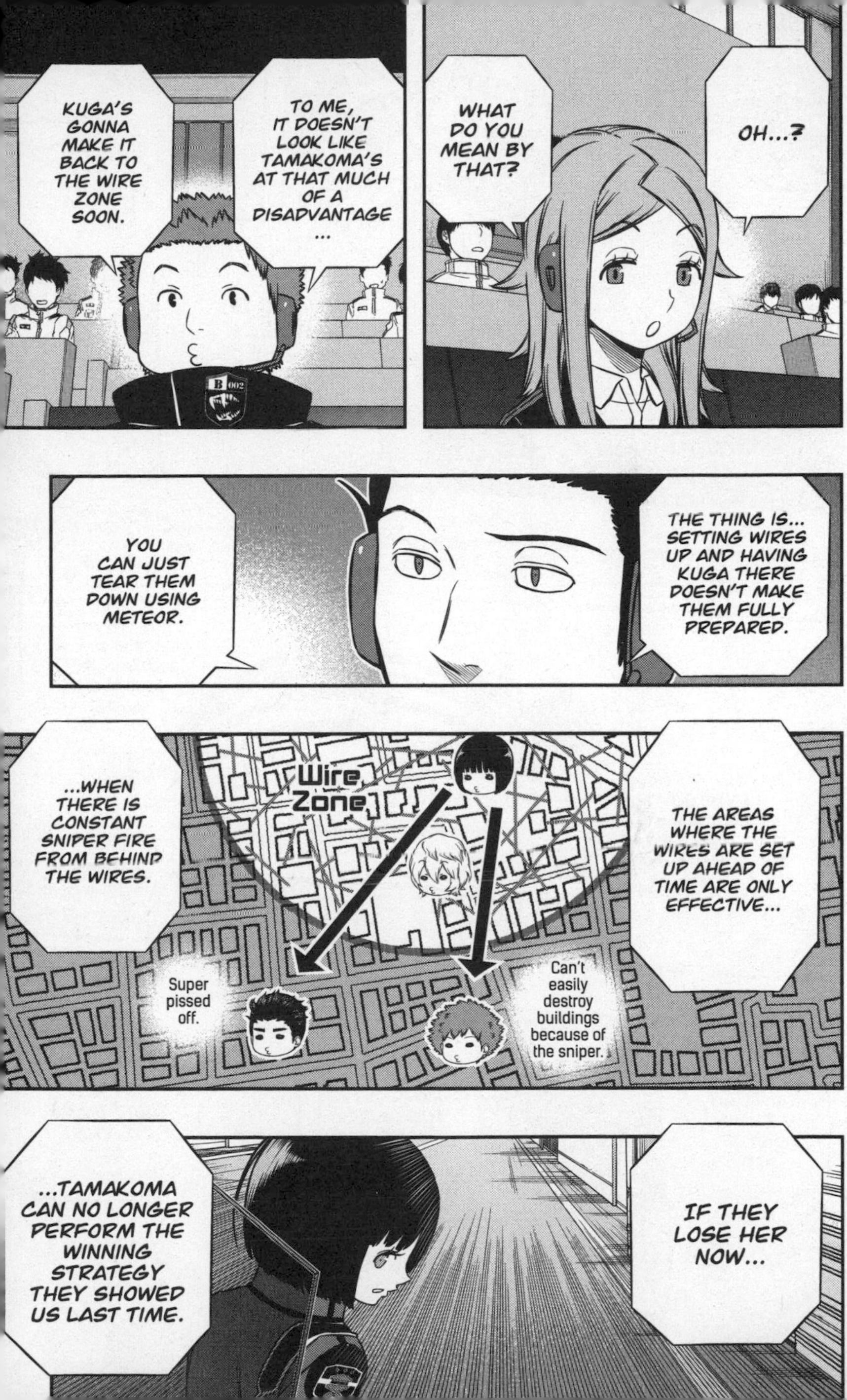
OH...?
WHAT DO YOU MEAN BY THAT?
TO ME, IT DOESN'T LOOK LIKE TAMAKOMA'S AT THAT MUCH OF A DISADVANTAGE...
KUGA'S GONNA MAKE IT BACK TO THE WIRE ZONE SOON.
THE THING IS... SETTING WIRES UP AND HAVING KUGA THERE DOESN'T MAKE THEM FULLY PREPARED.
YOU CAN JUST TEAR THEM DOWN USING METEOR.
THE AREAS WHERE THE WIRES ARE SET UP AHEAD OF TIME ARE ONLY EFFECTIVE...
Wire Zone
Can't easily destroy buildings because of the sniper.
Super pissed off.
...WHEN THERE IS CONSTANT SNIPER FIRE FROM BEHIND THE WIRES.
IF THEY LOSE HER NOW...
...TAMAKOMA CAN NO LONGER PERFORM THE WINNING STRATEGY THEY SHOWED US LAST TIME.

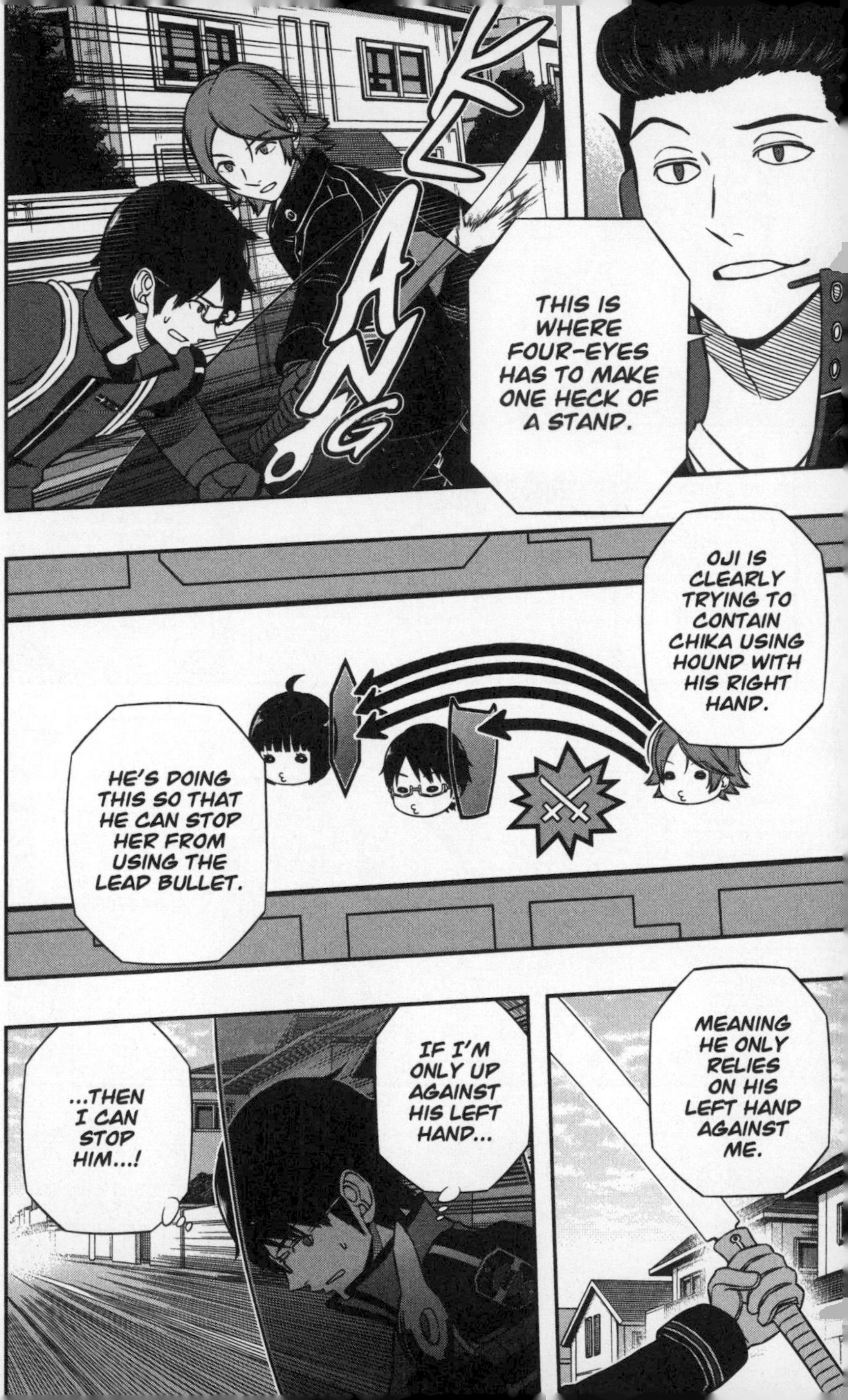
THIS IS WHERE FOUR-EYES HAS TO MAKE ONE HECK OF A STAND.
KLANG
OJI IS CLEARLY TRYING TO CONTAIN CHIKA USING HOUND WITH HIS RIGHT HAND.
HE'S DOING THIS SO THAT HE CAN STOP HER FROM USING THE LEAD BULLET.
MEANING HE ONLY RELIES ON HIS LEFT HAND AGAINST ME.
IF I'M ONLY UP AGAINST HIS LEFT HAND...
...THEN I CAN STOP HIM...!

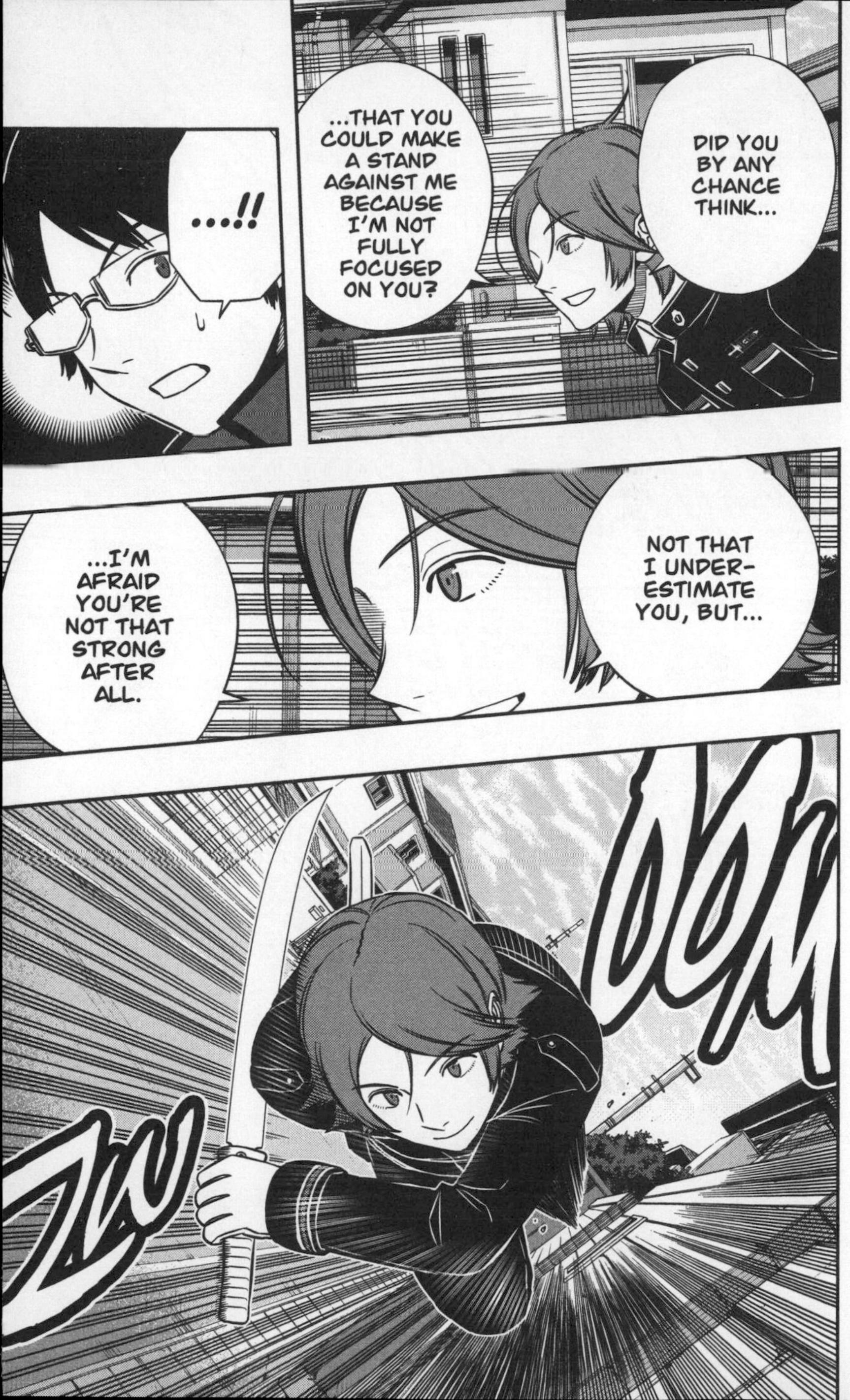
DID YOU BY ANY CHANCE THINK...
...THAT YOU COULD MAKE A STAND AGAINST ME BECAUSE I'M NOT FULLY FOCUSED ON YOU?
...!!
NOT THAT I UNDER-ESTIMATE YOU, BUT...
...I'M AFRAID YOU'RE NOT THAT STRONG AFTER ALL.
ZU

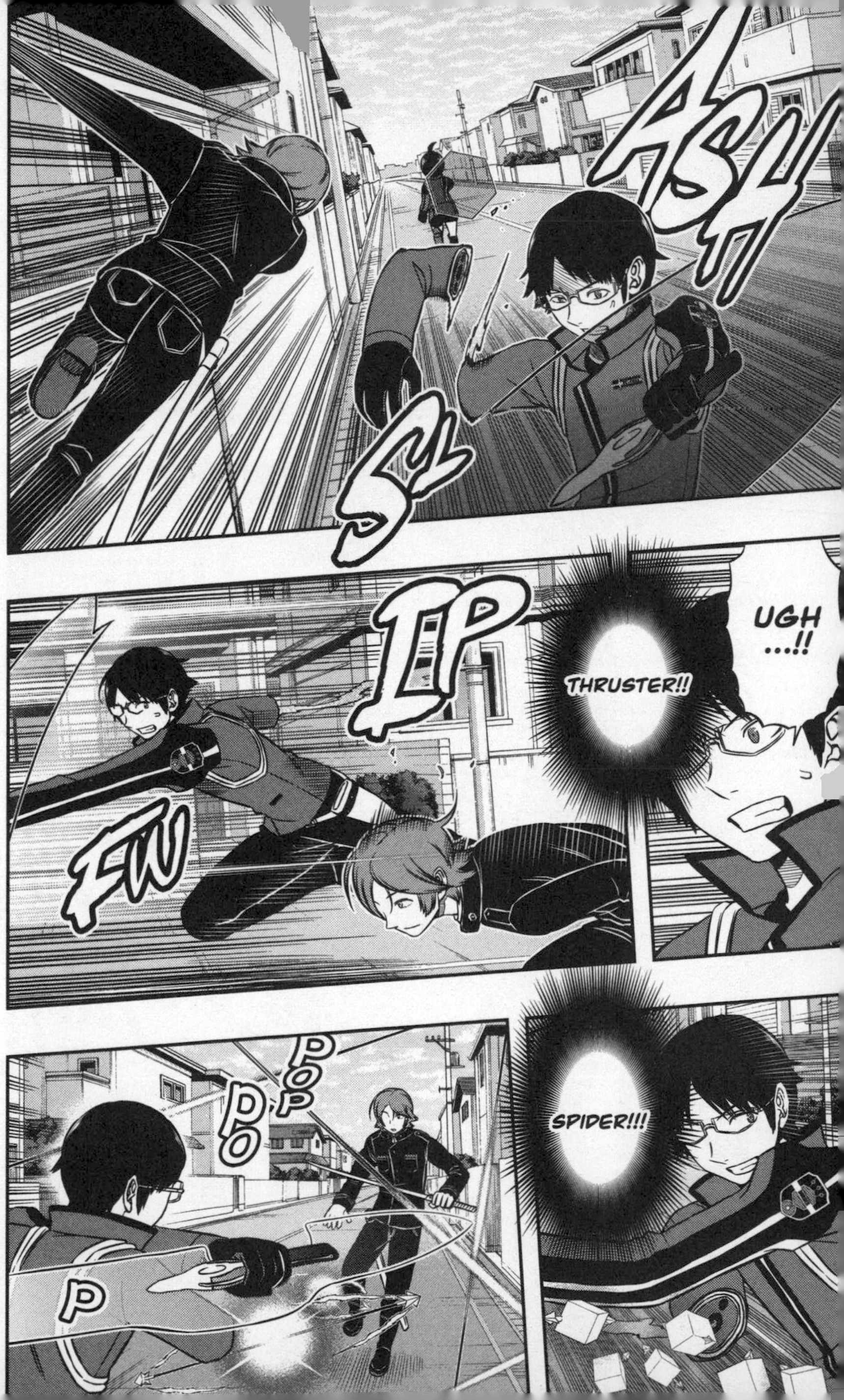
ASH
SL
UGH ...!!
THRUSTER!!
IP
FW
SPIDER!!!
POP
POP
P

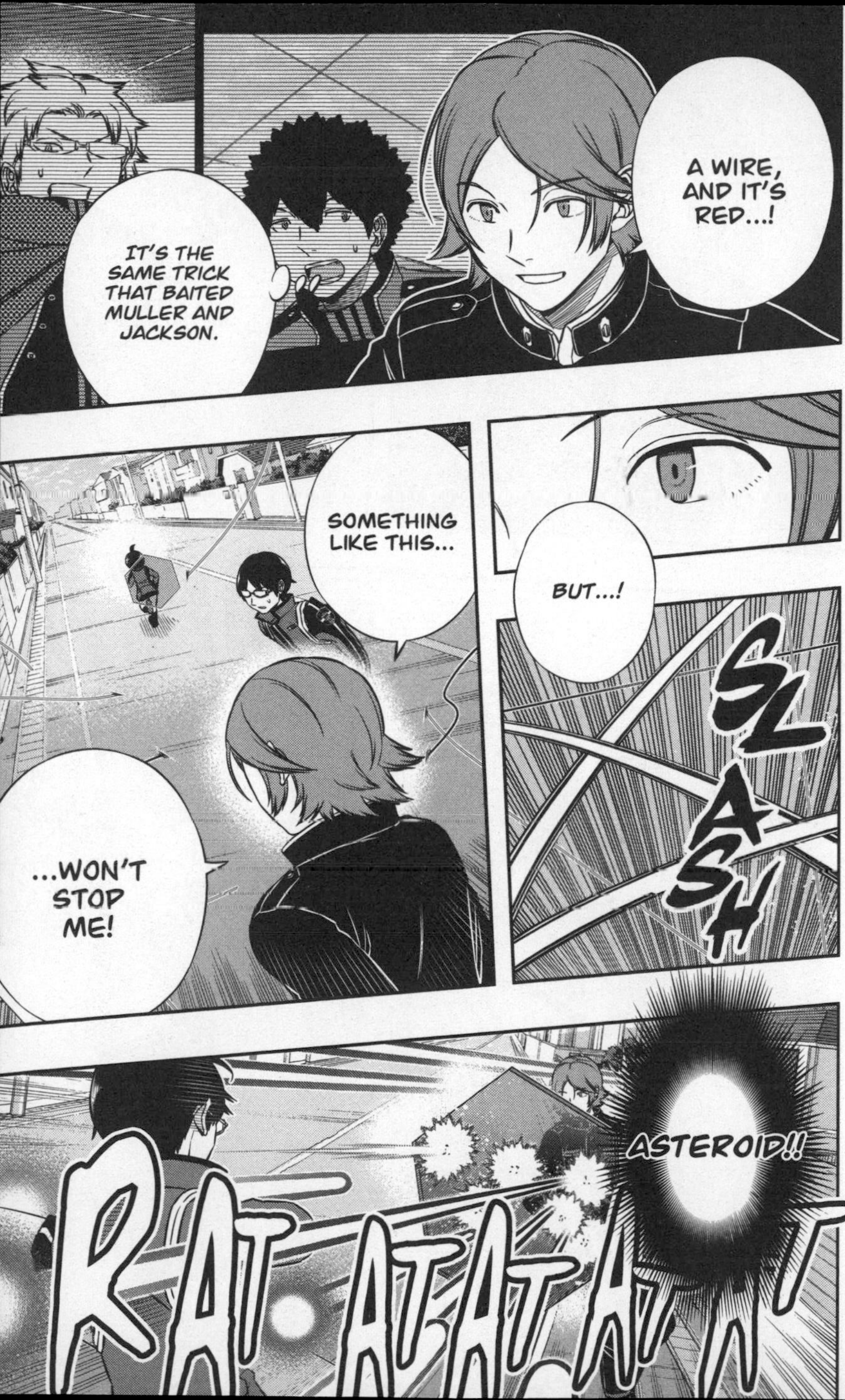
A WIRE, AND IT'S RED...!
IT'S THE SAME TRICK THAT BAITED MULLER AND JACKSON.
BUT...!
SLASH
SOMETHING LIKE THIS...
...WON'T STOP ME!
ASTEROID!!
RATATATAT

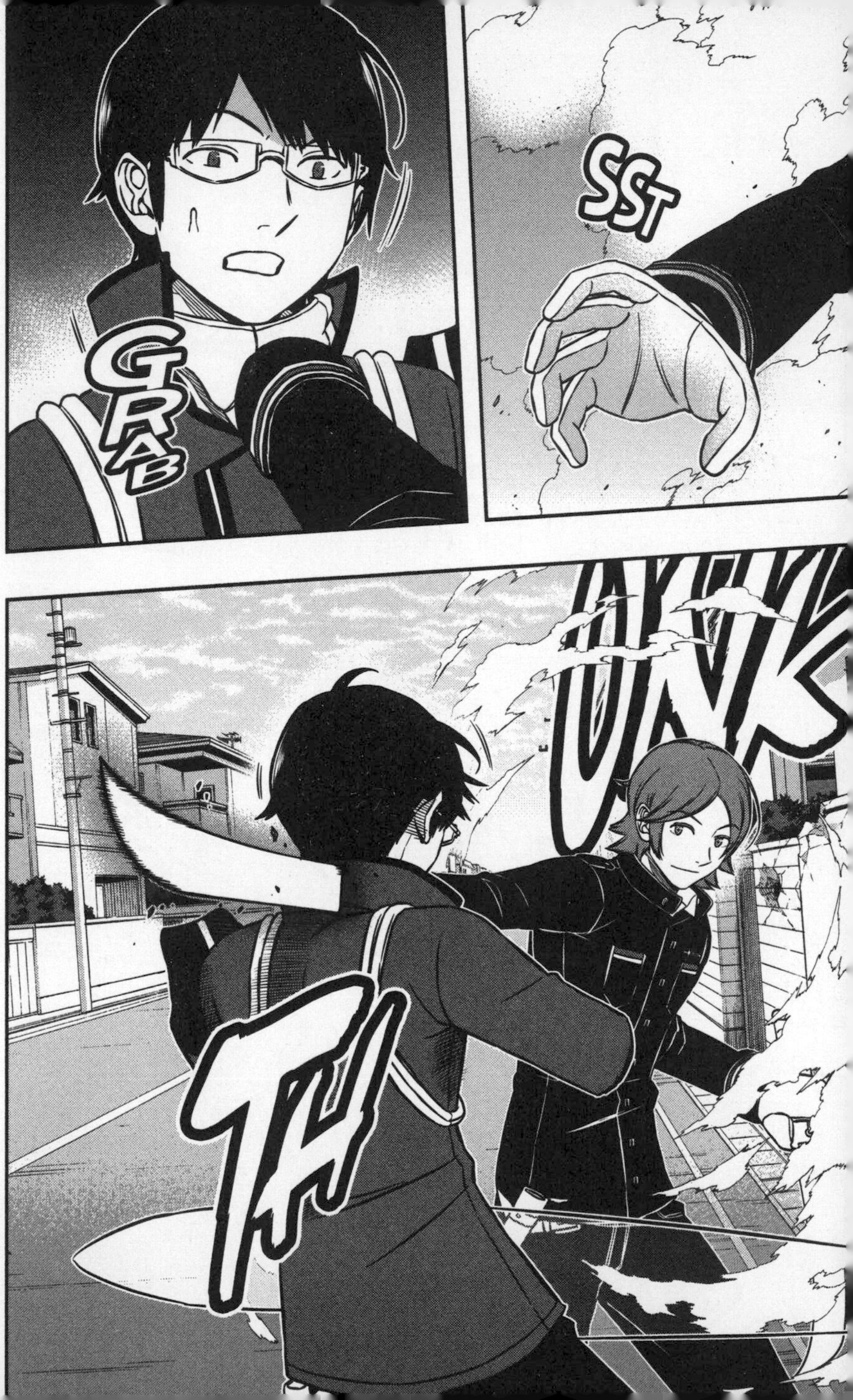
SST
GRAB

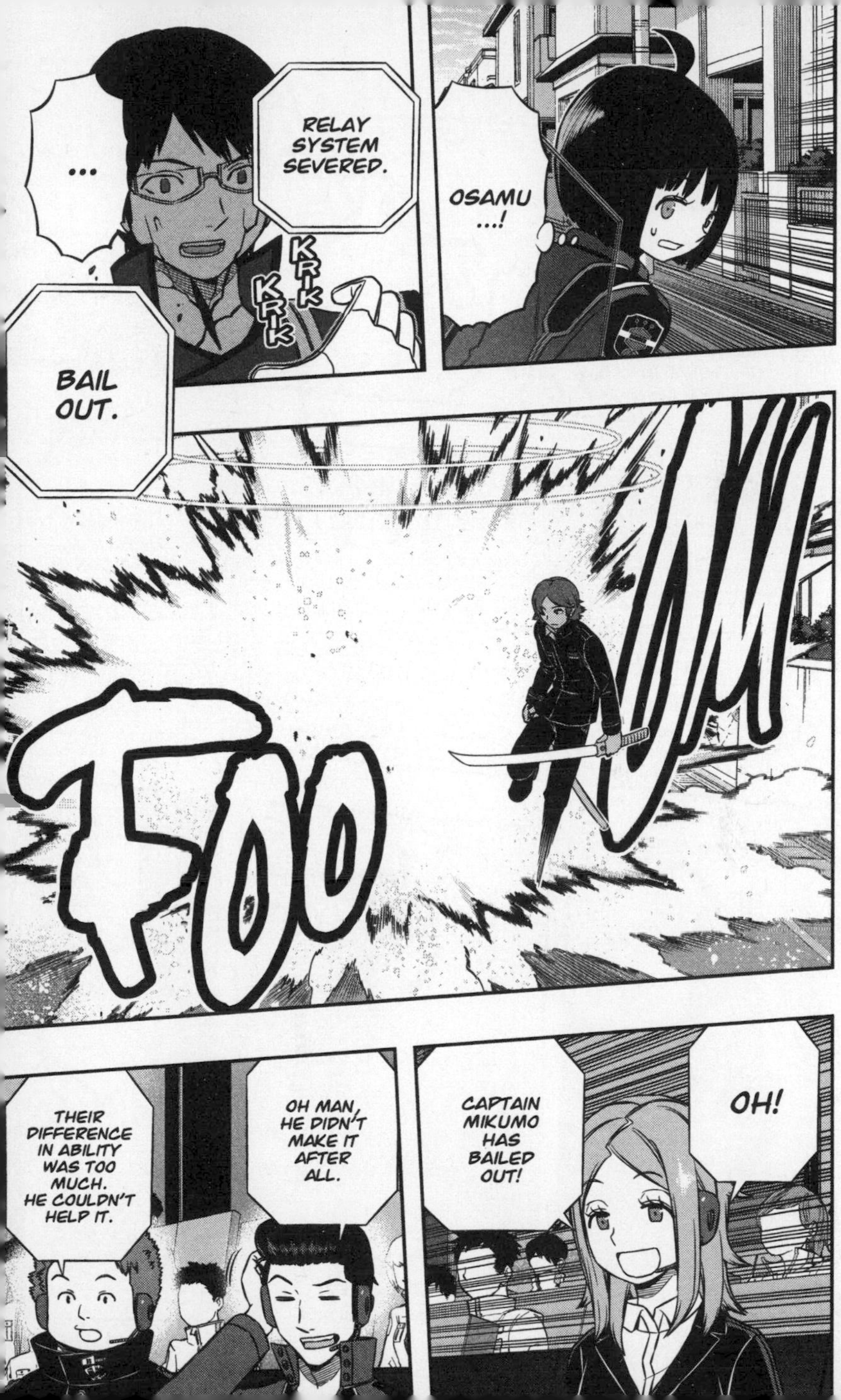
OSAMU ...!
RELAY SYSTEM SEVERED.
...
KRIK KRIK
BAIL OUT.
FOO
OM
OH!
CAPTAIN MIKUMO HAS BAILED OUT!
OH MAN, HE DIDN'T MAKE IT AFTER ALL.
THEIR DIFFERENCE IN ABILITY WAS TOO MUCH. HE COULDN'T HELP IT.

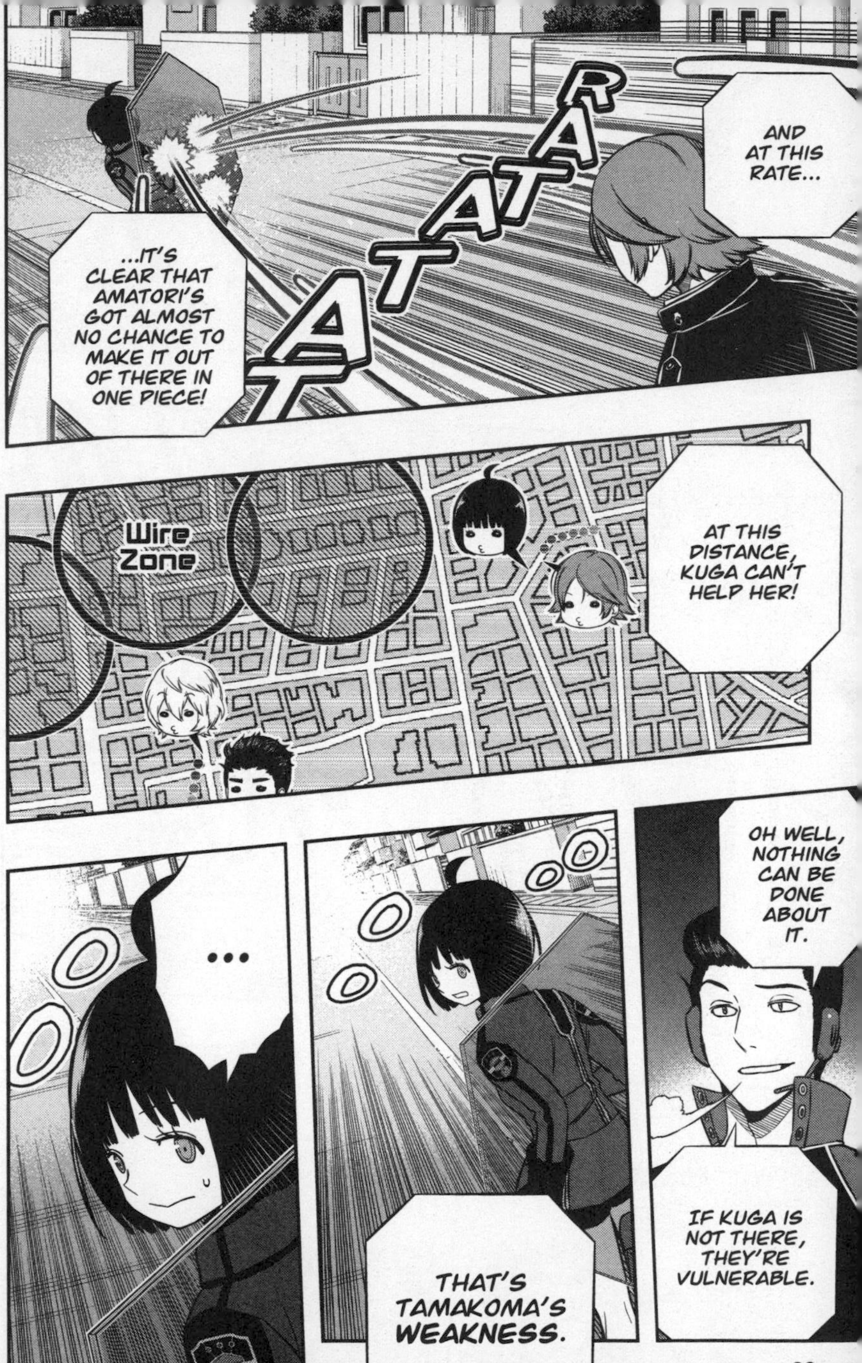
AND AT THIS RATE...
RATATAT
...IT'S CLEAR THAT AMATORI'S GOT ALMOST NO CHANCE TO MAKE IT OUT OF THERE IN ONE PIECE!
AT THIS DISTANCE, KUGA CAN'T HELP HER!
Wire Zone
OH WELL, NOTHING CAN BE DONE ABOUT IT.
IF KUGA IS NOT THERE, THEY'RE VULNERABLE.
THAT'S TAMAKOMA'S WEAKNESS.
...

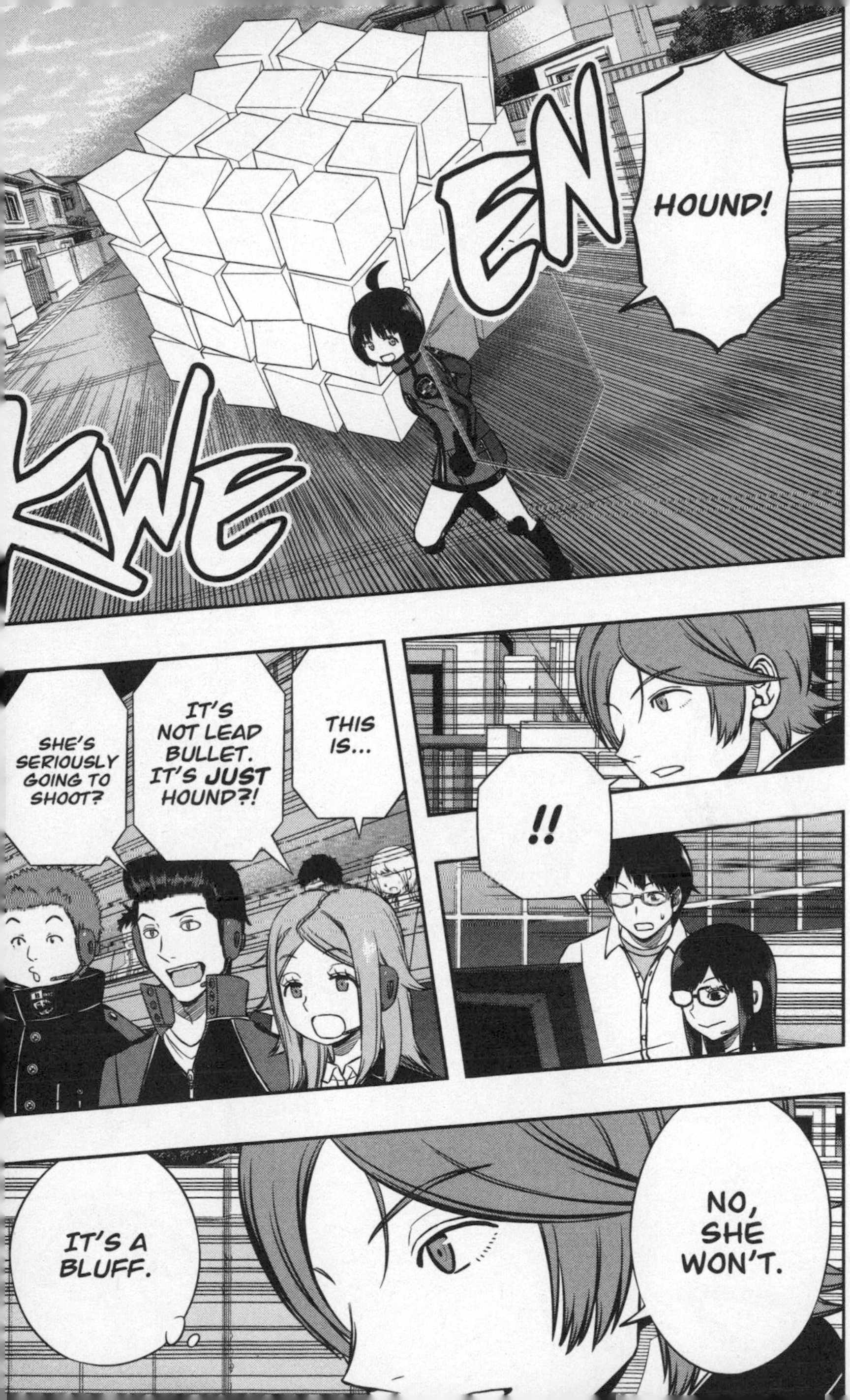
HOUND!
KWEEN
!!
THIS IS...
IT'S NOT LEAD BULLET. IT'S **JUST** HOUND?!
SHE'S SERIOUSLY GOING TO SHOOT?
NO, SHE WON'T.
IT'S A BLUFF.

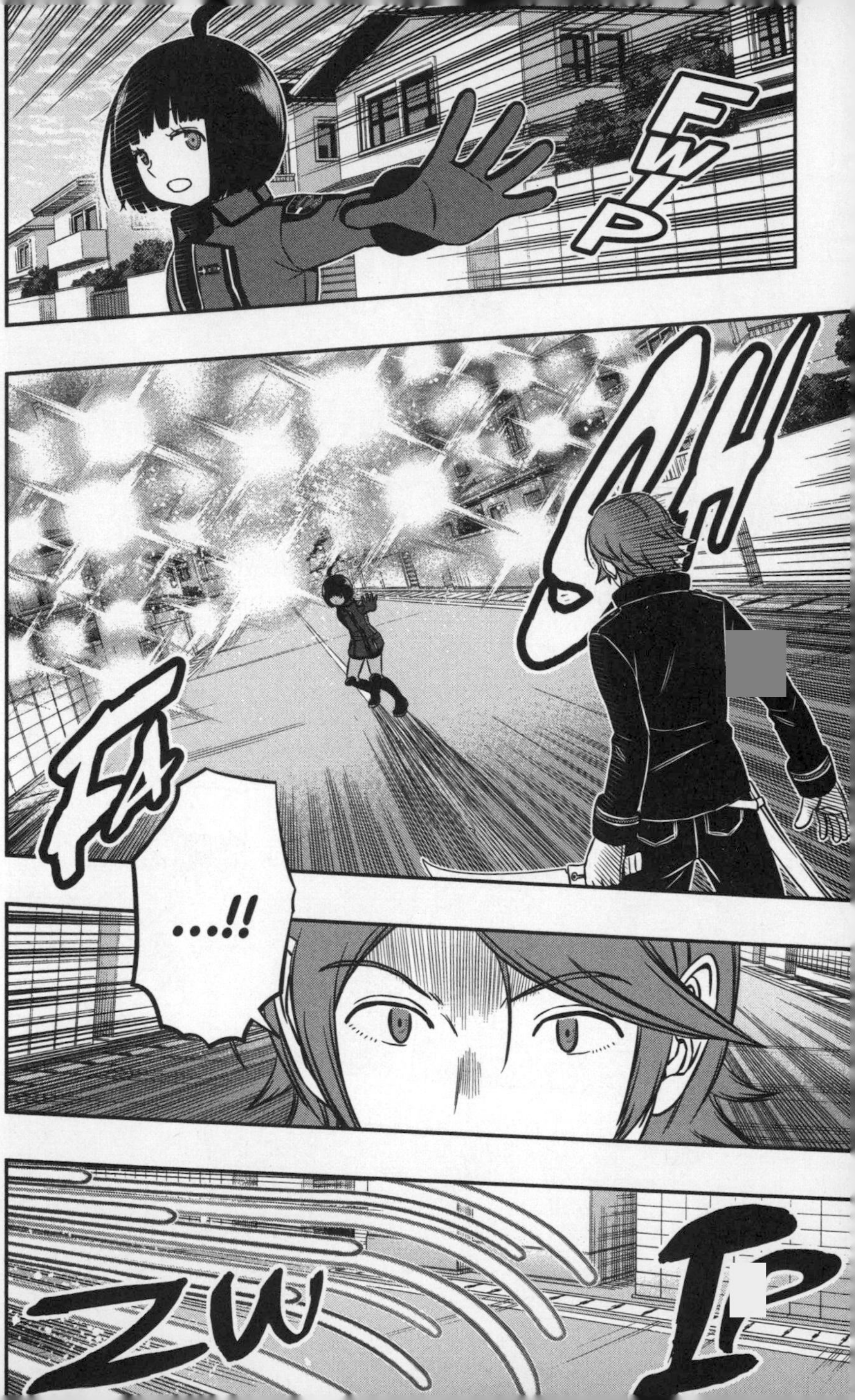
FWIP
...!!
ZWIP

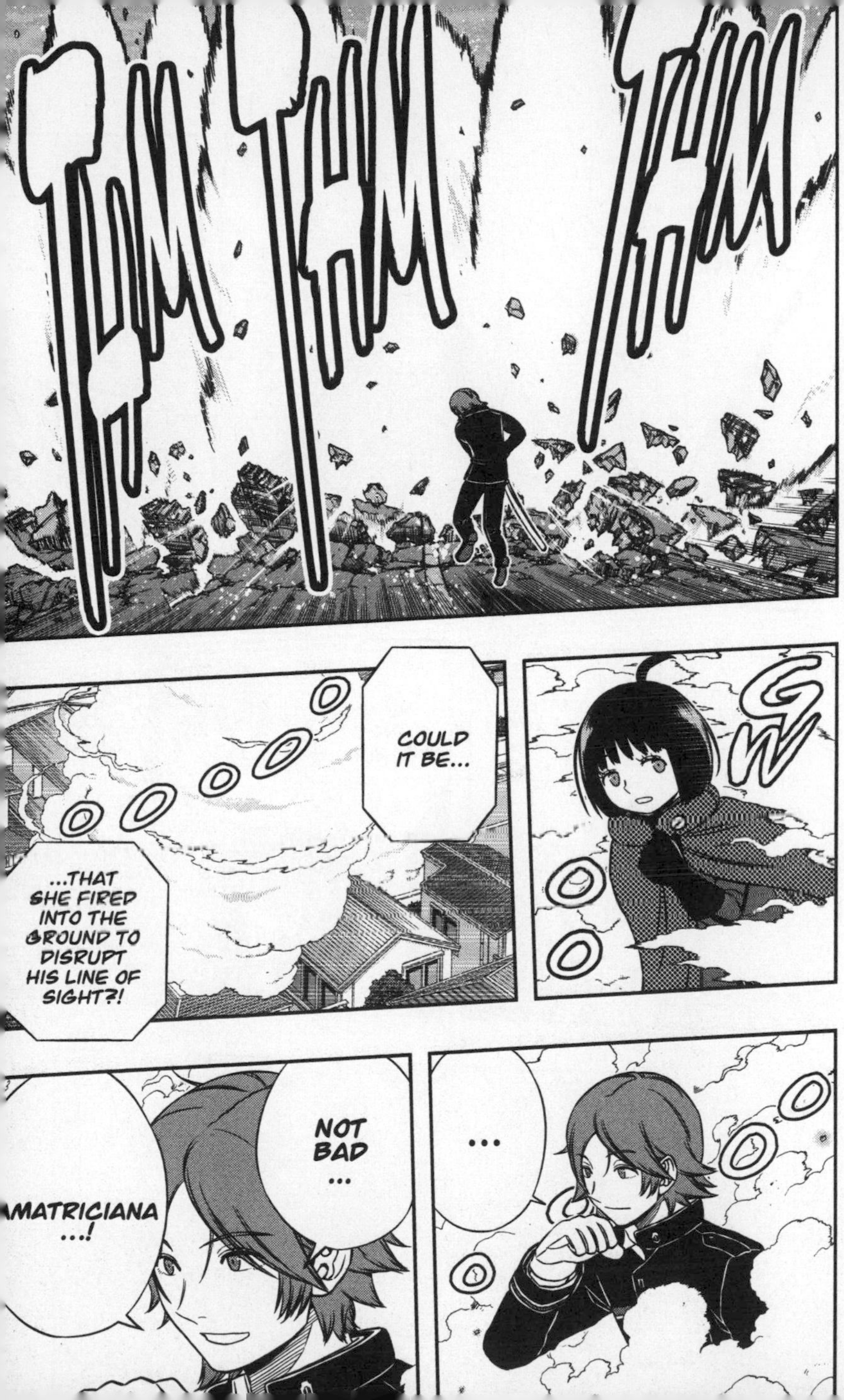
COULD IT BE...
...THAT SHE FIRED INTO THE GROUND TO DISRUPT HIS LINE OF SIGHT?!
...
NOT BAD ...
AMATRICIANA ...!

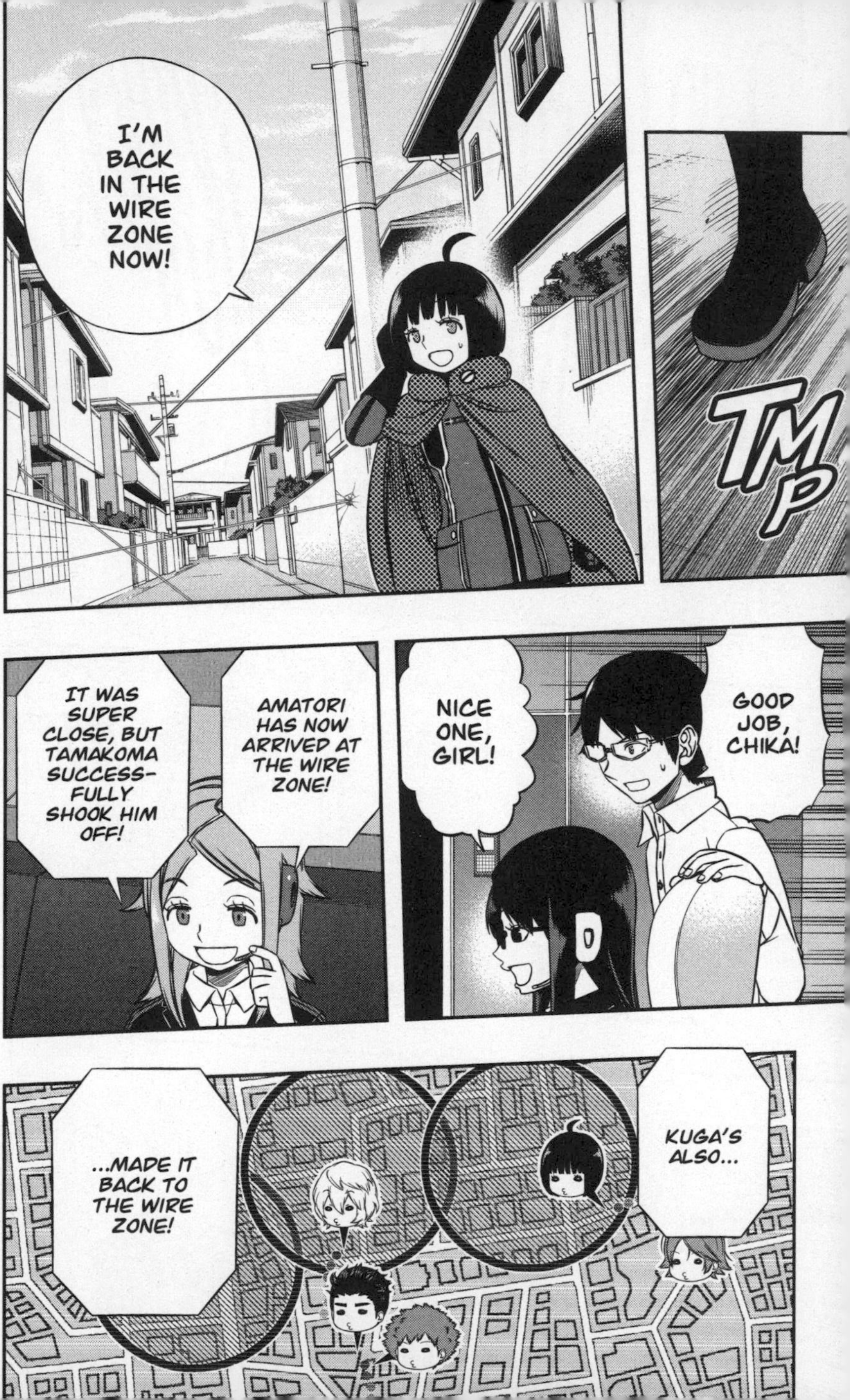
TMP
I'M BACK IN THE WIRE ZONE NOW!
GOOD JOB, CHIKA!
NICE ONE, GIRL!
AMATORI HAS NOW ARRIVED AT THE WIRE ZONE!
IT WAS SUPER CLOSE, BUT TAMAKOMA SUCCESS-FULLY SHOOK HIM OFF!
KUGA'S ALSO...
...MADE IT BACK TO THE WIRE ZONE!

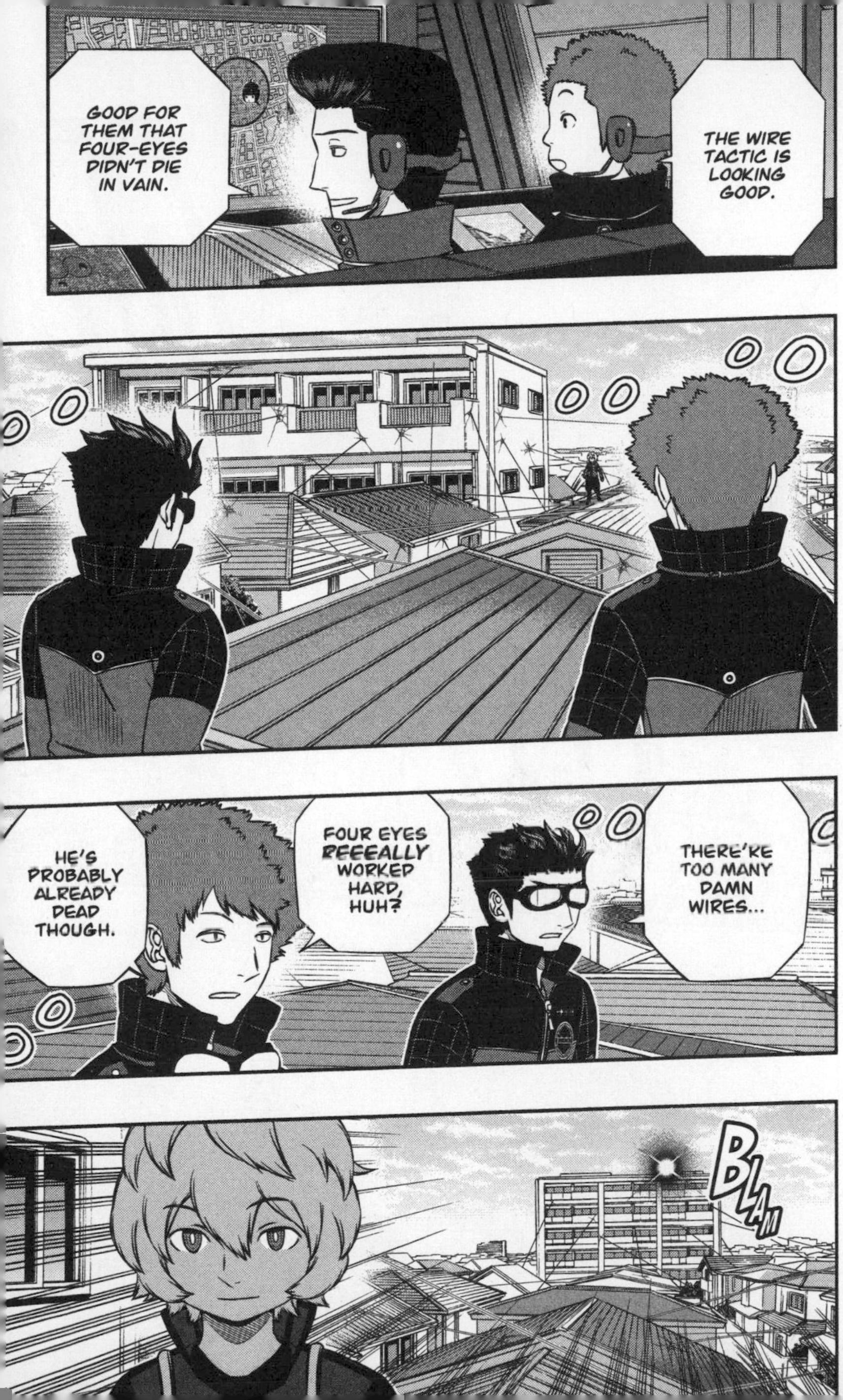
THE WIRE TACTIC IS LOOKING GOOD.
GOOD FOR THEM THAT FOUR-EYES DIDN'T DIE IN VAIN.
THERE'RE TOO MANY DAMN WIRES...
FOUR EYES REEEALLY WORKED HARD, HUH?
HE'S PROBABLY ALREADY DEAD THOUGH.
BLAM

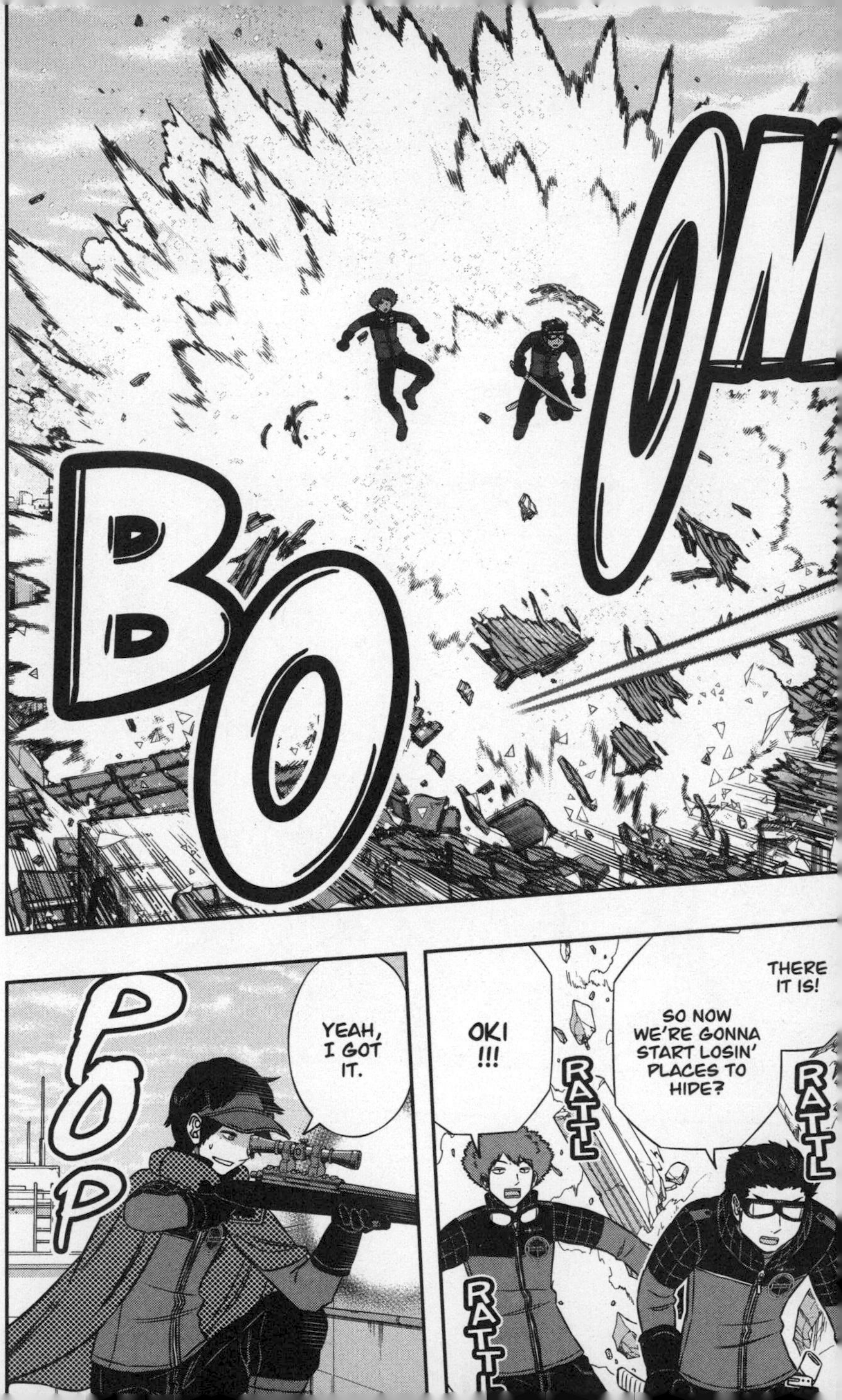

BOOM
THERE IT IS!
RATTL
SO NOW WE'RE GONNA START LOSIN' PLACES TO HIDE?
RATTL
OKI !!!
RATTL
YEAH, I GOT IT.
POP

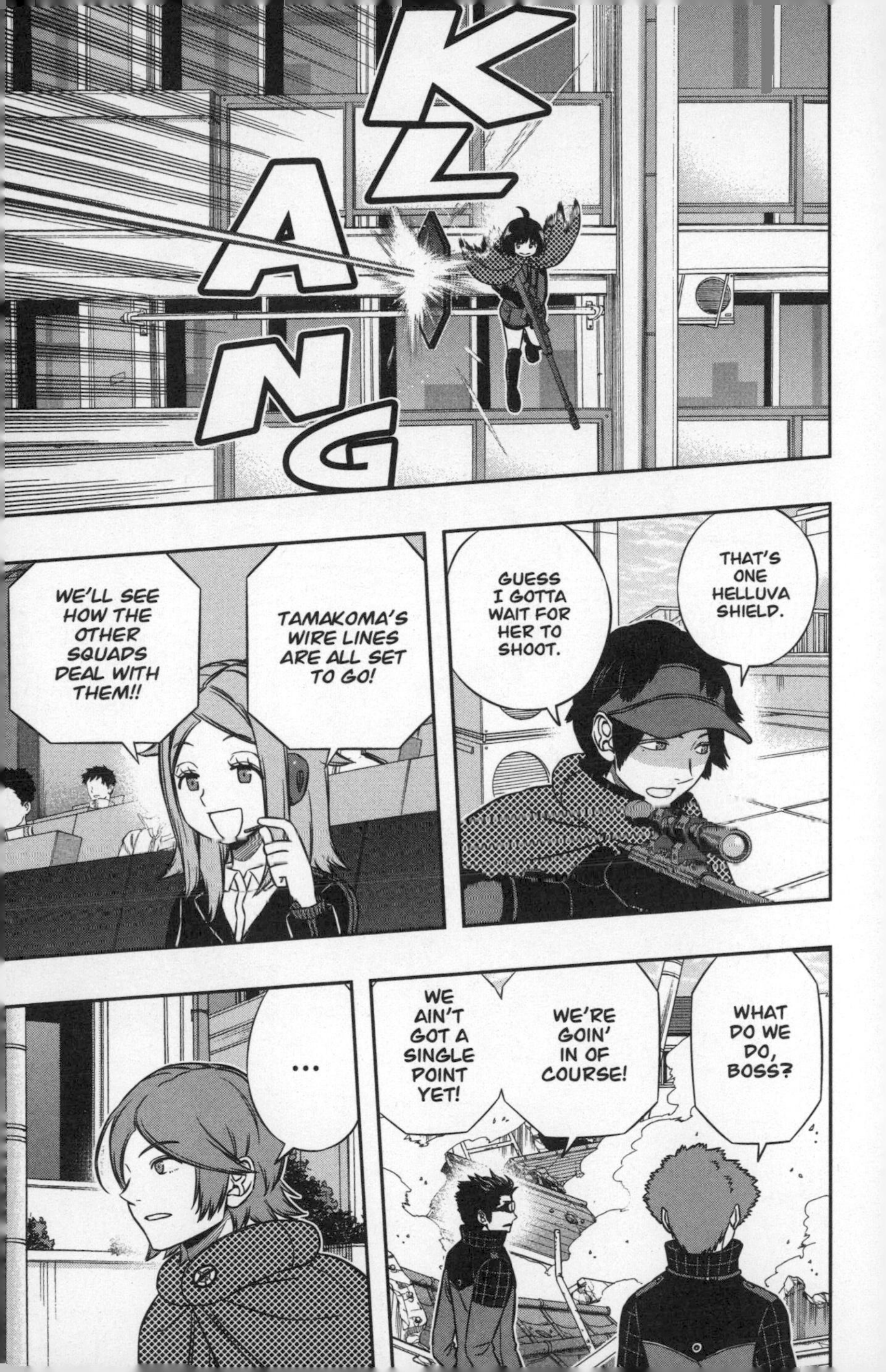
KLANG
THAT'S ONE HELLUVA SHIELD.
GUESS I GOTTA WAIT FOR HER TO SHOOT.
TAMAKOMA'S WIRE LINES ARE ALL SET TO GO!
WE'LL SEE HOW THE OTHER SQUADS DEAL WITH THEM!!
WHAT DO WE DO, BOSS?
WE'RE GOIN' IN OF COURSE!
WE AIN'T GOT A SINGLE POINT YET!
...

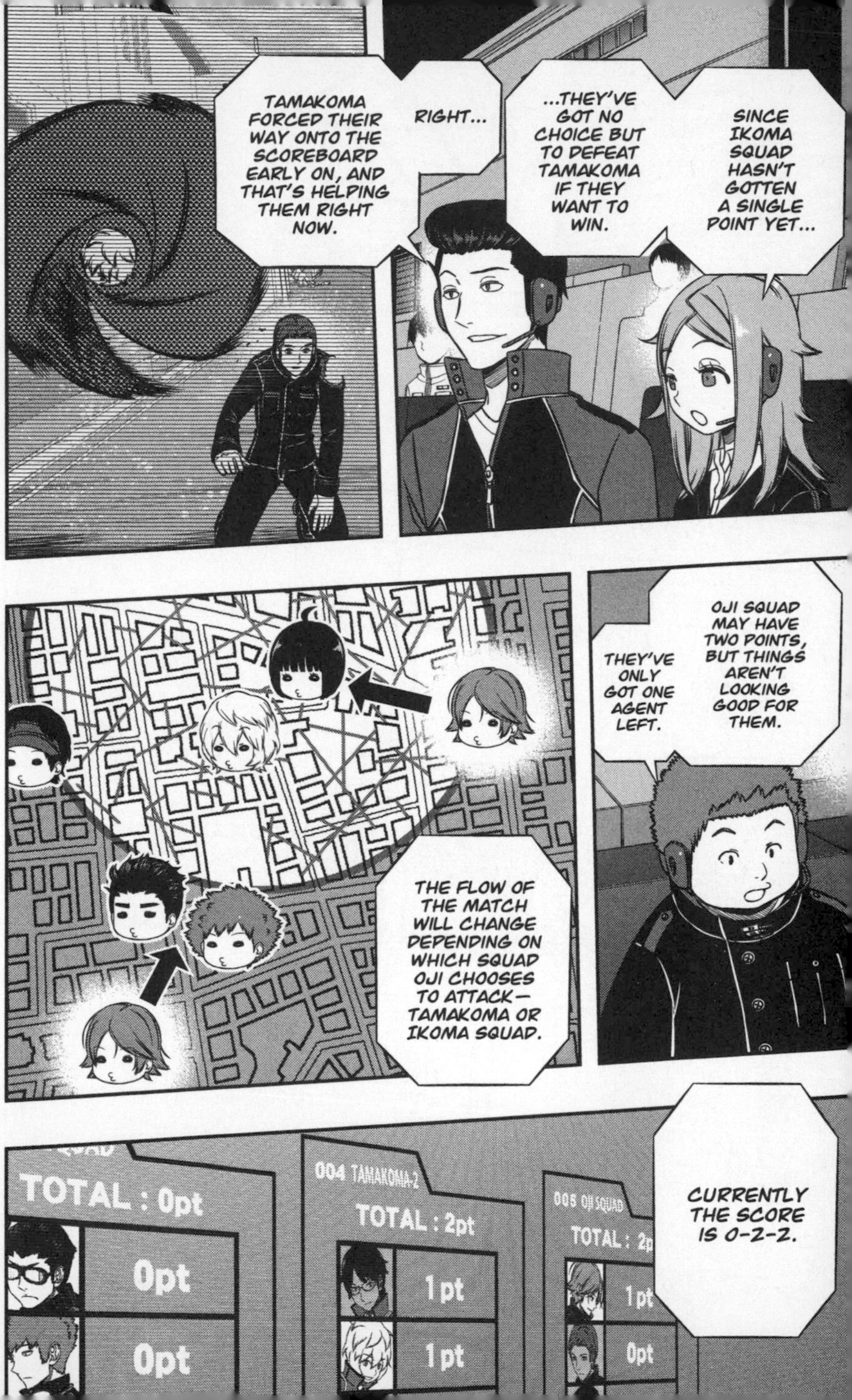
SINCE IKOMA SQUAD HASN'T GOTTEN A SINGLE POINT YET...
...THEY'VE GOT NO CHOICE BUT TO DEFEAT TAMAKOMA IF THEY WANT TO WIN.
RIGHT...
TAMAKOMA FORCED THEIR WAY ONTO THE SCOREBOARD EARLY ON, AND THAT'S HELPING THEM RIGHT NOW.
OJI SQUAD MAY HAVE TWO POINTS, BUT THINGS AREN'T LOOKING GOOD FOR THEM.
THEY'VE ONLY GOT ONE AGENT LEFT.
THE FLOW OF THE MATCH WILL CHANGE DEPENDING ON WHICH SQUAD OJI CHOOSES TO ATTACK—TAMAKOMA OR IKOMA SQUAD.
CURRENTLY THE SCORE IS 0-2-2.
005 OJI SQUAD
1pt
0pt
004 TAMAKOMA-2
TOTAL : 2pt
1pt
1pt
TOTAL : 0pt
0pt
0pt

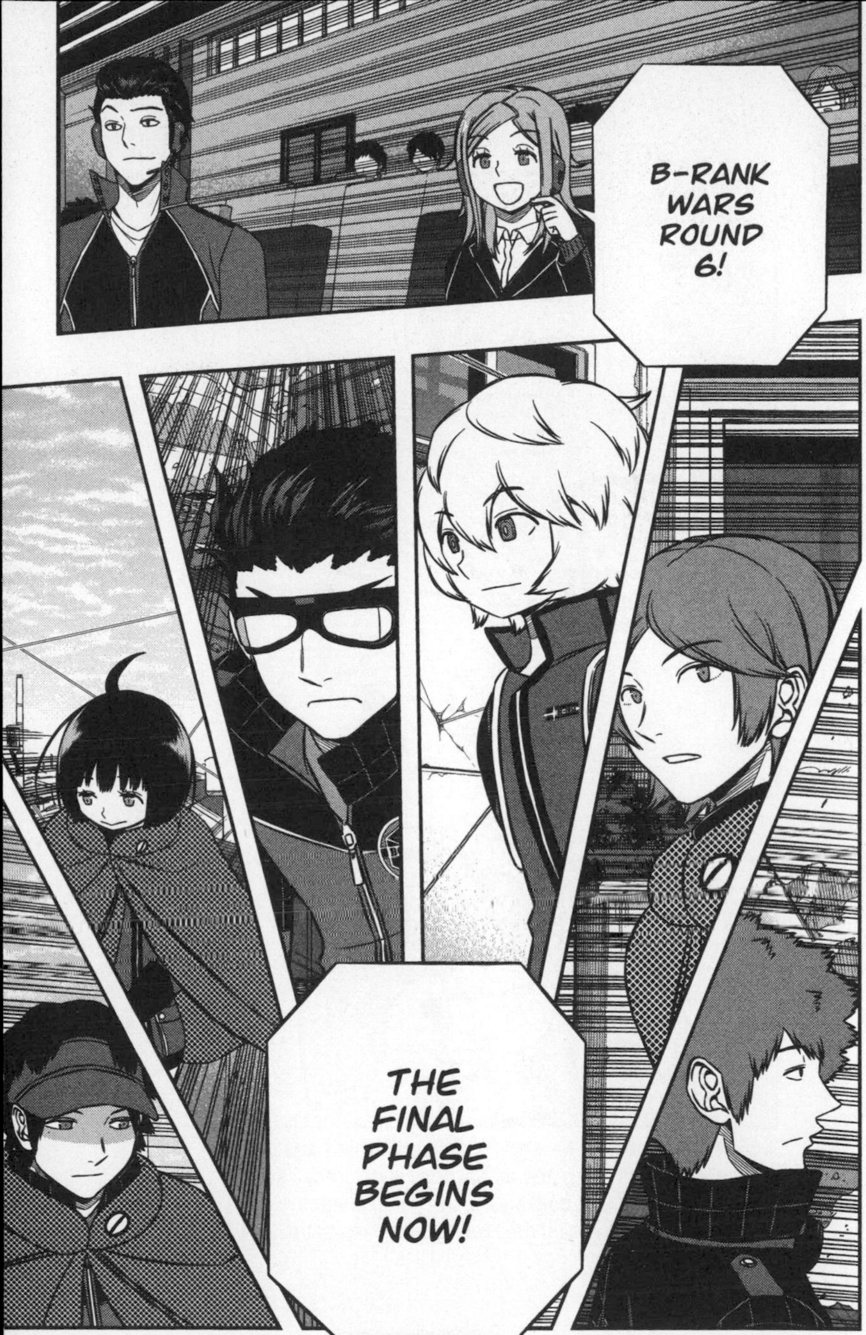
B-RANK WARS ROUND 6!
THE FINAL PHASE BEGINS NOW!

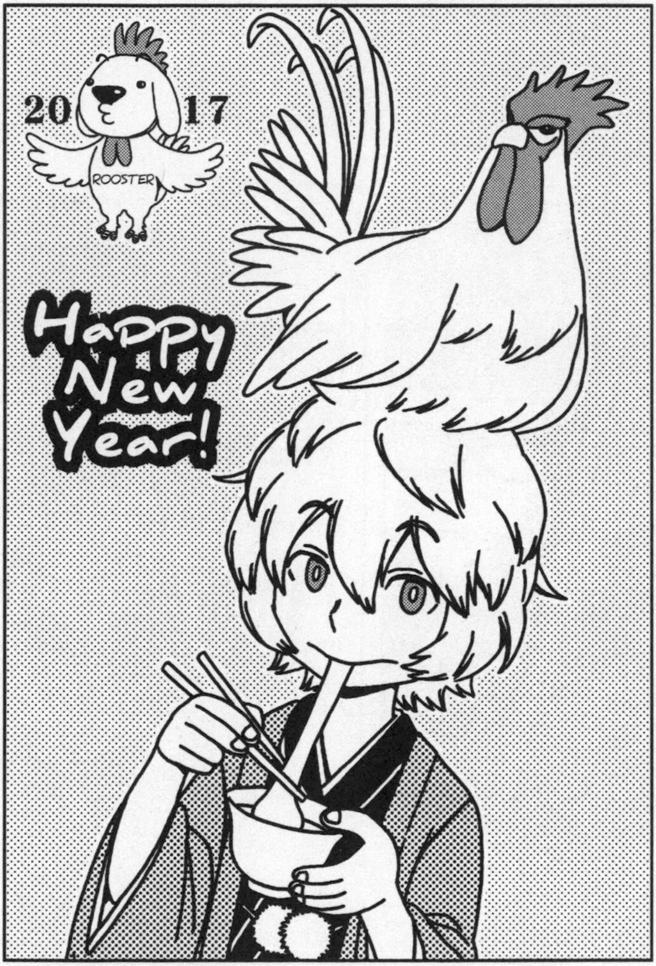
2017
ROOSTER
Happy New Year!

A drawing for the 2017 New Year's postcard, which was part of a collaboration piece (the actual copy is colored). I sent this to my friends and colleagues. The colored version of rooster-enthal gives off the feeling of bodysuit and it looks a bit creepy.

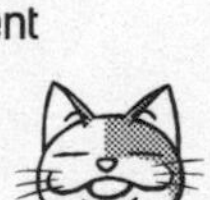

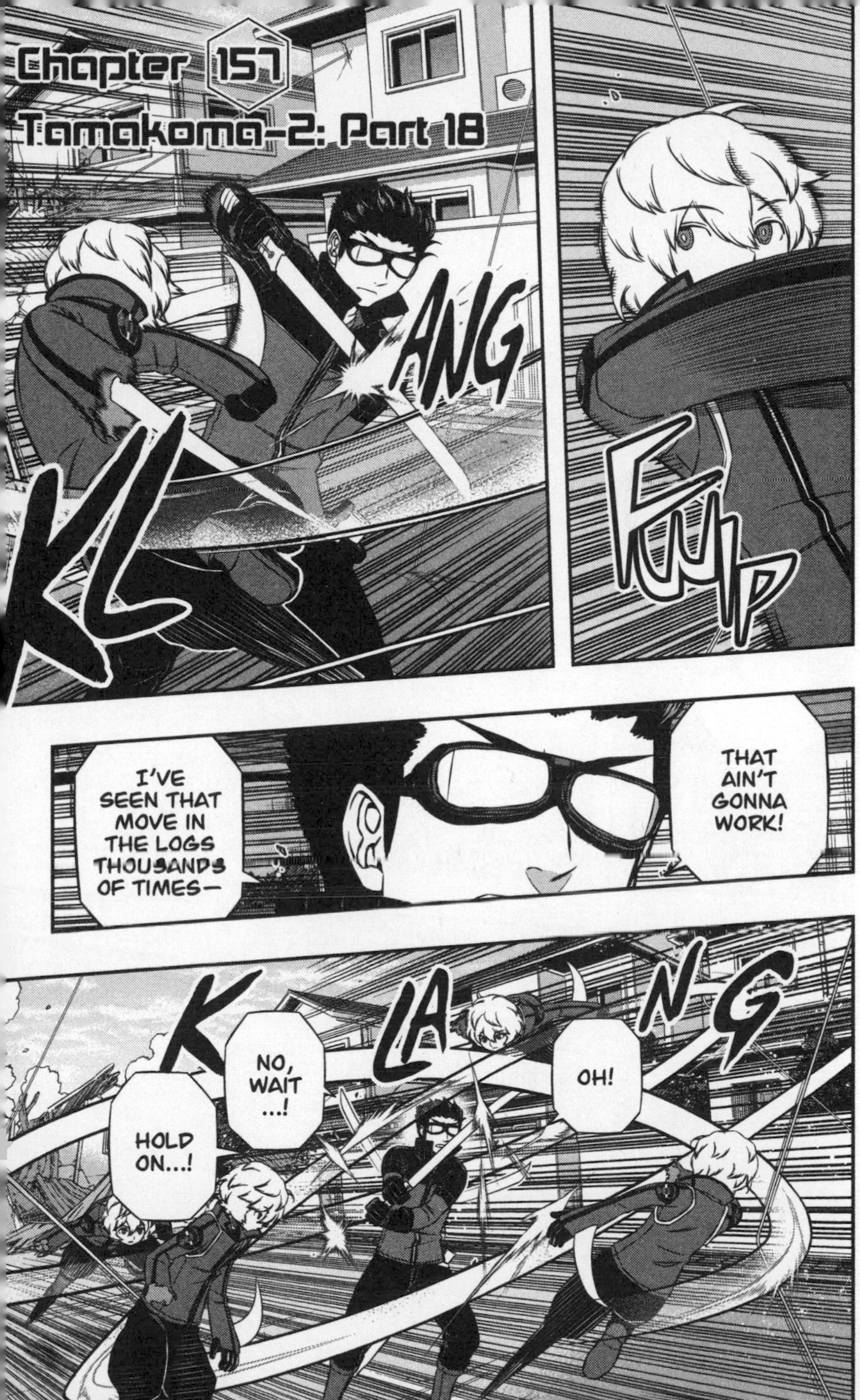

FWUP
Chapter 157
Tamakoma-2: Part 18
KLANG
THAT AIN'T GONNA WORK!
I'VE SEEN THAT MOVE IN THE LOGS THOUSANDS OF TIMES—
KLANG
OH!
NO, WAIT ...!
HOLD ON...!

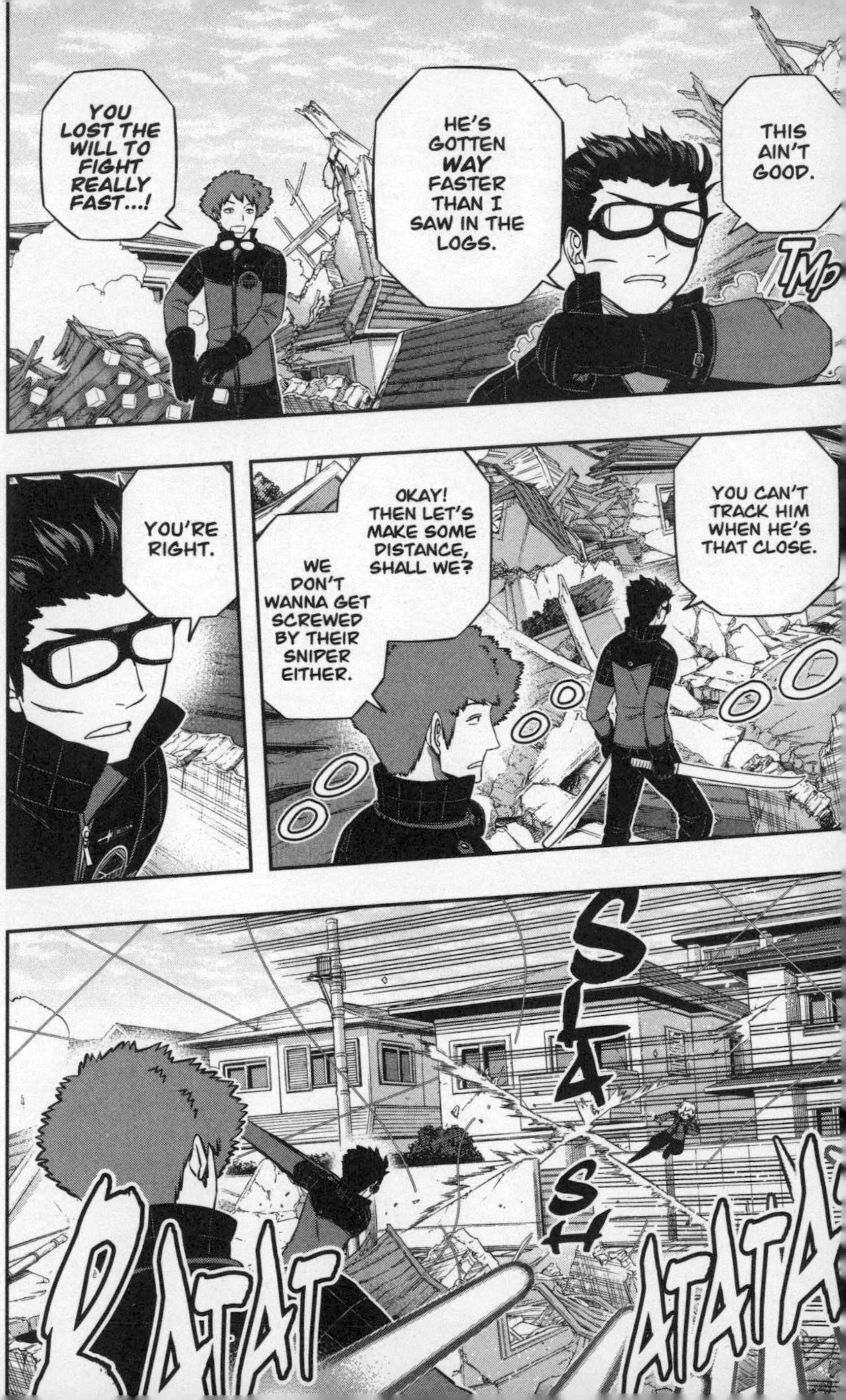
THIS AIN'T GOOD.
TMP
HE'S GOTTEN WAY FASTER THAN I SAW IN THE LOGS.
YOU LOST THE WILL TO FIGHT REALLY FAST...!
YOU CAN'T TRACK HIM WHEN HE'S THAT CLOSE.
OKAY! THEN LET'S MAKE SOME DISTANCE, SHALL WE?
WE DON'T WANNA GET SCREWED BY THEIR SNIPER EITHER.
YOU'RE RIGHT.
SLASH
ATATA
RATAT

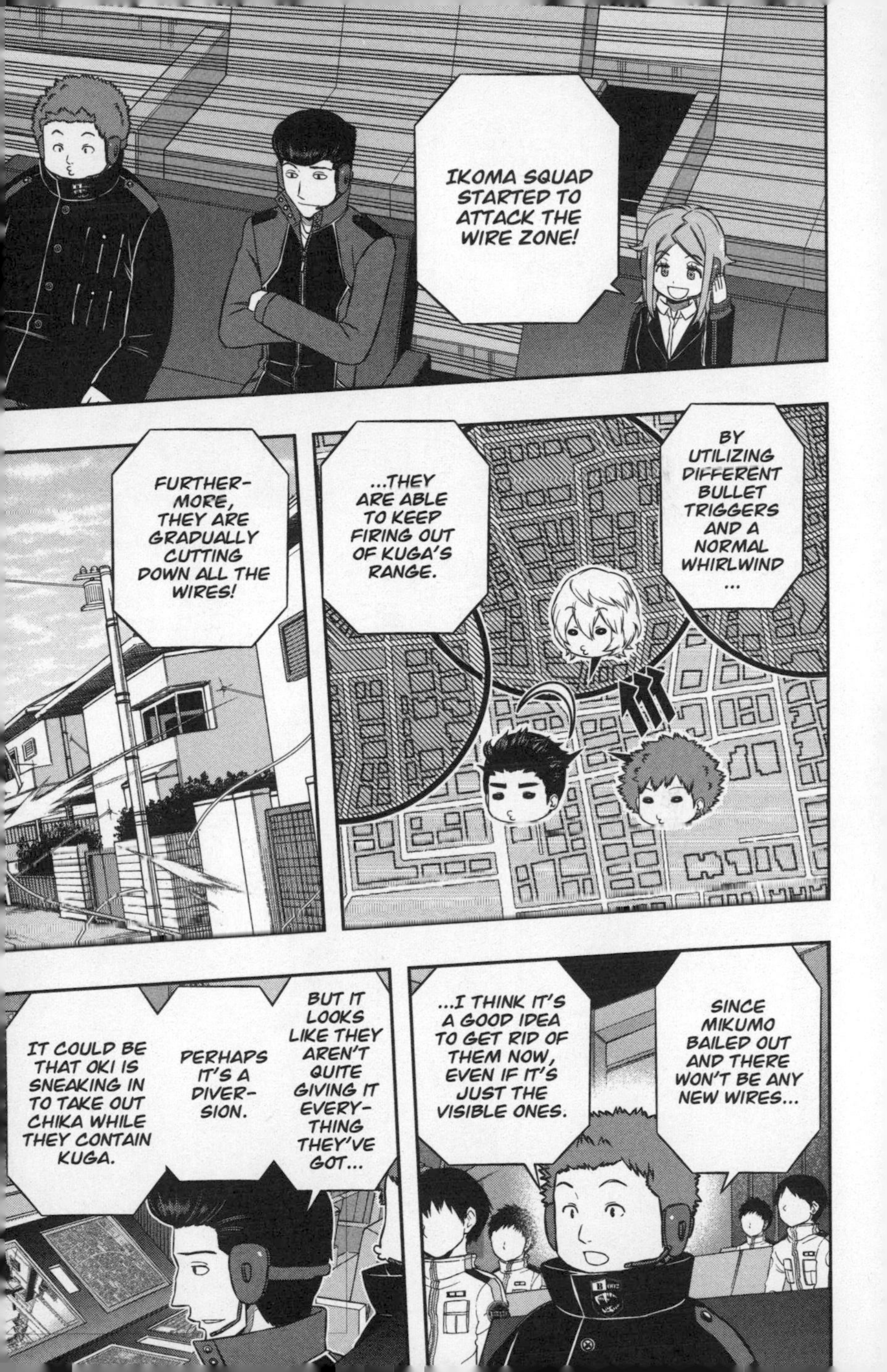
IKOMA SQUAD STARTED TO ATTACK THE WIRE ZONE!
BY UTILIZING DIFFERENT BULLET TRIGGERS AND A NORMAL WHIRLWIND ...
...THEY ARE ABLE TO KEEP FIRING OUT OF KUGA'S RANGE.
FURTHER-MORE, THEY ARE GRADUALLY CUTTING DOWN ALL THE WIRES!
SINCE MIKUMO BAILED OUT AND THERE WON'T BE ANY NEW WIRES...
...I THINK IT'S A GOOD IDEA TO GET RID OF THEM NOW, EVEN IF IT'S JUST THE VISIBLE ONES.
BUT IT LOOKS LIKE THEY AREN'T QUITE GIVING IT EVERY-THING THEY'VE GOT...
PERHAPS IT'S A DIVER-SION.
IT COULD BE THAT OKI IS SNEAKING IN TO TAKE OUT CHIKA WHILE THEY CONTAIN KUGA.

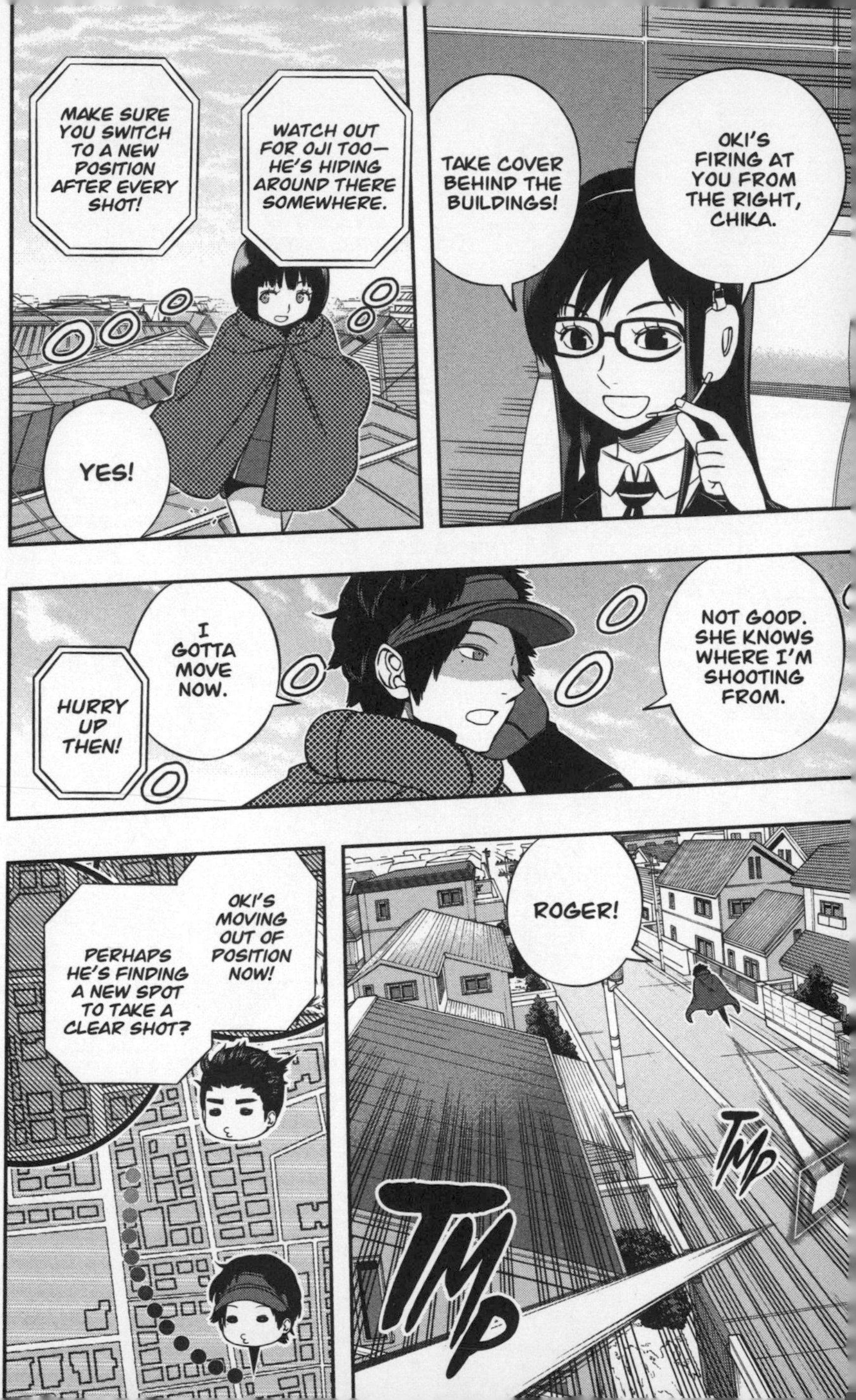
OKI'S FIRING AT YOU FROM THE RIGHT, CHIKA.
TAKE COVER BEHIND THE BUILDINGS!
WATCH OUT FOR OJI TOO— HE'S HIDING AROUND THERE SOMEWHERE.
MAKE SURE YOU SWITCH TO A NEW POSITION AFTER EVERY SHOT!
YES!
NOT GOOD. SHE KNOWS WHERE I'M SHOOTING FROM.
I GOTTA MOVE NOW.
HURRY UP THEN!
ROGER!
TMP
TMP
OKI'S MOVING OUT OF POSITION NOW!
PERHAPS HE'S FINDING A NEW SPOT TO TAKE A CLEAR SHOT?

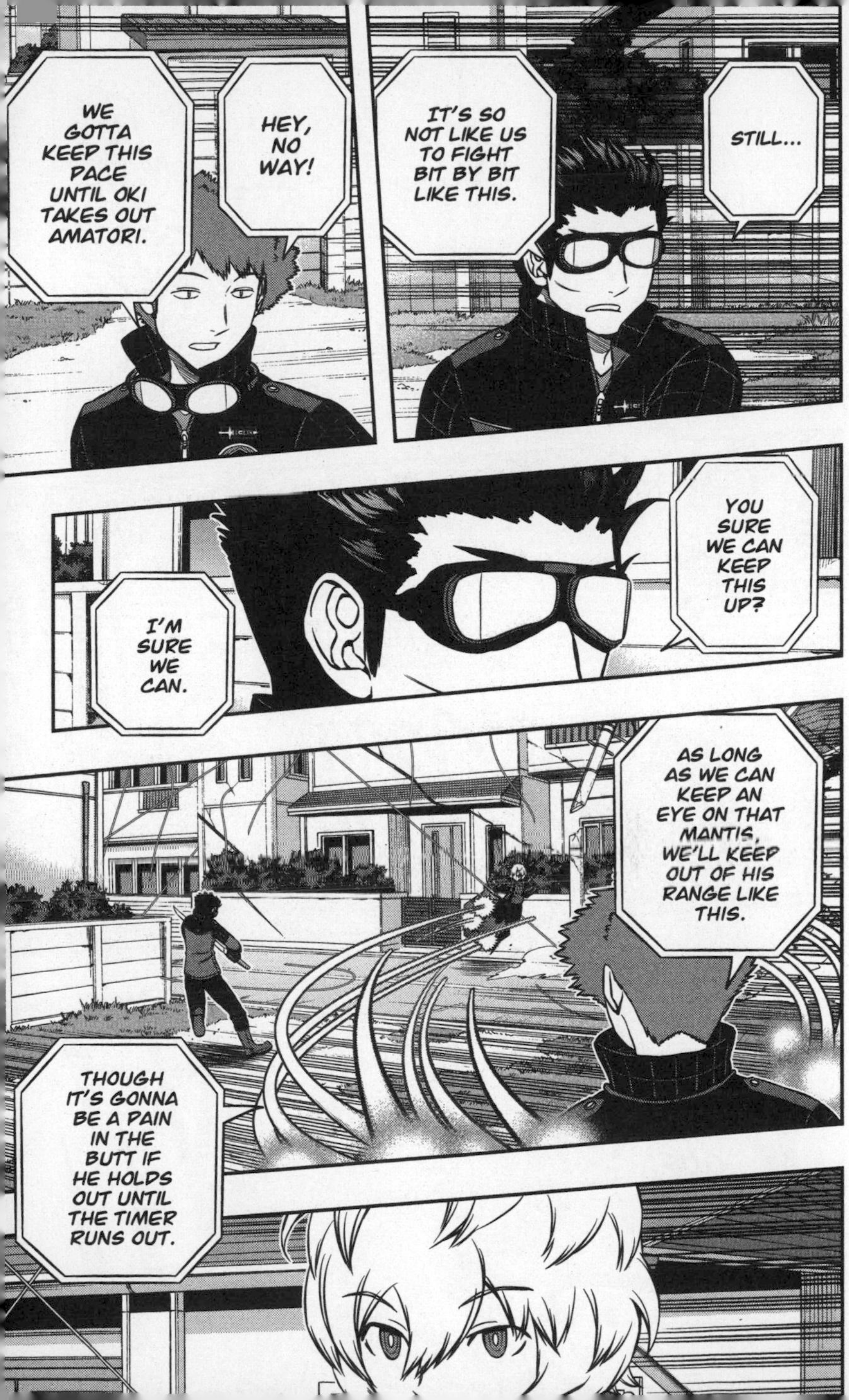
STILL...
IT'S SO NOT LIKE US TO FIGHT BIT BY BIT LIKE THIS.
HEY, NO WAY!
WE GOTTA KEEP THIS PACE UNTIL OKI TAKES OUT AMATORI.
YOU SURE WE CAN KEEP THIS UP?
I'M SURE WE CAN.
AS LONG AS WE CAN KEEP AN EYE ON THAT MANTIS, WE'LL KEEP OUT OF HIS RANGE LIKE THIS.
THOUGH IT'S GONNA BE A PAIN IN THE BUTT IF HE HOLDS OUT UNTIL THE TIMER RUNS OUT.

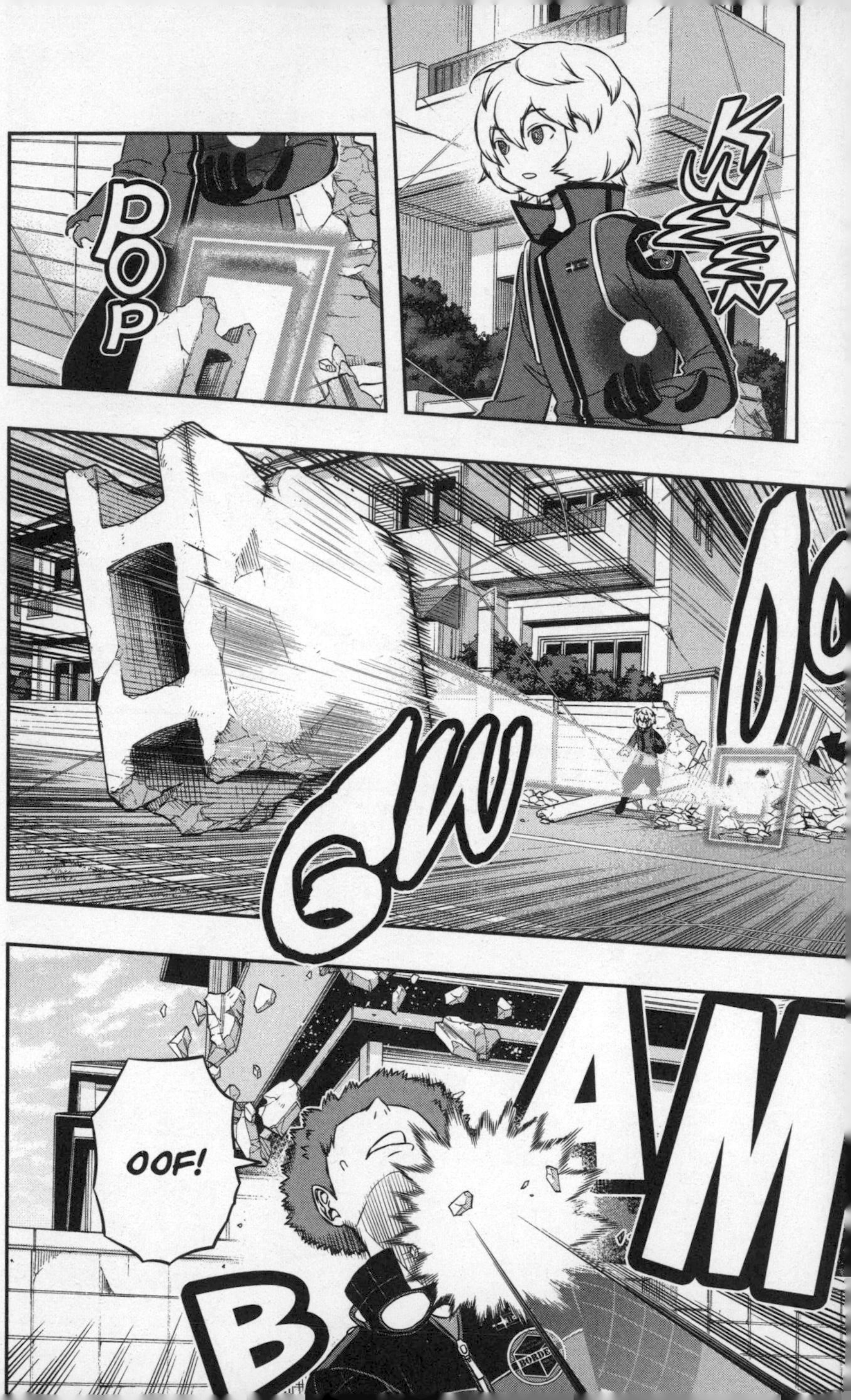
KWEEN
POP
GWOO
BAM
OOF!

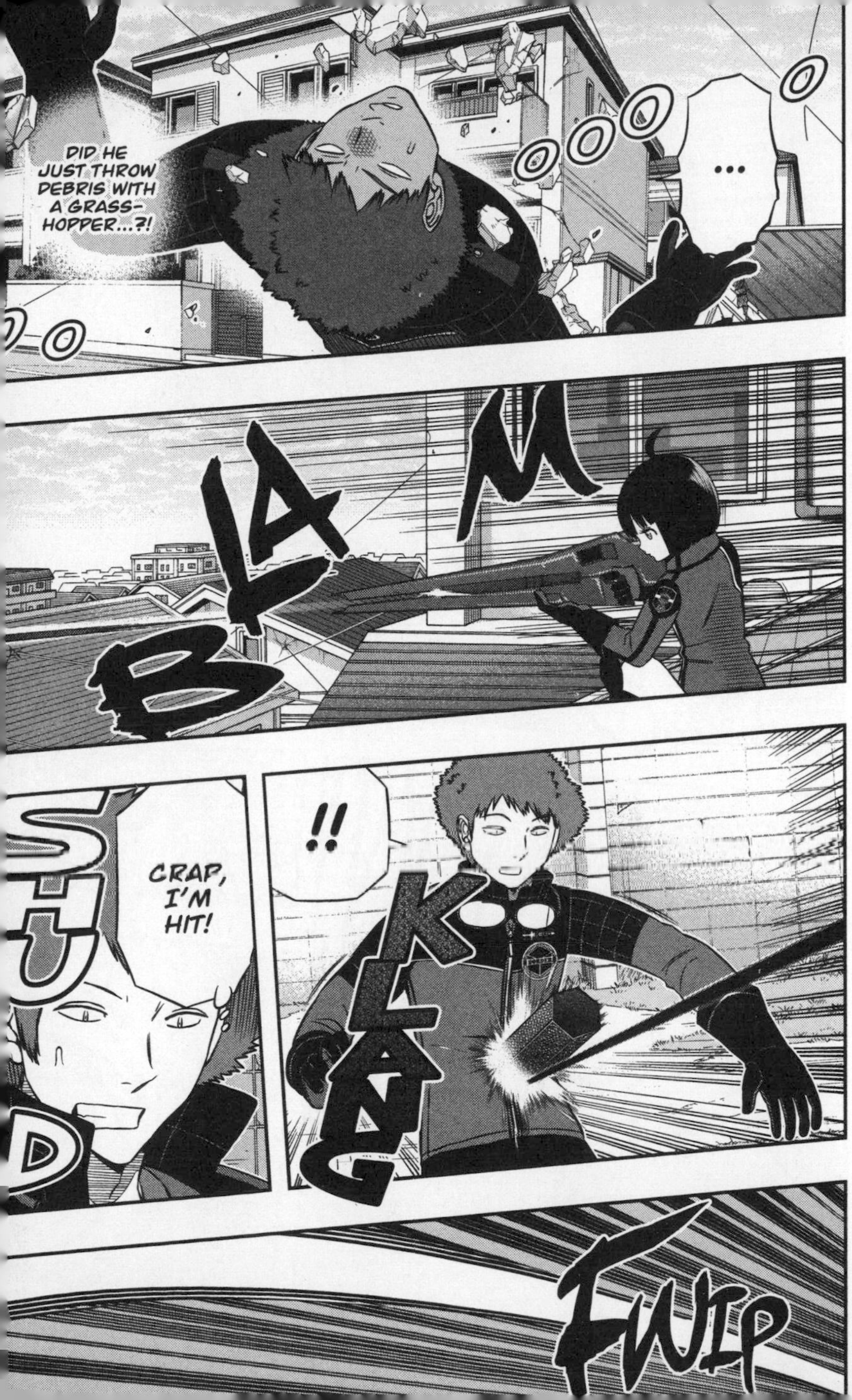
...
DID HE JUST THROW DEBRIS WITH A GRASS-HOPPER...?!
BAM
!!
KLANG
SHUD
CRAP, I'M HIT!
FWIP

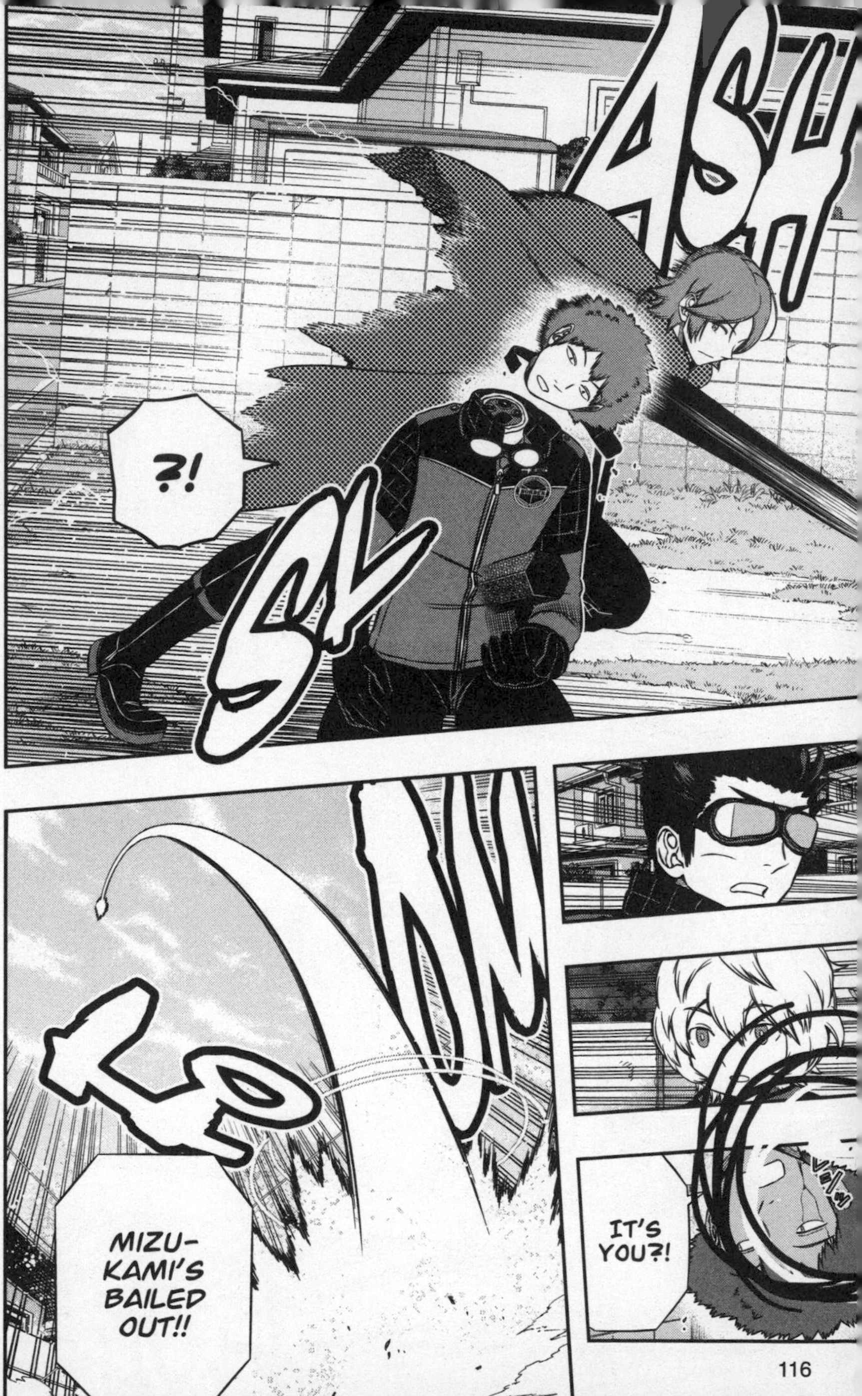
?!
IT'S YOU?!
MIZU-KAMI'S BAILED OUT!!

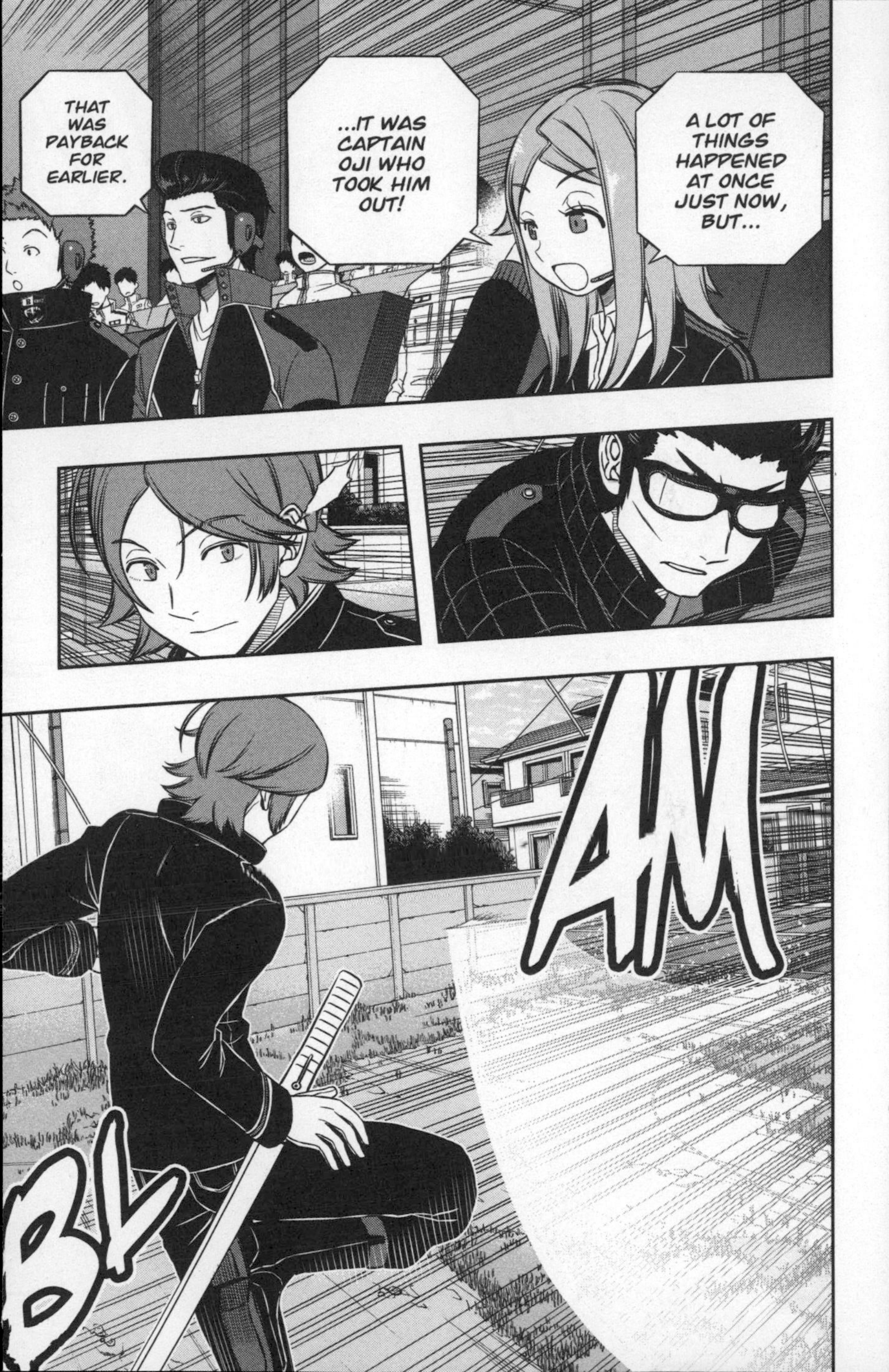
A LOT OF THINGS HAPPENED AT ONCE JUST NOW, BUT...
...IT WAS CAPTAIN OJI WHO TOOK HIM OUT!
THAT WAS PAYBACK FOR EARLIER.
AM
BL

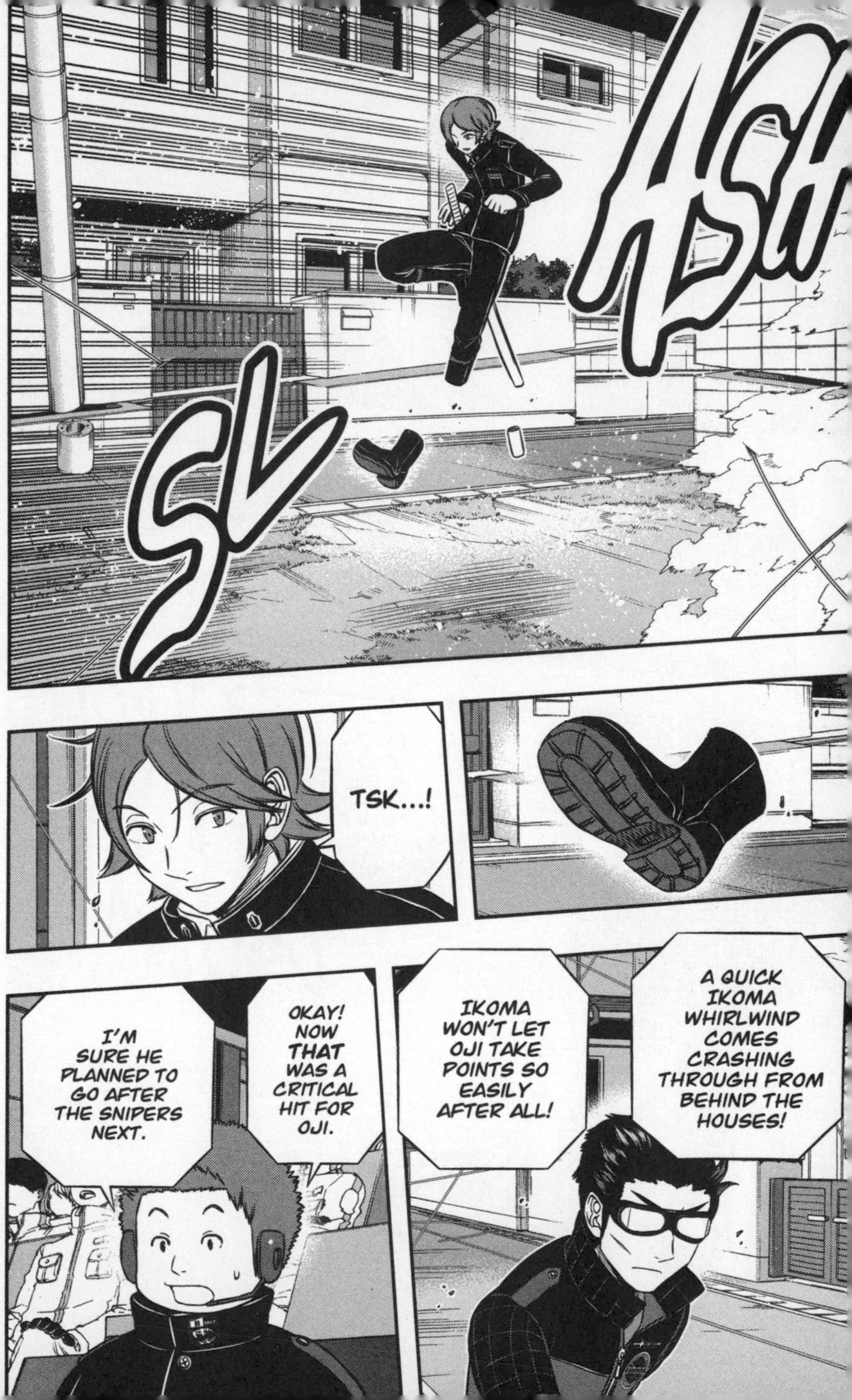

ASH
SL
TSK...!
A QUICK IKOMA WHIRLWIND COMES CRASHING THROUGH FROM BEHIND THE HOUSES!
IKOMA WON'T LET OJI TAKE POINTS SO EASILY AFTER ALL!
OKAY! NOW THAT WAS A CRITICAL HIT FOR OJI.
I'M SURE HE PLANNED TO GO AFTER THE SNIPERS NEXT.

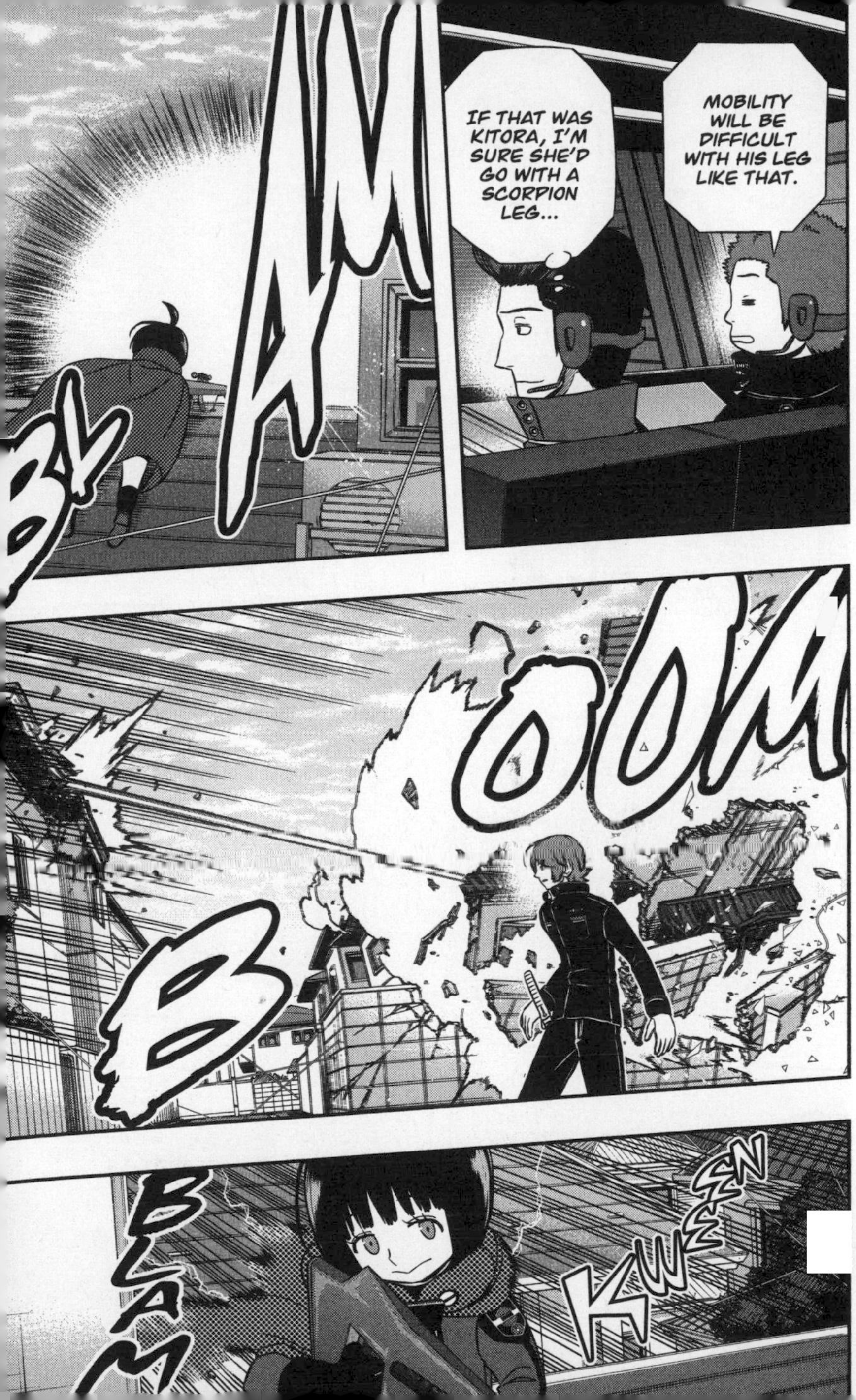
MOBILITY WILL BE DIFFICULT WITH HIS LEG LIKE THAT.
IF THAT WAS KITORA, I'M SURE SHE'D GO WITH A SCORPION LEG...
BAM
BOOM
BLAM

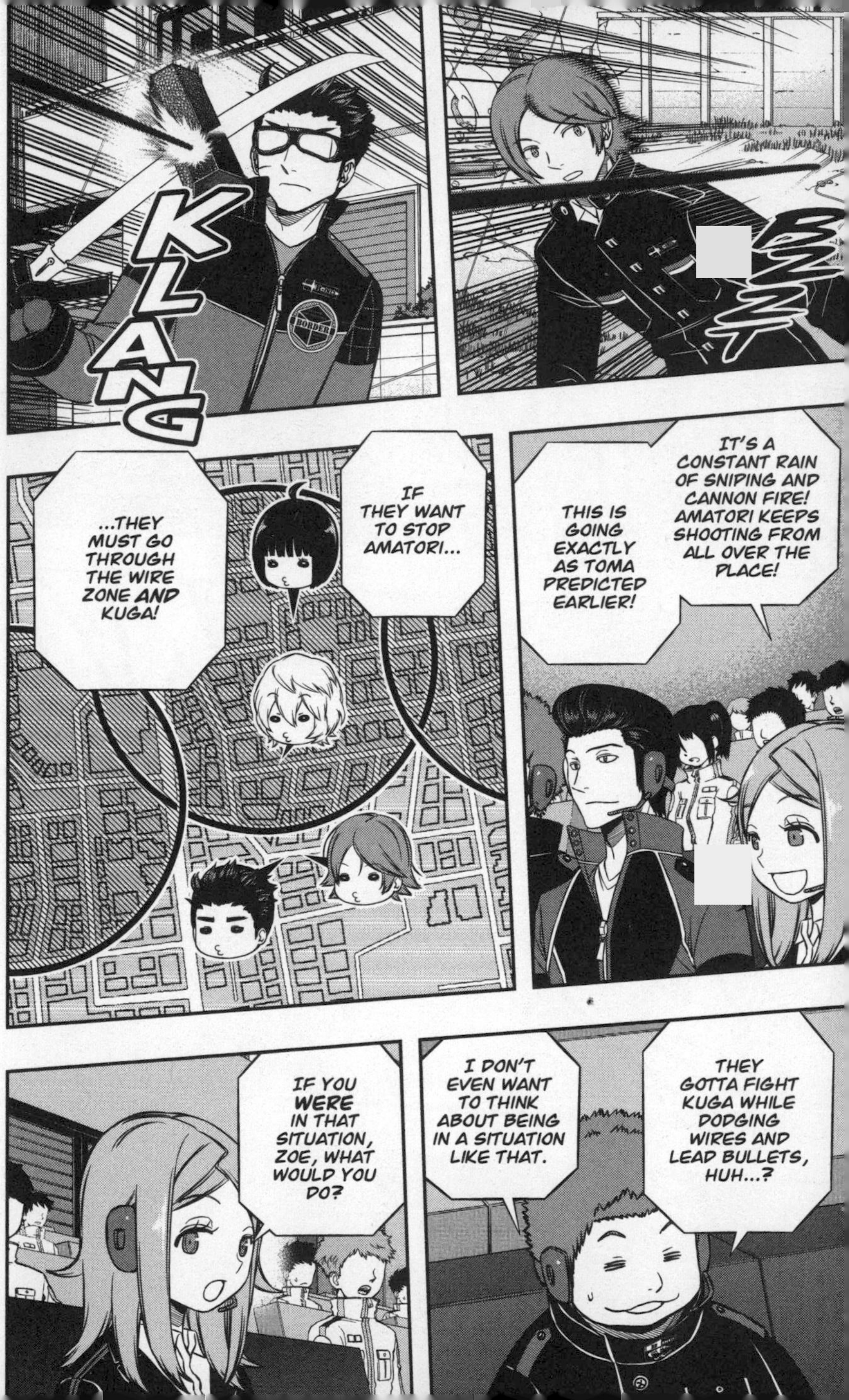
KLANG
IT'S A CONSTANT RAIN OF SNIPING AND CANNON FIRE! AMATORI KEEPS SHOOTING FROM ALL OVER THE PLACE!
THIS IS GOING EXACTLY AS TOMA PREDICTED EARLIER!
IF THEY WANT TO STOP AMATORI...
...THEY MUST GO THROUGH THE WIRE ZONE AND KUGA!
THEY GOTTA FIGHT KUGA WHILE DODGING WIRES AND LEAD BULLETS, HUH...?
I DON'T EVEN WANT TO THINK ABOUT BEING IN A SITUATION LIKE THAT.
IF YOU WERE IN THAT SITUATION, ZOE, WHAT WOULD YOU DO?

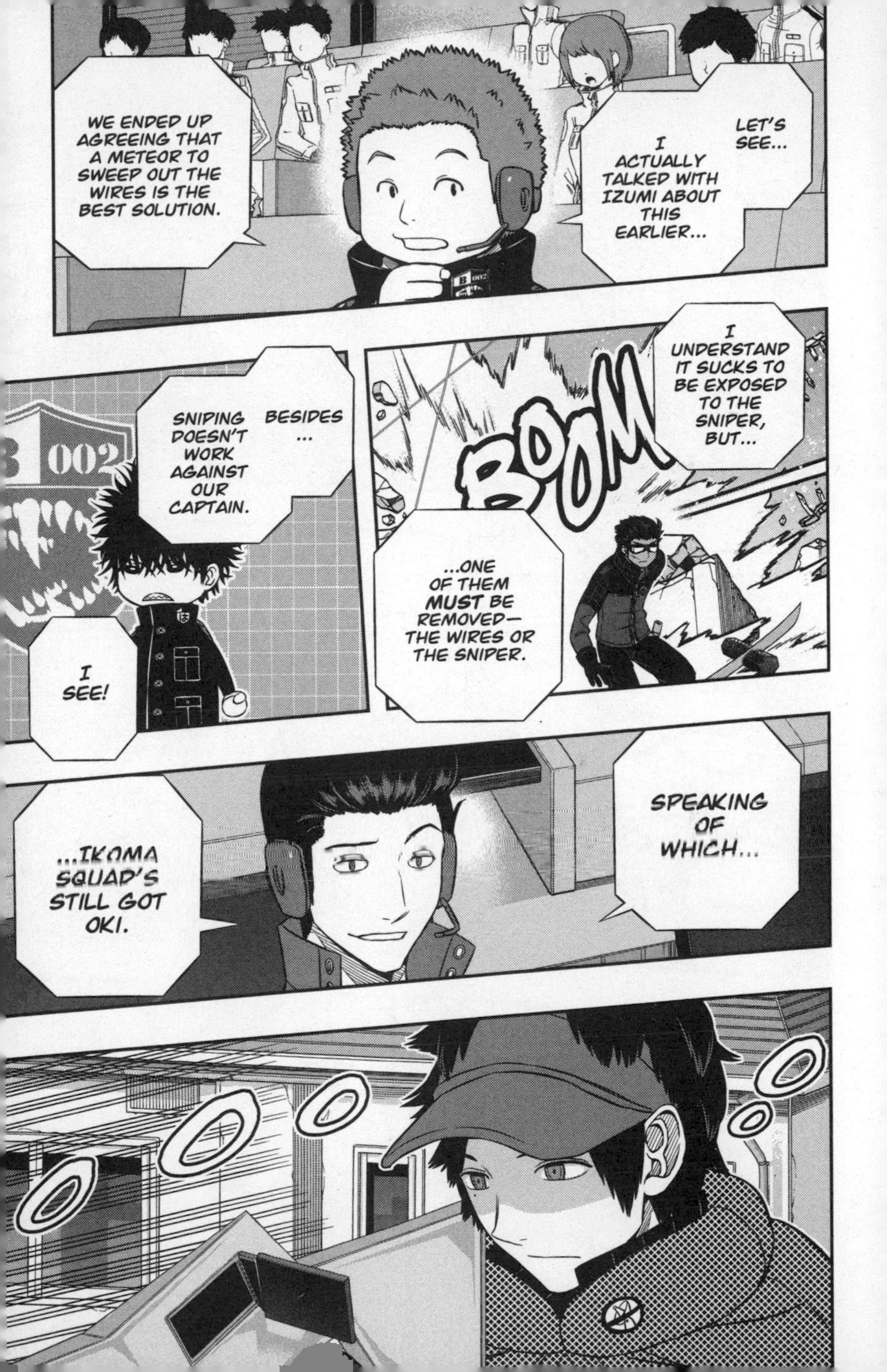
LET'S SEE...
I ACTUALLY TALKED WITH IZUMI ABOUT THIS EARLIER...
WE ENDED UP AGREEING THAT A METEOR TO SWEEP OUT THE WIRES IS THE BEST SOLUTION.
I UNDERSTAND IT SUCKS TO BE EXPOSED TO THE SNIPER, BUT...
BOOM
...ONE OF THEM MUST BE REMOVED—THE WIRES OR THE SNIPER.
BESIDES ...
SNIPING DOESN'T WORK AGAINST OUR CAPTAIN.
I SEE!
SPEAKING OF WHICH...
...IKOMA SQUAD'S STILL GOT OKI.

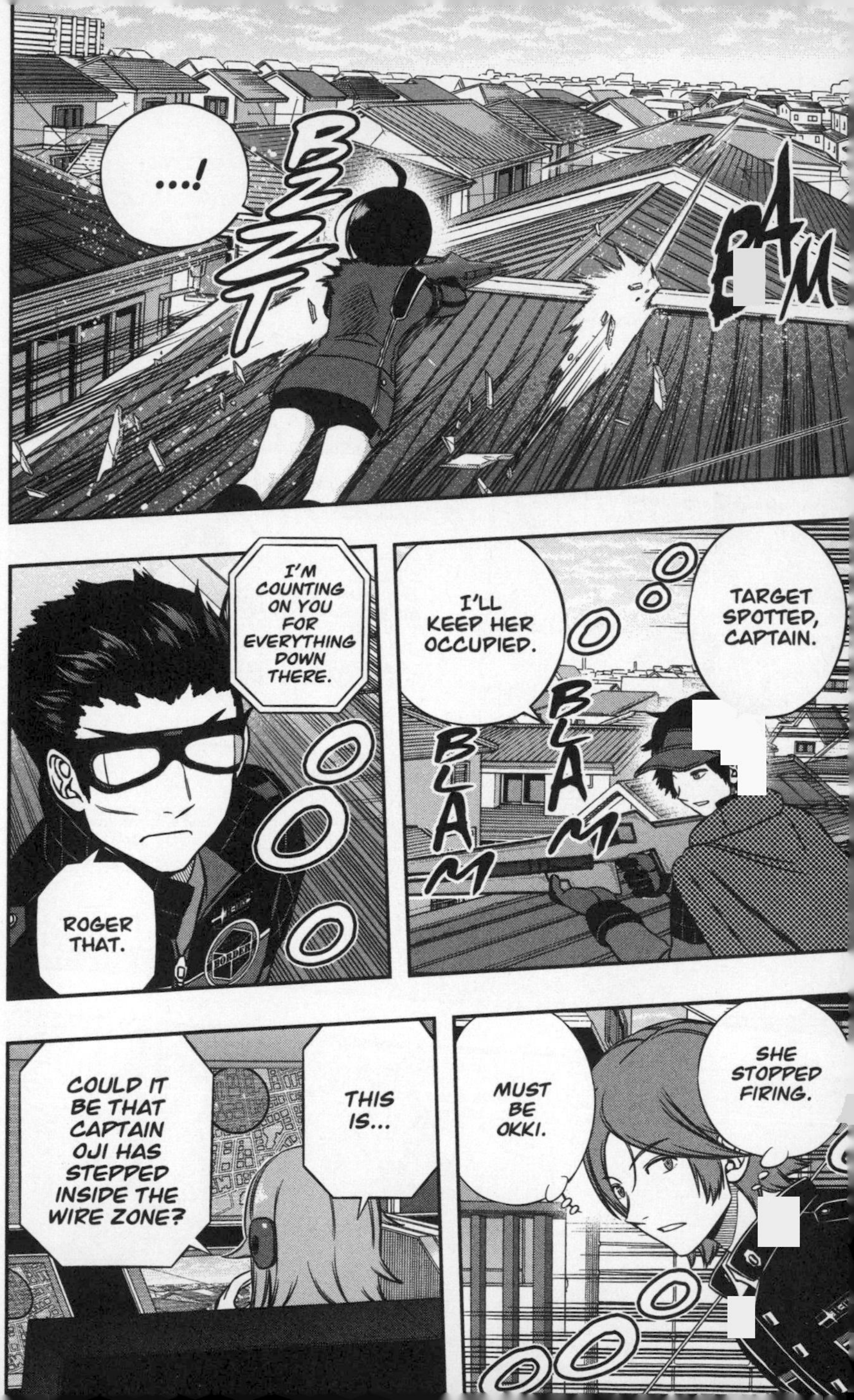
BZZZT
...!
TARGET SPOTTED, CAPTAIN.
I'LL KEEP HER OCCUPIED.
BLAM
BLAM
I'M COUNTING ON YOU FOR EVERYTHING DOWN THERE.
ROGER THAT.
SHE STOPPED FIRING.
MUST BE OKKI.
THIS IS...
COULD IT BE THAT CAPTAIN OJI HAS STEPPED INSIDE THE WIRE ZONE?

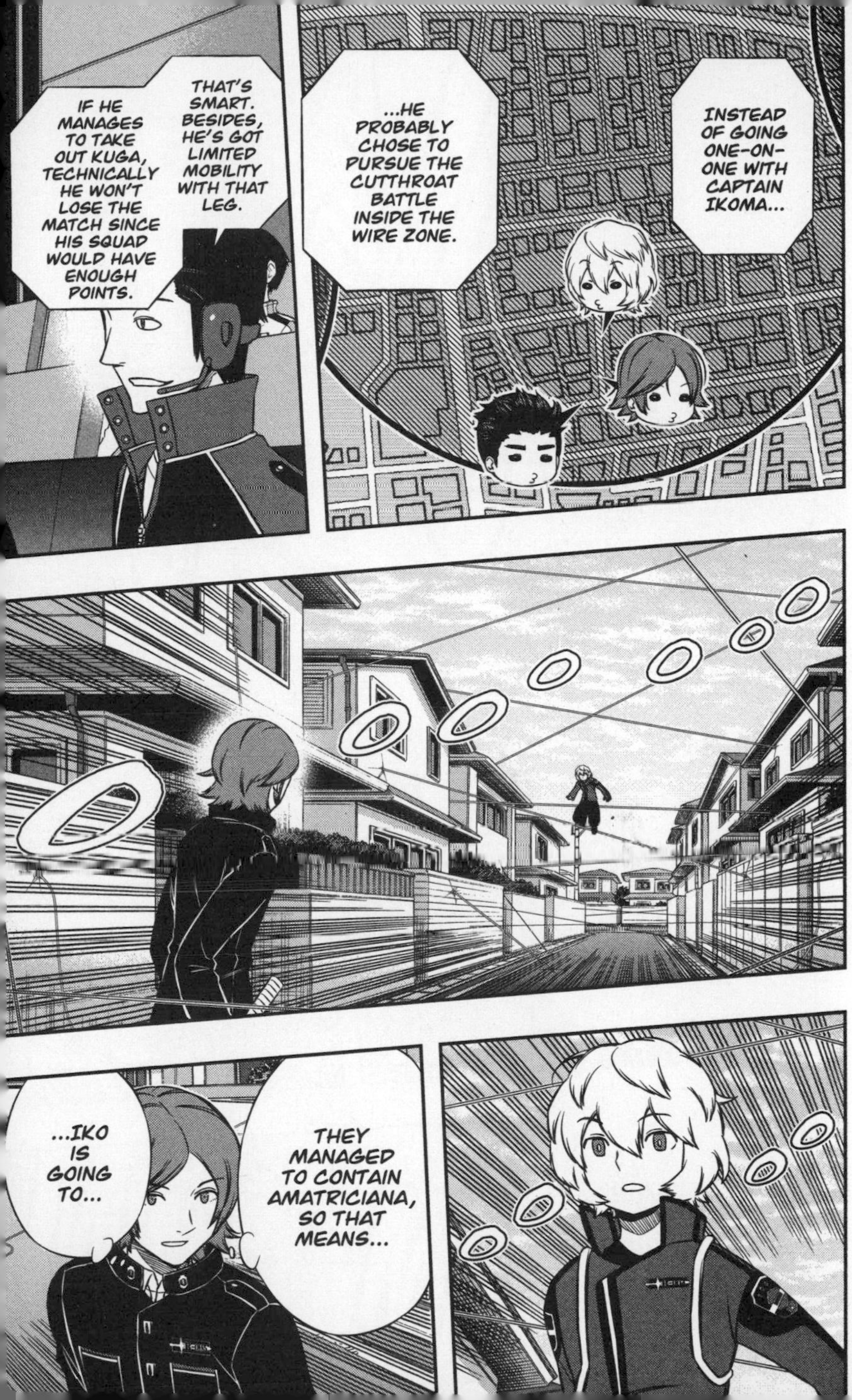
INSTEAD OF GOING ONE-ON-ONE WITH CAPTAIN IKOMA...
...HE PROBABLY CHOSE TO PURSUE THE CUTTHROAT BATTLE INSIDE THE WIRE ZONE.
THAT'S SMART. BESIDES, HE'S GOT LIMITED MOBILITY WITH THAT LEG.
IF HE MANAGES TO TAKE OUT KUGA, TECHNICALLY HE WON'T LOSE THE MATCH SINCE HIS SQUAD WOULD HAVE ENOUGH POINTS.
THEY MANAGED TO CONTAIN AMATRICIANA, SO THAT MEANS...
...IKO IS GOING TO...

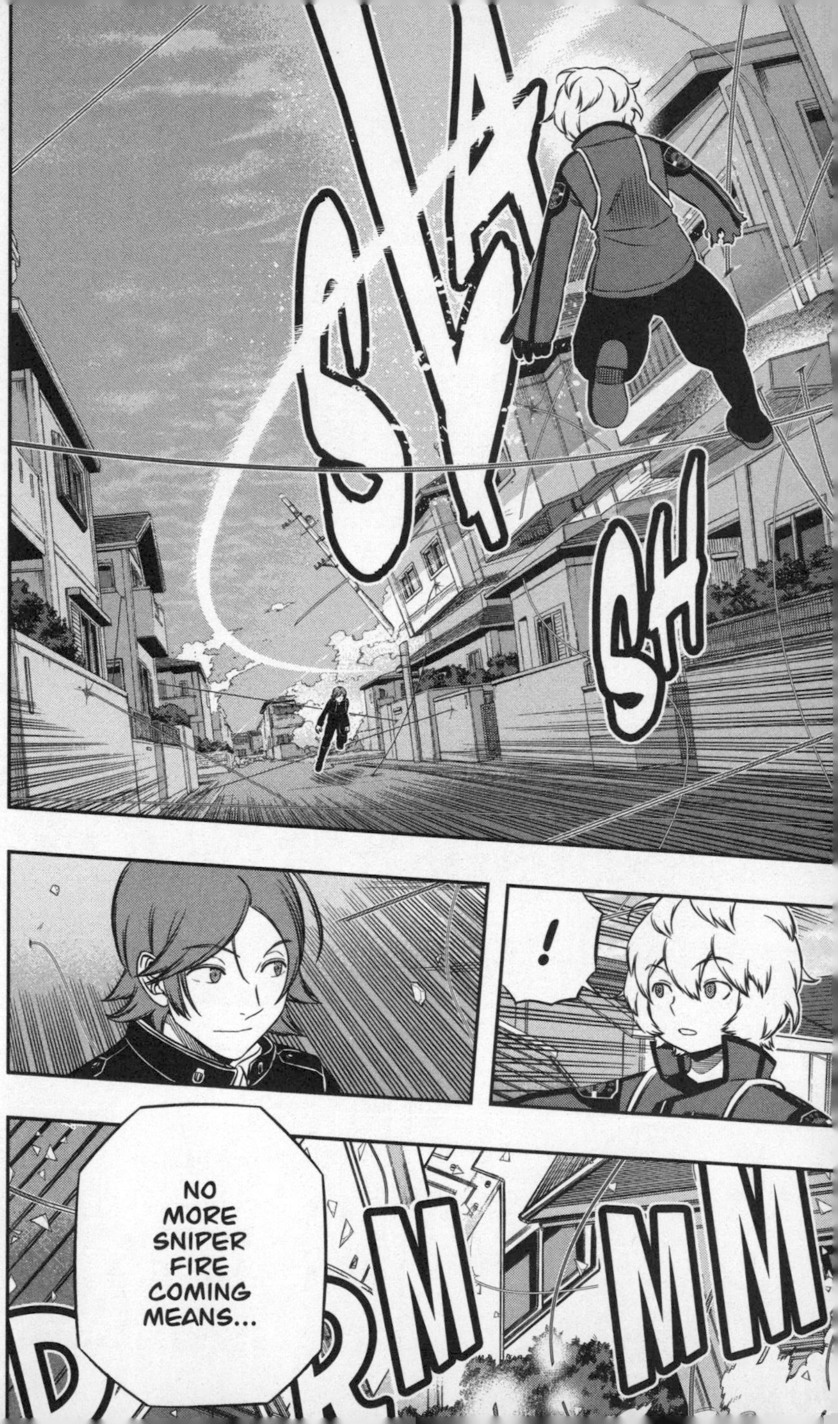
!
NO MORE SNIPER FIRE COMING MEANS...

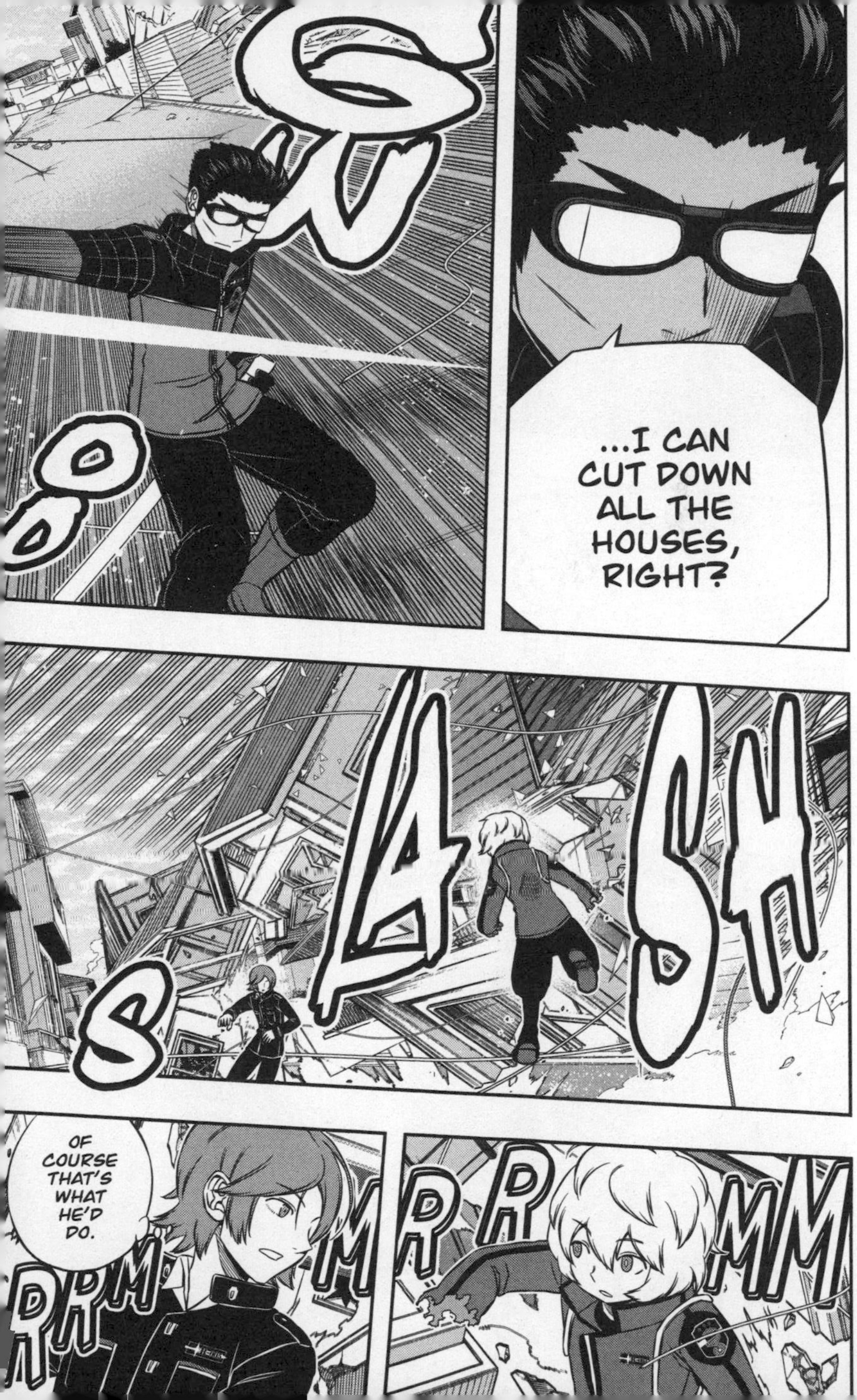
...I CAN CUT DOWN ALL THE HOUSES, RIGHT?
OF COURSE THAT'S WHAT HE'D DO.

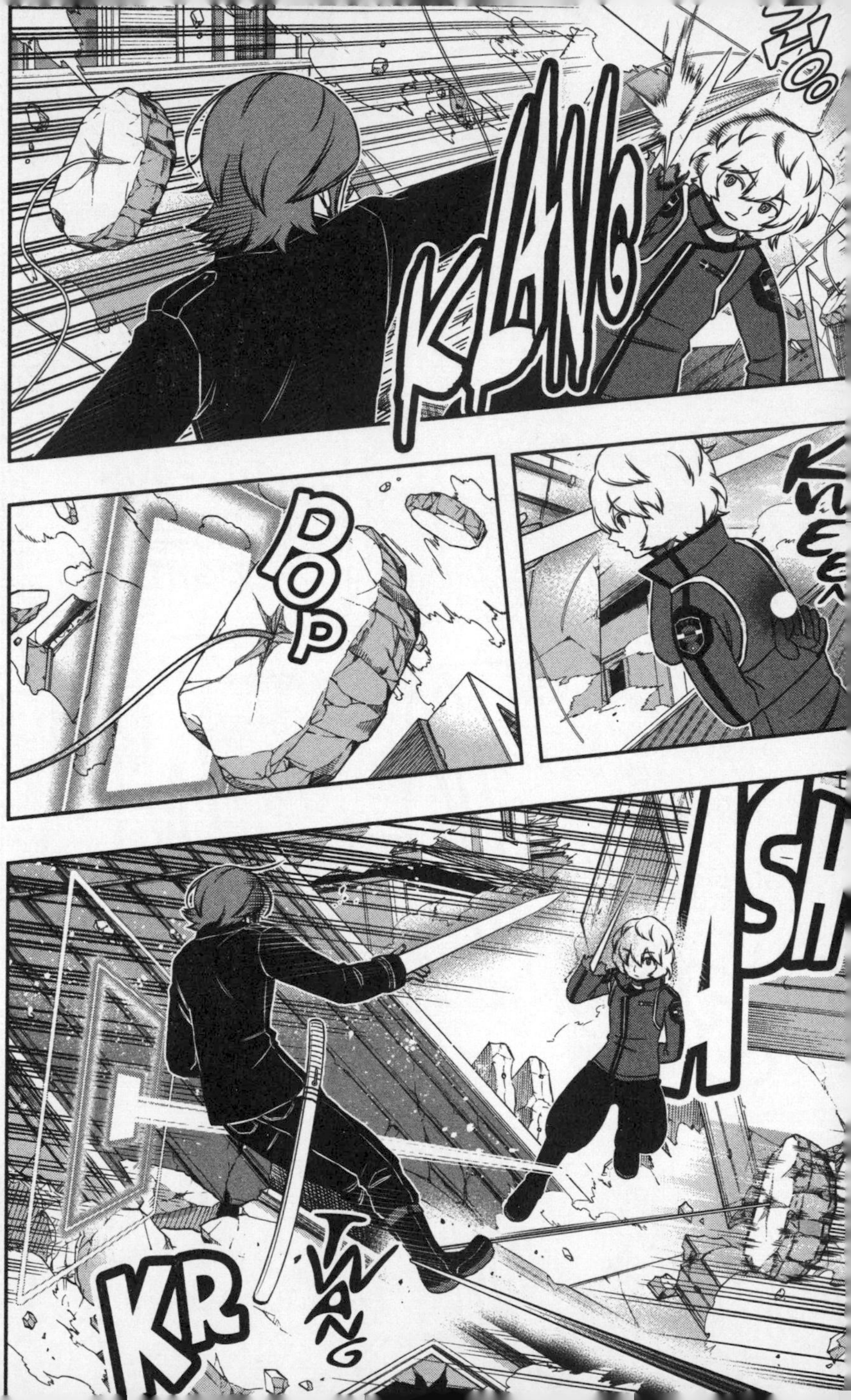
WHOO
KLANG
KNEE
POP
ASH
KR
TWANG

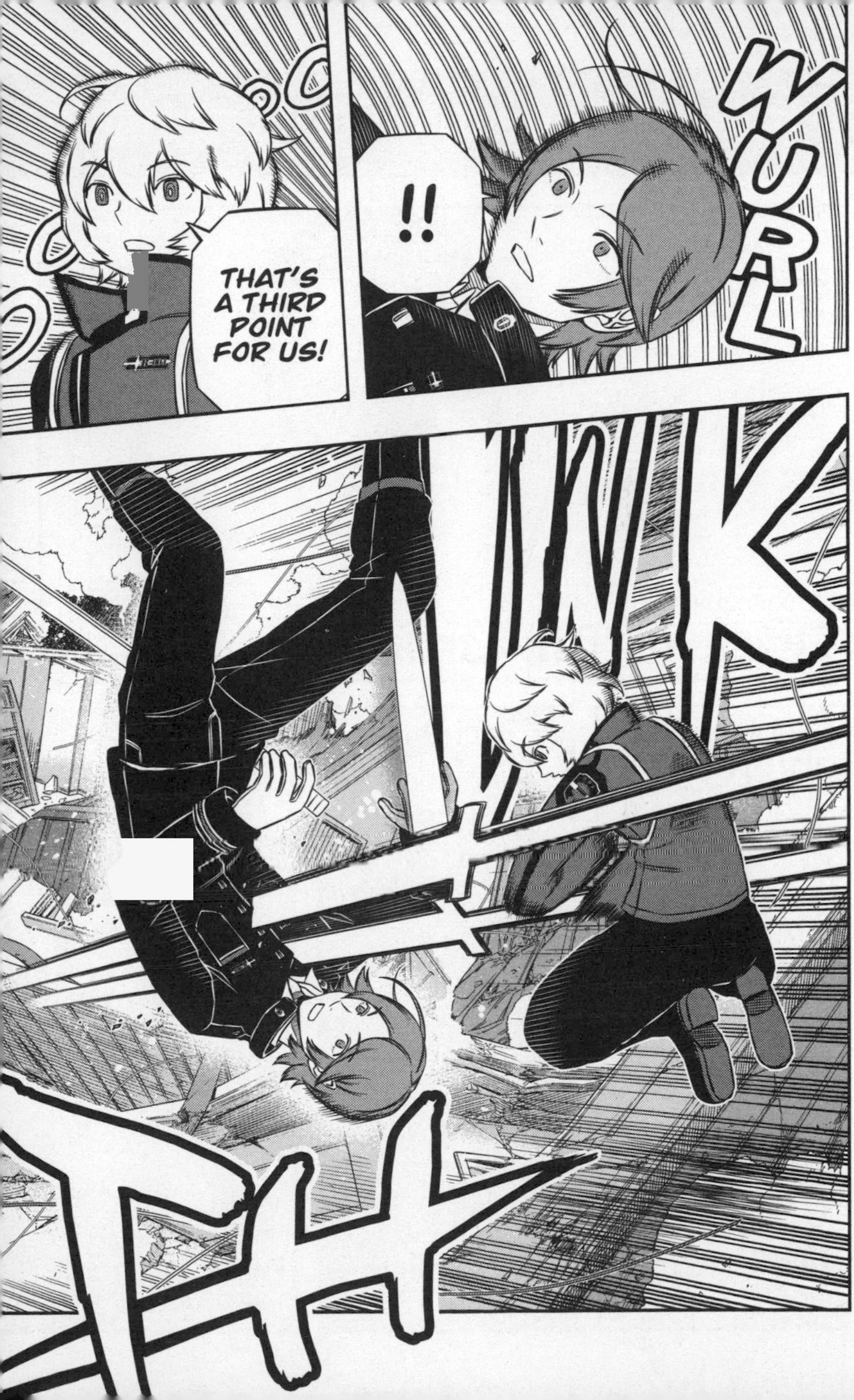
WURL
!!
THAT'S A THIRD POINT FOR US!

Second Popularity Poll Results!

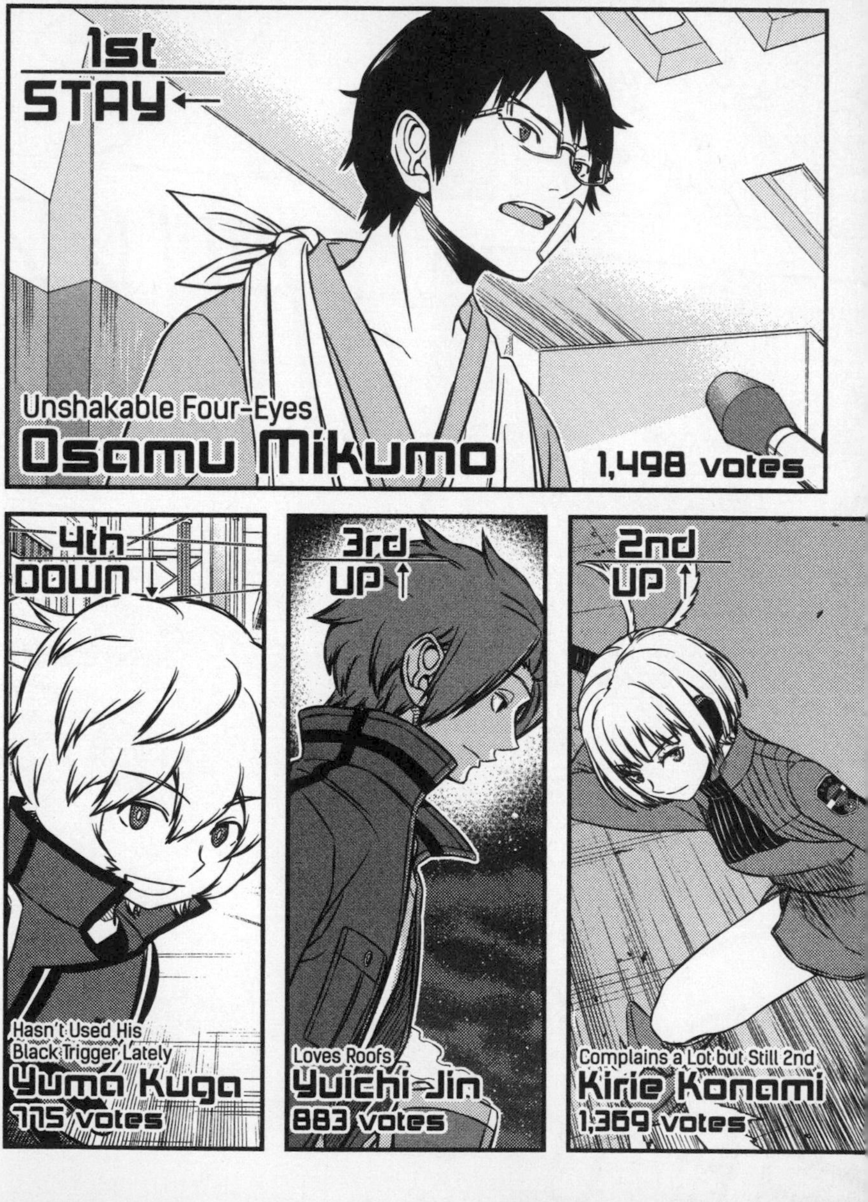
1st
STAY ←
Unshakable Four-Eyes
Osamu Mikumo
1,498 votes
2nd
UP ↑
Complains a Lot but Still 2nd
Kirie Konami
1,369 votes
3rd
UP ↑
Loves Roofs
Yuichi Jin
883 votes
4th
DOWN ↓
Hasn't Used His
Black Trigger Lately
Yuma Kuga
775 votes

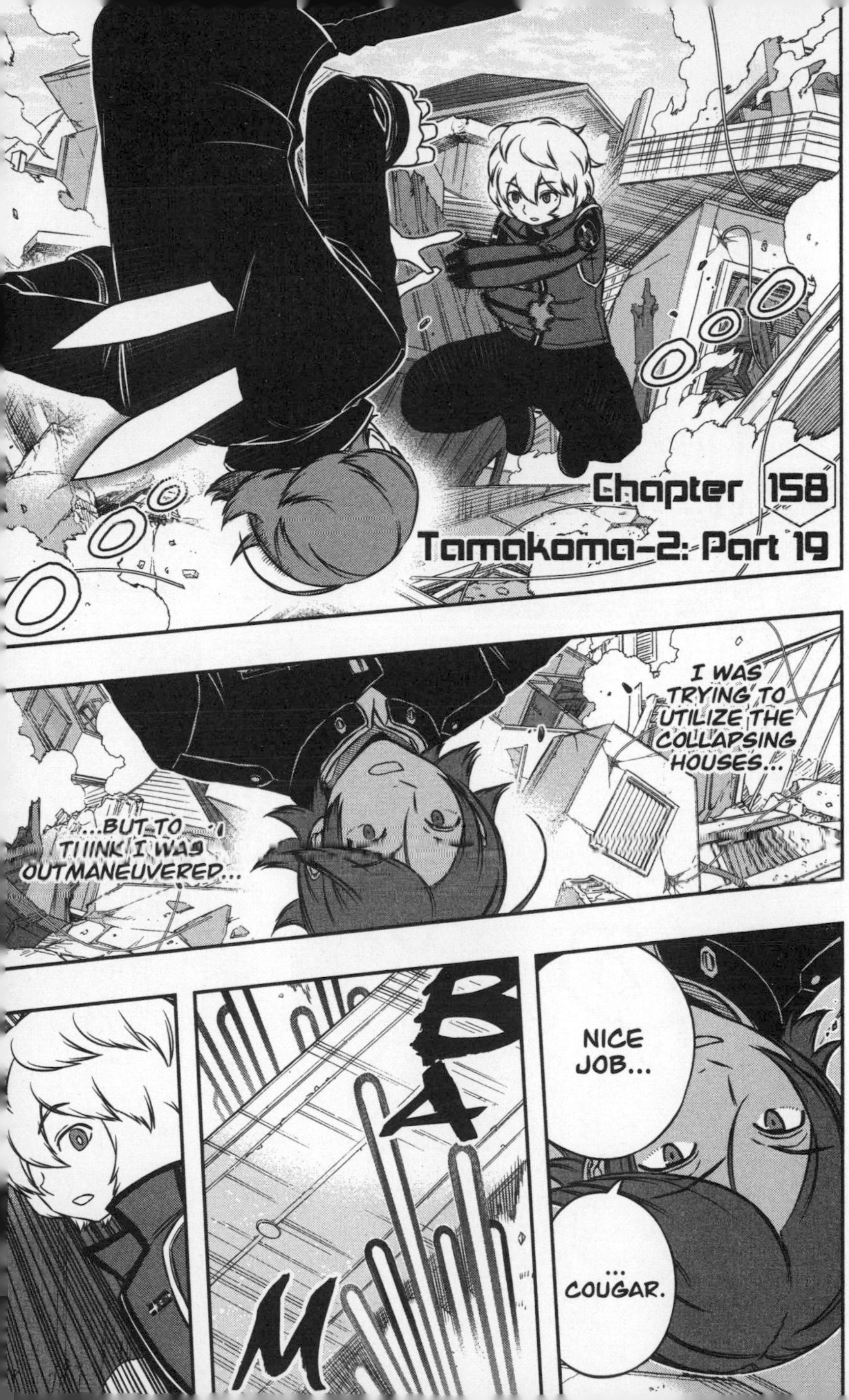
Chapter 158
Tamakoma-2: Part 19
I WAS TRYING TO UTILIZE THE COLLAPSING HOUSES...
...BUT TO THINK I WAS OUTMANEUVERED...
NICE JOB...
...COUGAR.
BAM

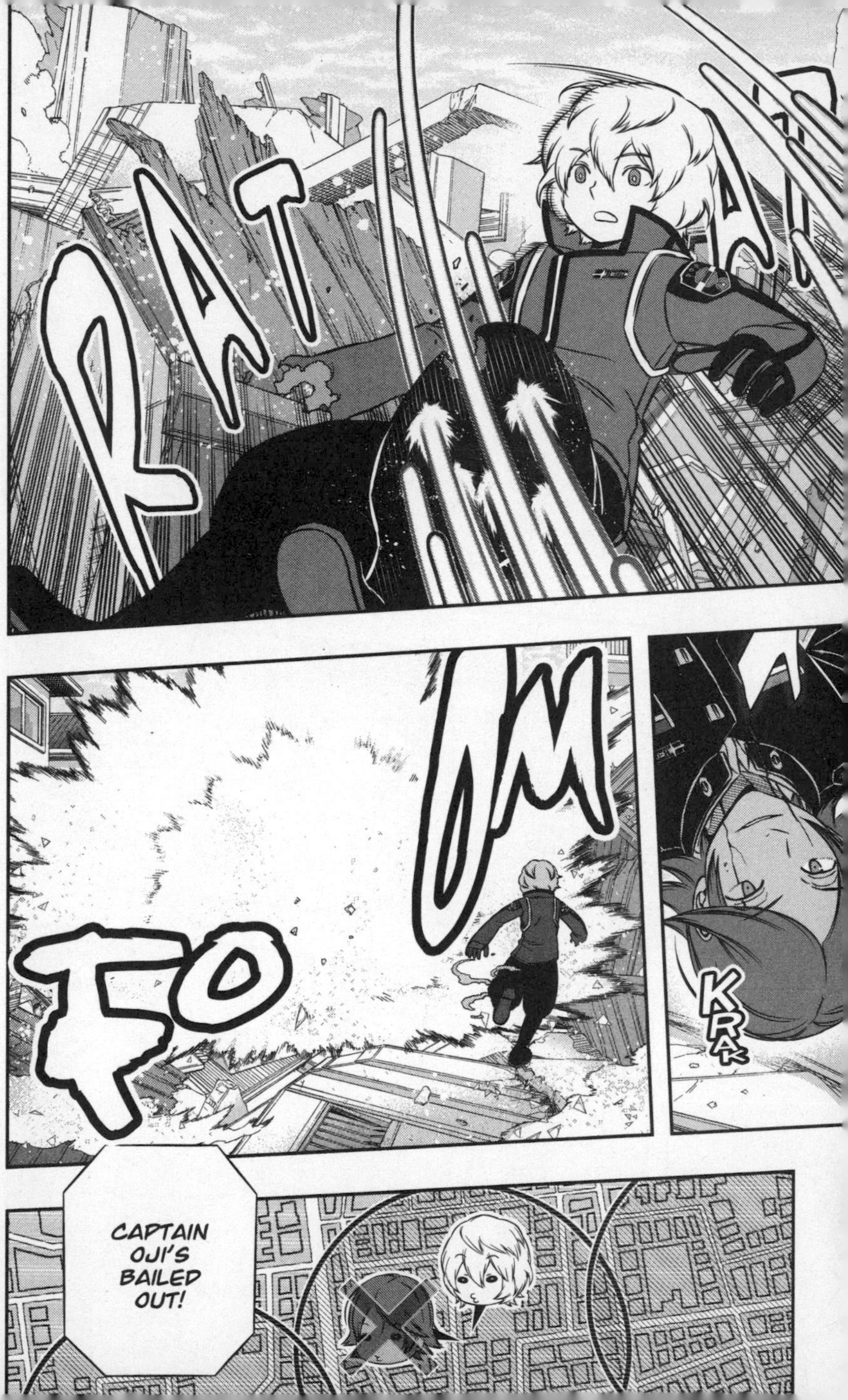
RAT
KRAK
FOOM
CAPTAIN OJI'S BAILED OUT!

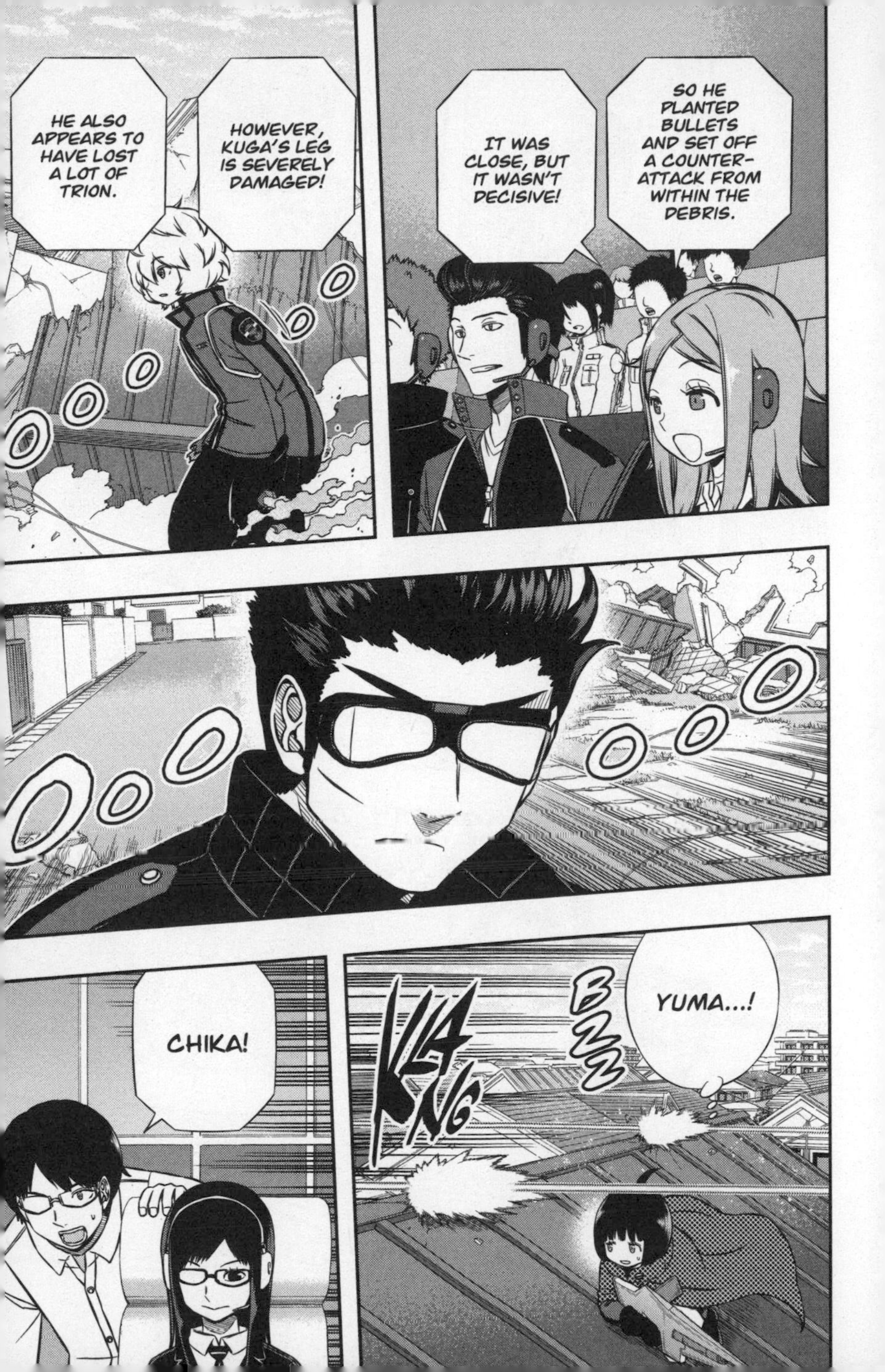
SO HE PLANTED BULLETS AND SET OFF A COUNTER-ATTACK FROM WITHIN THE DEBRIS.
IT WAS CLOSE, BUT IT WASN'T DECISIVE!
HOWEVER, KUGA'S LEG IS SEVERELY DAMAGED!
HE ALSO APPEARS TO HAVE LOST A LOT OF TRION.
KLANG
BZZZ
YUMA...!
CHIKA!

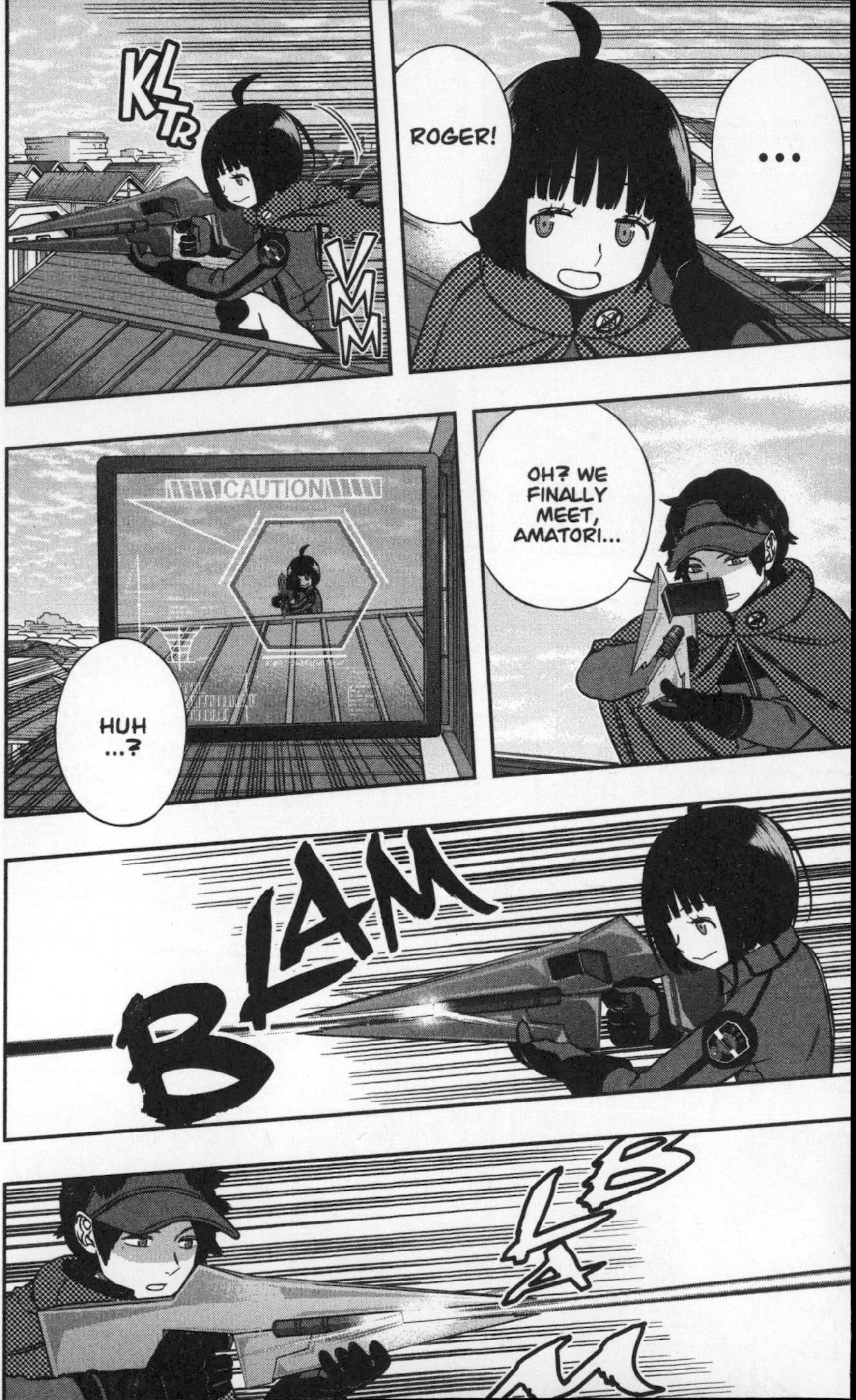
...
ROGER!
KLTR
VMMM
OH? WE FINALLY MEET, AMATORI...
CAUTION
HUH ...?
BLAM

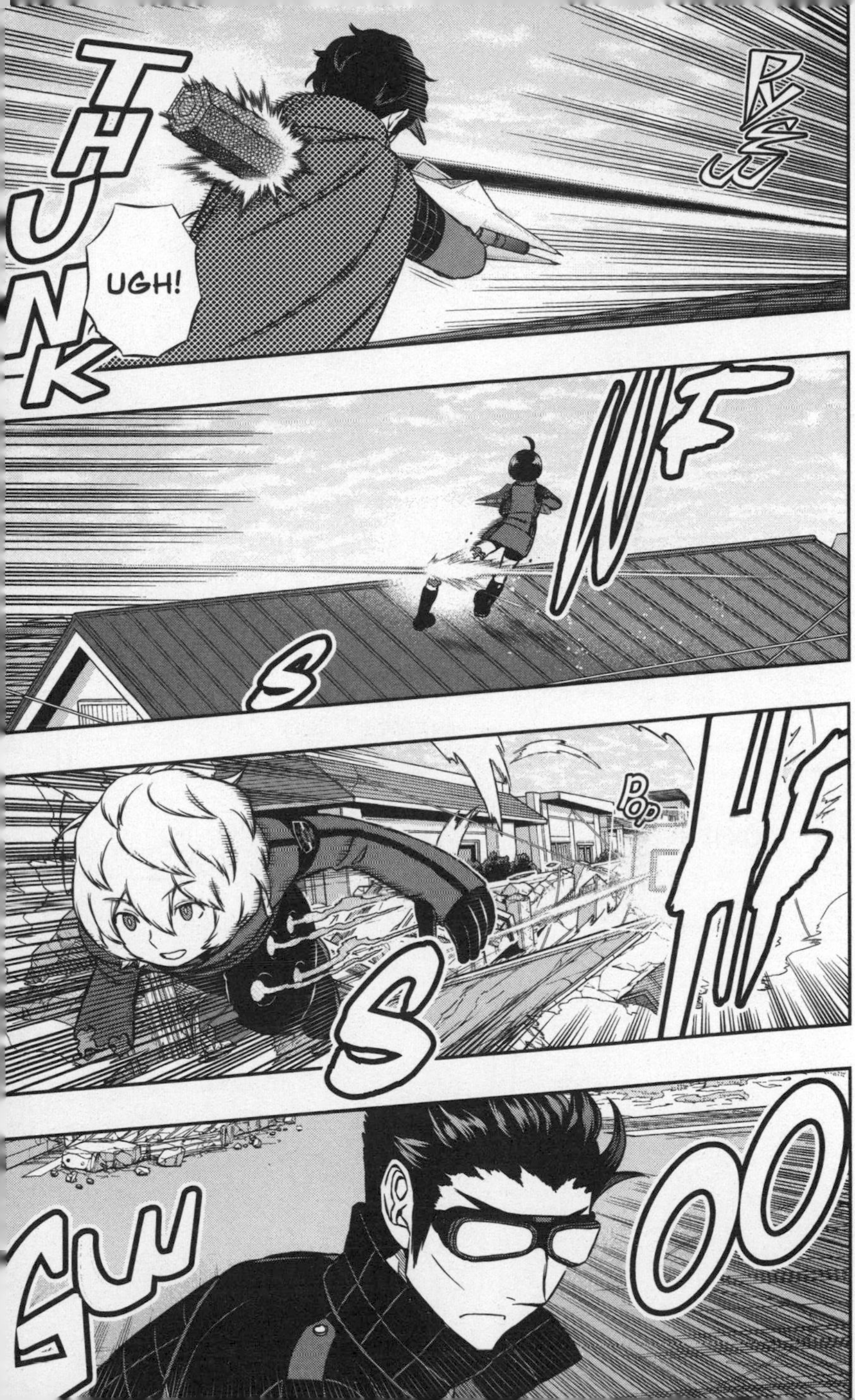
RYSU
THUNK
UGH!
WF
S
HF
POP
S
OO
GU

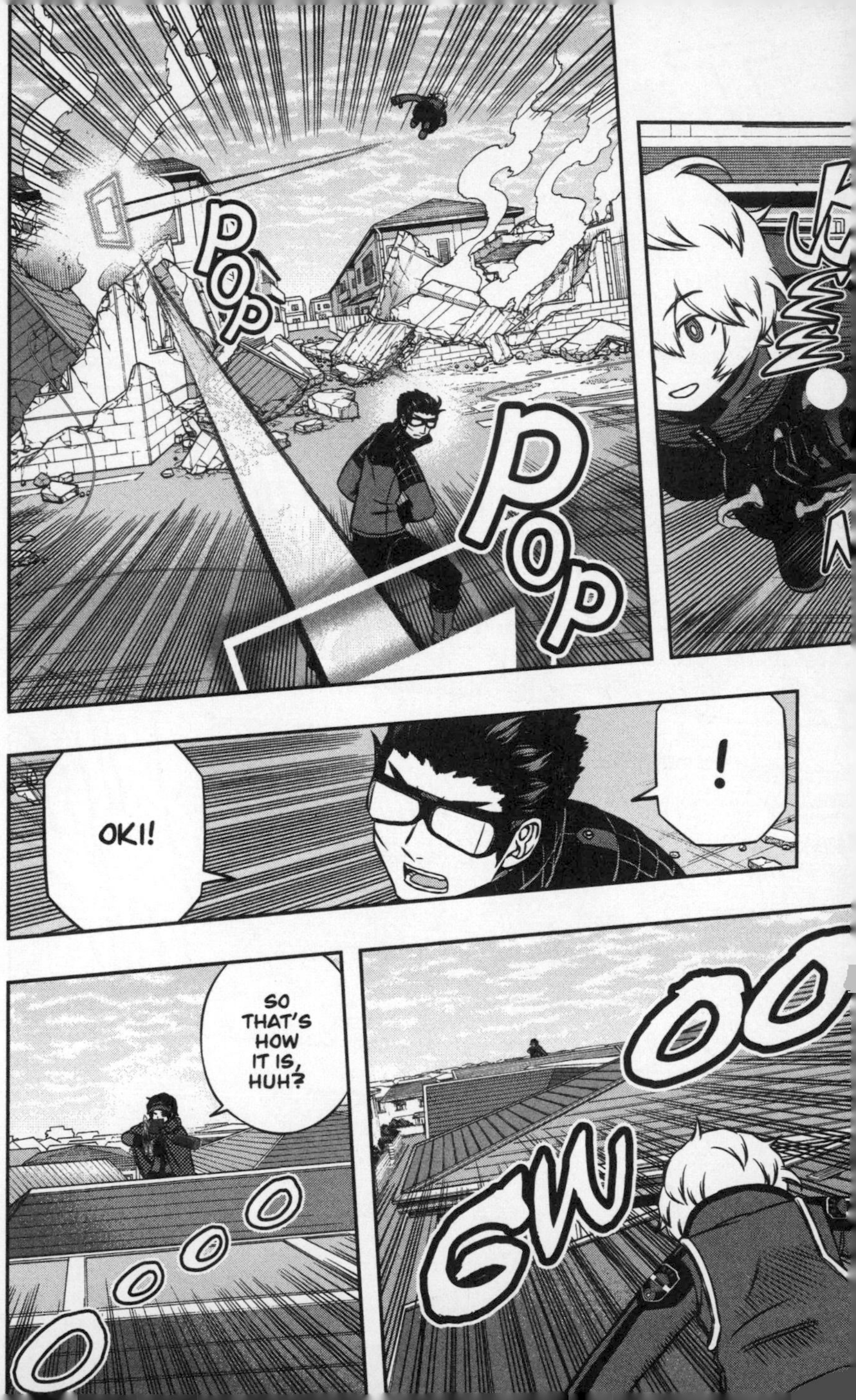
POP
POP
POP
POP
!
OKI!
SO THAT'S HOW IT IS, HUH?

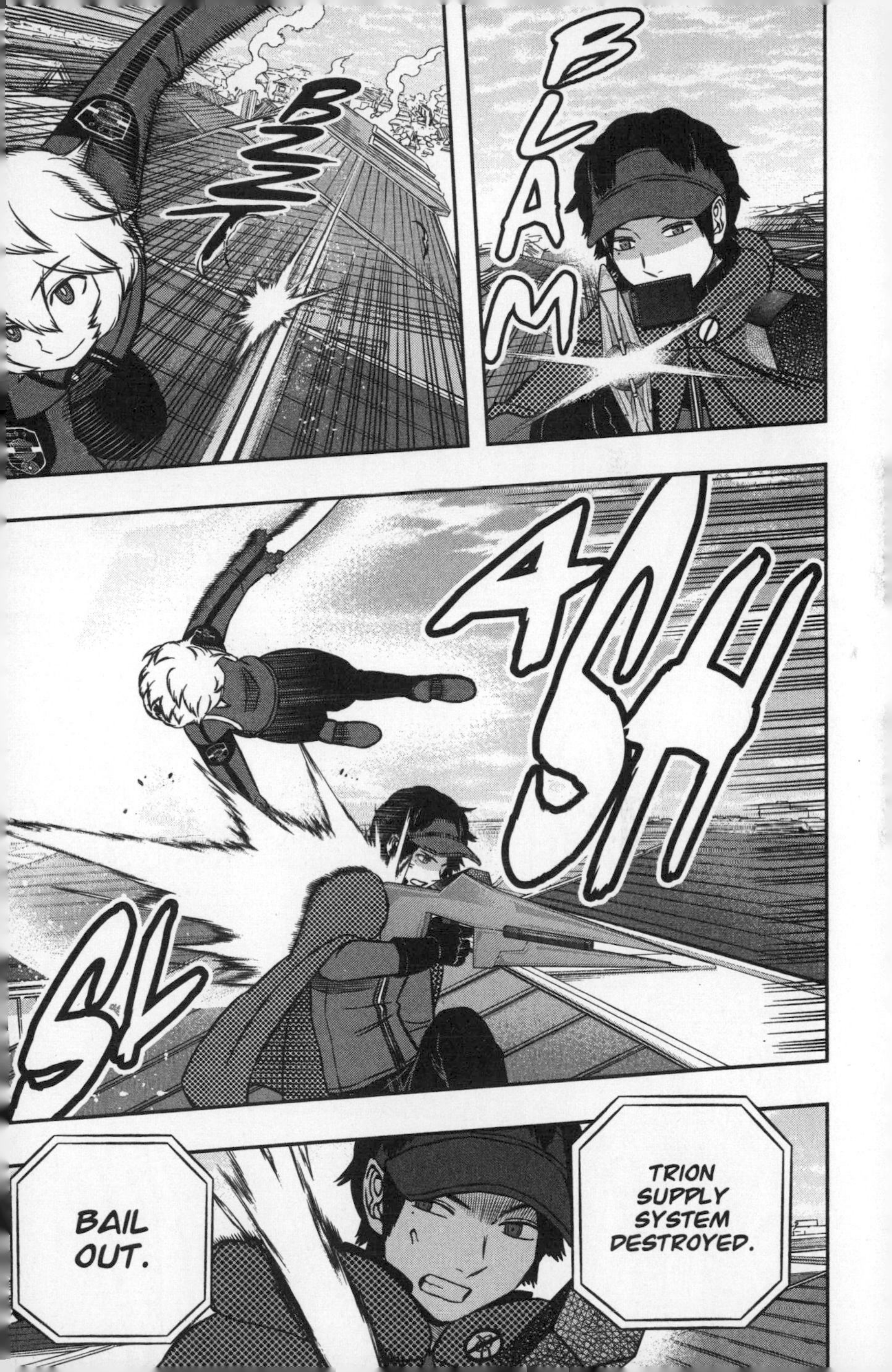
BLAM
BZZT
TRION SUPPLY SYSTEM DESTROYED.
BAIL OUT.

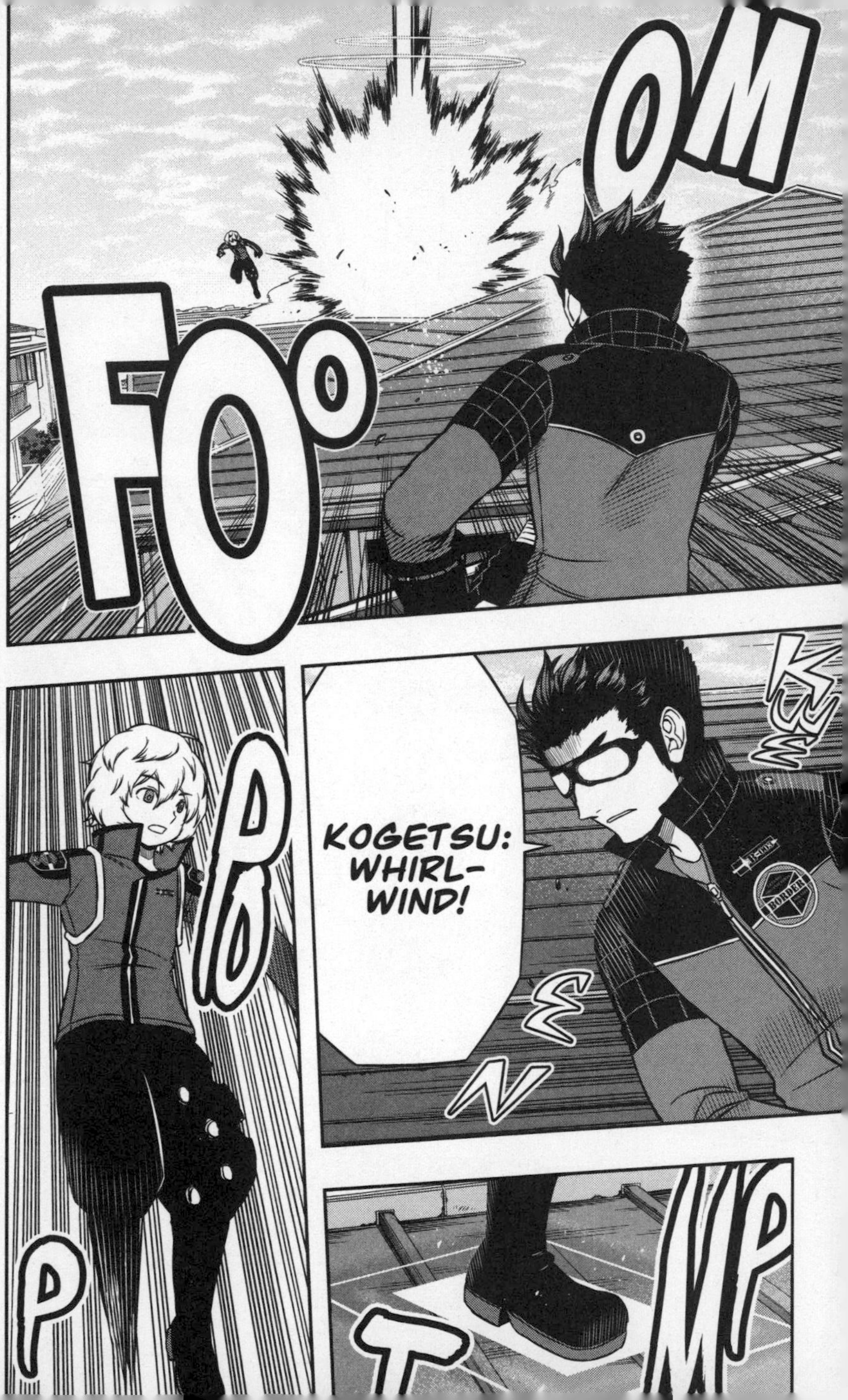
FOOOM
KOGETSU: WHIRL-WIND!
TMMP

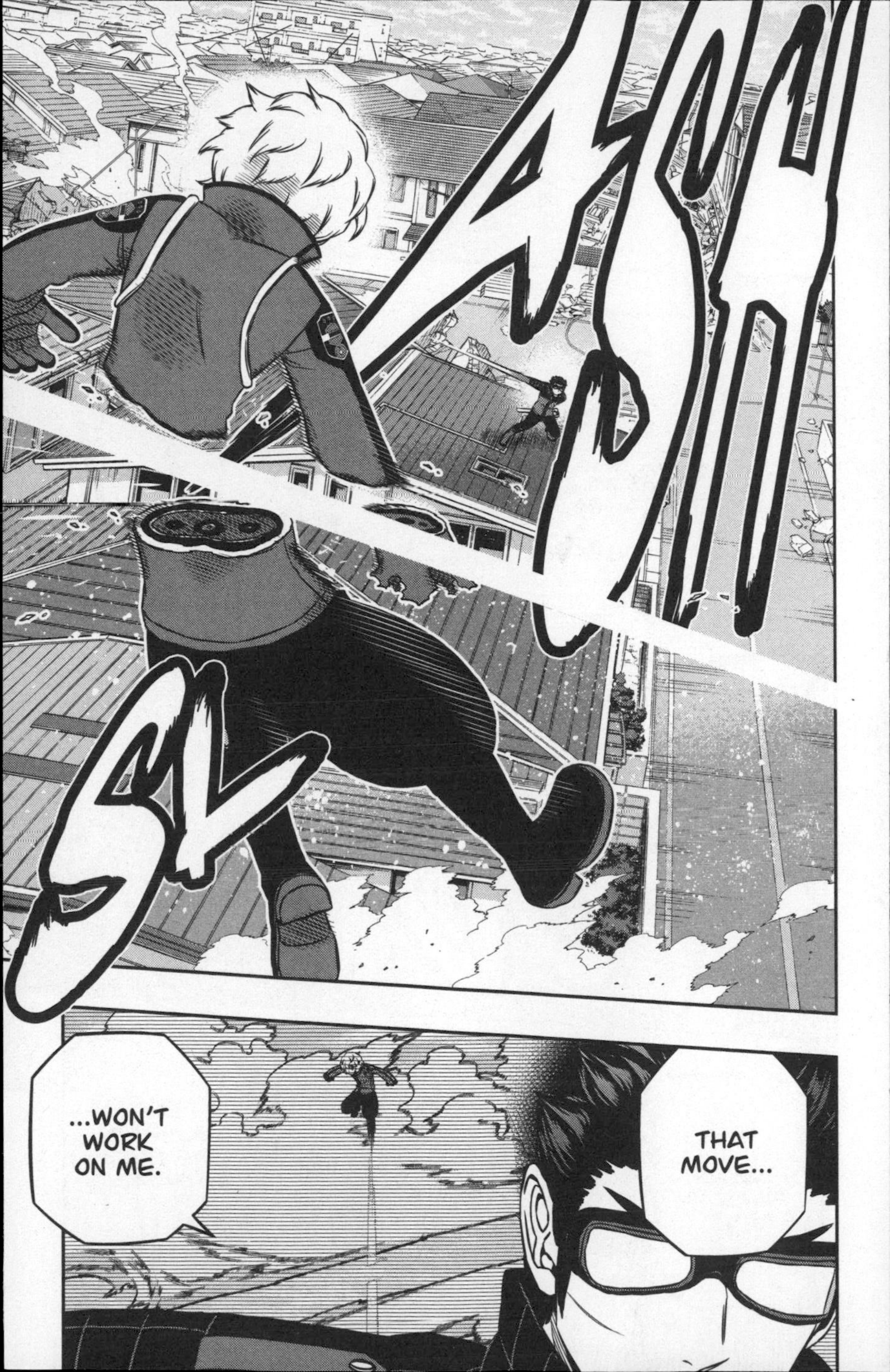
THAT MOVE...
...WON'T WORK ON ME.

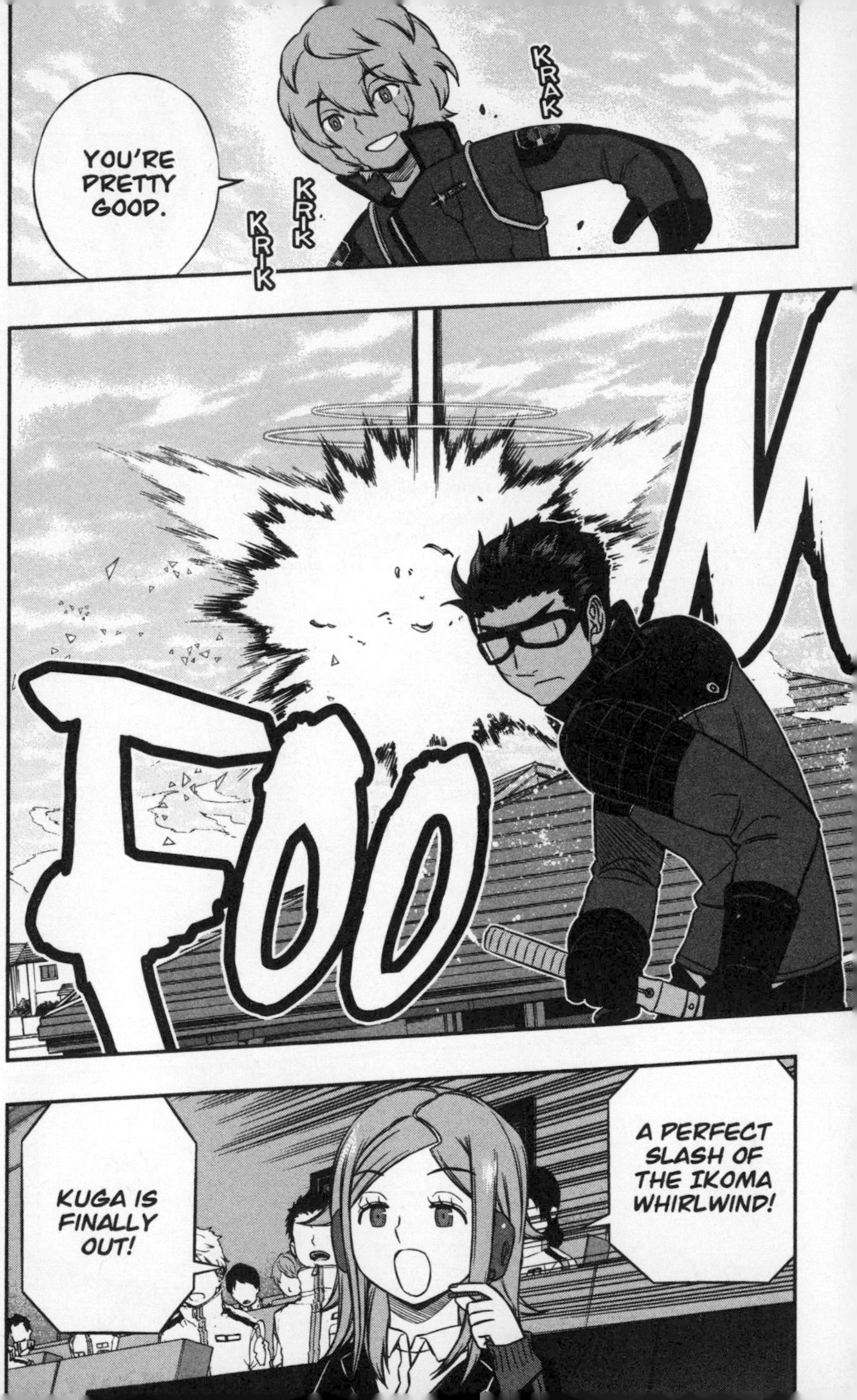
KRAK
KRIK
KRIK
YOU'RE PRETTY GOOD.
FOOM
A PERFECT SLASH OF THE IKOMA WHIRLWIND!
KUGA IS FINALLY OUT!

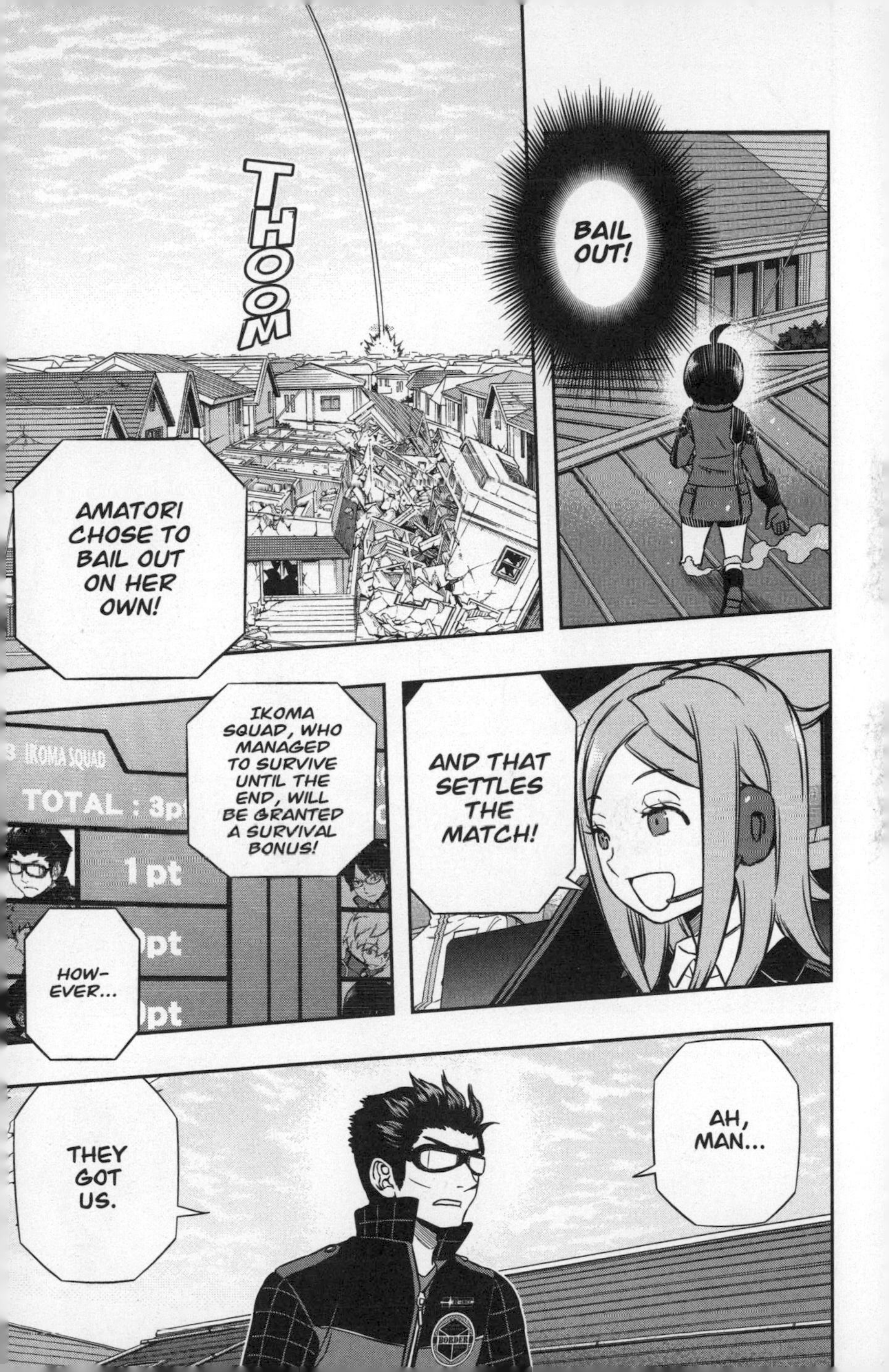
BAIL OUT!
THOOM
AMATORI CHOSE TO BAIL OUT ON HER OWN!
AND THAT SETTLES THE MATCH!
IKOMA SQUAD
1 pt
IKOMA SQUAD, WHO MANAGED TO SURVIVE UNTIL THE END, WILL BE GRANTED A SURVIVAL BONUS!
HOW-EVER...
AH, MAN...
THEY GOT US.

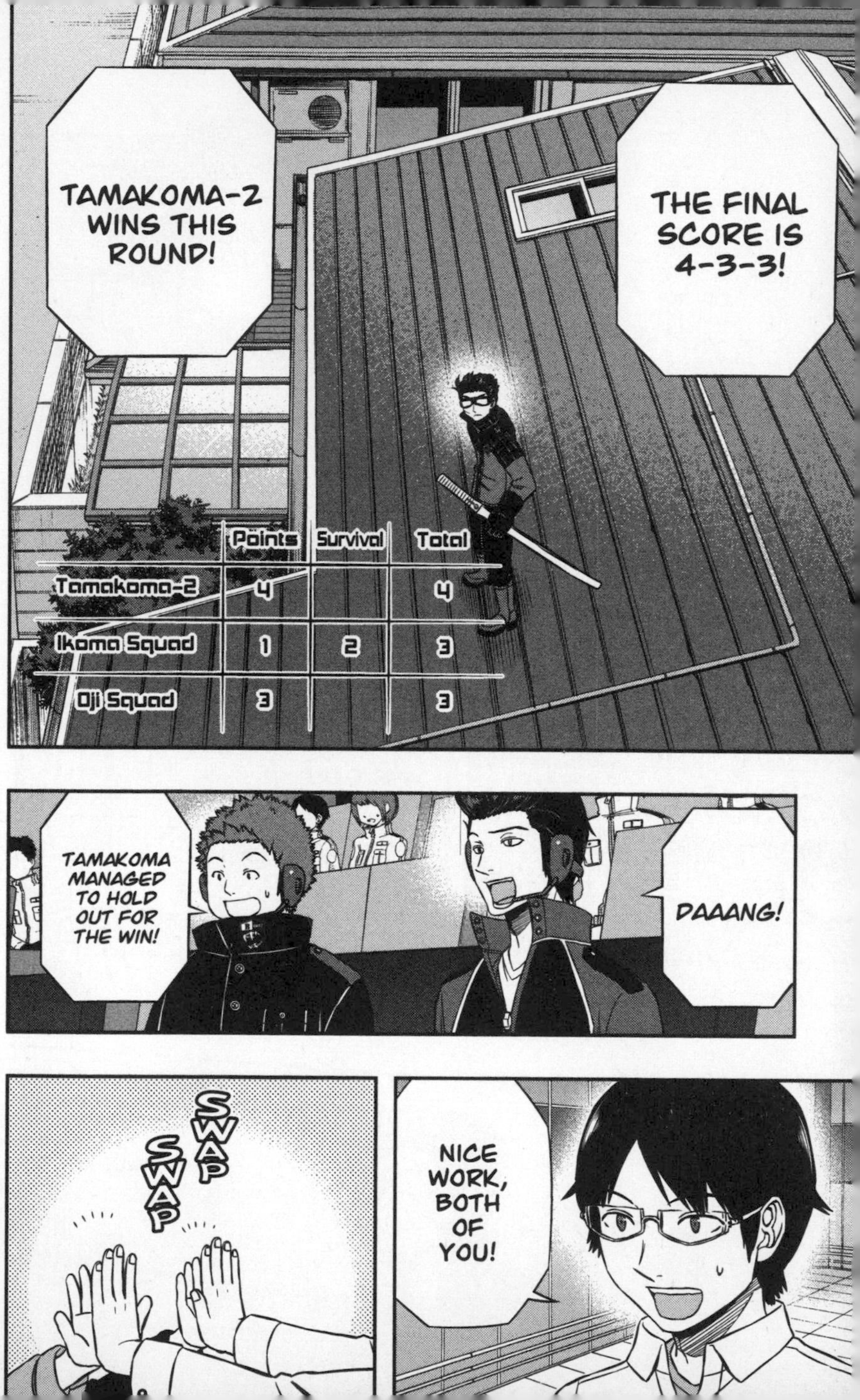
THE FINAL SCORE IS 4-3-3!
TAMAKOMA-2 WINS THIS ROUND!
Points Survival Total
Tamakoma-2 4 4
Ikoma Squad 1 2 3
Oji Squad 3 3
DAAANG!
TAMAKOMA MANAGED TO HOLD OUT FOR THE WIN!
NICE WORK, BOTH OF YOU!
SWAP
SWAP

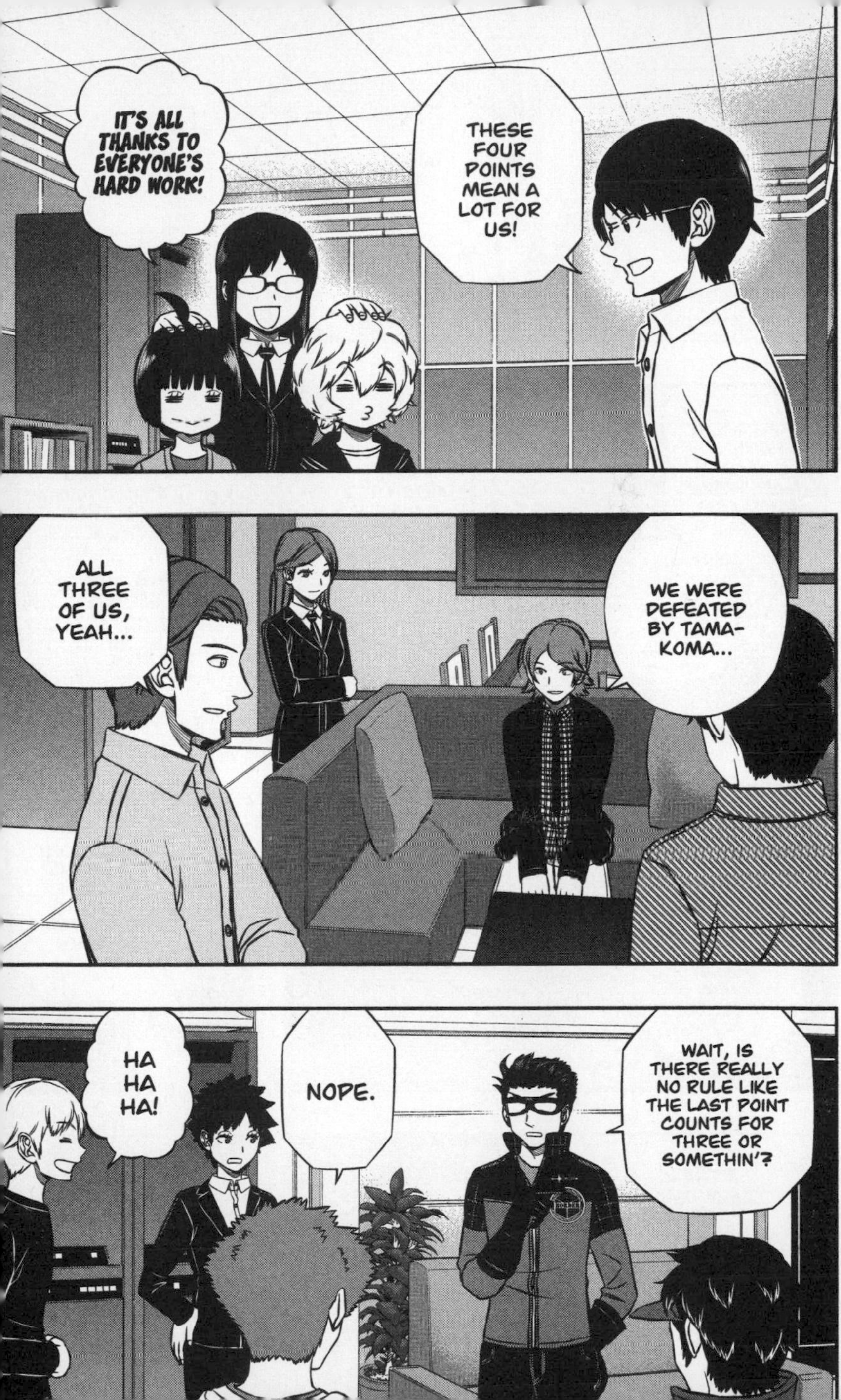
THESE FOUR POINTS MEAN A LOT FOR US!
IT'S ALL THANKS TO EVERYONE'S HARD WORK!
WE WERE DEFEATED BY TAMA-KOMA...
ALL THREE OF US, YEAH...
WAIT, IS THERE REALLY NO RULE LIKE THE LAST POINT COUNTS FOR THREE OR SOMETHIN'?
NOPE.
HA HA HA!

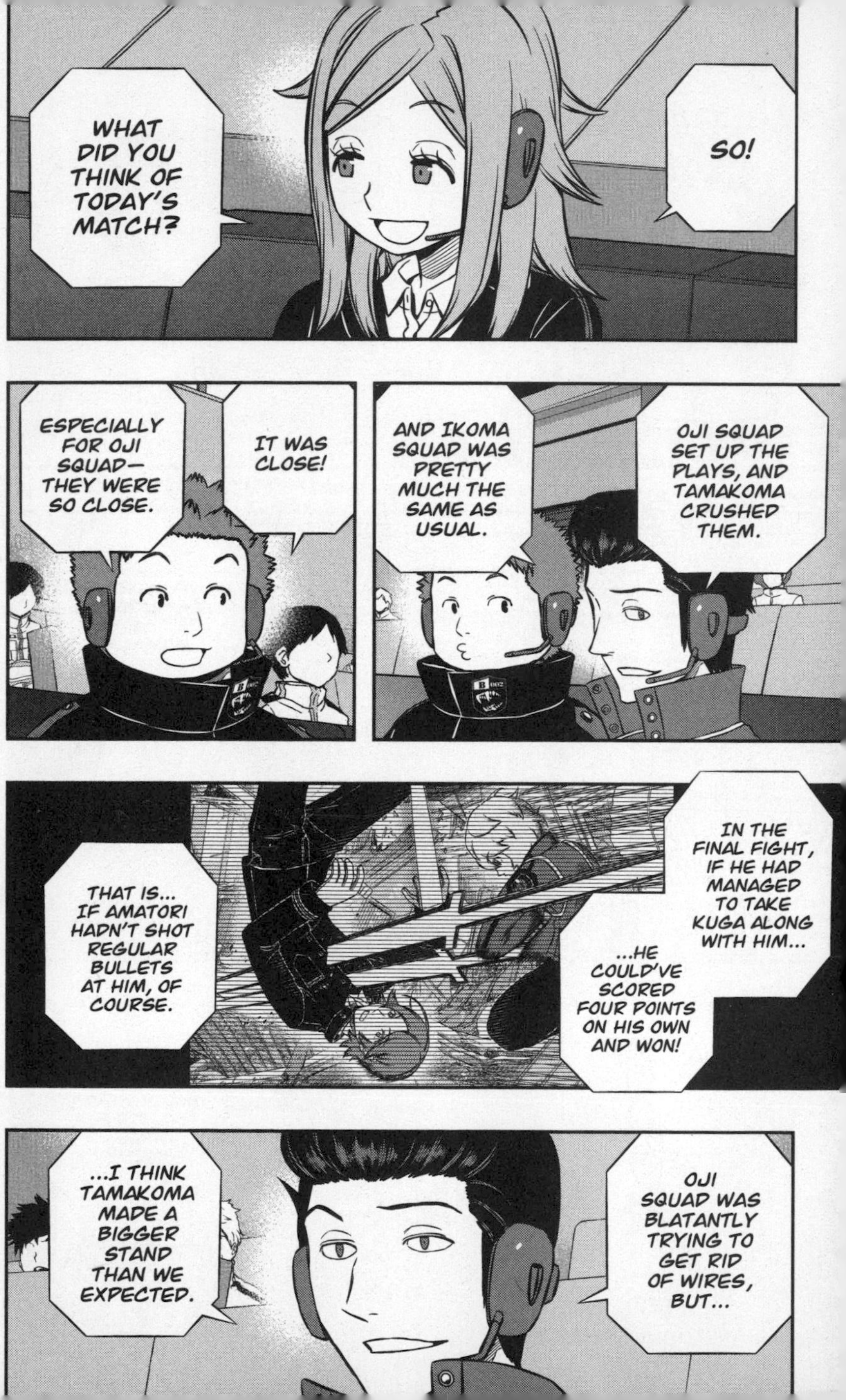
SO!
WHAT DID YOU THINK OF TODAY'S MATCH?
OJI SQUAD SET UP THE PLAYS, AND TAMAKOMA CRUSHED THEM.
AND IKOMA SQUAD WAS PRETTY MUCH THE SAME AS USUAL.
IT WAS CLOSE!
ESPECIALLY FOR OJI SQUAD—THEY WERE SO CLOSE.
IN THE FINAL FIGHT, IF HE HAD MANAGED TO TAKE KUGA ALONG WITH HIM...
...HE COULD'VE SCORED FOUR POINTS ON HIS OWN AND WON!
THAT IS... IF AMATORI HADN'T SHOT REGULAR BULLETS AT HIM, OF COURSE.
OJI SQUAD WAS BLATANTLY TRYING TO GET RID OF WIRES, BUT...
...I THINK TAMAKOMA MADE A BIGGER STAND THAN WE EXPECTED.

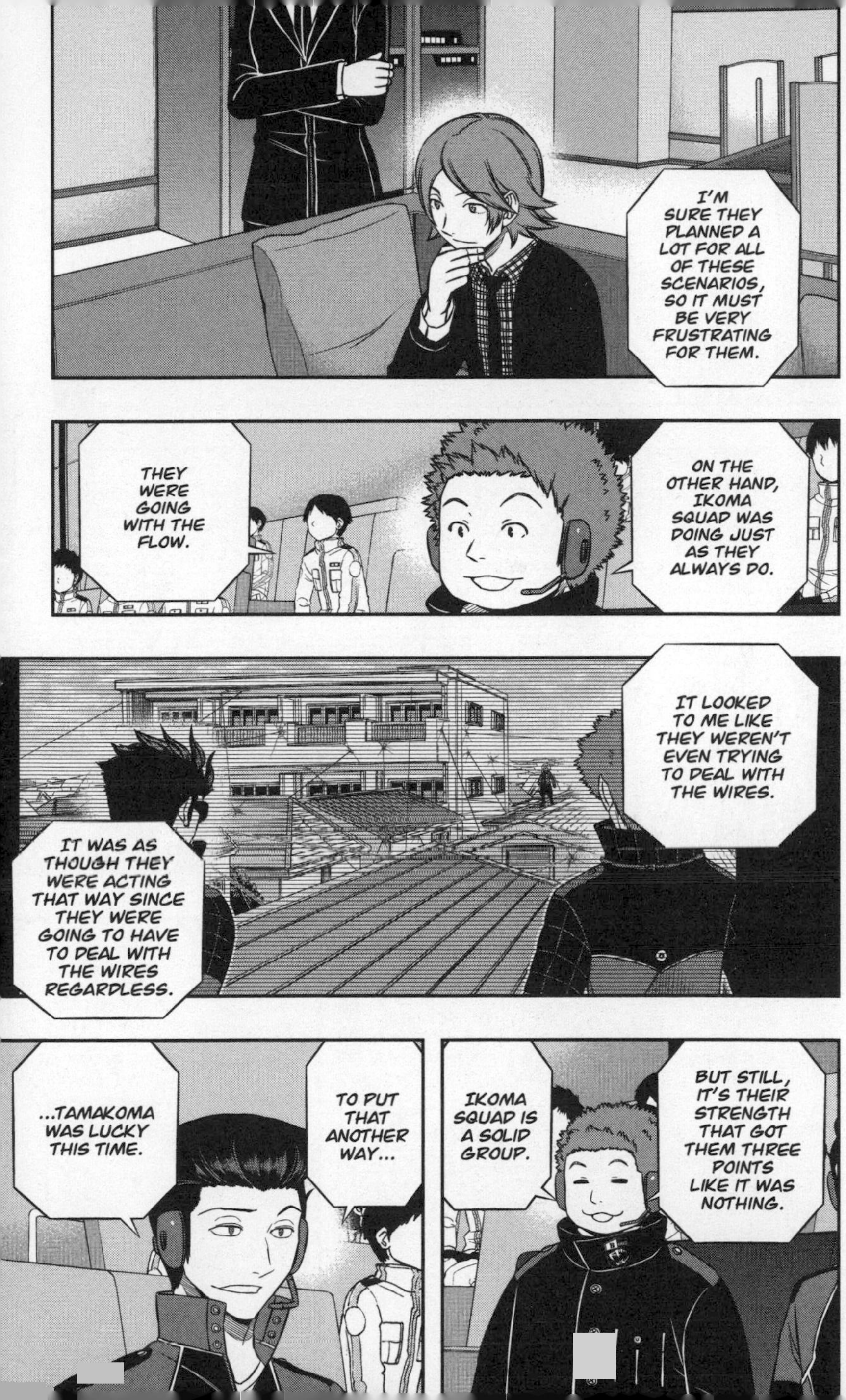
I'M SURE THEY PLANNED A LOT FOR ALL OF THESE SCENARIOS, SO IT MUST BE VERY FRUSTRATING FOR THEM.
ON THE OTHER HAND, IKOMA SQUAD WAS DOING JUST AS THEY ALWAYS DO.
THEY WERE GOING WITH THE FLOW.
IT LOOKED TO ME LIKE THEY WEREN'T EVEN TRYING TO DEAL WITH THE WIRES.
IT WAS AS THOUGH THEY WERE ACTING THAT WAY SINCE THEY WERE GOING TO HAVE TO DEAL WITH THE WIRES REGARDLESS.
BUT STILL, IT'S THEIR STRENGTH THAT GOT THEM THREE POINTS LIKE IT WAS NOTHING.
IKOMA SQUAD IS A SOLID GROUP.
TO PUT THAT ANOTHER WAY...
...TAMAKOMA WAS LUCKY THIS TIME.

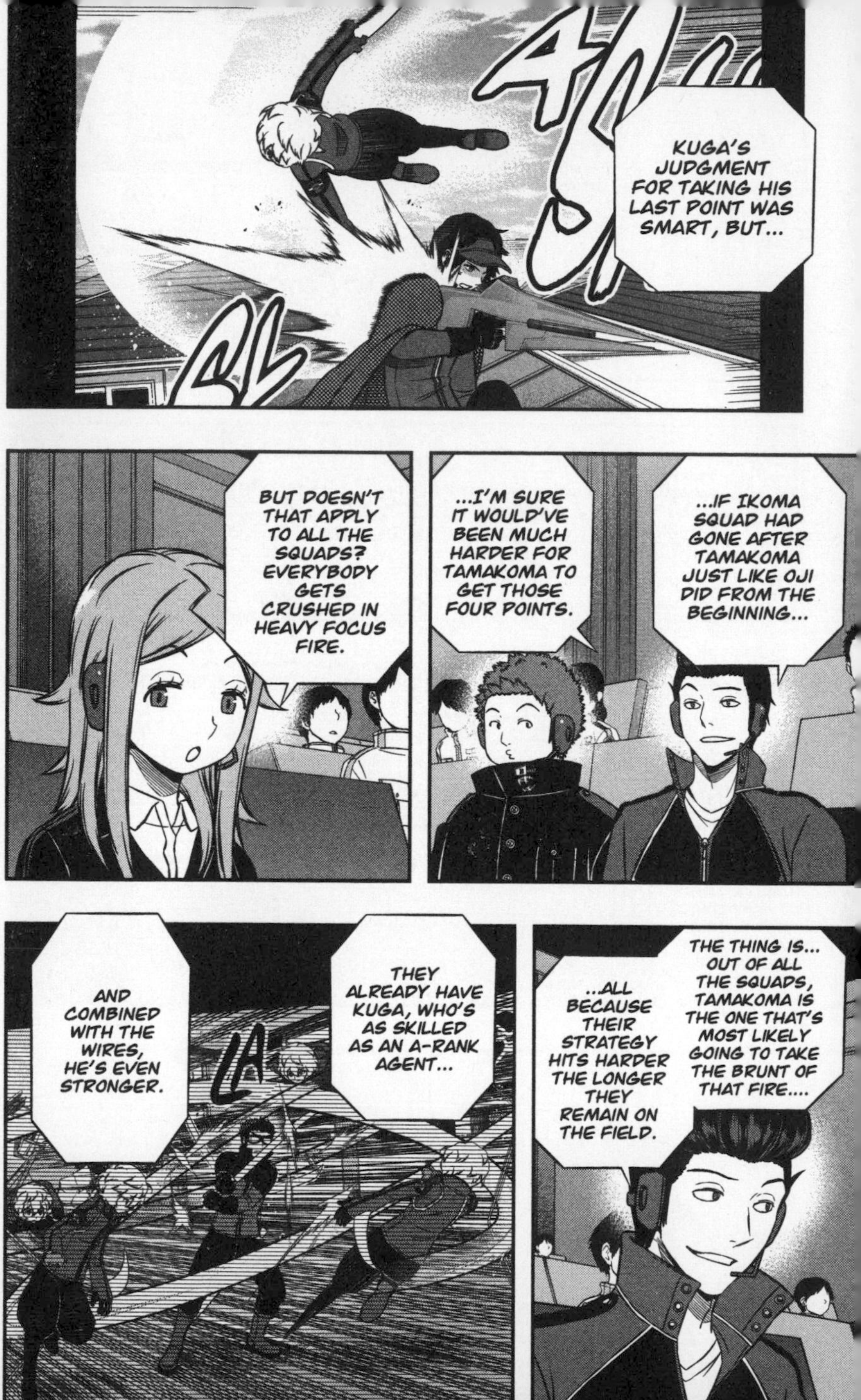
KUGA'S JUDGMENT FOR TAKING HIS LAST POINT WAS SMART, BUT...
...IF IKOMA SQUAD HAD GONE AFTER TAMAKOMA JUST LIKE OJI DID FROM THE BEGINNING...
...I'M SURE IT WOULD'VE BEEN MUCH HARDER FOR TAMAKOMA TO GET THOSE FOUR POINTS.
BUT DOESN'T THAT APPLY TO ALL THE SQUADS? EVERYBODY GETS CRUSHED IN HEAVY FOCUS FIRE.
THE THING IS... OUT OF ALL THE SQUADS, TAMAKOMA IS THE ONE THAT'S MOST LIKELY GOING TO TAKE THE BRUNT OF THAT FIRE....
...ALL BECAUSE THEIR STRATEGY HITS HARDER THE LONGER THEY REMAIN ON THE FIELD.
THEY ALREADY HAVE KUGA, WHO'S AS SKILLED AS AN A-RANK AGENT...
AND COMBINED WITH THE WIRES, HE'S EVEN STRONGER.

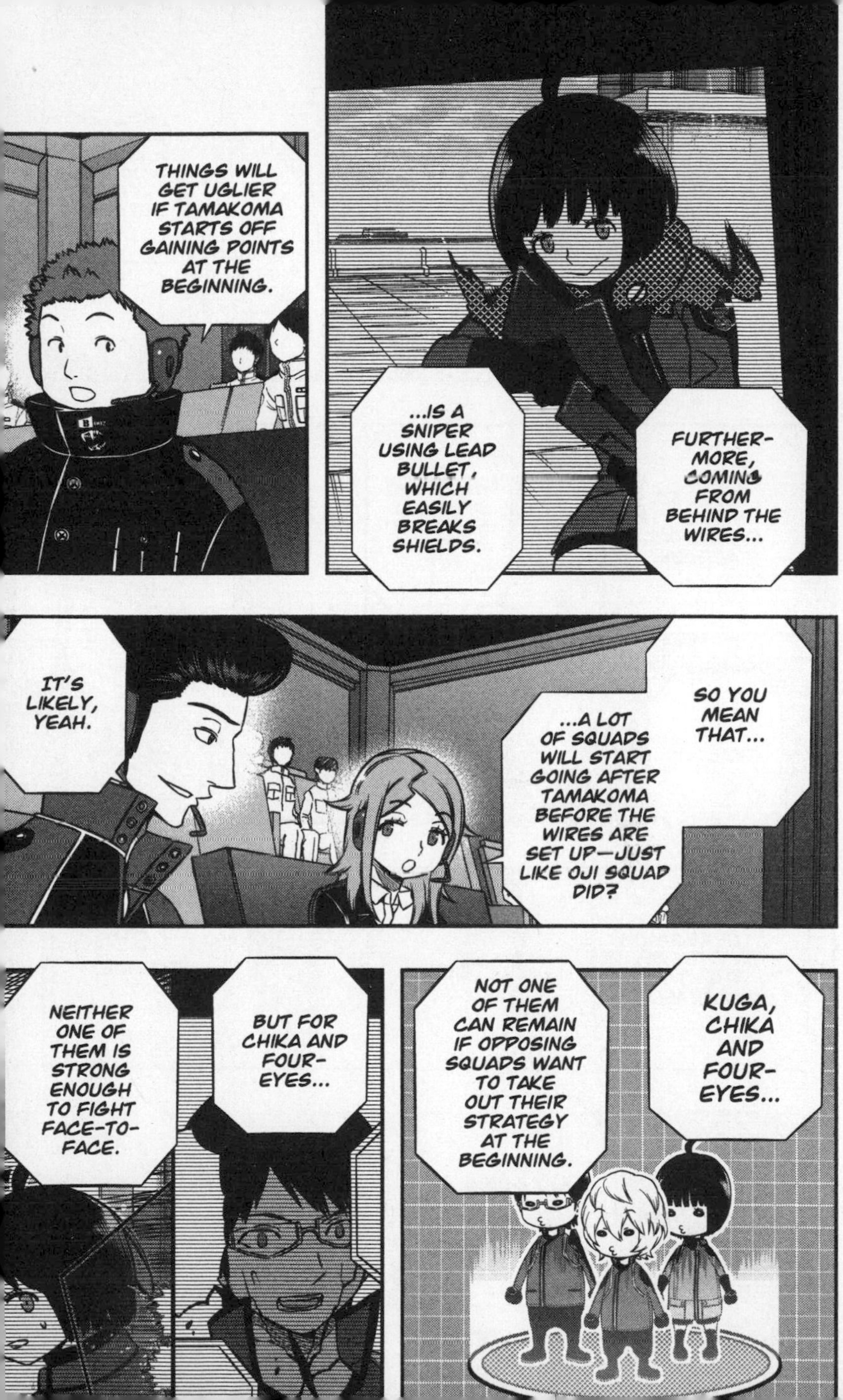
FURTHER-MORE, COMING FROM BEHIND THE WIRES...
...IS A SNIPER USING LEAD BULLET, WHICH EASILY BREAKS SHIELDS.
THINGS WILL GET UGLIER IF TAMAKOMA STARTS OFF GAINING POINTS AT THE BEGINNING.
SO YOU MEAN THAT...
...A LOT OF SQUADS WILL START GOING AFTER TAMAKOMA BEFORE THE WIRES ARE SET UP—JUST LIKE OJI SQUAD DID?
IT'S LIKELY, YEAH.
KUGA, CHIKA AND FOUR-EYES...
NOT ONE OF THEM CAN REMAIN IF OPPOSING SQUADS WANT TO TAKE OUT THEIR STRATEGY AT THE BEGINNING.
BUT FOR CHIKA AND FOUR-EYES...
NEITHER ONE OF THEM IS STRONG ENOUGH TO FIGHT FACE-TO-FACE.

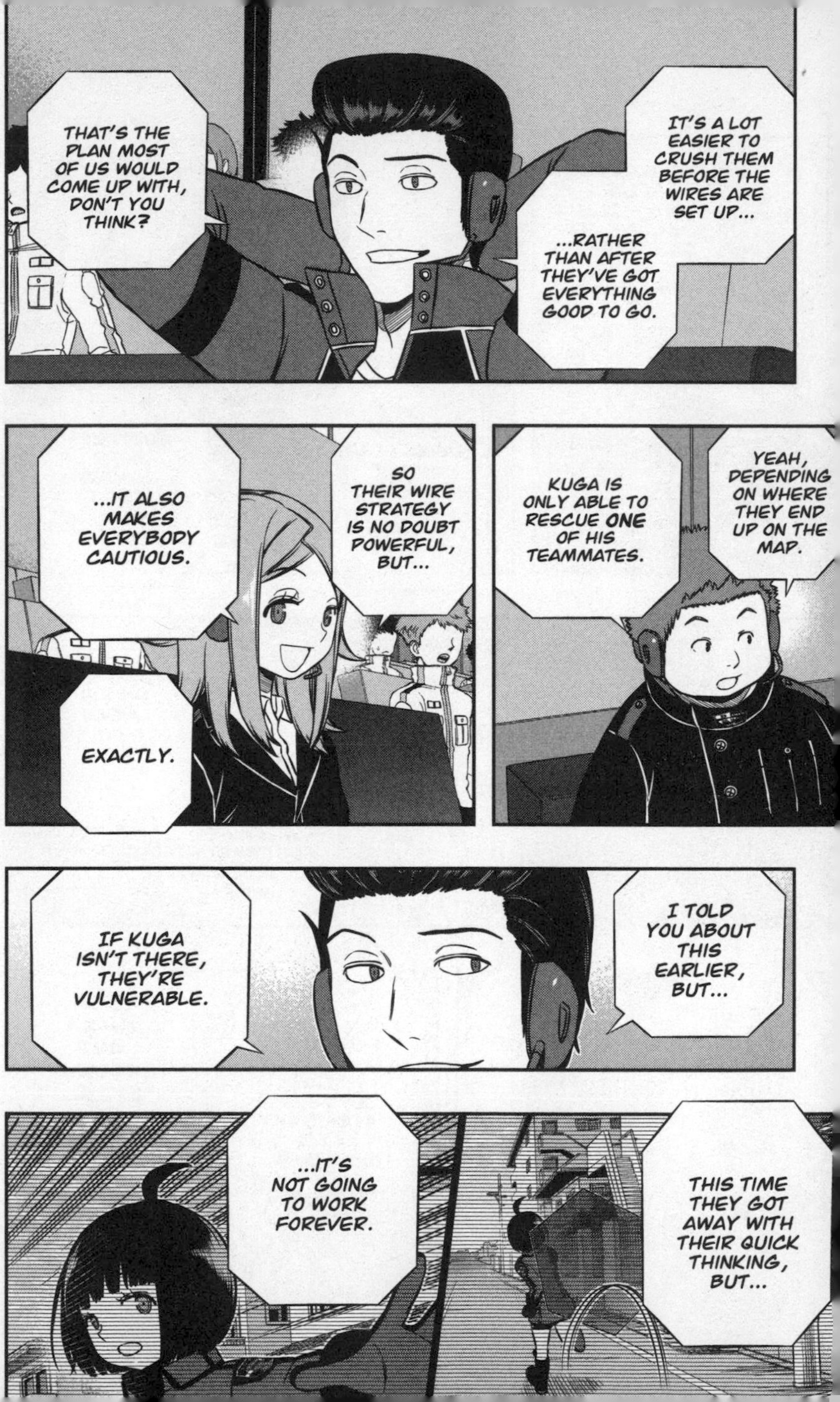
IT'S A LOT EASIER TO CRUSH THEM BEFORE THE WIRES ARE SET UP...
...RATHER THAN AFTER THEY'VE GOT EVERYTHING GOOD TO GO.
THAT'S THE PLAN MOST OF US WOULD COME UP WITH, DON'T YOU THINK?
YEAH, DEPENDING ON WHERE THEY END UP ON THE MAP.
KUGA IS ONLY ABLE TO RESCUE ONE OF HIS TEAMMATES.
SO THEIR WIRE STRATEGY IS NO DOUBT POWERFUL, BUT...
...IT ALSO MAKES EVERYBODY CAUTIOUS.
EXACTLY.
I TOLD YOU ABOUT THIS EARLIER, BUT...
IF KUGA ISN'T THERE, THEY'RE VULNERABLE.
THIS TIME THEY GOT AWAY WITH THEIR QUICK THINKING, BUT...
...IT'S NOT GOING TO WORK FOREVER.

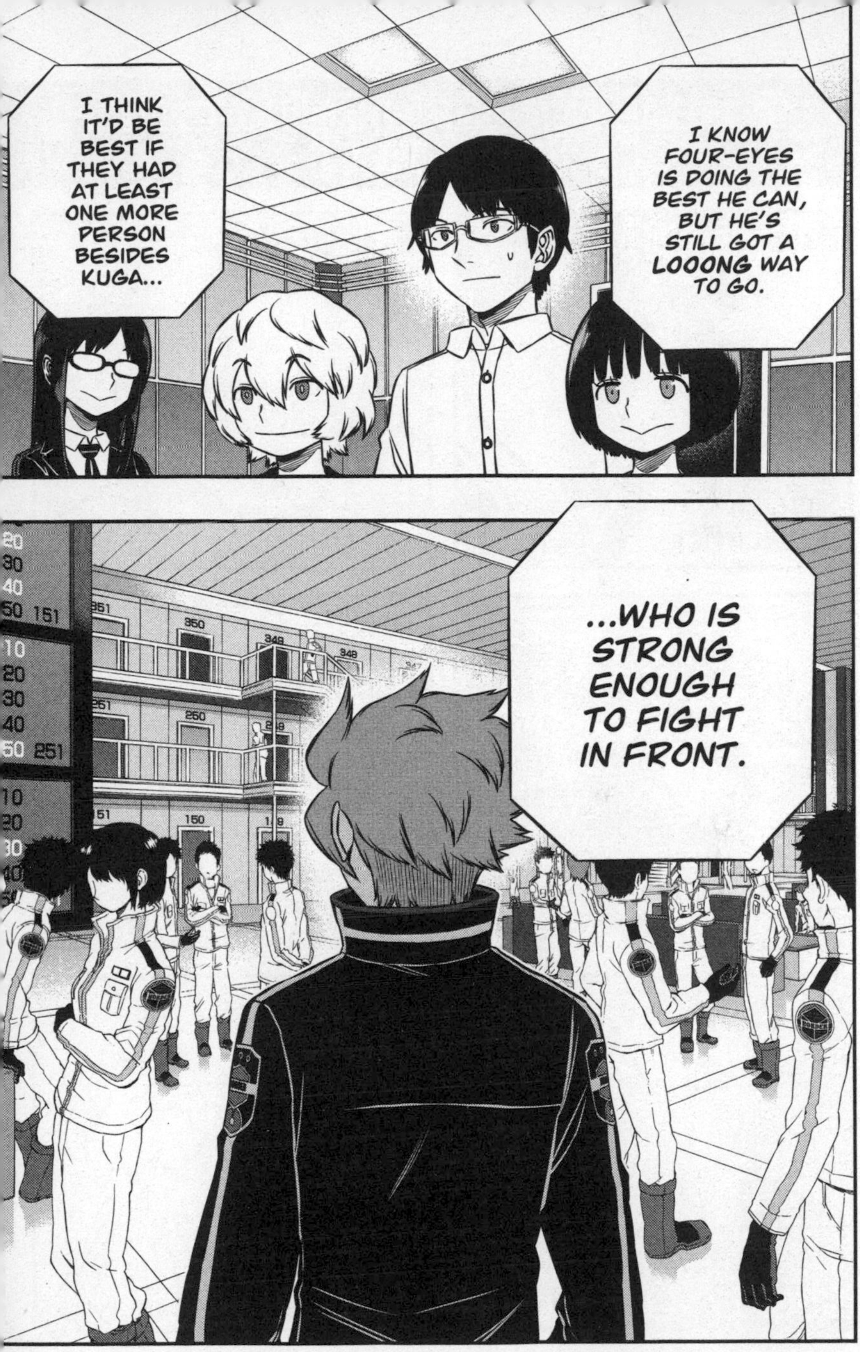
I KNOW FOUR-EYES IS DOING THE BEST HE CAN, BUT HE'S STILL GOT A LOOONG WAY TO GO.
I THINK IT'D BE BEST IF THEY HAD AT LEAST ONE MORE PERSON BESIDES KUGA...
...WHO IS STRONG ENOUGH TO FIGHT IN FRONT.

Second Popularity Poll Results! (Continued)

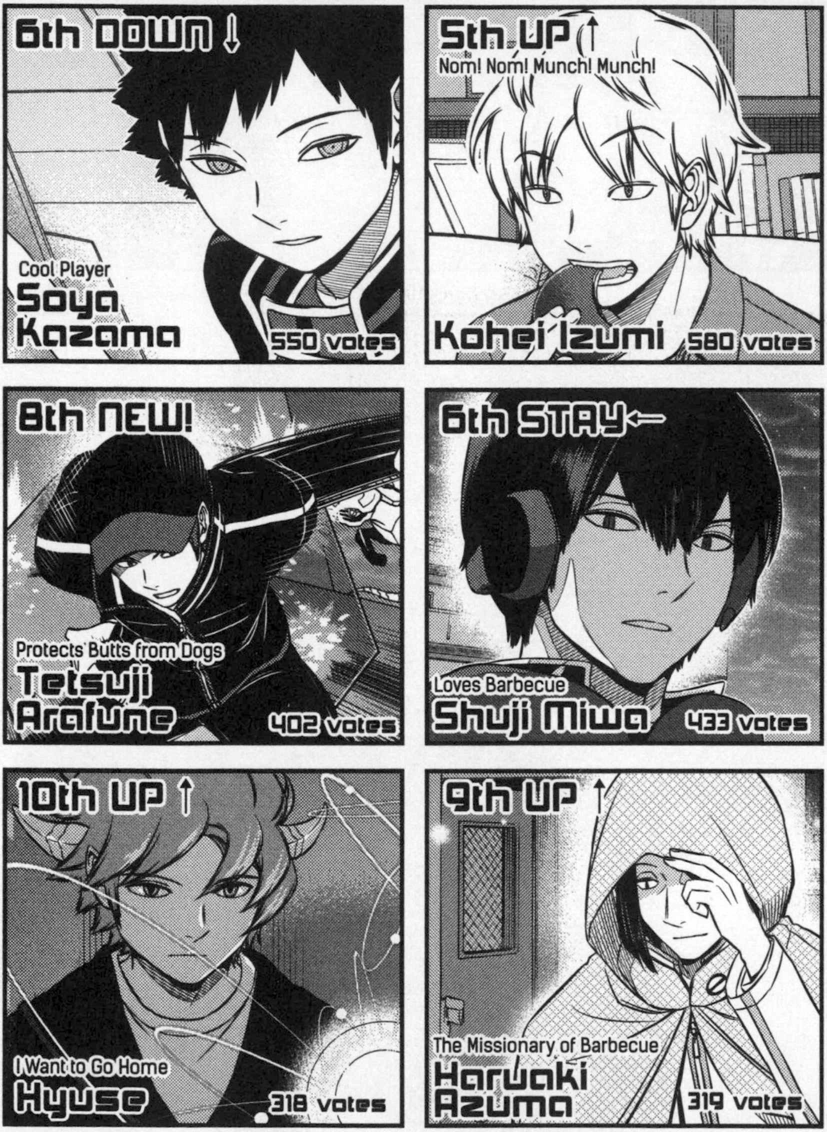

5th UP ↑
Nom! Nom! Munch! Munch!
Kohei Izumi
580 votes
6th DOWN ↓
Cool Player
Soya Kazama
550 votes
6th STAY ←
Loves Barbecue
Shuji Miwa
433 votes
8th NEW!
Protects Butts from Dogs
Tetsuji Arafune
402 votes
9th UP ↑
The Missionary of Barbecue
Haruaki Azuma
319 votes
10th UP ↑
I Want to Go Home
Hyuse
318 votes

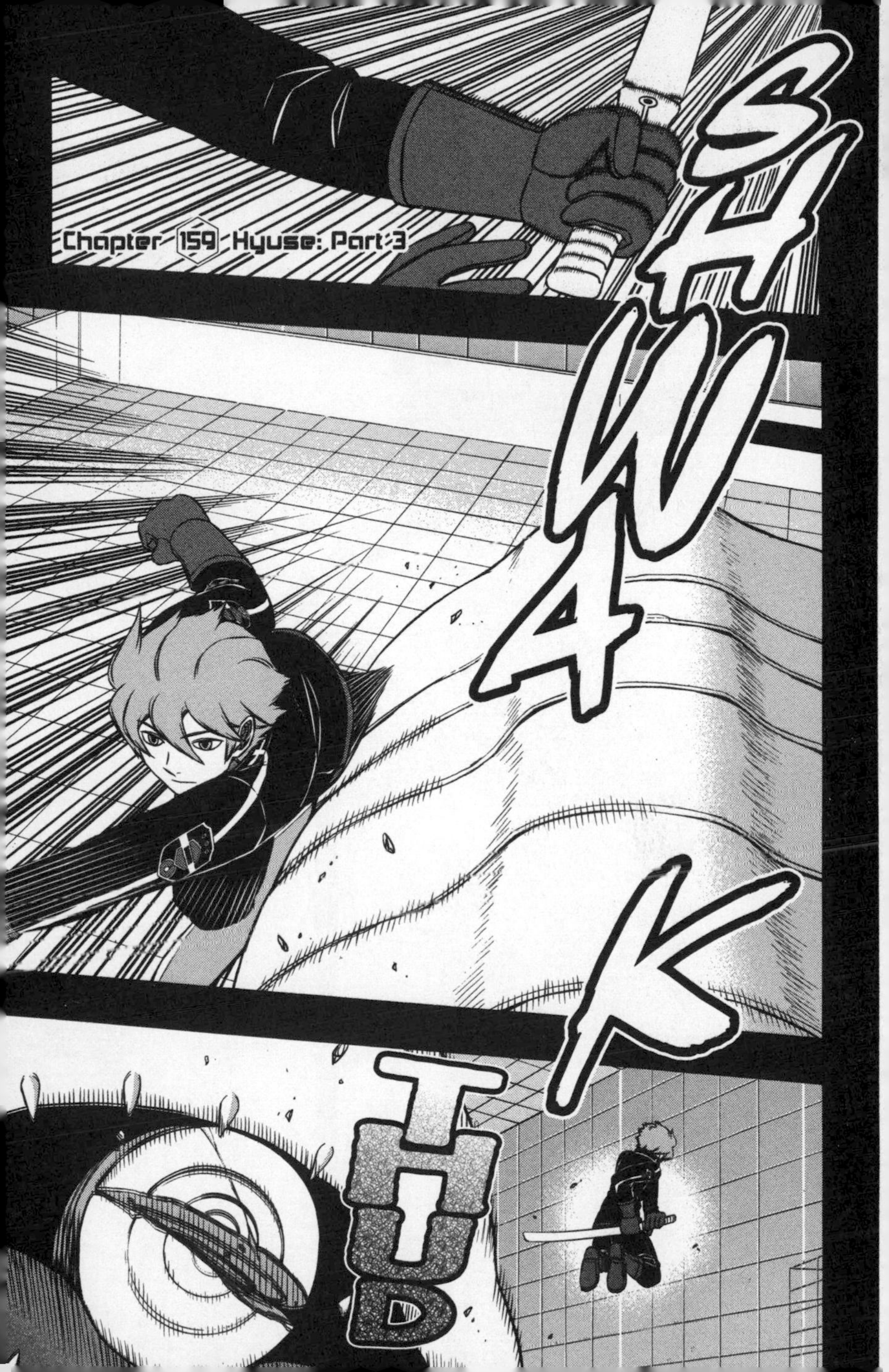
Chapter 159 Hyuse: Part 3
SHWAK
THUD

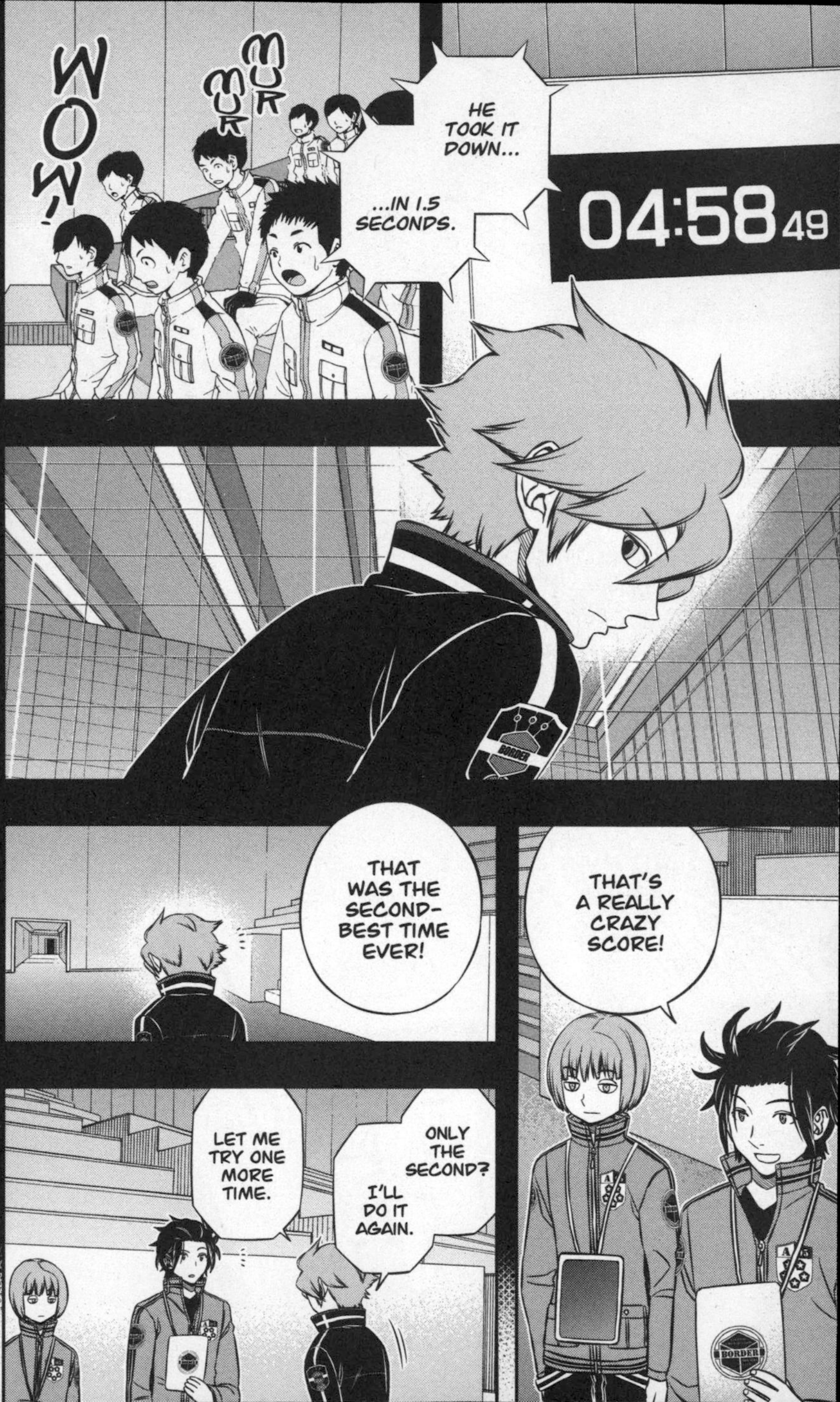
HE TOOK IT DOWN...
...IN 1.5 SECONDS.
04:58 49
MUR MUR
WOW!
THAT'S A REALLY CRAZY SCORE!
THAT WAS THE SECOND-BEST TIME EVER!
ONLY THE SECOND?
I'LL DO IT AGAIN.
LET ME TRY ONE MORE TIME.

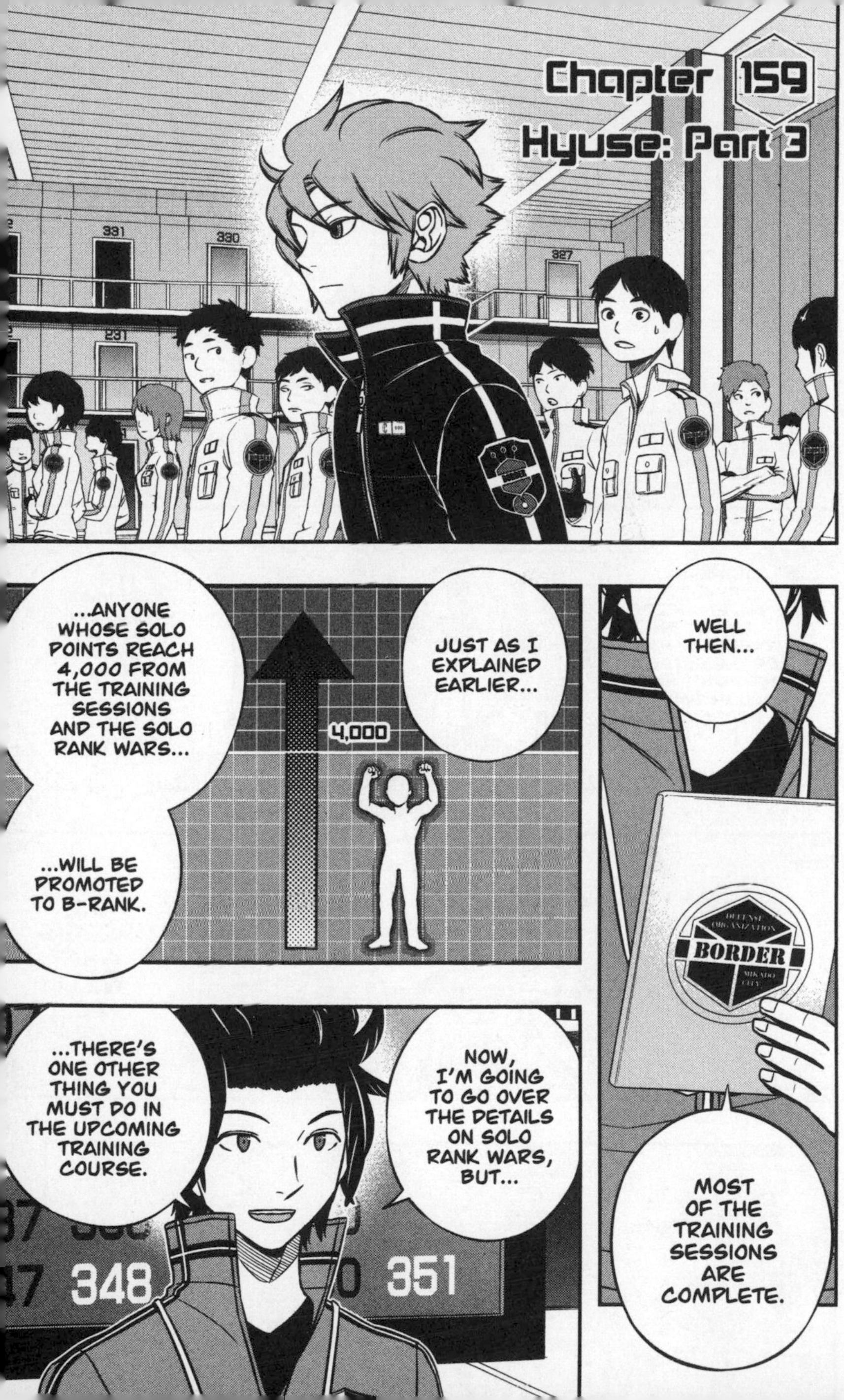
Chapter 159
Hyuse: Part 3
WELL THEN...
BORDER
MOST OF THE TRAINING SESSIONS ARE COMPLETE.
JUST AS I EXPLAINED EARLIER...
...ANYONE WHOSE SOLO POINTS REACH 4,000 FROM THE TRAINING SESSIONS AND THE SOLO RANK WARS...
4,000
...WILL BE PROMOTED TO B-RANK.
NOW, I'M GOING TO GO OVER THE DETAILS ON SOLO RANK WARS, BUT...
...THERE'S ONE OTHER THING YOU MUST DO IN THE UPCOMING TRAINING COURSE.
348
351

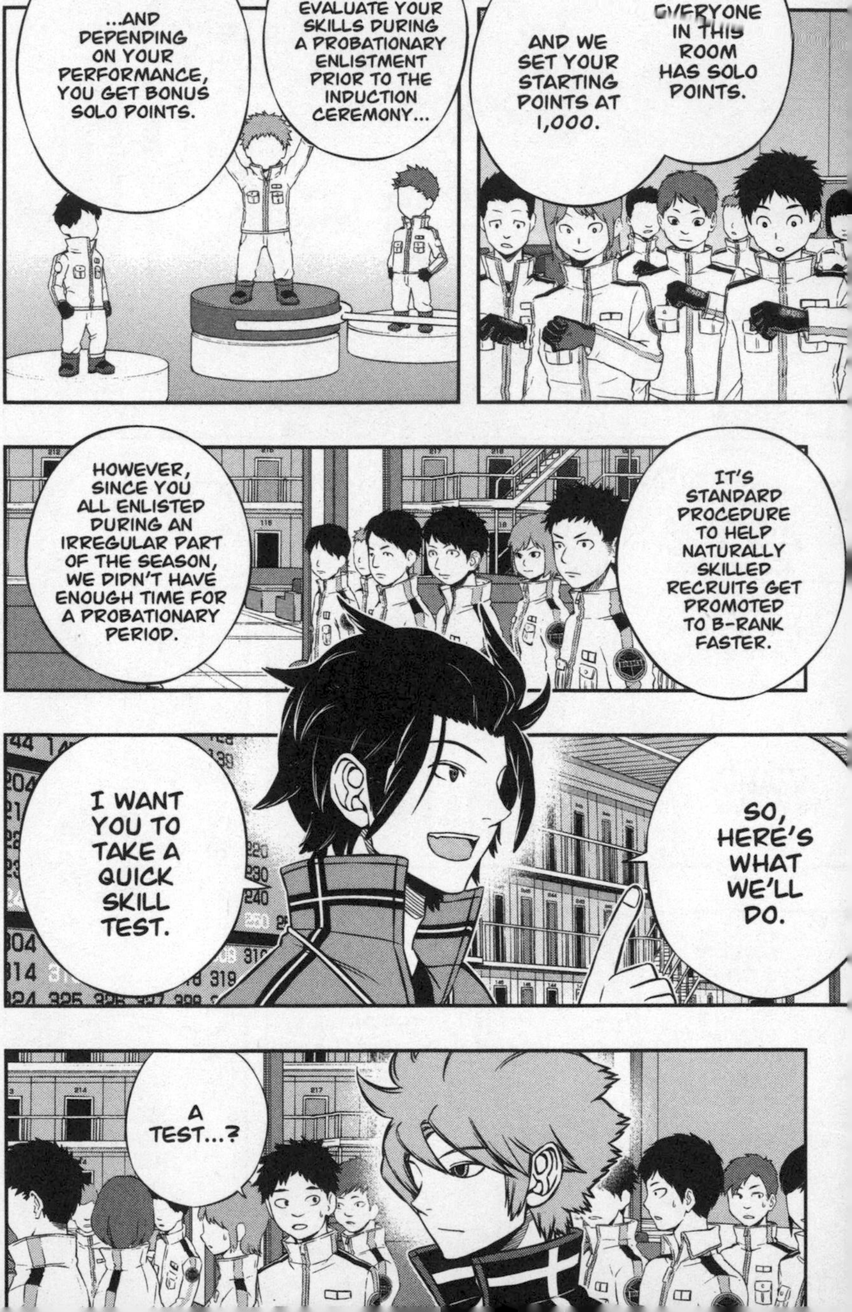
EVERYONE IN THIS ROOM HAS SOLO POINTS.
AND WE SET YOUR STARTING POINTS AT 1,000.
NORMALLY WHAT WE DO IS EVALUATE YOUR SKILLS DURING A PROBATIONARY ENLISTMENT PRIOR TO THE INDUCTION CEREMONY...
...AND DEPENDING ON YOUR PERFORMANCE, YOU GET BONUS SOLO POINTS.
IT'S STANDARD PROCEDURE TO HELP NATURALLY SKILLED RECRUITS GET PROMOTED TO B-RANK FASTER.
HOWEVER, SINCE YOU ALL ENLISTED DURING AN IRREGULAR PART OF THE SEASON, WE DIDN'T HAVE ENOUGH TIME FOR A PROBATIONARY PERIOD.
SO, HERE'S WHAT WE'LL DO.
I WANT YOU TO TAKE A QUICK SKILL TEST.
A TEST...?

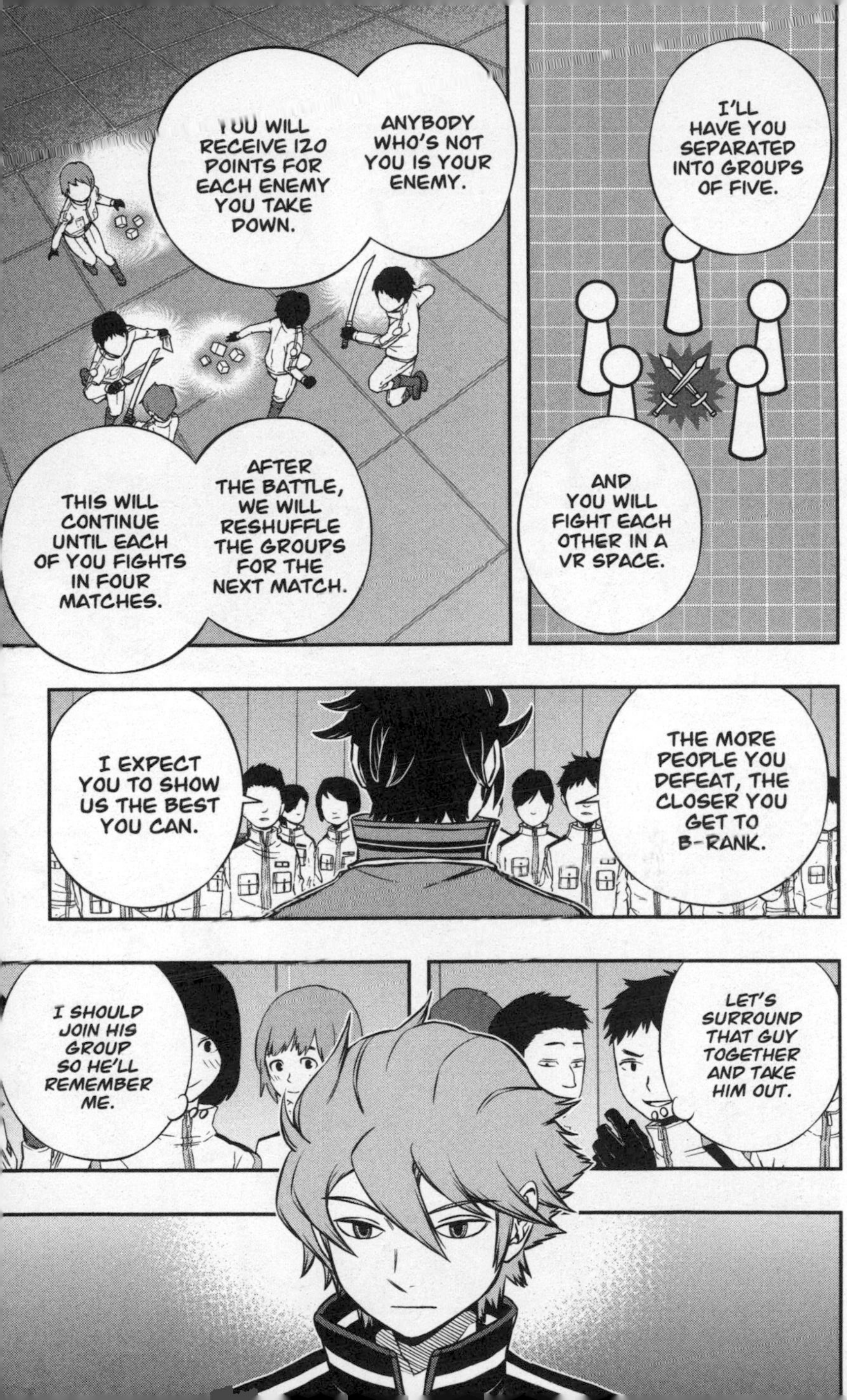
I'LL HAVE YOU SEPARATED INTO GROUPS OF FIVE.
AND YOU WILL FIGHT EACH OTHER IN A VR SPACE.
ANYBODY WHO'S NOT YOU IS YOUR ENEMY.
YOU WILL RECEIVE 120 POINTS FOR EACH ENEMY YOU TAKE DOWN.
AFTER THE BATTLE, WE WILL RESHUFFLE THE GROUPS FOR THE NEXT MATCH.
THIS WILL CONTINUE UNTIL EACH OF YOU FIGHTS IN FOUR MATCHES.
THE MORE PEOPLE YOU DEFEAT, THE CLOSER YOU GET TO B-RANK.
I EXPECT YOU TO SHOW US THE BEST YOU CAN.
LET'S SURROUND THAT GUY TOGETHER AND TAKE HIM OUT.
I SHOULD JOIN HIS GROUP SO HE'LL REMEMBER ME.

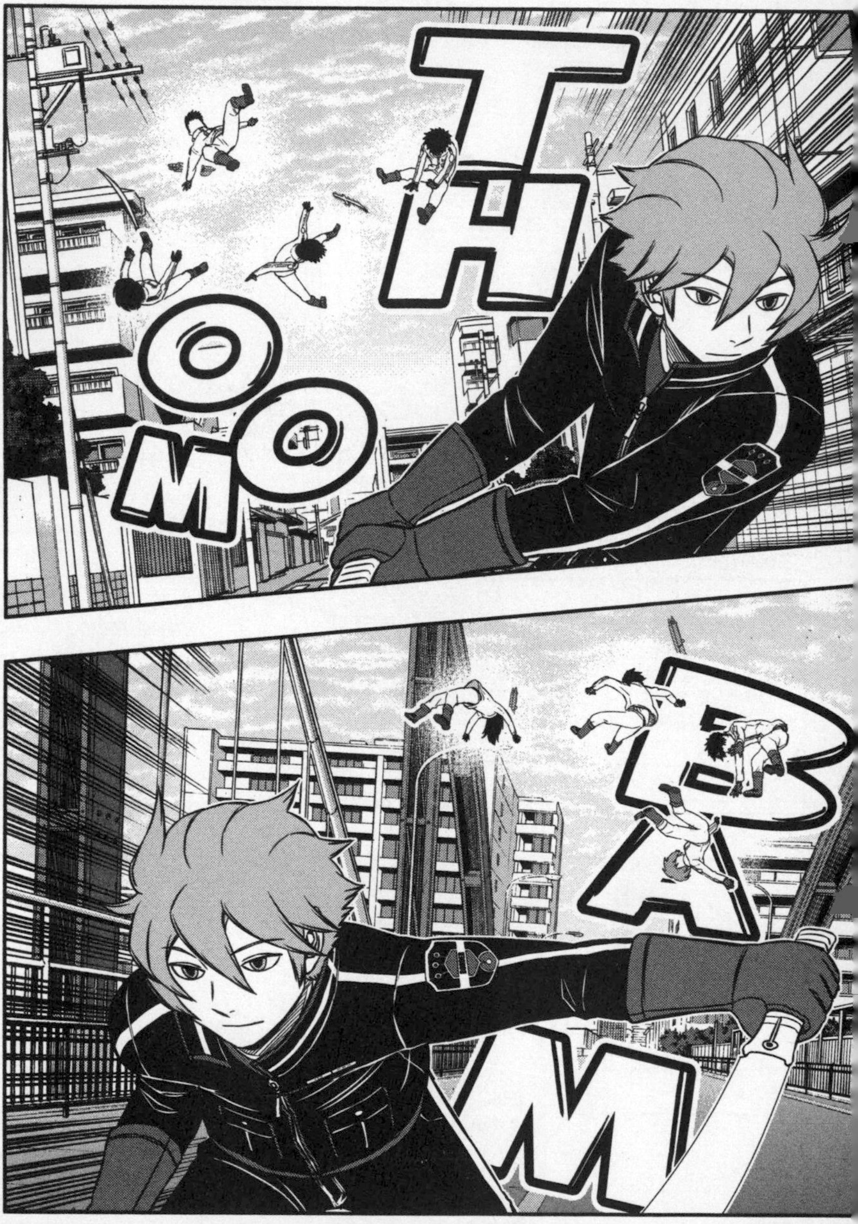
THOOM
BAM

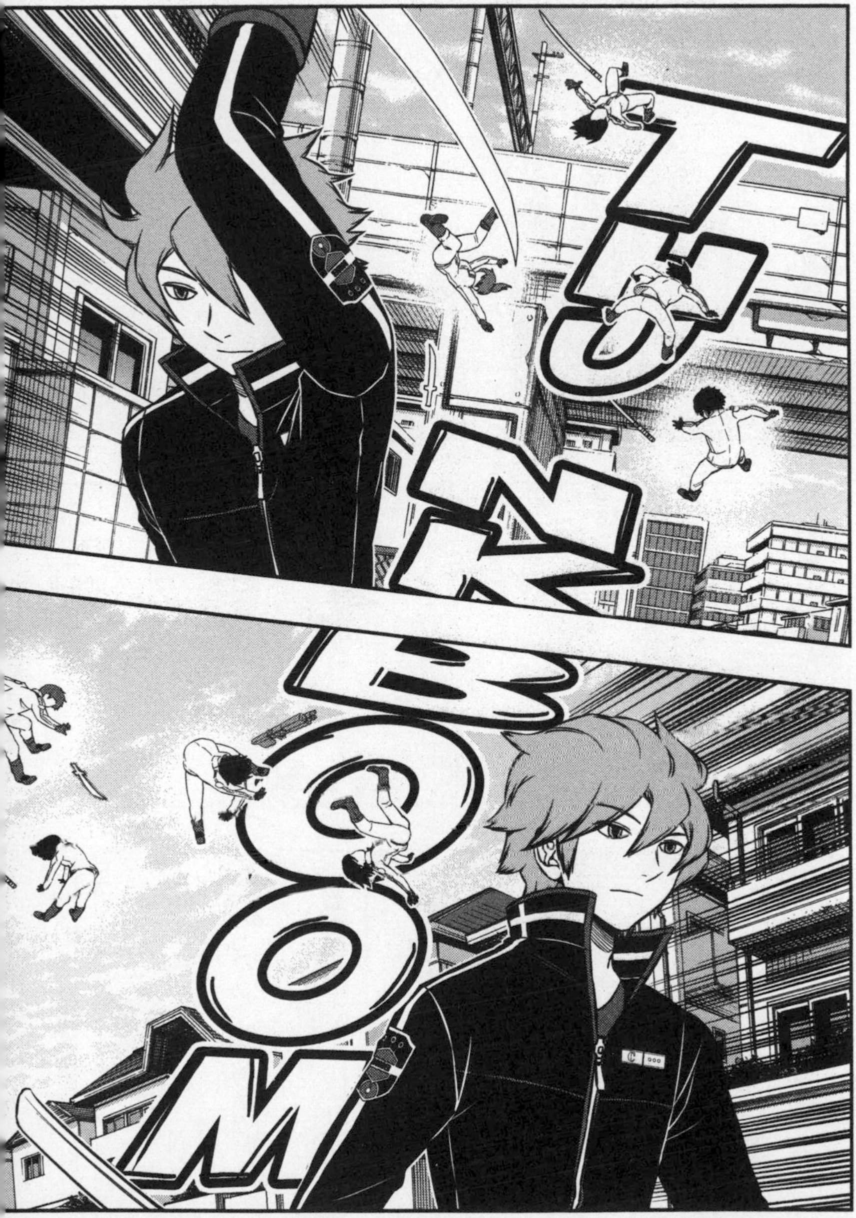
BOOM

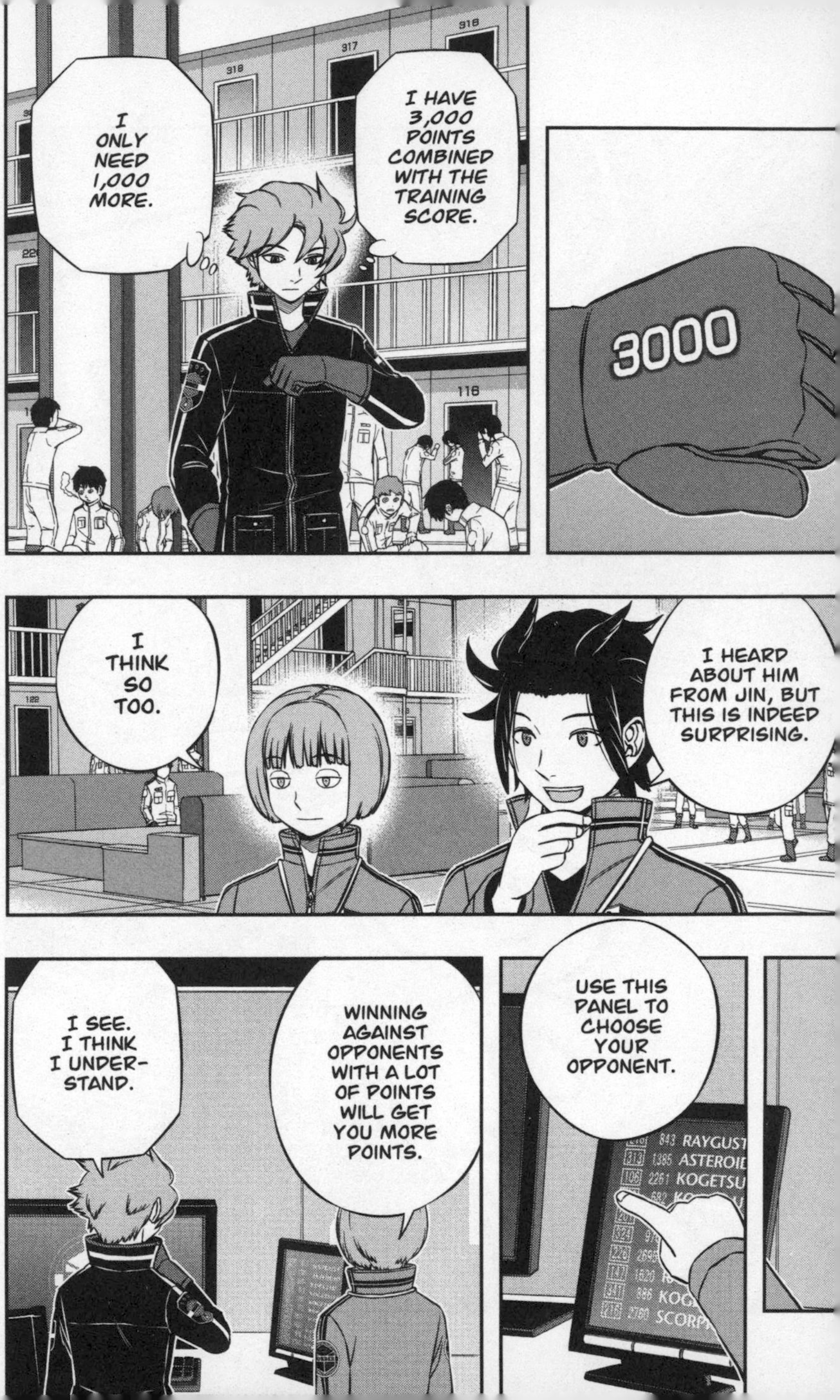

3000
I HAVE 3,000 POINTS COMBINED WITH THE TRAINING SCORE.
I ONLY NEED 1,000 MORE.
I HEARD ABOUT HIM FROM JIN, BUT THIS IS INDEED SURPRISING.
I THINK SO TOO.
USE THIS PANEL TO CHOOSE YOUR OPPONENT.
WINNING AGAINST OPPONENTS WITH A LOT OF POINTS WILL GET YOU MORE POINTS.
I SEE. I THINK I UNDER-STAND.

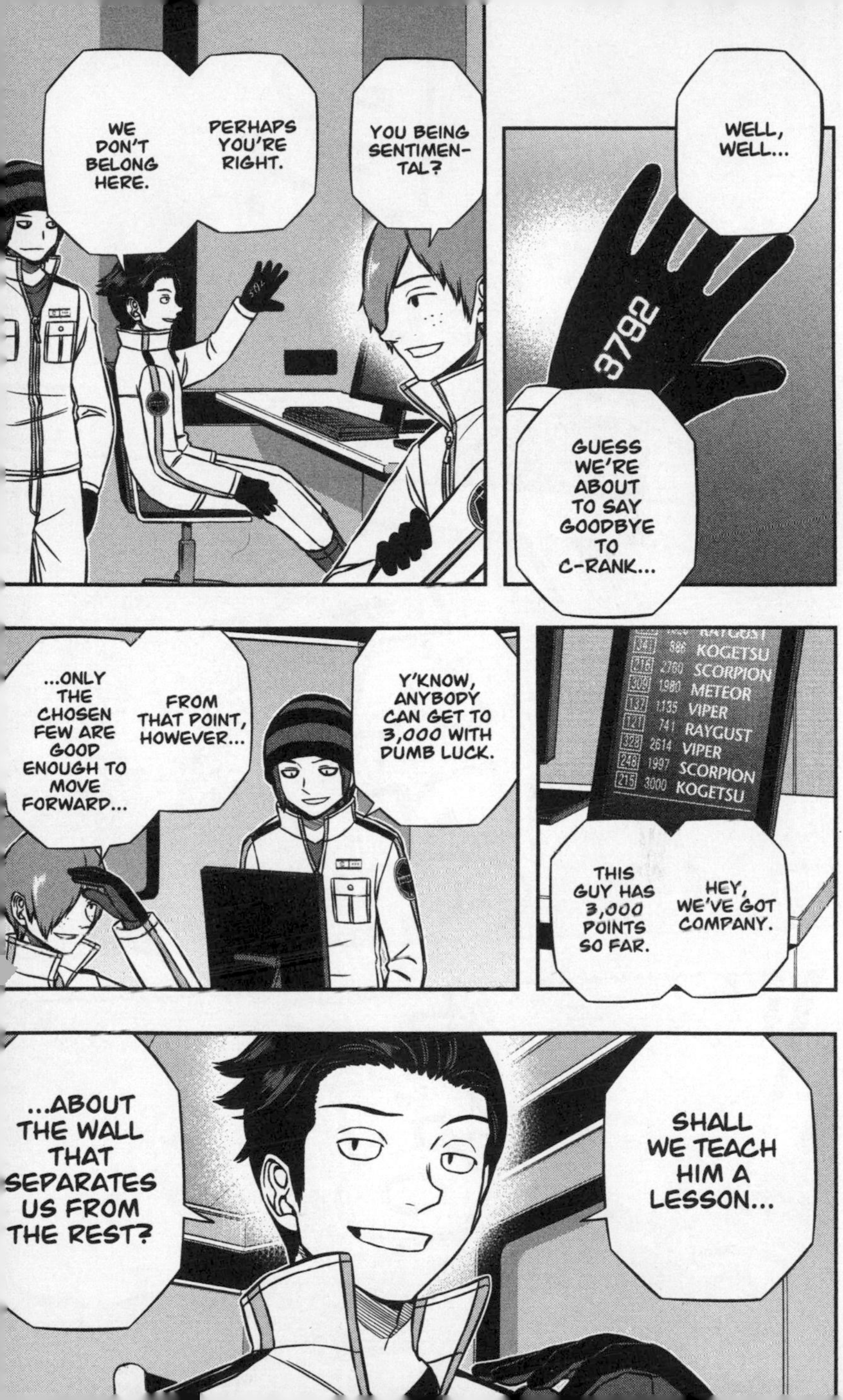
WELL, WELL...
3792
GUESS WE'RE ABOUT TO SAY GOODBYE TO C-RANK...
YOU BEING SENTIMEN-TAL?
PERHAPS YOU'RE RIGHT.
WE DON'T BELONG HERE.
341 986 KOGETSU
216 2760 SCORPION
309 1980 METEOR
137 1135 VIPER
121 741 RAYGUST
328 2614 VIPER
248 1997 SCORPION
215 3000 KOGETSU
HEY, WE'VE GOT COMPANY.
THIS GUY HAS 3,000 POINTS SO FAR.
Y'KNOW, ANYBODY CAN GET TO 3,000 WITH DUMB LUCK.
FROM THAT POINT, HOWEVER...
...ONLY THE CHOSEN FEW ARE GOOD ENOUGH TO MOVE FORWARD...
SHALL WE TEACH HIM A LESSON...
...ABOUT THE WALL THAT SEPARATES US FROM THE REST?

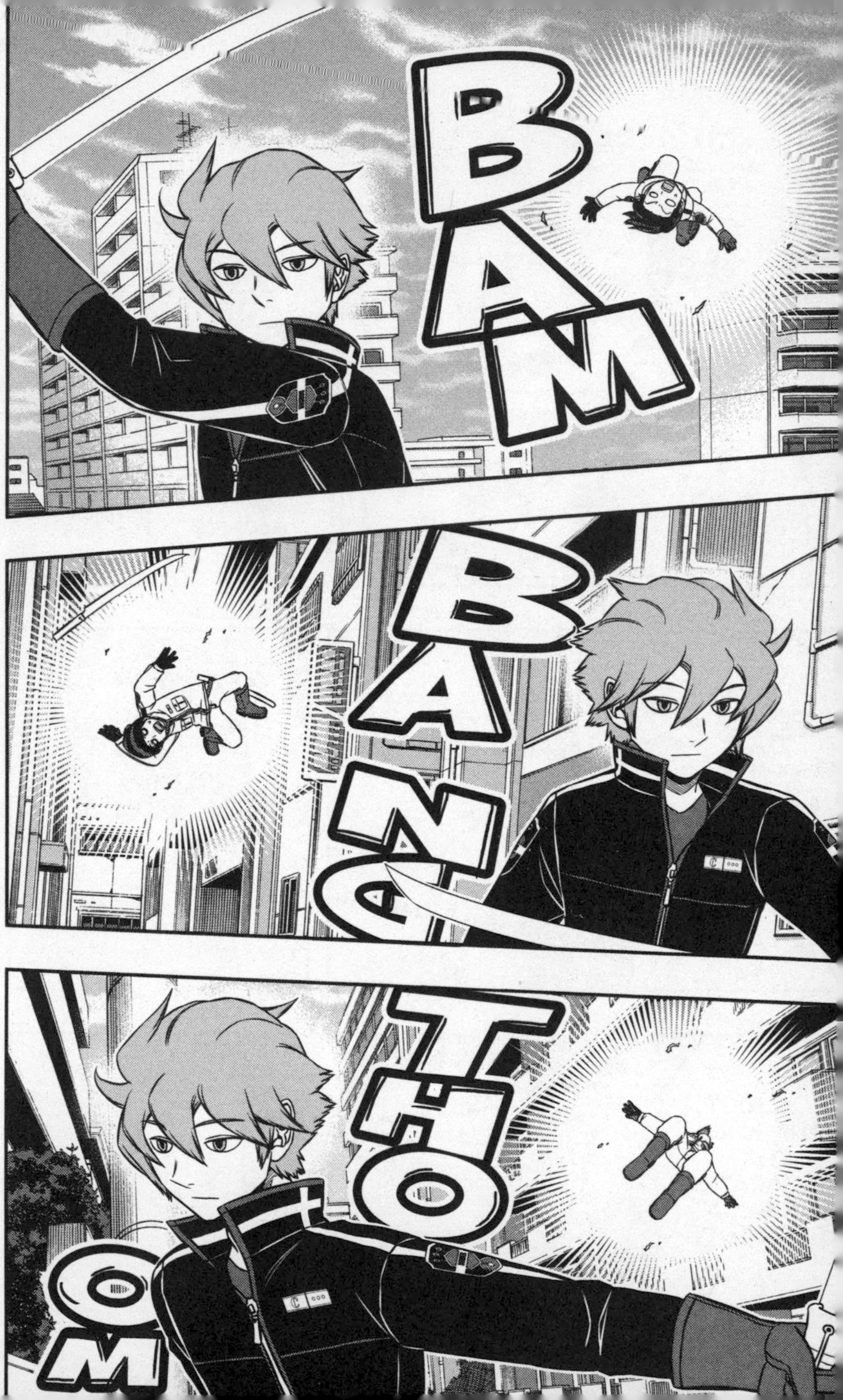
BAM
BANG
THOOM

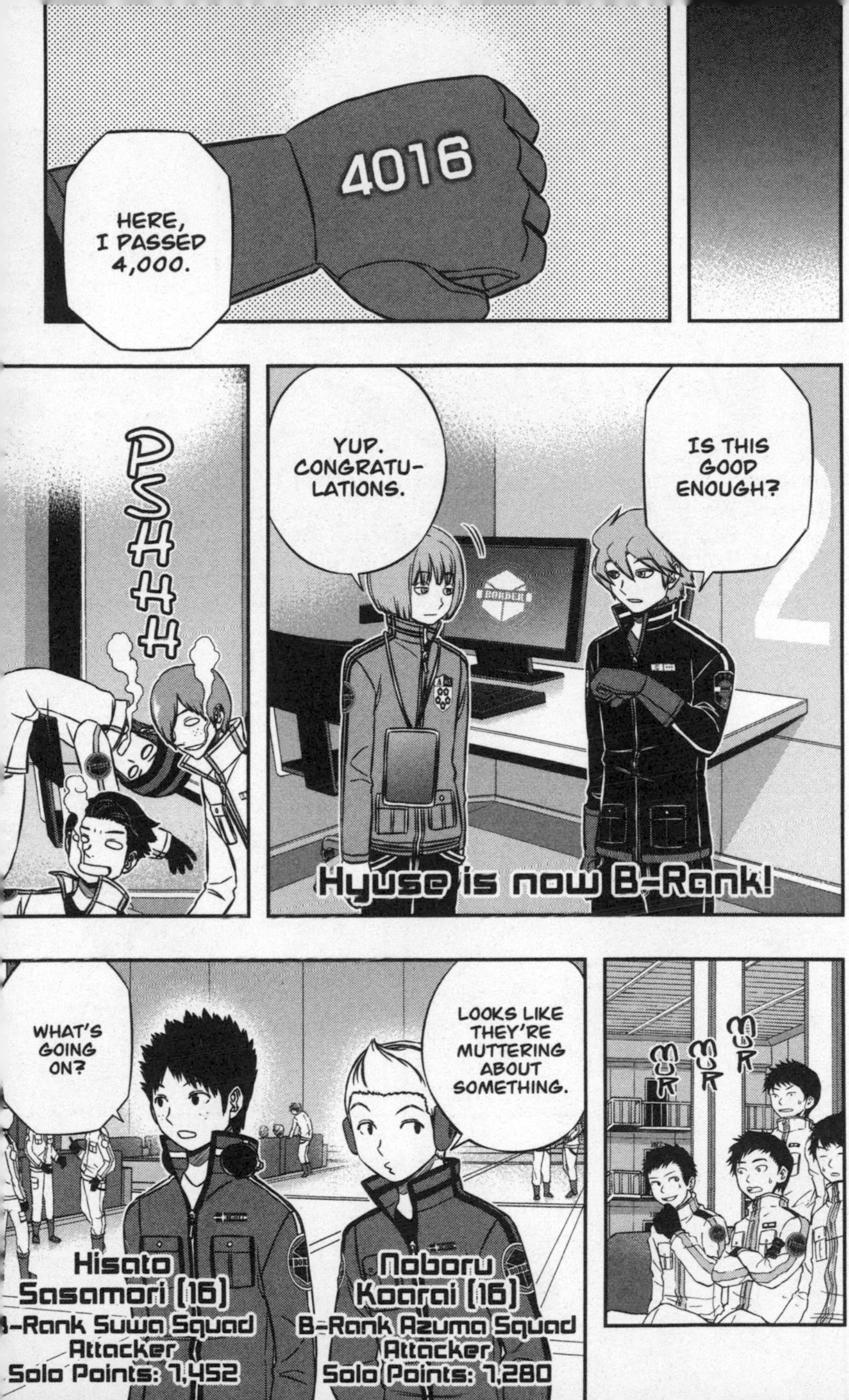
4016
HERE, I PASSED 4,000.
IS THIS GOOD ENOUGH?
YUP. CONGRATULATIONS.
Hyuse is now B-Rank!
PSHHHH
MUR MUR MUR
LOOKS LIKE THEY'RE MUTTERING ABOUT SOMETHING.
Noboru Koarai (16) B-Rank Azuma Squad Attacker Solo Points: 7,280
WHAT'S GOING ON?
Hisato Sasamori (16) B-Rank Suwa Squad Attacker Solo Points: 7,452

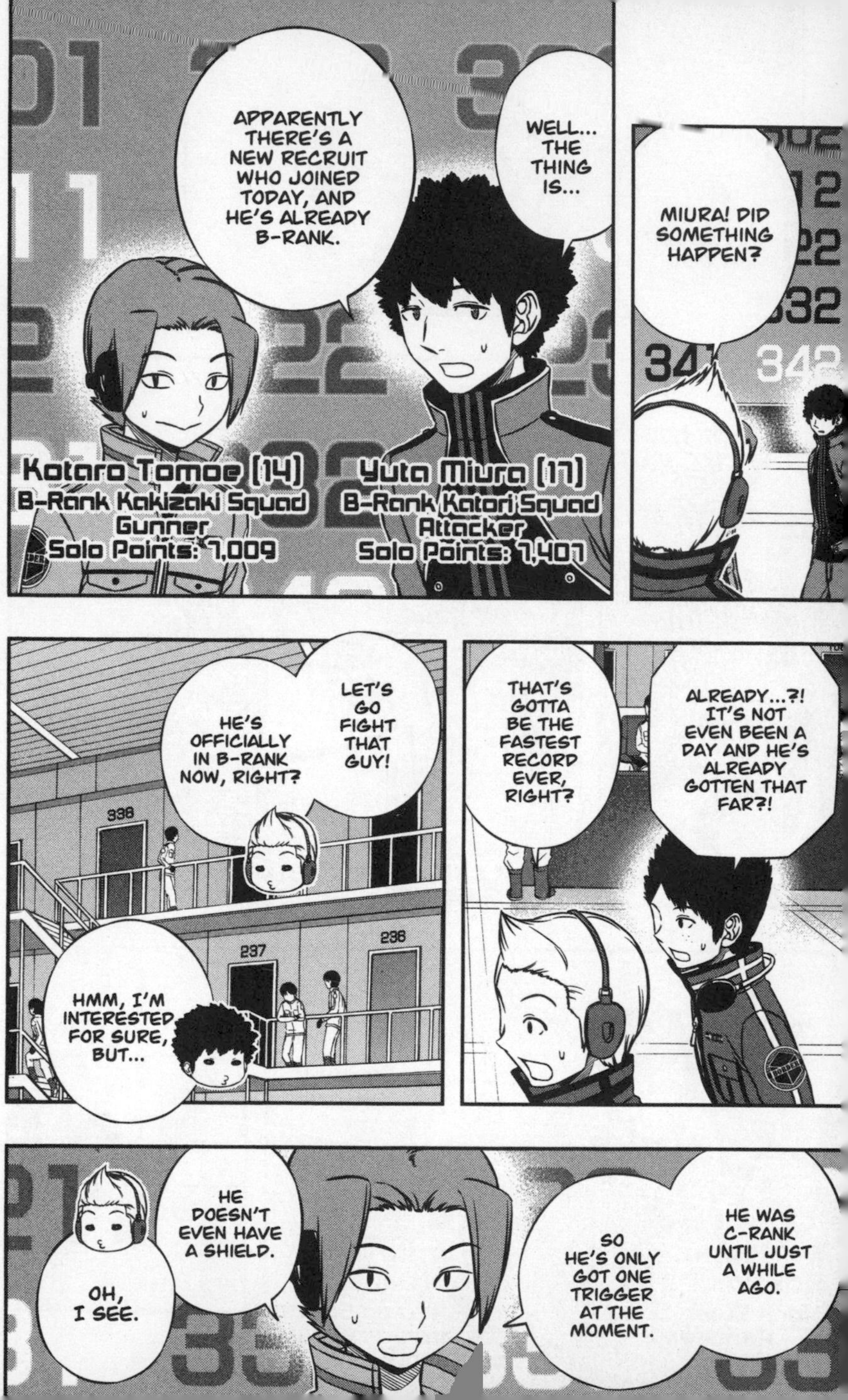
MIURA! DID SOMETHING HAPPEN?
WELL... THE THING IS...
APPARENTLY THERE'S A NEW RECRUIT WHO JOINED TODAY, AND HE'S ALREADY B-RANK.
Yuta Miura (17)
B-Rank Katori Squad
Attacker
Solo Points: 7,401
Kotaro Tomoe (14)
B-Rank Kakizaki Squad
Gunner
Solo Points: 7,009
ALREADY...?! IT'S NOT EVEN BEEN A DAY AND HE'S ALREADY GOTTEN THAT FAR?!
THAT'S GOTTA BE THE FASTEST RECORD EVER, RIGHT?
LET'S GO FIGHT THAT GUY!
HE'S OFFICIALLY IN B-RANK NOW, RIGHT?
HMM, I'M INTERESTED FOR SURE, BUT...
HE WAS C-RANK UNTIL JUST A WHILE AGO.
SO HE'S ONLY GOT ONE TRIGGER AT THE MOMENT.
HE DOESN'T EVEN HAVE A SHIELD.
OH, I SEE.

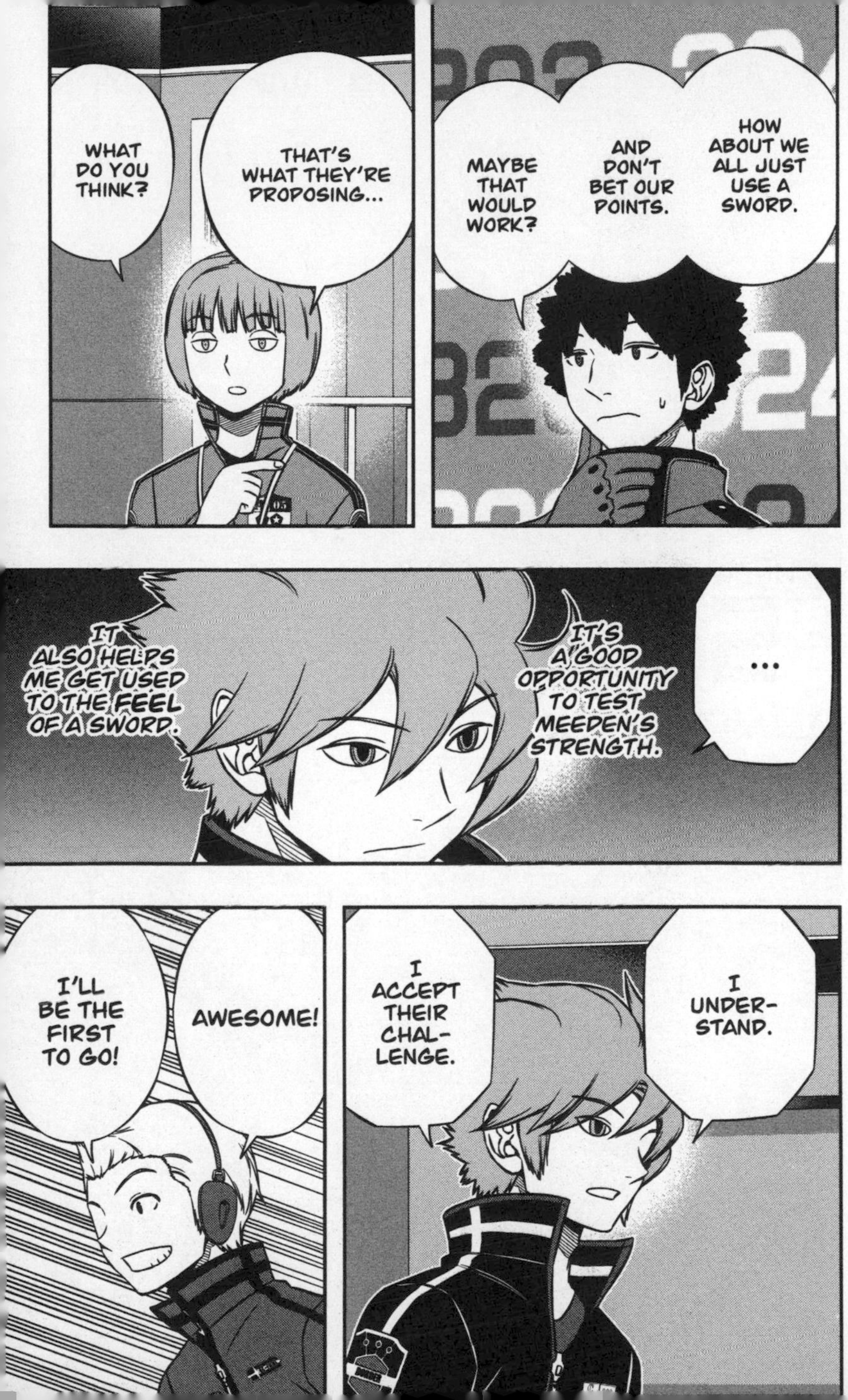
HOW ABOUT WE ALL JUST USE A SWORD.
AND DON'T BET OUR POINTS.
MAYBE THAT WOULD WORK?
THAT'S WHAT THEY'RE PROPOSING...
WHAT DO YOU THINK?
...
IT'S A GOOD OPPORTUNITY TO TEST MEEDEN'S STRENGTH.
IT ALSO HELPS ME GET USED TO THE FEEL OF A SWORD.
I UNDER-STAND.
I ACCEPT THEIR CHAL-LENGE.
AWESOME!
I'LL BE THE FIRST TO GO!

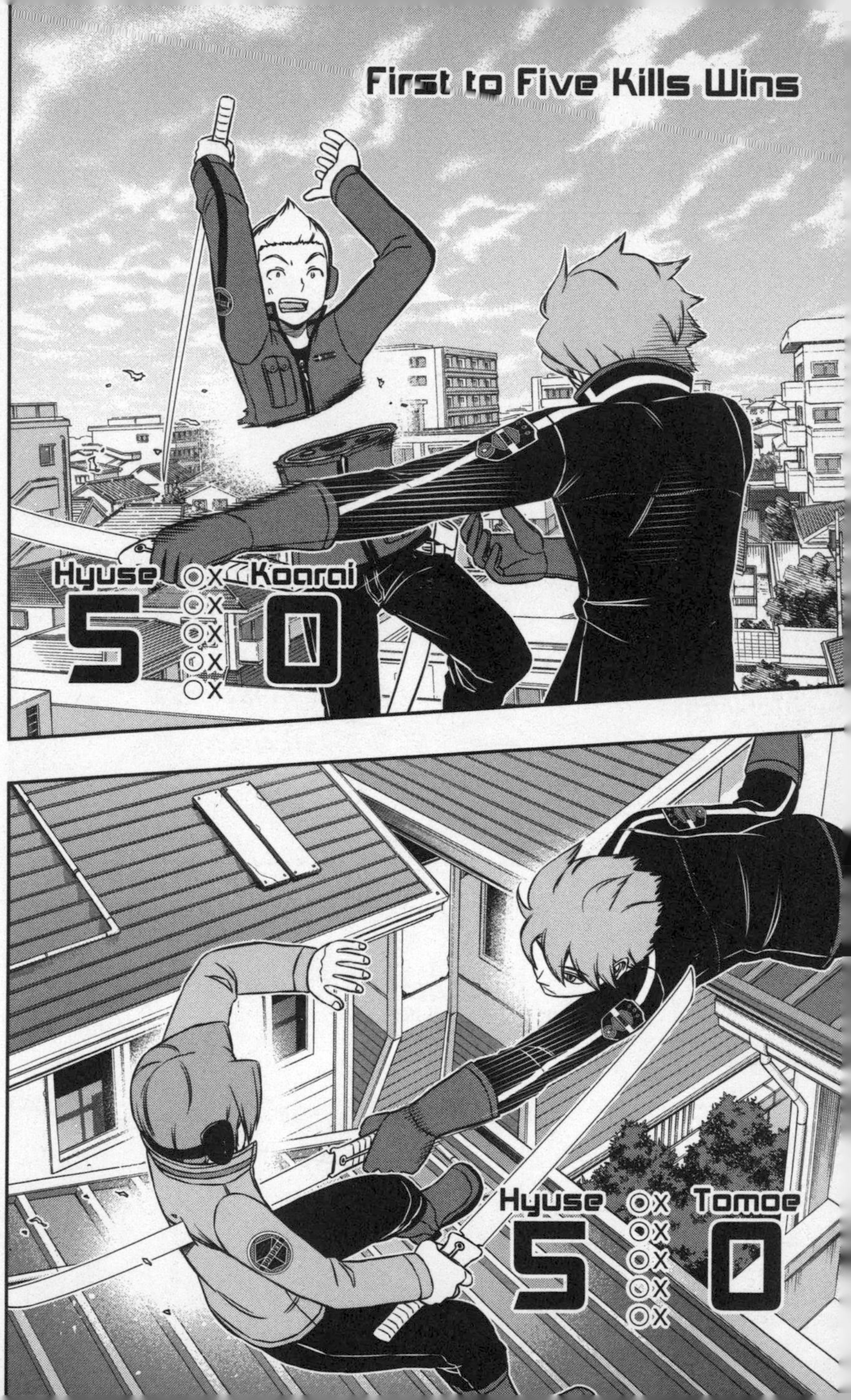
First to Five Kills Wins
Hyuse
5
Koarai
0
Hyuse
5
Tomoe
0

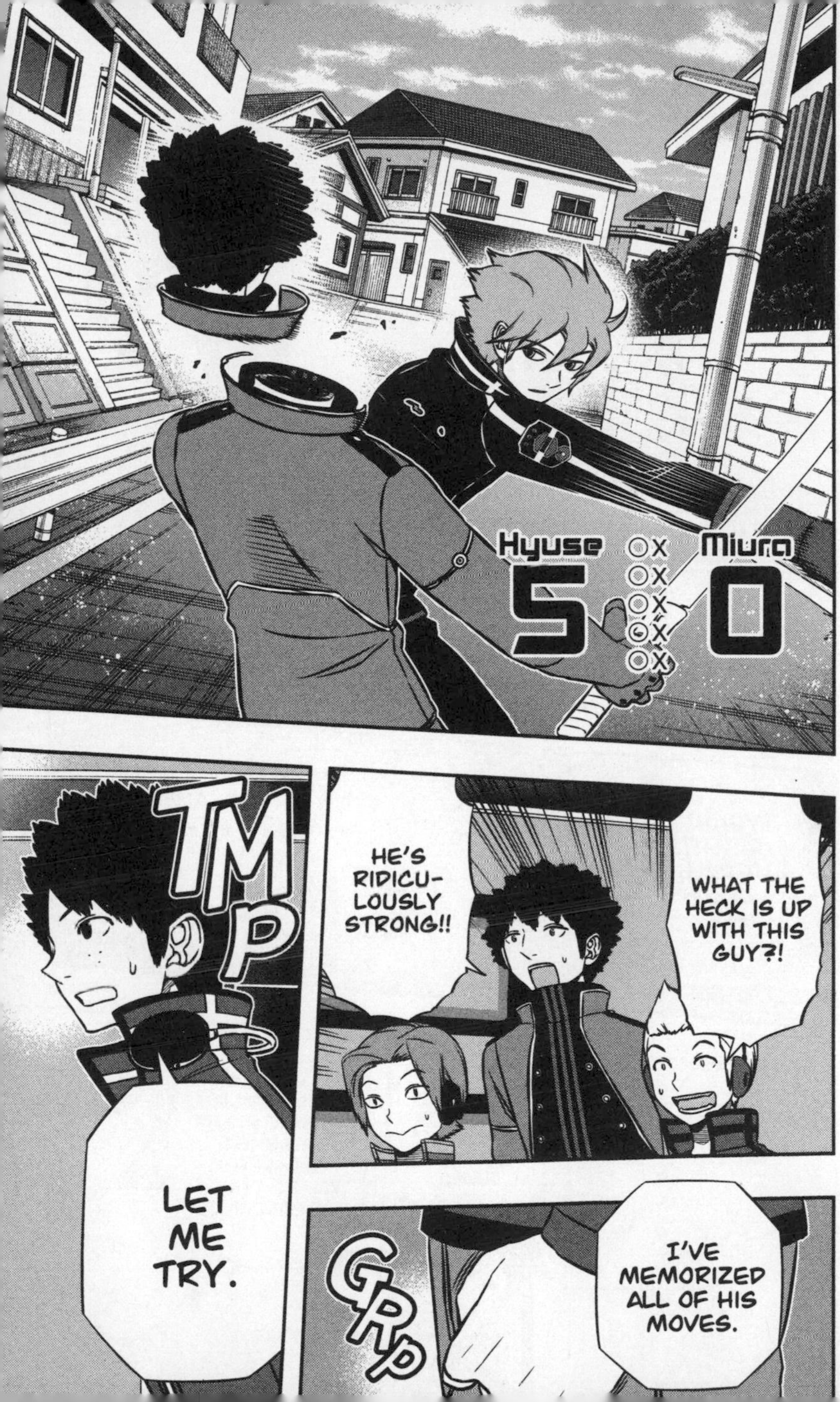
Hyuse
5
Miura
0
WHAT THE HECK IS UP WITH THIS GUY?!
HE'S RIDICU-LOUSLY STRONG!!
I'VE MEMORIZED ALL OF HIS MOVES.
GRP
TMP
LET ME TRY.

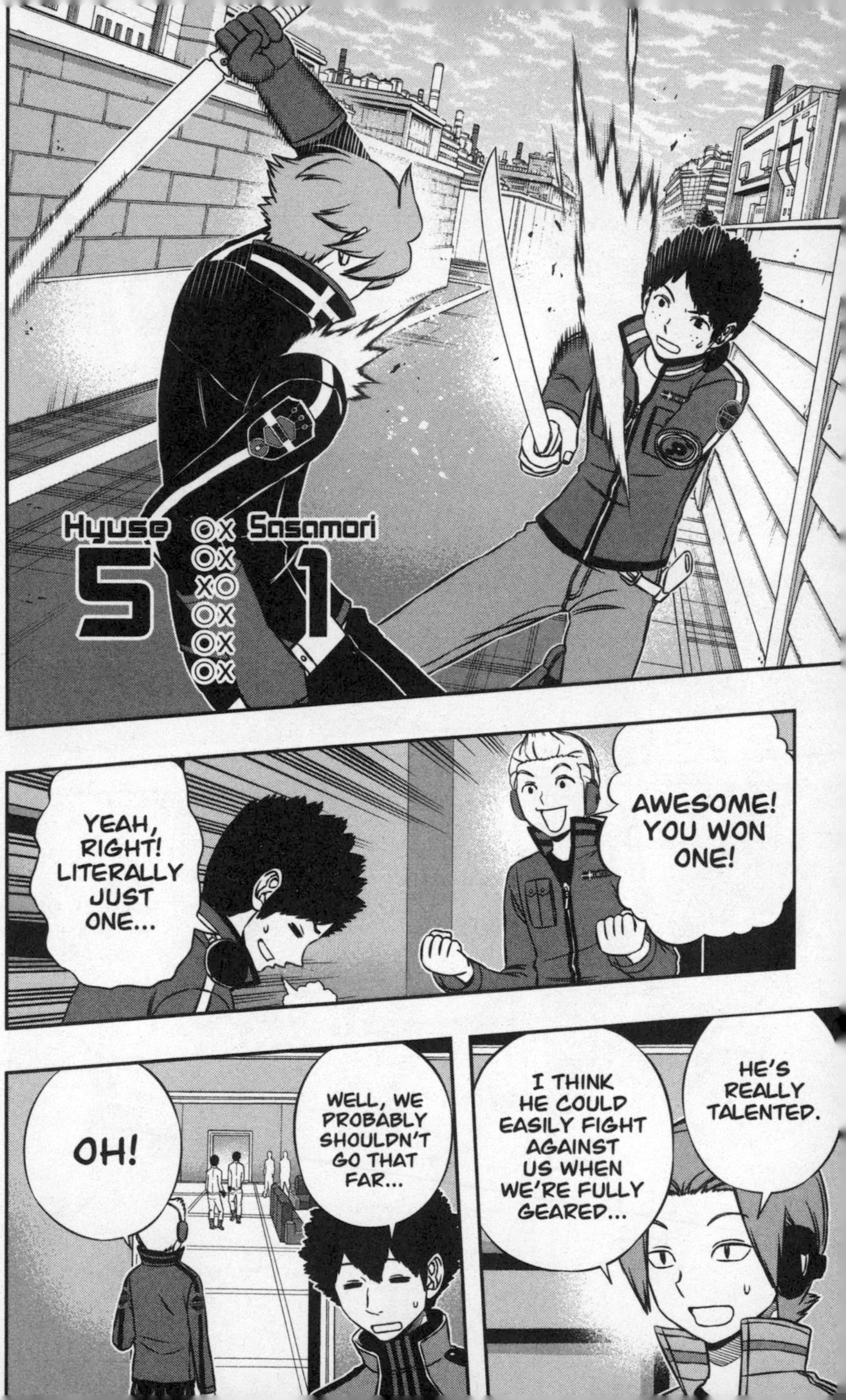
Hyuse
Sasamori
5
1
AWESOME! YOU WON ONE!
YEAH, RIGHT! LITERALLY JUST ONE...
HE'S REALLY TALENTED.
I THINK HE COULD EASILY FIGHT AGAINST US WHEN WE'RE FULLY GEARED...
WELL, WE PROBABLY SHOULDN'T GO THAT FAR...
OH!

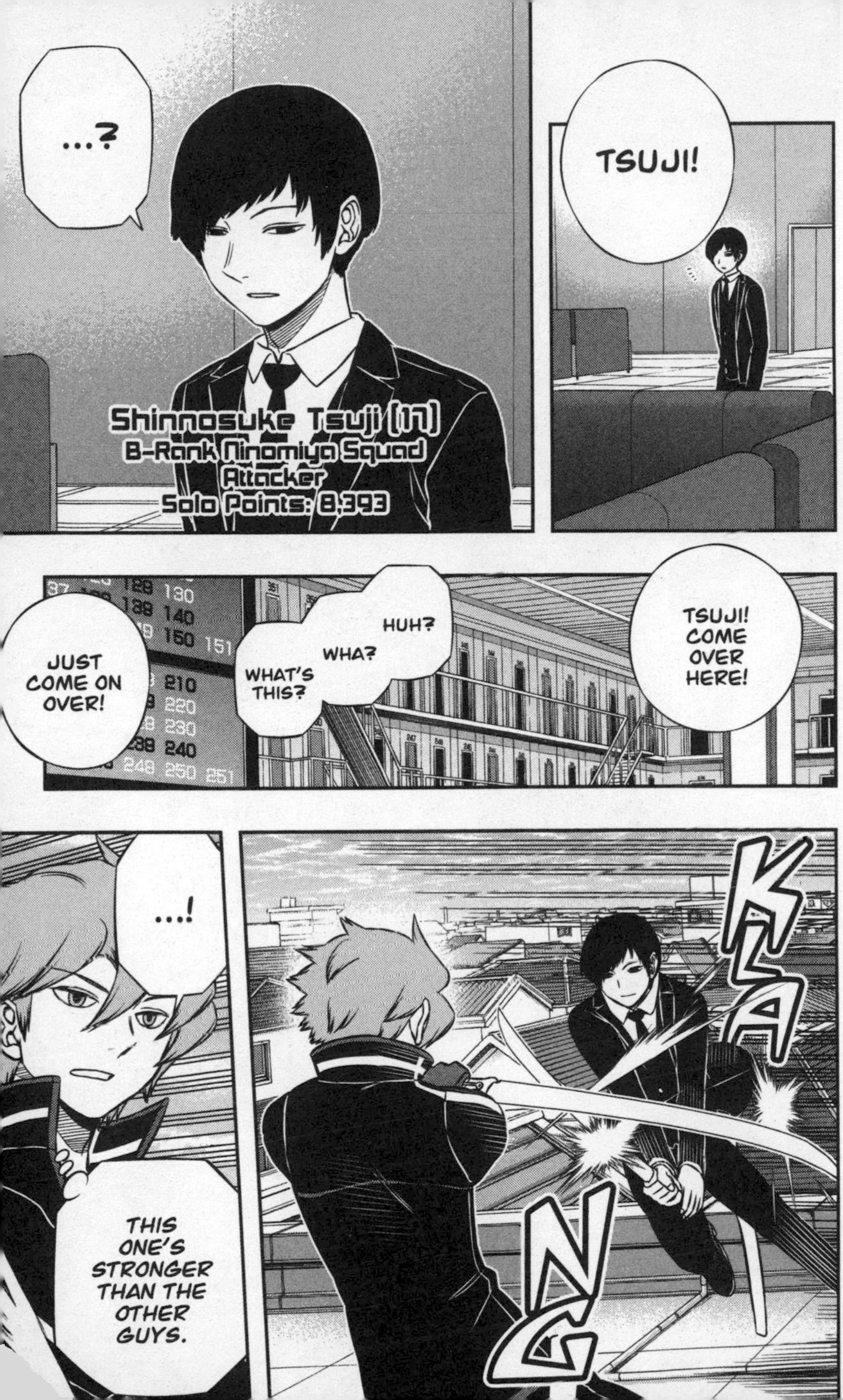
TSUJI!
...?
Shinnosuke Tsuji (17)
B-Rank Ninomiya Squad
Attacker
Solo Points: 8,393
TSUJI! COME OVER HERE!
HUH?
WHA?
WHAT'S THIS?
JUST COME ON OVER!
KLANG
...!
THIS ONE'S STRONGER THAN THE OTHER GUYS.

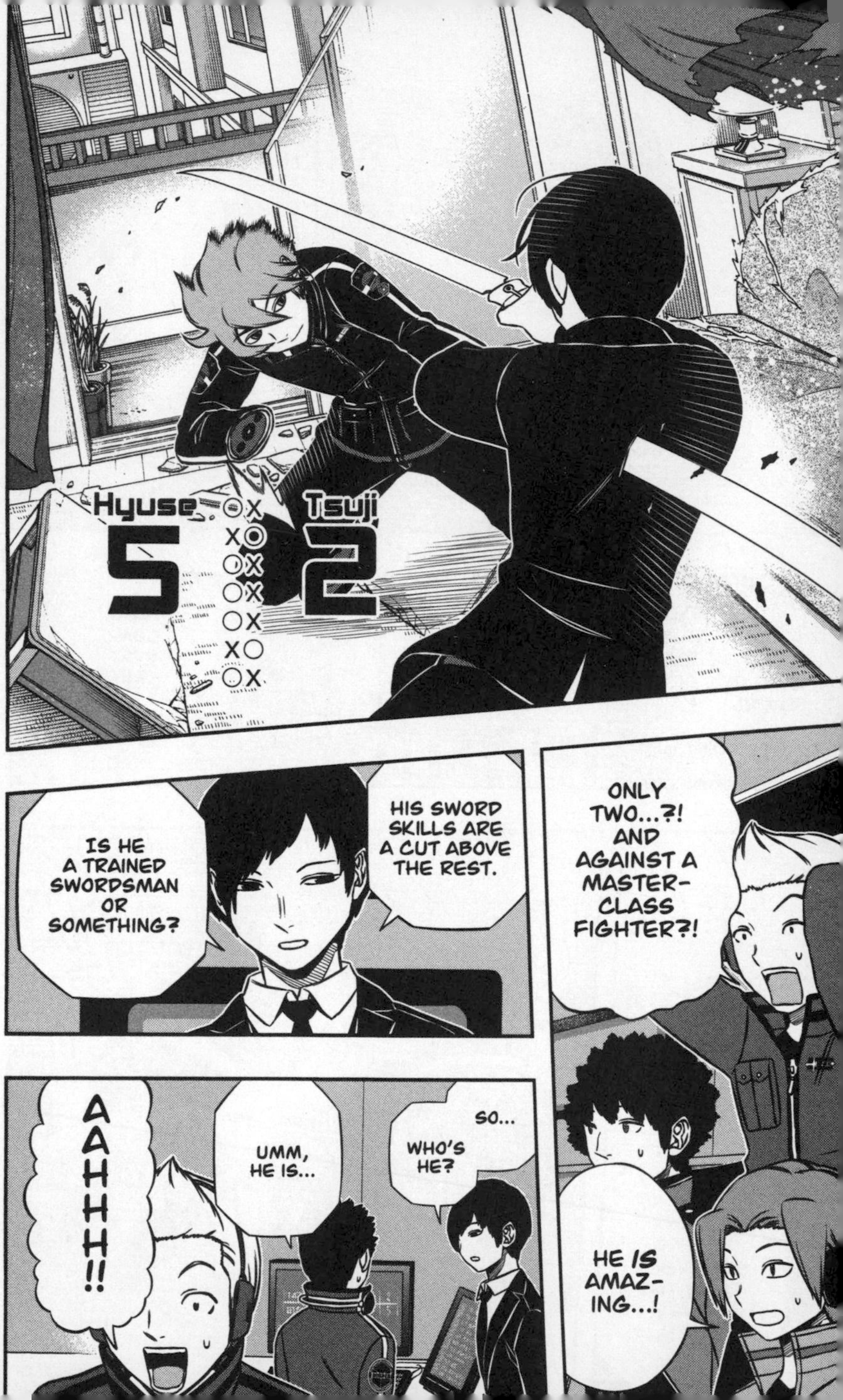

Hyuse
5
Tsuji
2
○X
X○
○X
○X
○X
X○
○X
ONLY TWO...?! AND AGAINST A MASTER-CLASS FIGHTER?!
HE IS AMAZING...!
HIS SWORD SKILLS ARE A CUT ABOVE THE REST.
IS HE A TRAINED SWORDSMAN OR SOMETHING?
SO...
WHO'S HE?
UMM, HE IS...
AAHHHH!!

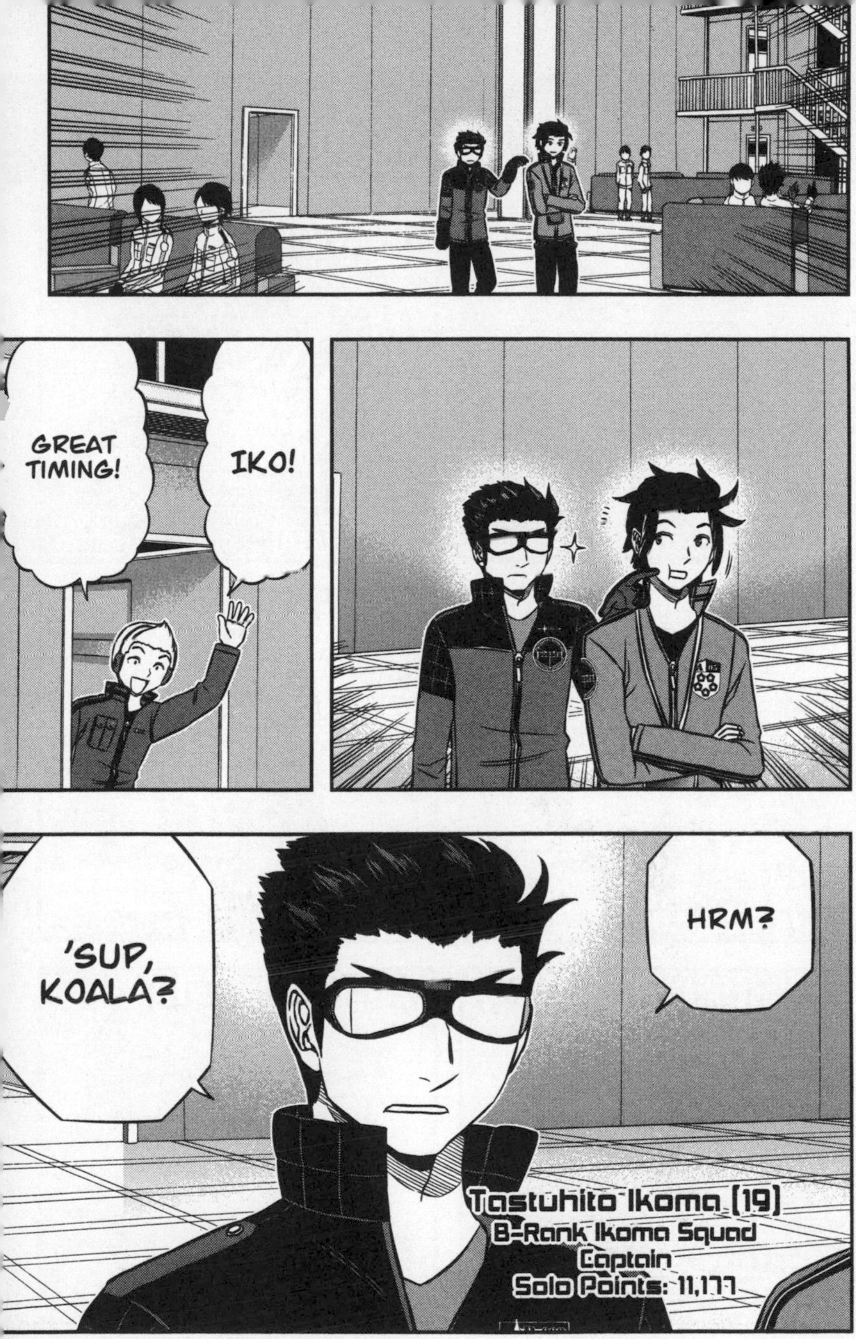
IKO!
GREAT TIMING!
HRM?
'SUP, KOALA?
Tastuhito Ikoma (19)
B-Rank Ikoma Squad
Captain
Solo Points: 11,177

Second Popularity Poll Results! (Continued)

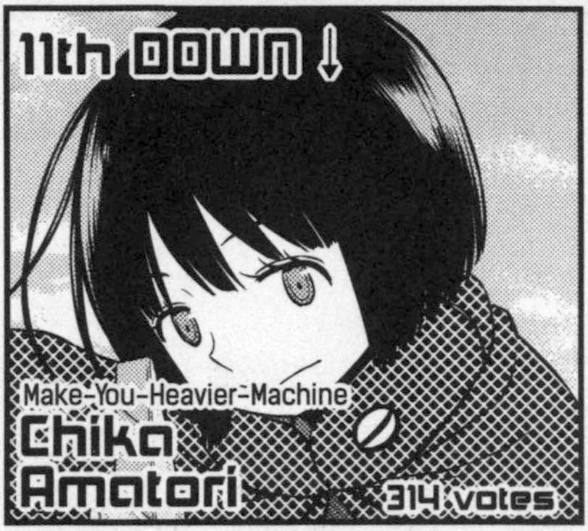
11th DOWN ↓
Make-You-Heavier-Machine
Chika Amatori
314 votes

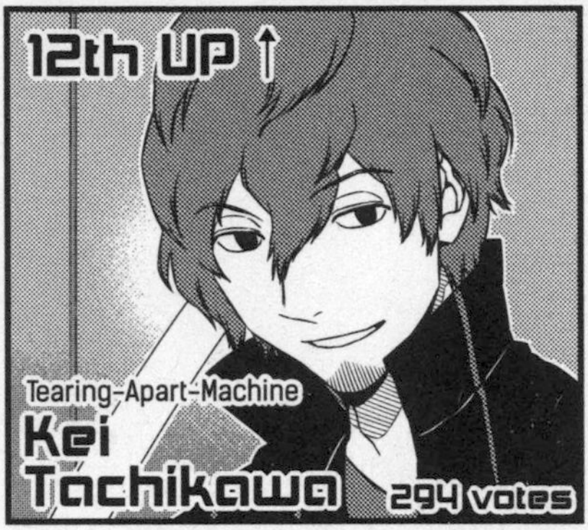
12th UP ↑
Tearing-Apart-Machine
Kei Tachikawa
294 votes

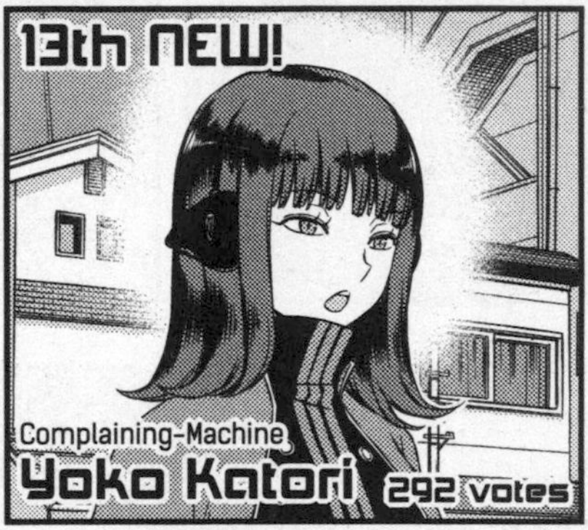
13th NEW!
Complaining-Machine
Yoko Katori
292 votes

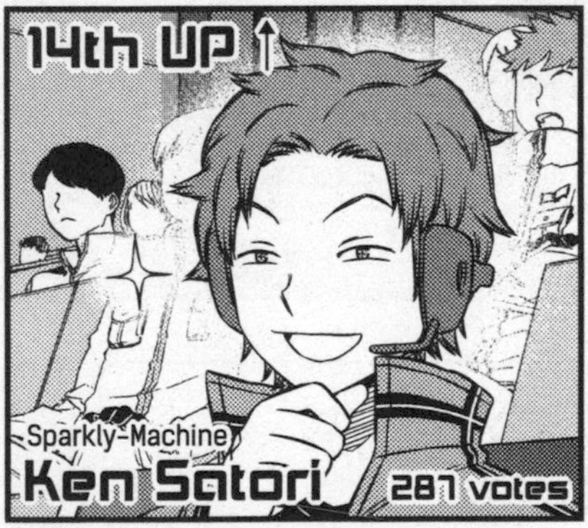
14th UP ↑
Sparkly-Machine
Ken Satori
287 votes

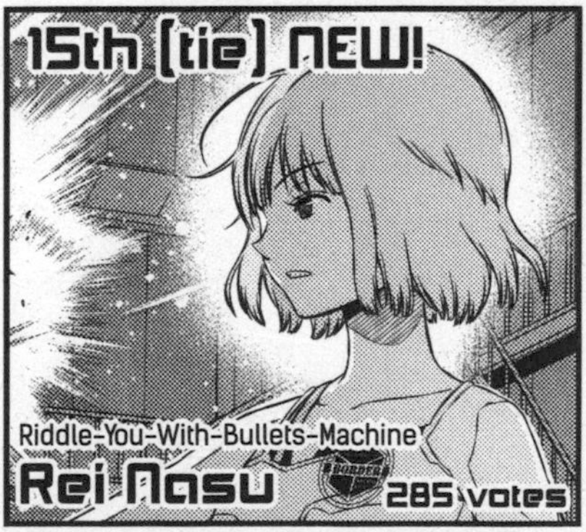
15th (tie) NEW!
Riddle-You-With-Bullets-Machine
Rei Nasu
285 votes

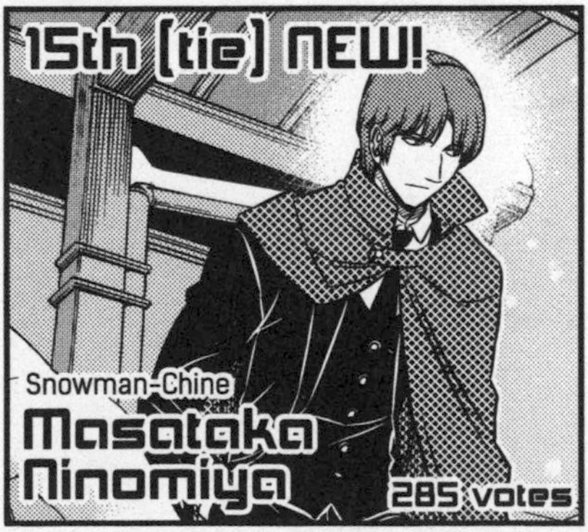
15th (tie) NEW!
Snowman-Chine
Masataka Ninomiya
285 votes

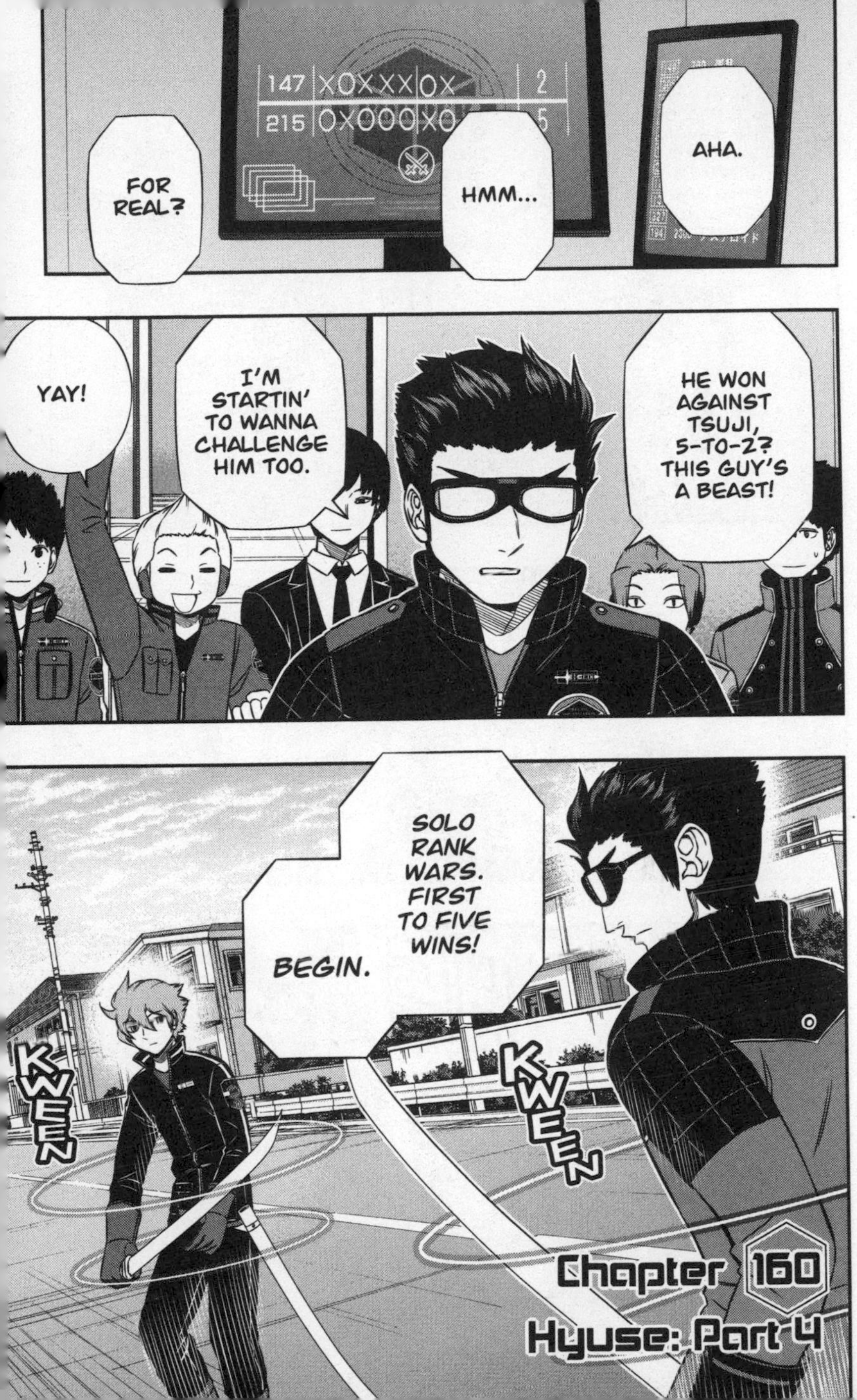
147 XOXXXOX 2
215 OXOOOXO 5
AHA.
HMM...
FOR REAL?
HE WON AGAINST TSUJI, 5-TO-2? THIS GUY'S A BEAST!
I'M STARTIN' TO WANNA CHALLENGE HIM TOO.
YAY!
SOLO RANK WARS. FIRST TO FIVE WINS!
BEGIN.
KWEEN
KWEEN
Chapter 160
Hyuse: Part 4

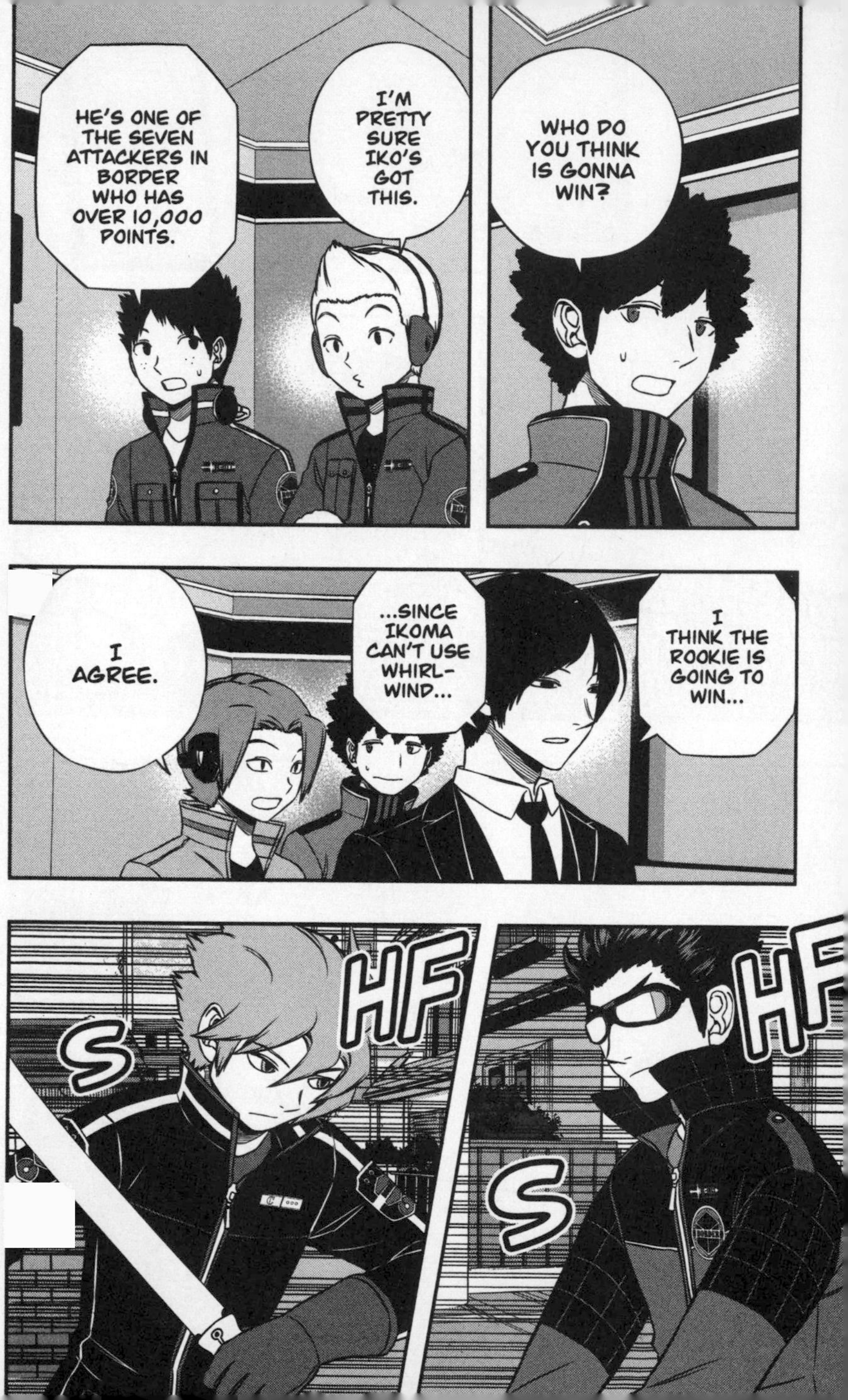
WHO DO YOU THINK IS GONNA WIN?
I'M PRETTY SURE IKO'S GOT THIS.
HE'S ONE OF THE SEVEN ATTACKERS IN BORDER WHO HAS OVER 10,000 POINTS.
I THINK THE ROOKIE IS GOING TO WIN...
...SINCE IKOMA CAN'T USE WHIRL-WIND...
I AGREE.
HF
S
HF
S

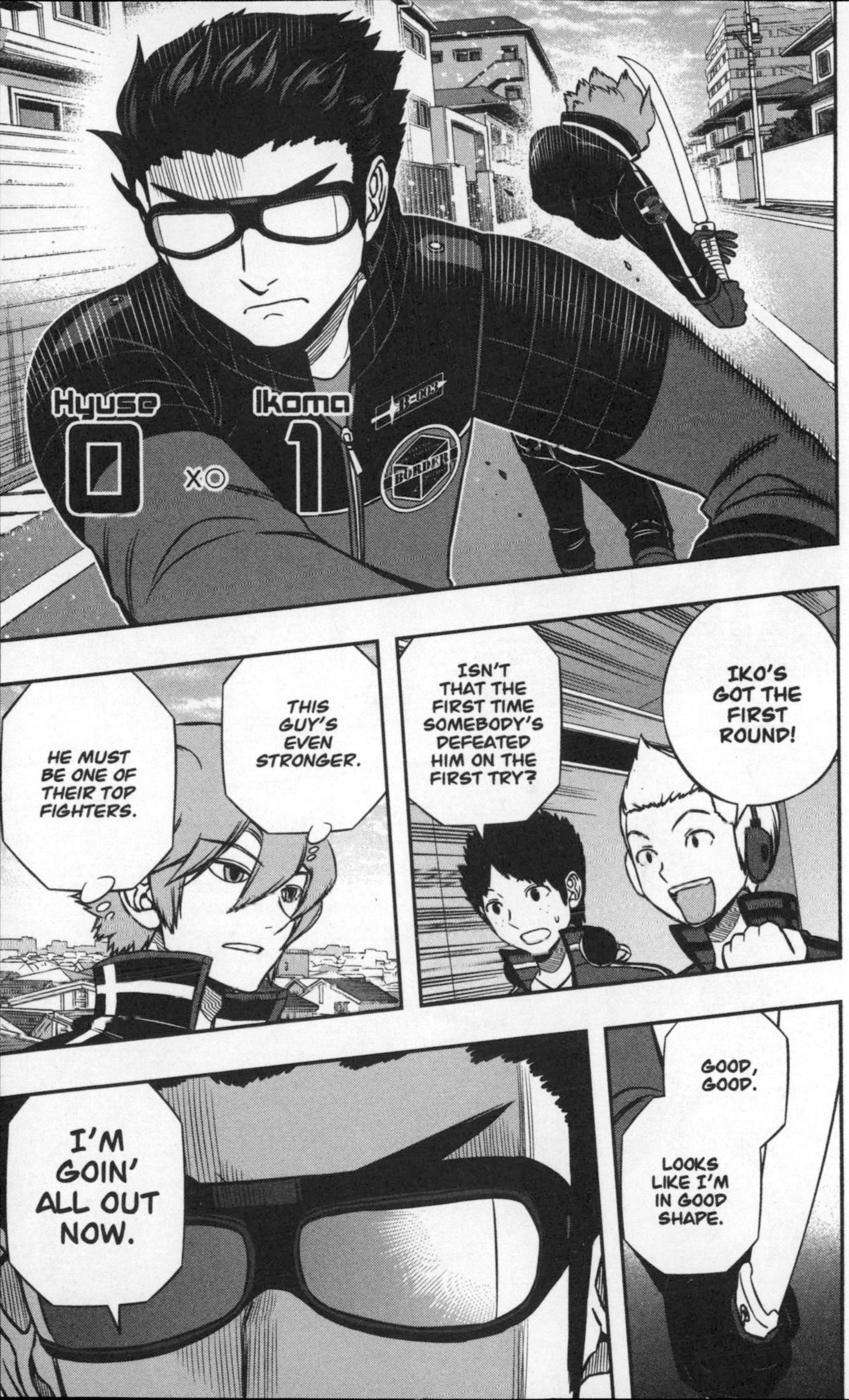
Hyuse
0
XO
Ikoma
1
BORDER
IKO'S GOT THE FIRST ROUND!
ISN'T THAT THE FIRST TIME SOMEBODY'S DEFEATED HIM ON THE FIRST TRY?
THIS GUY'S EVEN STRONGER.
HE MUST BE ONE OF THEIR TOP FIGHTERS.
GOOD, GOOD.
LOOKS LIKE I'M IN GOOD SHAPE.
I'M GOIN' ALL OUT NOW.

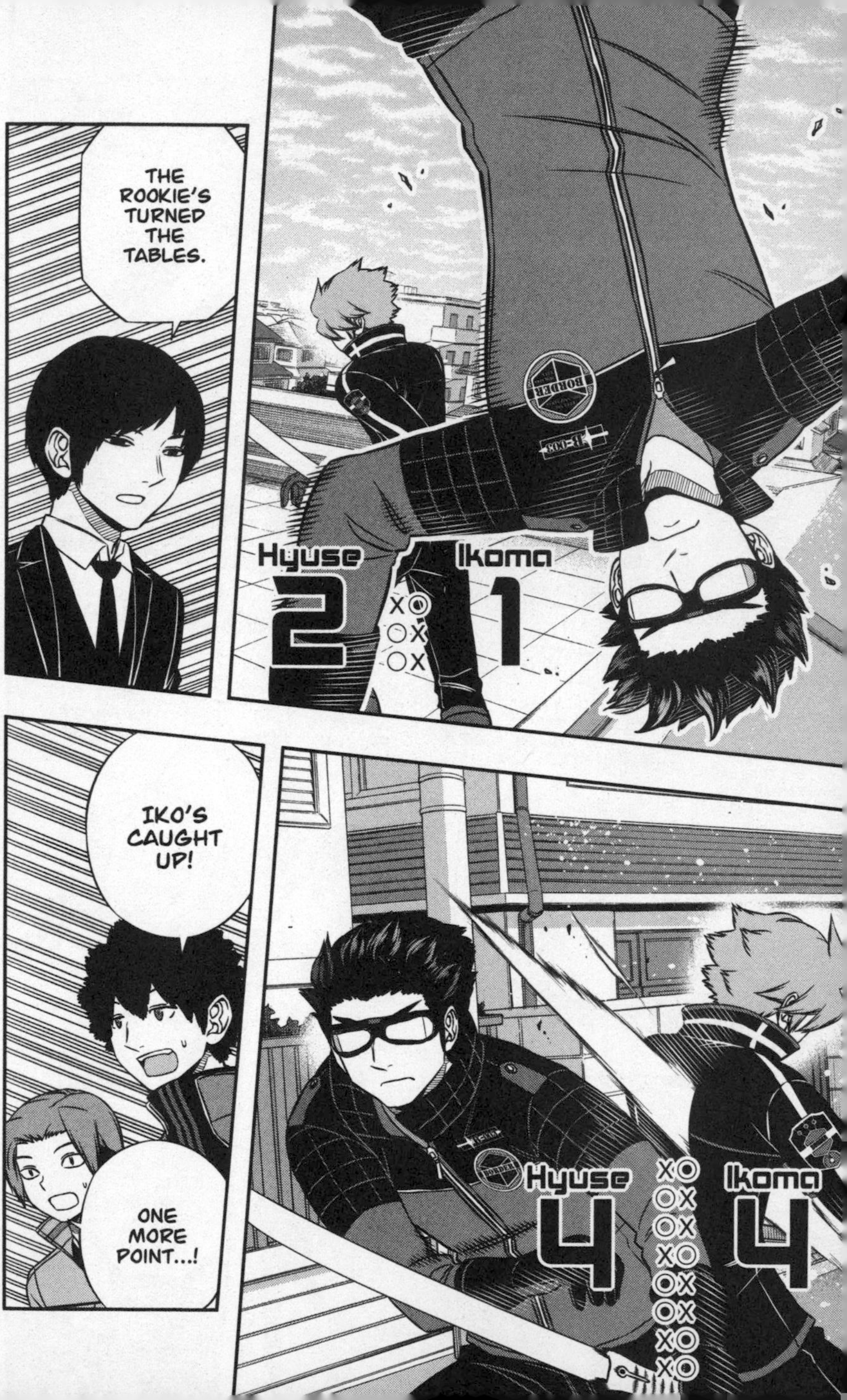
Hyuse
2
Ikoma
1
XO
OX
OX
THE ROOKIE'S TURNED THE TABLES.
Hyuse
4
Ikoma
4
XO
OX
OX
XO
OX
OX
XO
XO
IKO'S CAUGHT UP!
ONE MORE POINT...!

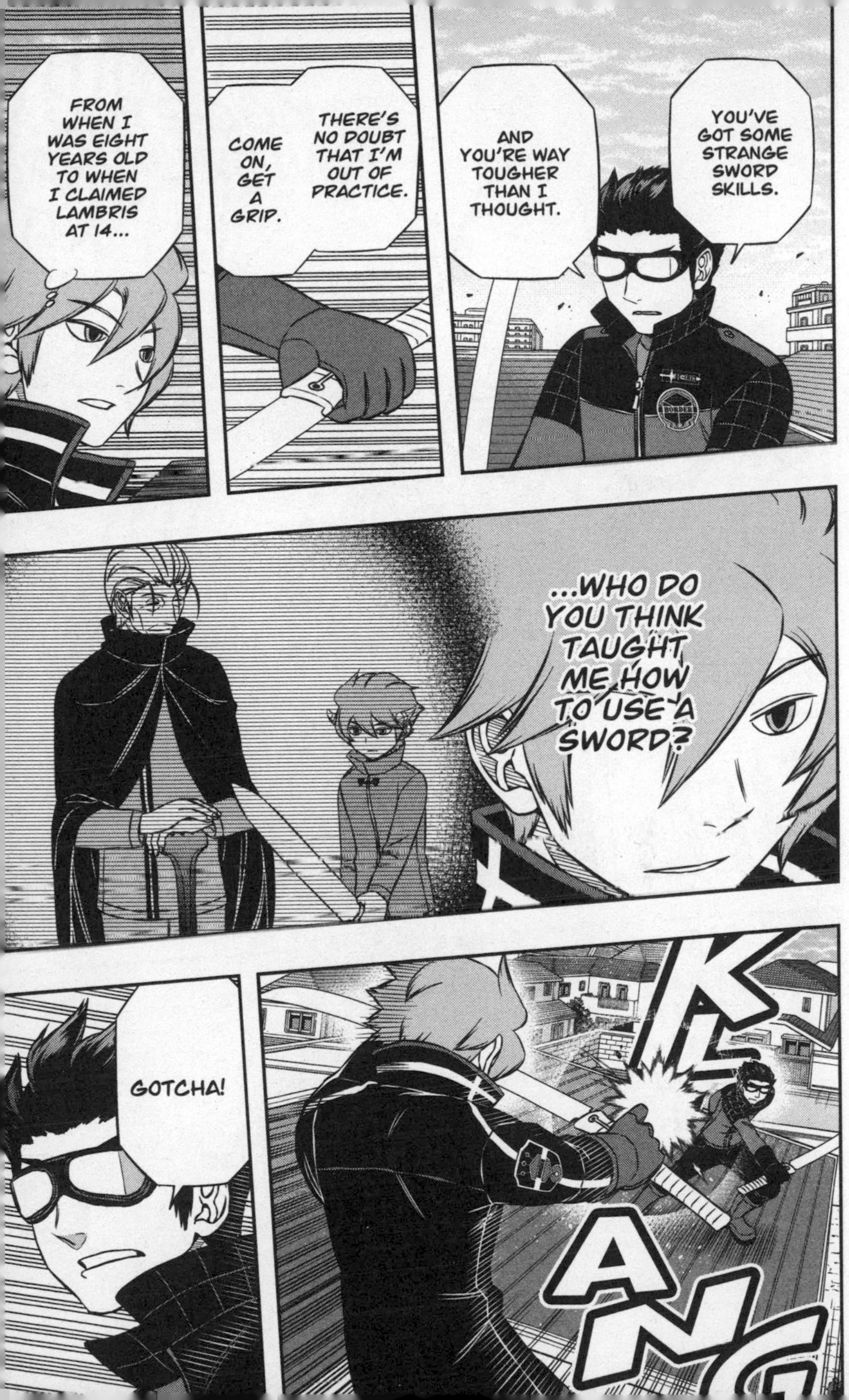

YOU'VE GOT SOME STRANGE SWORD SKILLS.
AND YOU'RE WAY TOUGHER THAN I THOUGHT.
THERE'S NO DOUBT THAT I'M OUT OF PRACTICE.
COME ON, GET A GRIP.
FROM WHEN I WAS EIGHT YEARS OLD TO WHEN I CLAIMED LAMBRIS AT 14...
...WHO DO YOU THINK TAUGHT ME HOW TO USE A SWORD?
KLANG
GOTCHA!

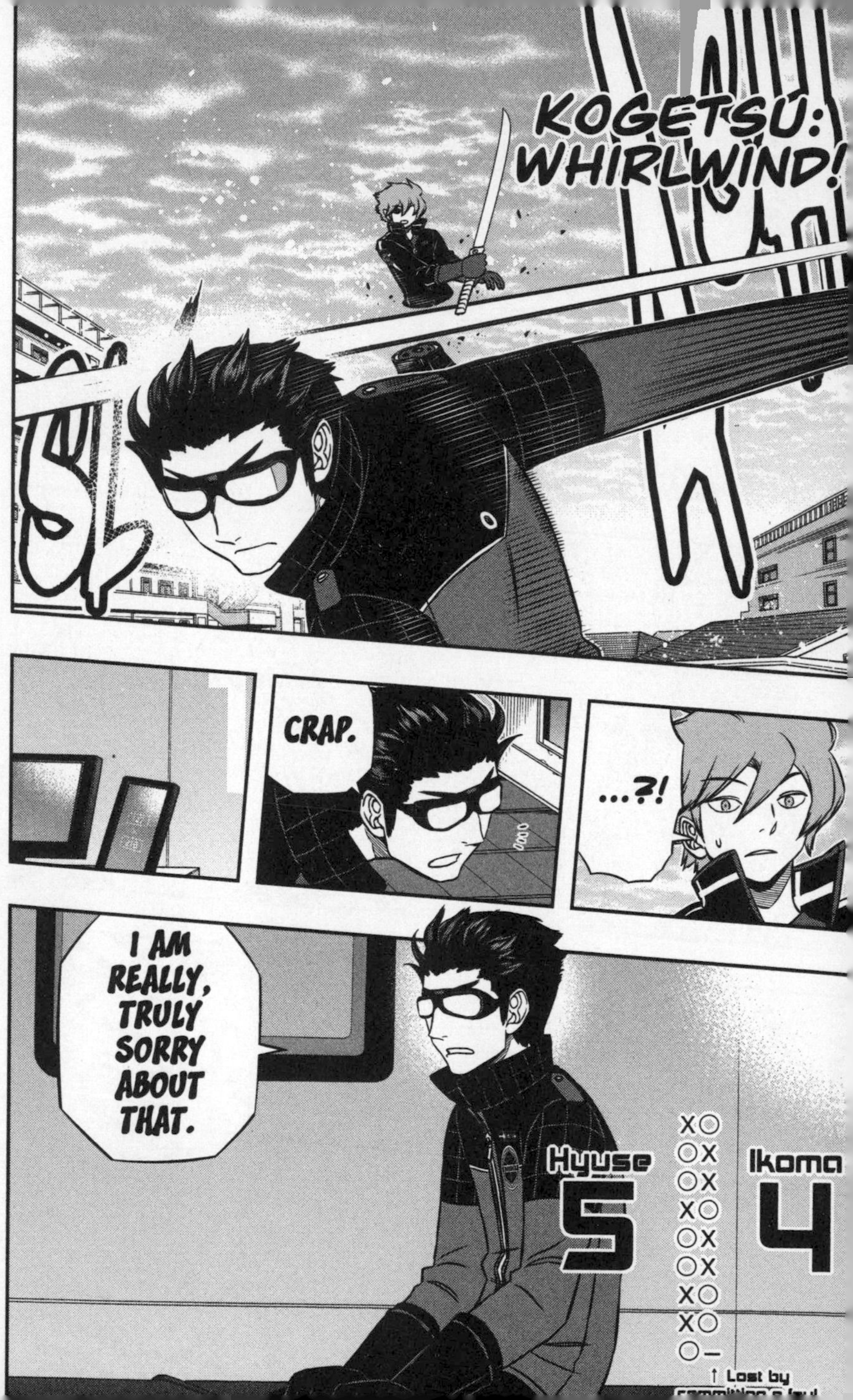
KOGETSU: WHIRLWIND!
...?!
CRAP.
I AM REALLY, TRULY SORRY ABOUT THAT.
Hyuse
5
Ikoma
4
X○
○X
○X
X○
○X
○X
X○
X○
○–
↑ Lost by

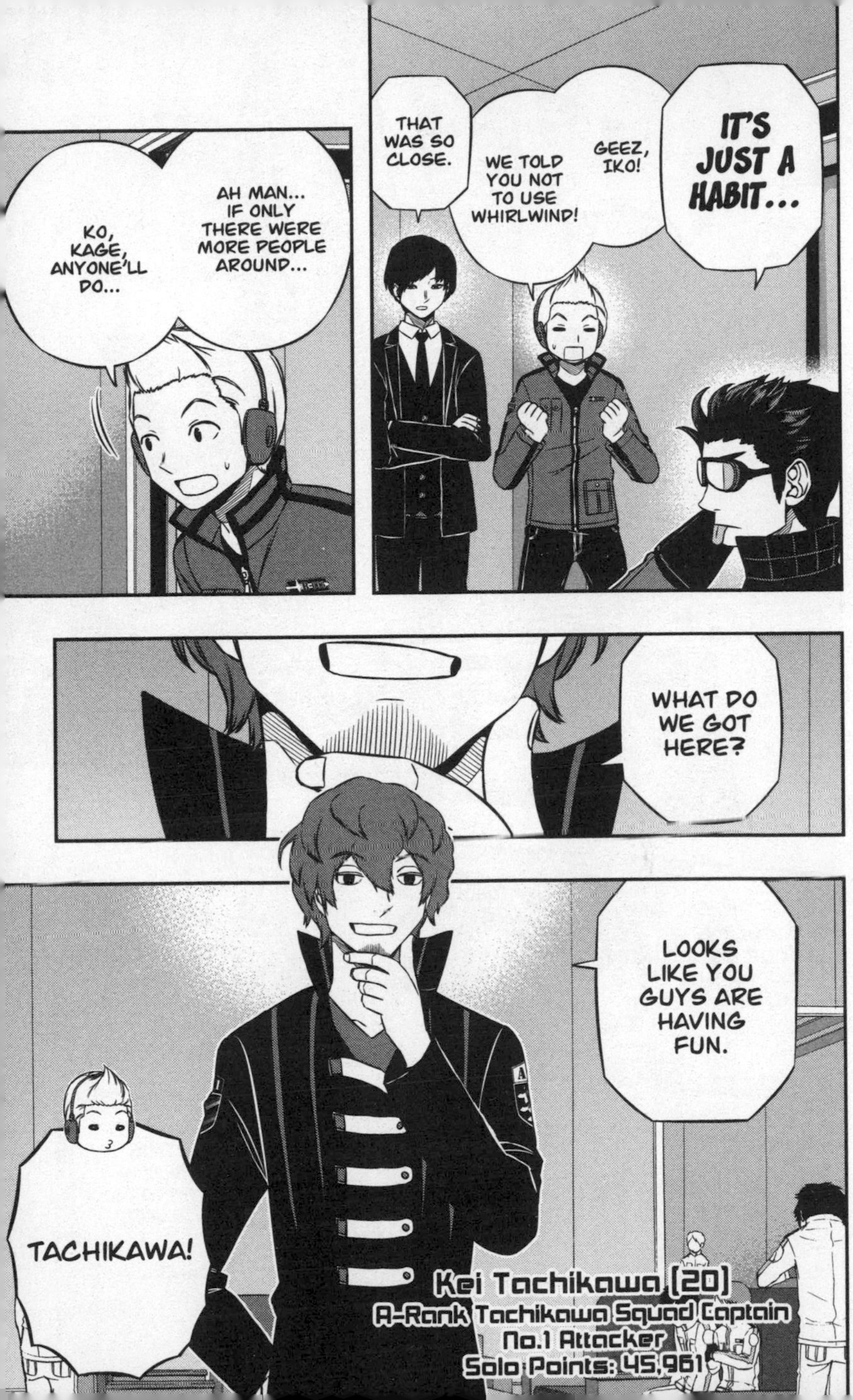

IT'S JUST A HABIT...
GEEZ, IKO!
WE TOLD YOU NOT TO USE WHIRLWIND!
THAT WAS SO CLOSE.
AH MAN... IF ONLY THERE WERE MORE PEOPLE AROUND...
KO, KAGE, ANYONE'LL DO...
WHAT DO WE GOT HERE?
LOOKS LIKE YOU GUYS ARE HAVING FUN.
TACHIKAWA!
Kei Tachikawa (20)
A-Rank Tachikawa Squad Captain
No.1 Attacker
Solo Points: 45,961

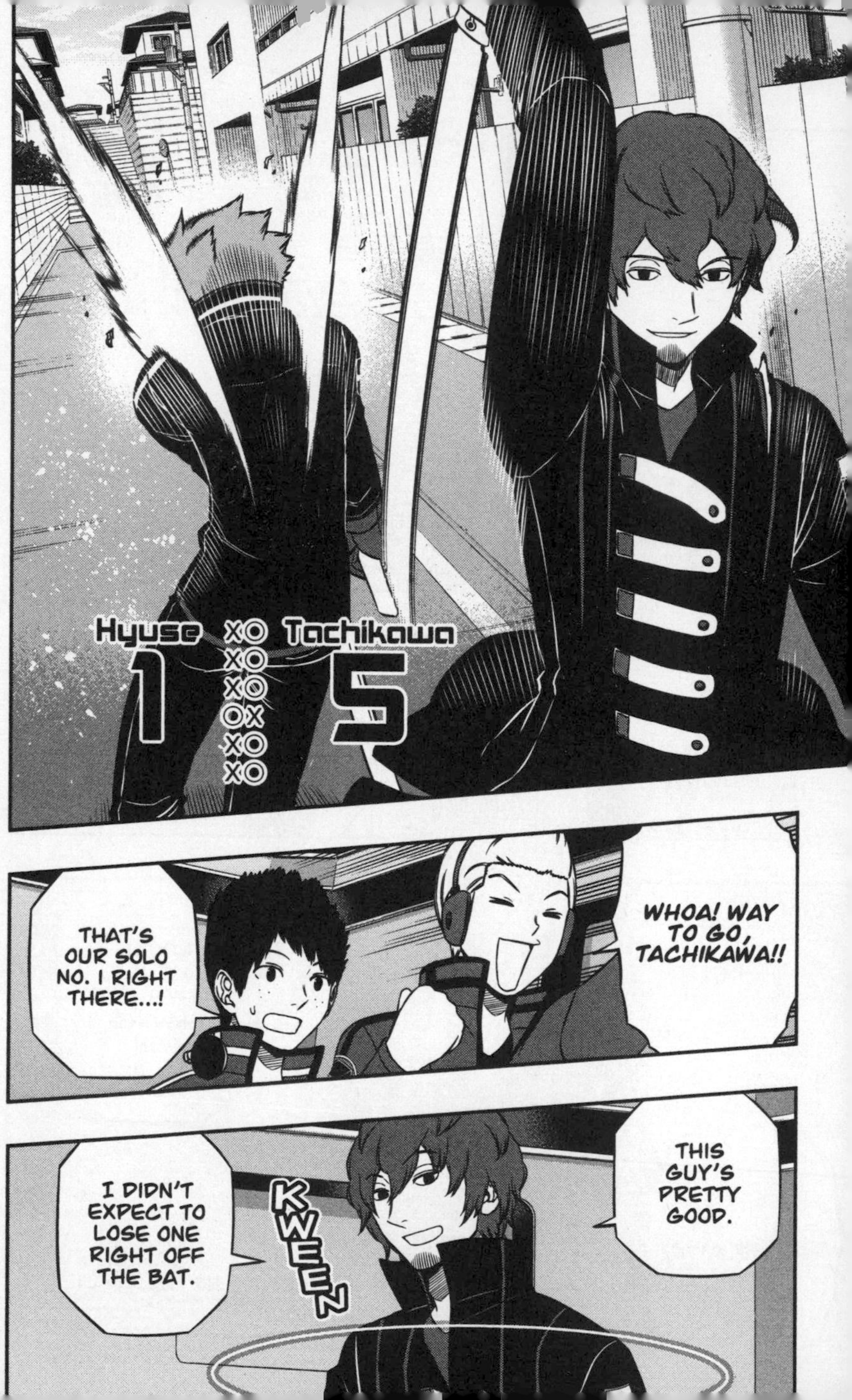
Hyuse
1
XO
XO
XO
OX
XO
XO
Tachikawa
5
WHOA! WAY TO GO, TACHIKAWA!!
THAT'S OUR SOLO NO. 1 RIGHT THERE...!
THIS GUY'S PRETTY GOOD.
KWEEN
I DIDN'T EXPECT TO LOSE ONE RIGHT OFF THE BAT.

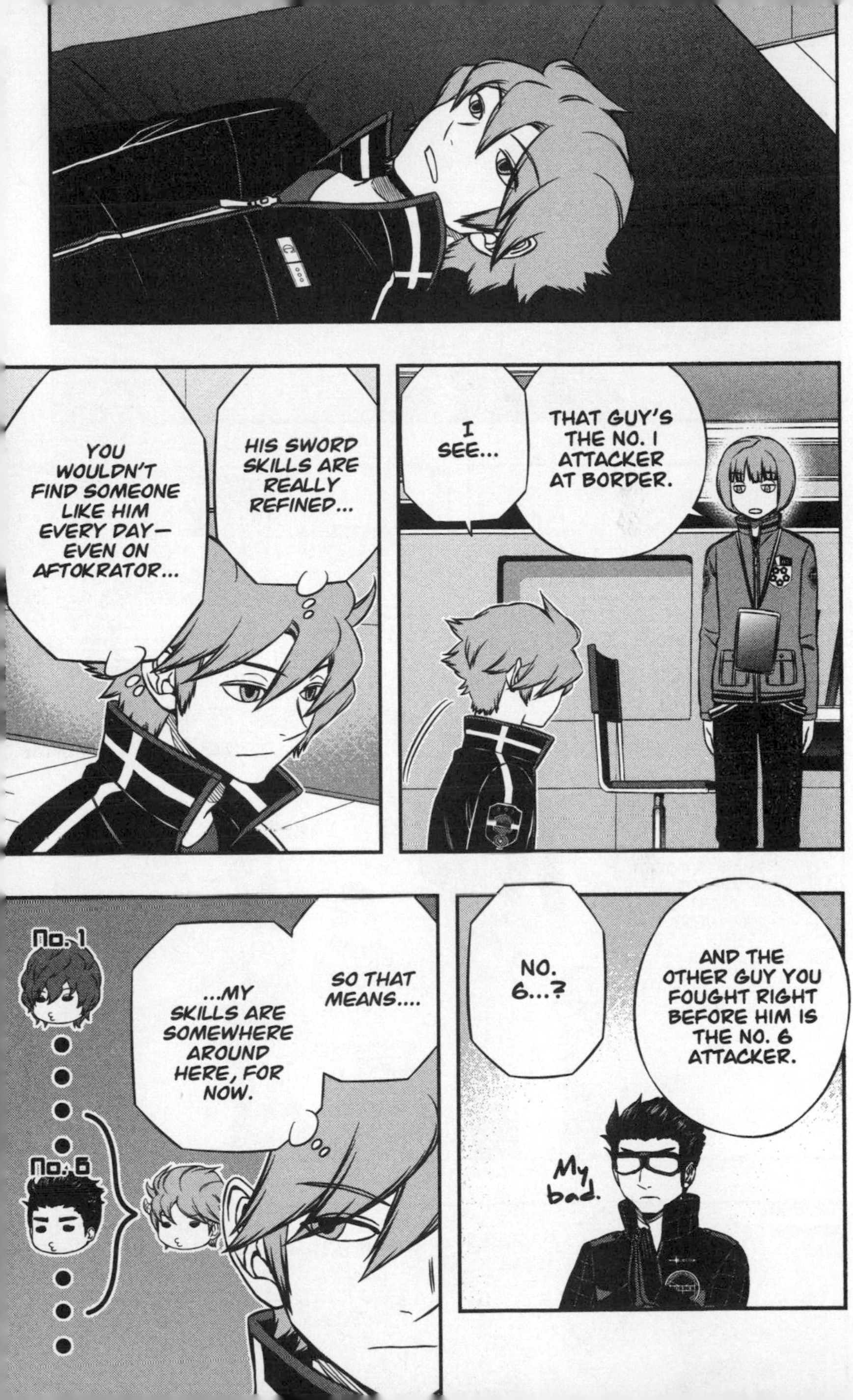
THAT GUY'S THE NO. 1 ATTACKER AT BORDER.
I SEE...
HIS SWORD SKILLS ARE REALLY REFINED...
YOU WOULDN'T FIND SOMEONE LIKE HIM EVERY DAY— EVEN ON AFTOKRATOR...
AND THE OTHER GUY YOU FOUGHT RIGHT BEFORE HIM IS THE NO. 6 ATTACKER.
NO. 6...?
My bad.
SO THAT MEANS....
...MY SKILLS ARE SOMEWHERE AROUND HERE, FOR NOW.
No. 1
No. 6

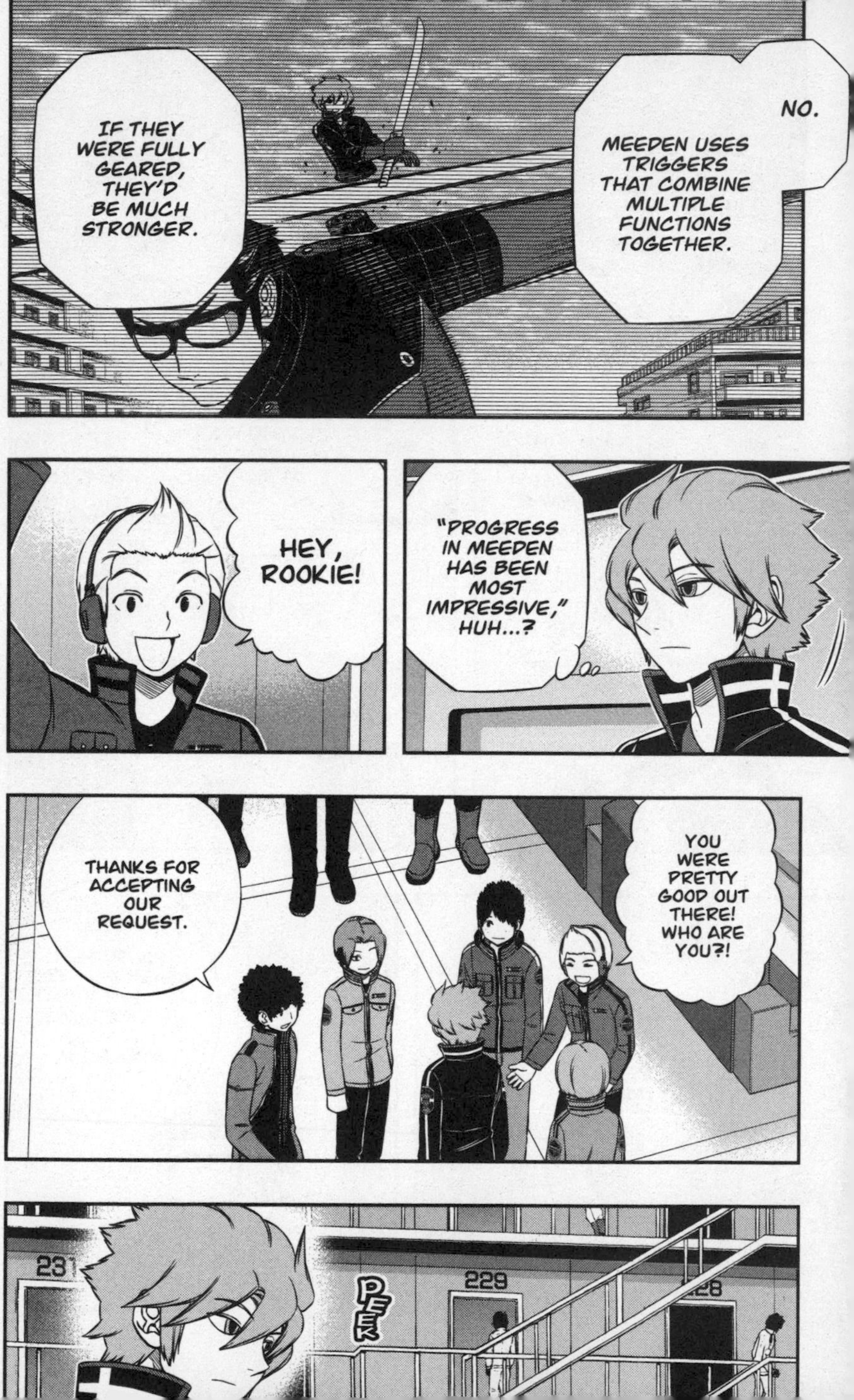
NO.
MEEDEN USES TRIGGERS THAT COMBINE MULTIPLE FUNCTIONS TOGETHER.
IF THEY WERE FULLY GEARED, THEY'D BE MUCH STRONGER.
"PROGRESS IN MEEDEN HAS BEEN MOST IMPRESSIVE," HUH...?
HEY, ROOKIE!
YOU WERE PRETTY GOOD OUT THERE! WHO ARE YOU?!
THANKS FOR ACCEPTING OUR REQUEST.
231
229
228
PEEK

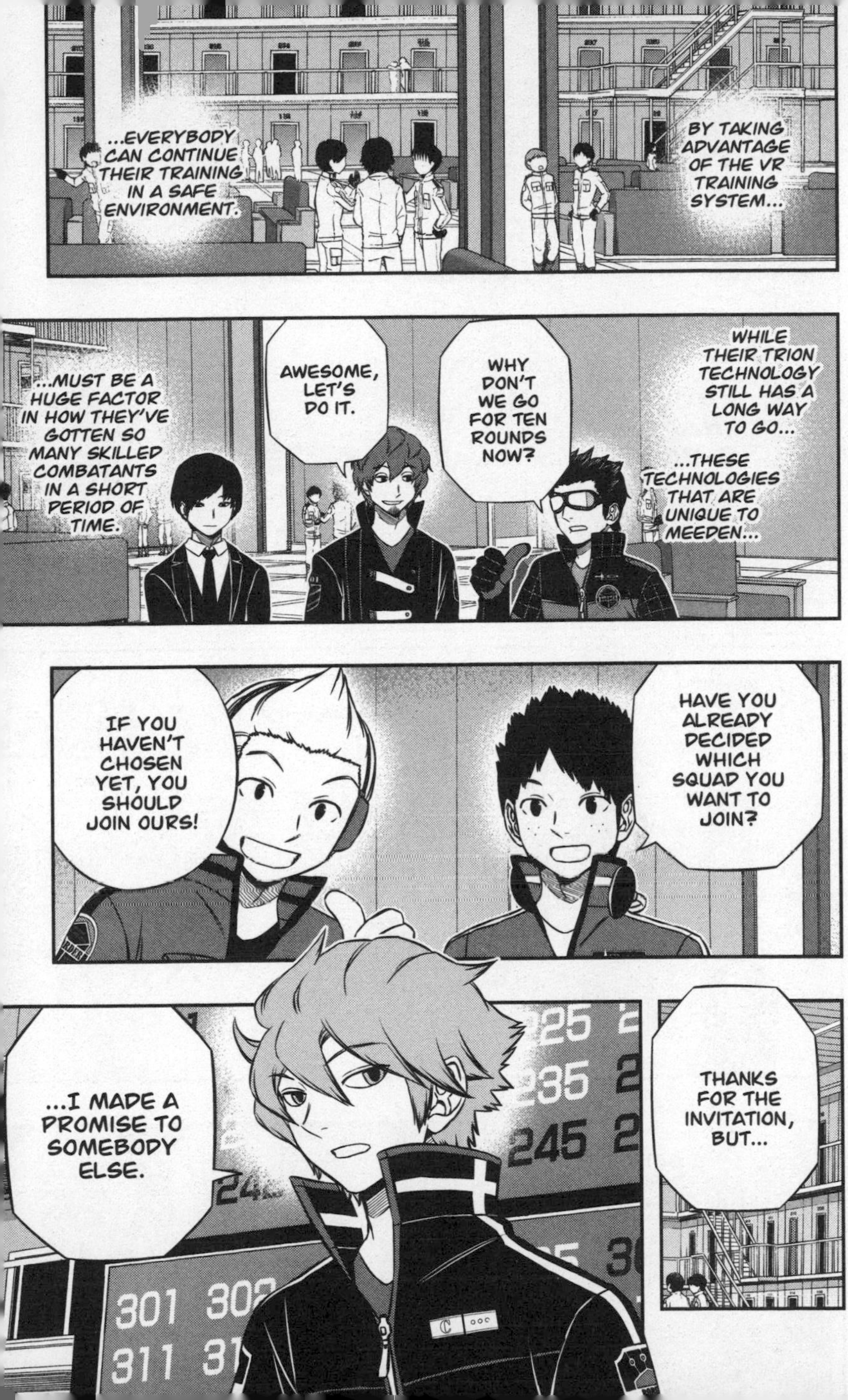
BY TAKING ADVANTAGE OF THE VR TRAINING SYSTEM...
...EVERYBODY CAN CONTINUE THEIR TRAINING IN A SAFE ENVIRONMENT.
WHILE THEIR TRION TECHNOLOGY STILL HAS A LONG WAY TO GO...
...THESE TECHNOLOGIES THAT ARE UNIQUE TO MEEDEN...
WHY DON'T WE GO FOR TEN ROUNDS NOW?
AWESOME, LET'S DO IT.
...MUST BE A HUGE FACTOR IN HOW THEY'VE GOTTEN SO MANY SKILLED COMBATANTS IN A SHORT PERIOD OF TIME.
HAVE YOU ALREADY DECIDED WHICH SQUAD YOU WANT TO JOIN?
IF YOU HAVEN'T CHOSEN YET, YOU SHOULD JOIN OURS!
THANKS FOR THE INVITATION, BUT...
...I MADE A PROMISE TO SOMEBODY ELSE.

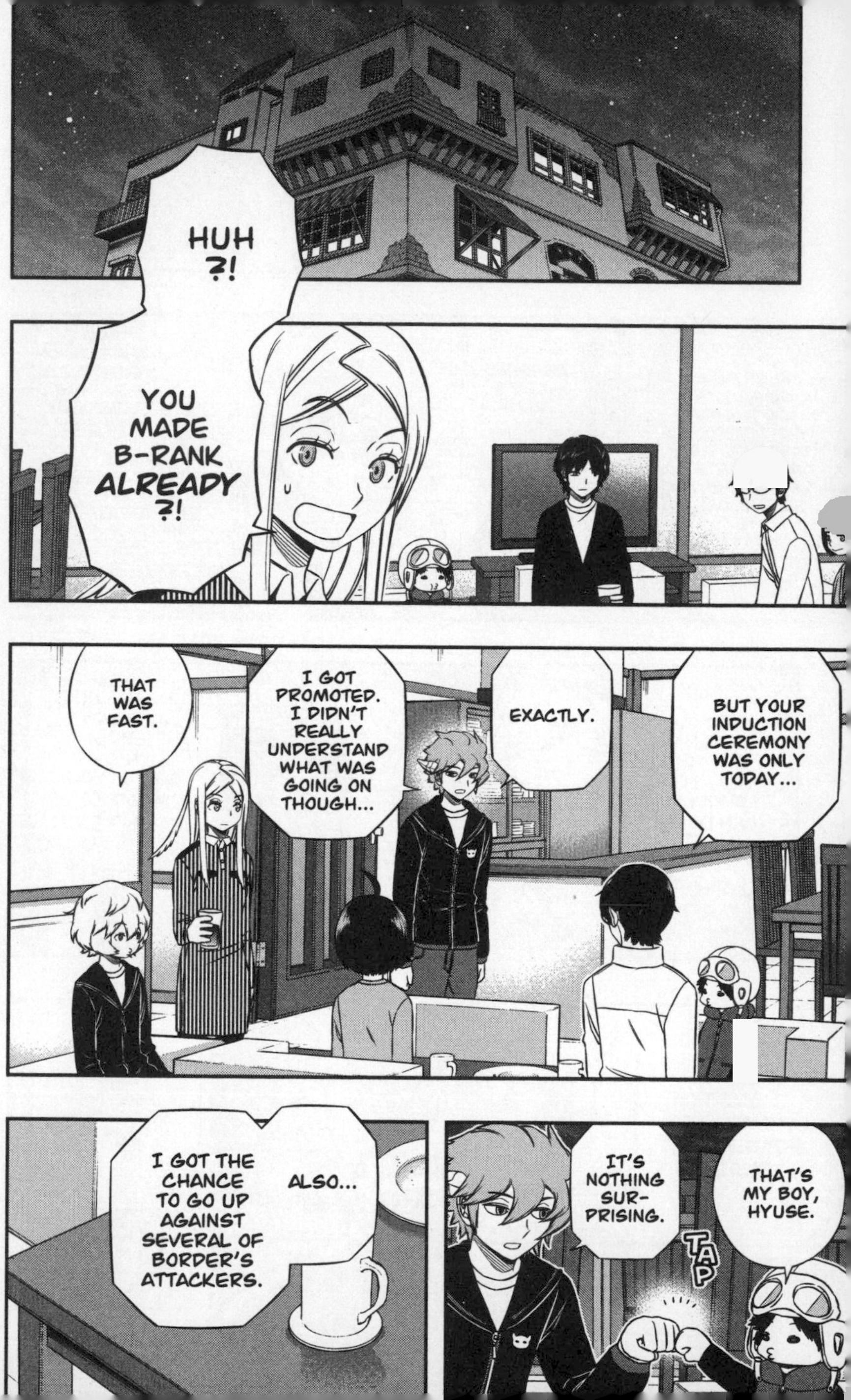
HUH ?!
YOU MADE B-RANK ALREADY ?!
BUT YOUR INDUCTION CEREMONY WAS ONLY TODAY...
EXACTLY.
I GOT PROMOTED. I DIDN'T REALLY UNDERSTAND WHAT WAS GOING ON THOUGH...
THAT WAS FAST.
THAT'S MY BOY, HYUSE.
TAP
IT'S NOTHING SUR-PRISING.
ALSO...
I GOT THE CHANCE TO GO UP AGAINST SEVERAL OF BORDER'S ATTACKERS.

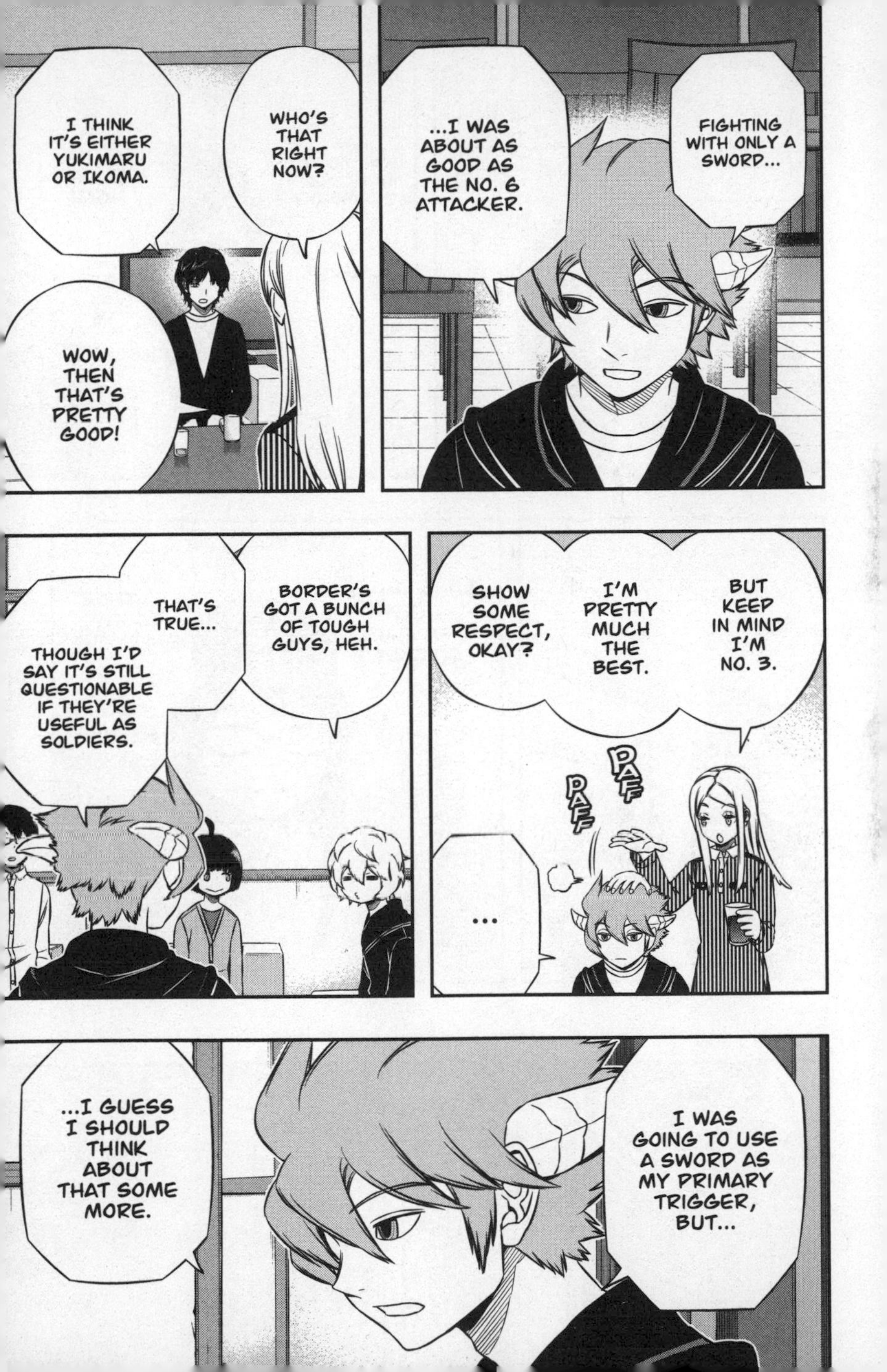
FIGHTING WITH ONLY A SWORD...
...I WAS ABOUT AS GOOD AS THE NO. 6 ATTACKER.
WHO'S THAT RIGHT NOW?
I THINK IT'S EITHER YUKIMARU OR IKOMA.
WOW, THEN THAT'S PRETTY GOOD!
BUT KEEP IN MIND I'M NO. 3.
I'M PRETTY MUCH THE BEST.
SHOW SOME RESPECT, OKAY?
PAFF
PAFF
...
BORDER'S GOT A BUNCH OF TOUGH GUYS, HEH.
THAT'S TRUE...
THOUGH I'D SAY IT'S STILL QUESTIONABLE IF THEY'RE USEFUL AS SOLDIERS.
I WAS GOING TO USE A SWORD AS MY PRIMARY TRIGGER, BUT...
...I GUESS I SHOULD THINK ABOUT THAT SOME MORE.

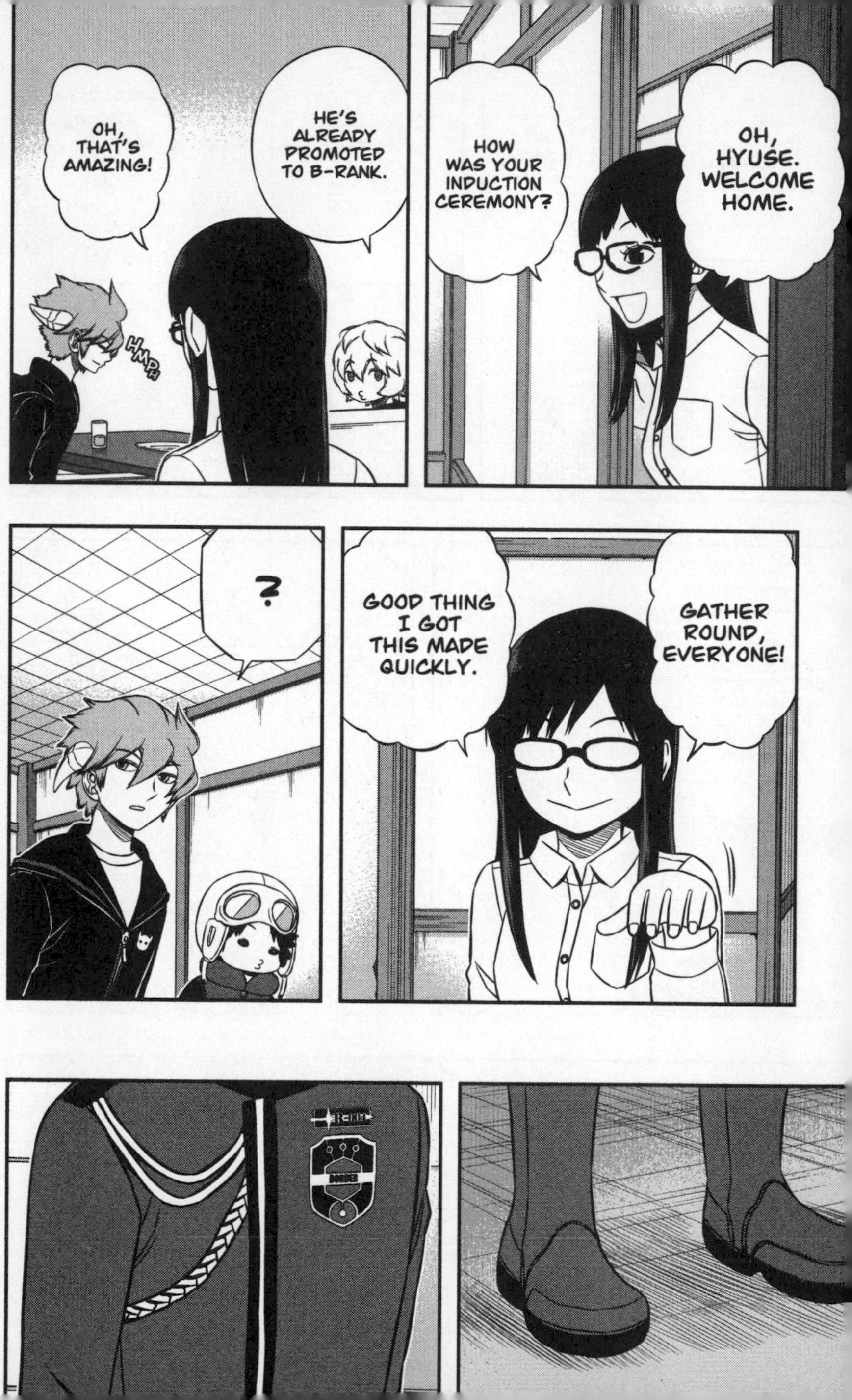
OH, HYUSE. WELCOME HOME.
HOW WAS YOUR INDUCTION CEREMONY?
HE'S ALREADY PROMOTED TO B-RANK.
OH, THAT'S AMAZING!
HMPH
GATHER ROUND, EVERYONE!
GOOD THING I GOT THIS MADE QUICKLY.
?

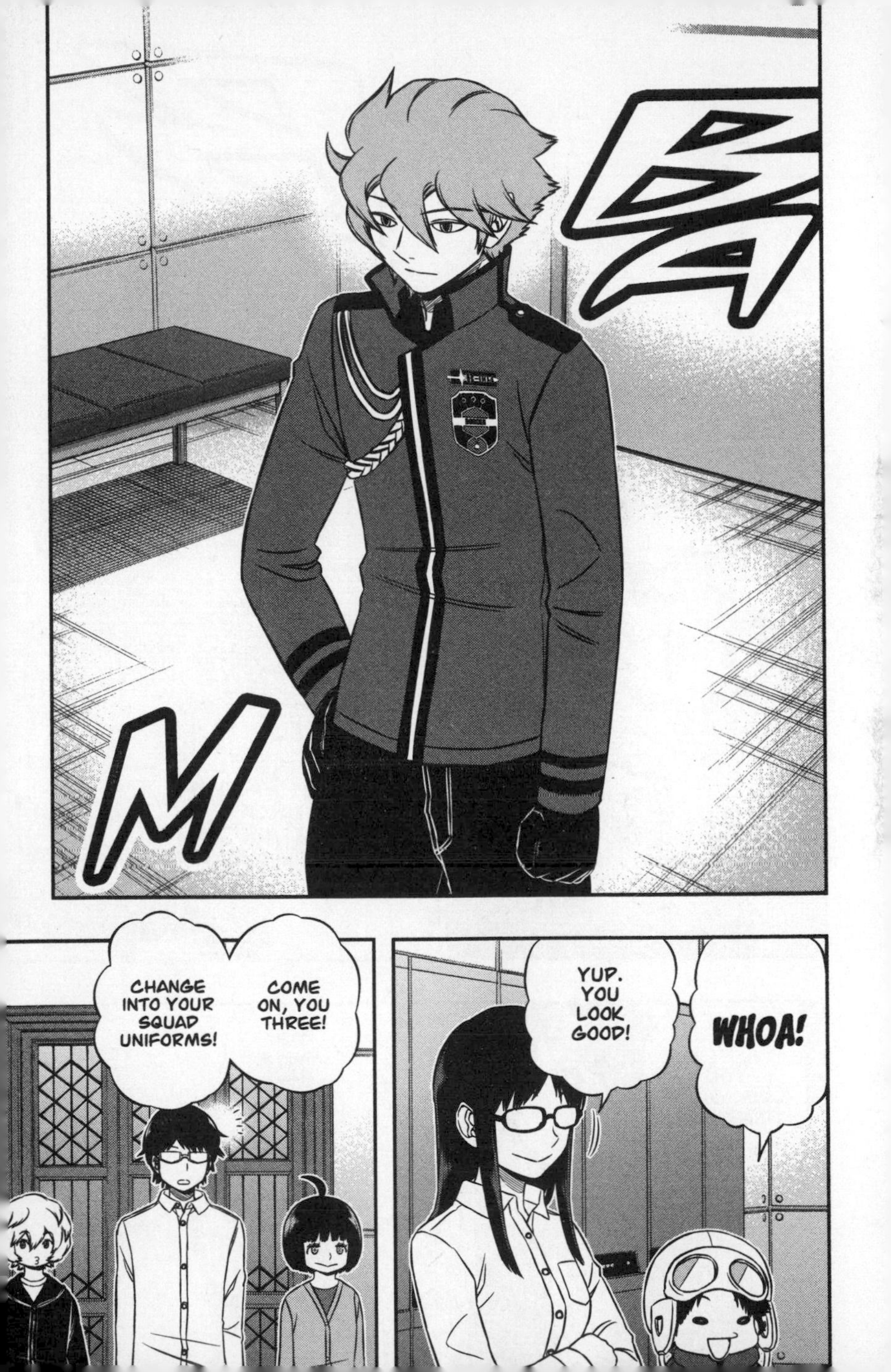
WHOA!
YUP. YOU LOOK GOOD!
COME ON, YOU THREE!
CHANGE INTO YOUR SQUAD UNIFORMS!

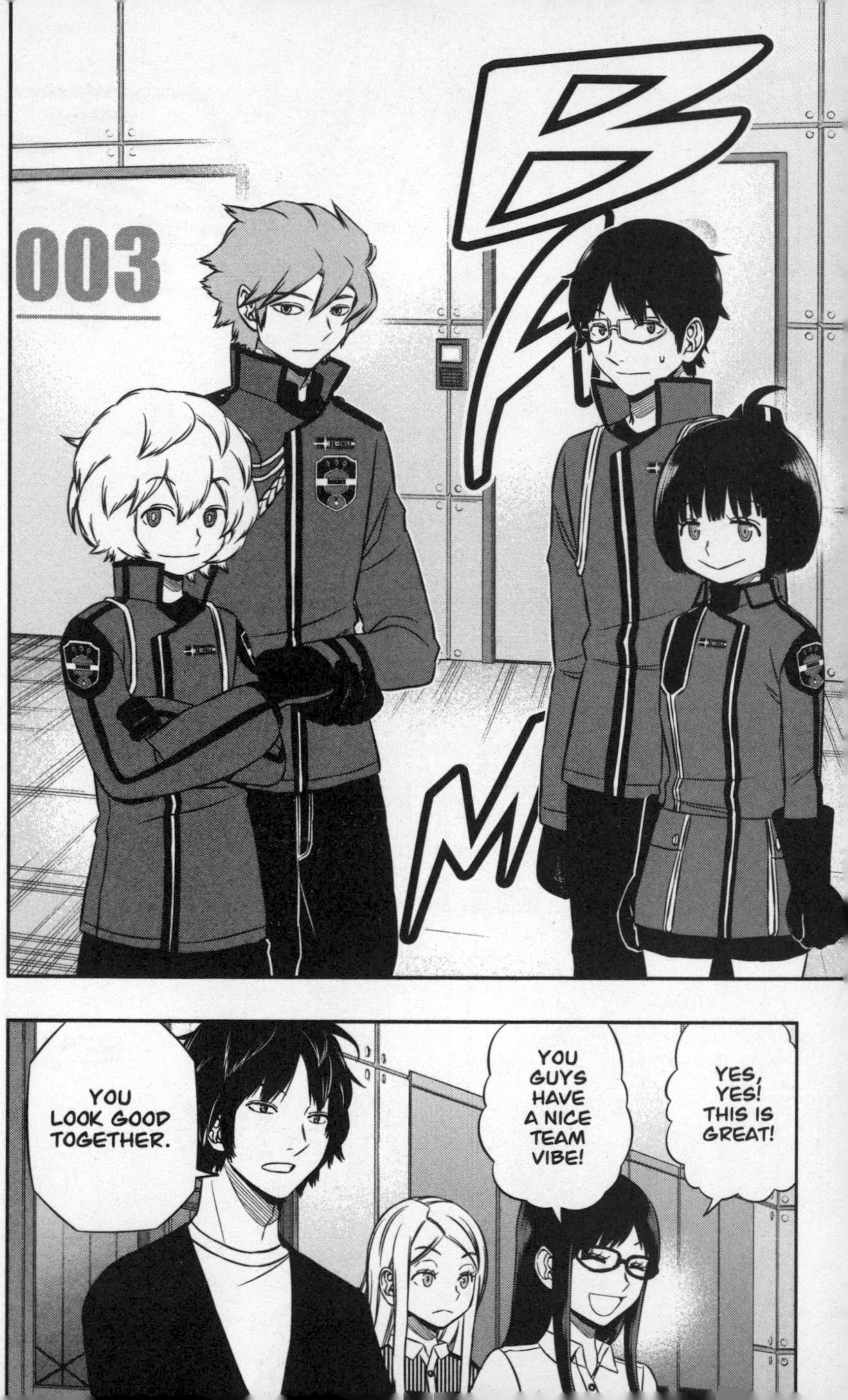
003
BAM
YES, YES! THIS IS GREAT!
YOU GUYS HAVE A NICE TEAM VIBE!
YOU LOOK GOOD TOGETHER.

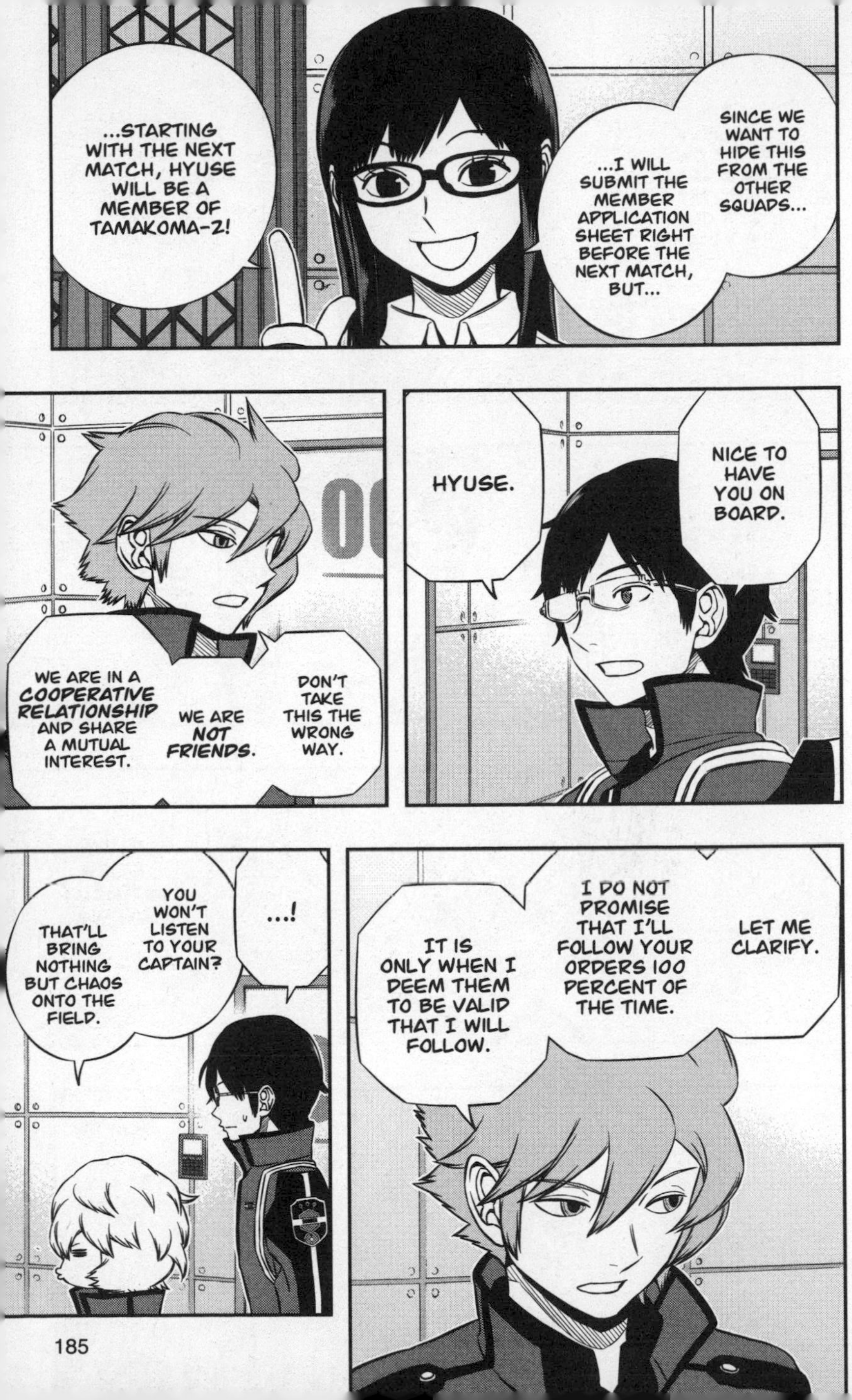
SINCE WE WANT TO HIDE THIS FROM THE OTHER SQUADS...
...I WILL SUBMIT THE MEMBER APPLICATION SHEET RIGHT BEFORE THE NEXT MATCH, BUT...
...STARTING WITH THE NEXT MATCH, HYUSE WILL BE A MEMBER OF TAMAKOMA-2!
NICE TO HAVE YOU ON BOARD.
HYUSE.
DON'T TAKE THIS THE WRONG WAY.
WE ARE *NOT FRIENDS*.
WE ARE IN A *COOPERATIVE RELATIONSHIP* AND SHARE A MUTUAL INTEREST.
LET ME CLARIFY.
I DO NOT PROMISE THAT I'LL FOLLOW YOUR ORDERS 100 PERCENT OF THE TIME.
IT IS ONLY WHEN I DEEM THEM TO BE VALID THAT I WILL FOLLOW.
...!
YOU WON'T LISTEN TO YOUR CAPTAIN?
THAT'LL BRING NOTHING BUT CHAOS ONTO THE FIELD.

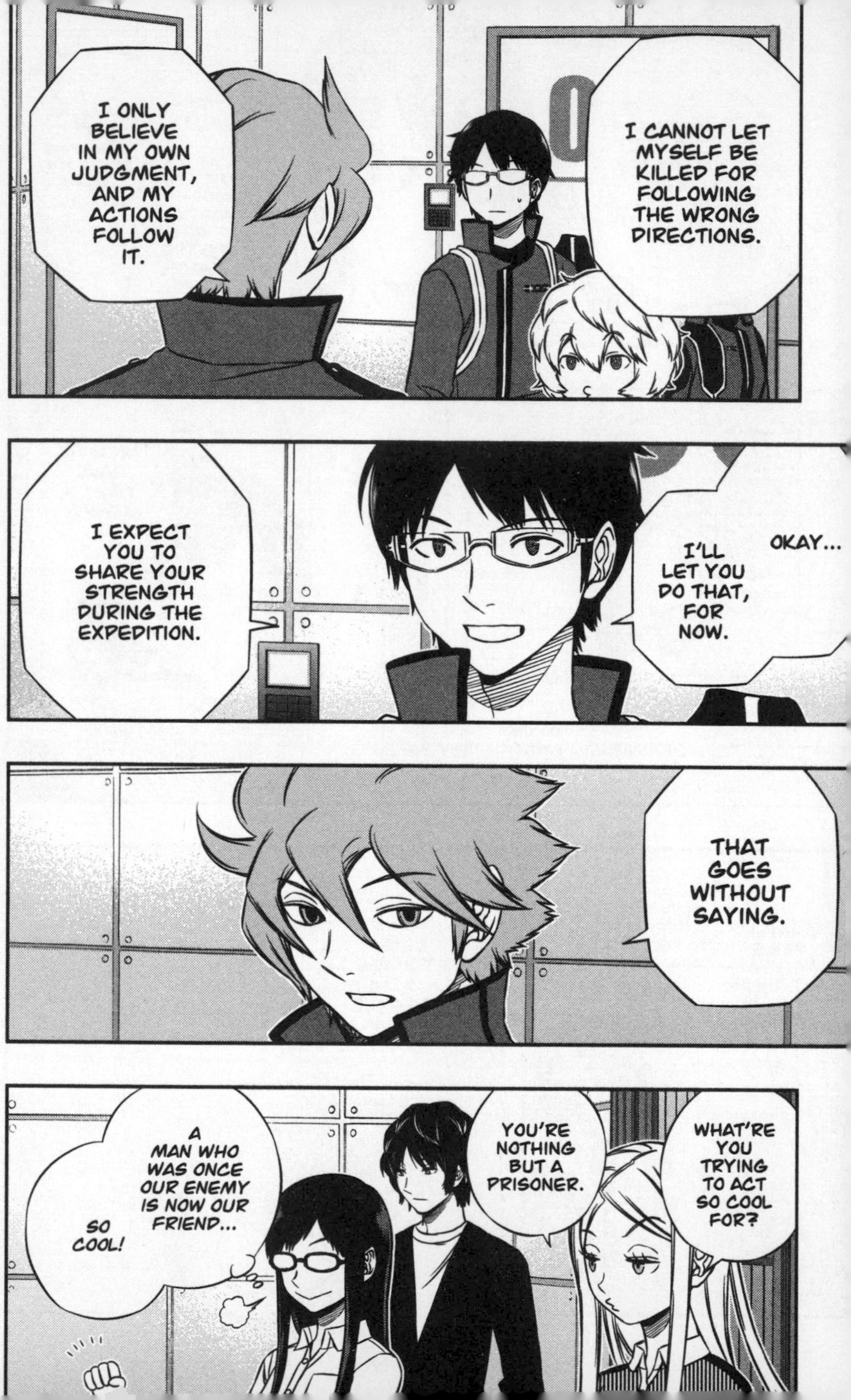
I CANNOT LET MYSELF BE KILLED FOR FOLLOWING THE WRONG DIRECTIONS.
I ONLY BELIEVE IN MY OWN JUDGMENT, AND MY ACTIONS FOLLOW IT.
OKAY...
I'LL LET YOU DO THAT, FOR NOW.
I EXPECT YOU TO SHARE YOUR STRENGTH DURING THE EXPEDITION.
THAT GOES WITHOUT SAYING.
WHAT'RE YOU TRYING TO ACT SO COOL FOR?
YOU'RE NOTHING BUT A PRISONER.
A MAN WHO WAS ONCE OUR ENEMY IS NOW OUR FRIEND...
SO COOL!

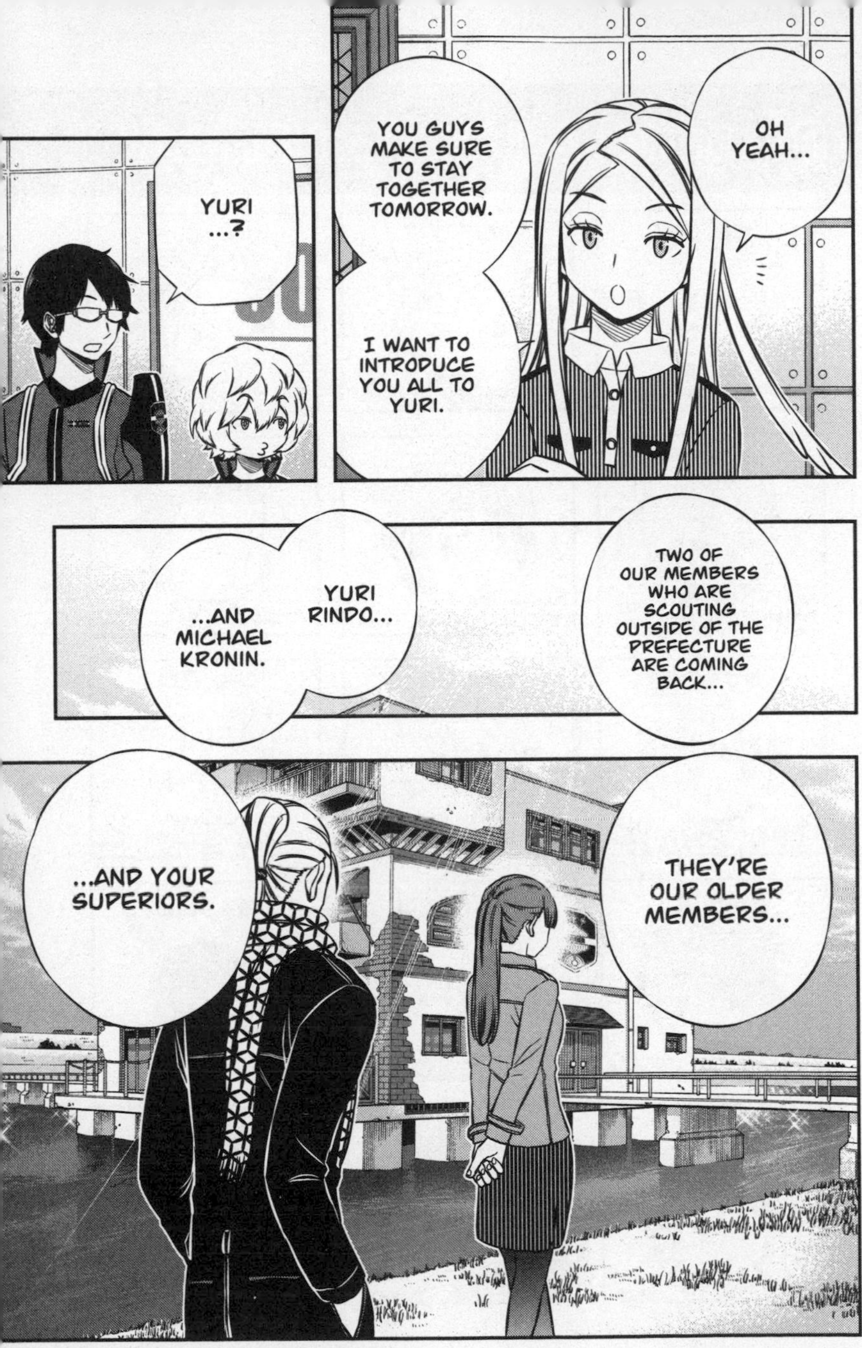
OH YEAH...
YOU GUYS MAKE SURE TO STAY TOGETHER TOMORROW.
I WANT TO INTRODUCE YOU ALL TO YURI.
YURI ...?
TWO OF OUR MEMBERS WHO ARE SCOUTING OUTSIDE OF THE PREFECTURE ARE COMING BACK...
YURI RINDO...
...AND MICHAEL KRONIN.
THEY'RE OUR OLDER MEMBERS...
...AND YOUR SUPERIORS.

To Be Continued In ***World Trigger*** 19!

Popularity Poll Results! (Under 17)

17th UP↑	18th UP↑	19th DOWN↓
Kotaro Suwa 264 votes	Ko Murakami 245 votes	Jun Arashiyama 236 votes

20th UP↑	21st DOWN↓	22nd DOWN↓
Shiro Kikuchihara 224 votes	Kyosuke Karasuma 217 votes	Yosuke Yoneya 200 votes

23rd DOWN↓	24th NEW!	25th UP↑
Mitsuru Tokieda 190 votes	Sumiharu Inukai 187 votes	Tatsuya Kuruma 186 votes

26th NEW!	27th NEW	28th DOWN↓
Masato Kageura 183 votes	Yuzuru Ema 181 votes	Replica 178 votes

29th UP↑	30th DOWN↓	31st DOWN↓
Tsukihiko Amo 177 votes	Masafumi Shinoda 174 votes	Ai Kitora 156 votes

Character Popularity Vote No.2 Results (Continuing)

32nd Shiori Usami
33rd Yotaro Rindo
34th Toru Narasaka
35th Shinnosuke Tsuji
36th Reiji Kizaki
37th Hikari Nire
38th (tie) Futaba Kuroe
38th (tie) Shun Midorikawa
40th Shohei Kodera
41st Fumika Teruya
42nd Isami Toma
43rd Daisuke Ashihara
44th Hatohara Mirai
45th (tie) Enedorad
45th (tie) Yuko Kumagai
47th Rinji Amatori
48th Yu Kunichika
49th Takeru Yuiga
50th Atsushi Hokari
51st Shinji Fuyushima
52nd Ryo Utagawa
53rd Haruka Ayatsuji
54th (tie) Viza
54th (tie) Nozomi Kako
56th (tie) Hiro Kitazoe
56th (tie) Yoshito Hanzaki
58th Kaho Mikami
59th Raizo Terashima
60th Taichi Betsuyaku
61st (tie) Hyrein
61st (tie) Mira
63rd (tie) Yuka Kon
63rd (tie) Hisato Sasamori
63rd (tie) Izuho Natsume
66th Katsumi Karasawa
67th (tie) Masamune Kido
67th (tie) Reghindetz
69th (tie) Enedora
69th (tie) Kuniharu Kakizaki
69th (tie) Raijin-maru
72nd (tie) Wataru Urushima
72nd (tie) Hana Somei
74th Makoto Chano
75th Akane Hiura
76th (tie) Madoka Ui
76th (tie) Rilienthal
76th (tie) Rokuro Wakamura
79th Daichi Tsutsumi
80th (tie) Sakurako Taketomi
80th (tie) Ren Tsukimi
82nd (tie) Sayoko Shiki
82nd (tie) Ranbanein
84th (tie) Motokichi Kinuta
84th (tie) Kyoko Sawamura
84th (tie) Kotaro Tomoe
87th (tie) Rin Kagami
87th (tie) Kasumi Mikumo
89th Yomi
(The rest are omitted...)

I'd like to express my gratitude to all of the readers who voted in the popularity poll.

The character count almost doubled since the first poll. How was this one?

The last popularity vote had a system that allowed for a maximum of three characters per letter. Other ongoing series have a similar system, but I heard that the staff nearly broke down due to the number of votes we received. That's why this time we made a new rule stating one character per letter.

Nevertheless, we received 14,433 letters in total and I wonder if it really made our staff's job any easier.

Also, it seems like some readers cast votes by purchasing multiple *JUMP* magazines and volumes that included the survey. I wonder if everyone's wallets are doing okay...

We also counted the votes by "single votes counting" method that omits some of the excessive multiple votes. In this result, Osamu got first, Yuma got second, Jin got third, Kazama got fourth, Izumi got fifth, Konami got sixth, Miwa got seventh, Arafune got eighth, Chika got ninth, and Ninomiya got tenth....

What's interesting is that Tetsuji Arafune came in eighth for both the multiple vote counts and the single counting system. I wonder how this guy, whose relationship to the main characters is distant at best, got to be so popular?

Did you notice he's even more popular than Hyuse and Tachikawa?

Now that I think about it, he also placed high in the Valentine's Day poll, now that I remember...

Maybe a lot of people were attracted to his macho plan.

Maybe there is something that makes people want to support characters whose ideologies are clear enough and trying to make the best "now" for the sake of future.

Thank you very much for such a huge number of votes!

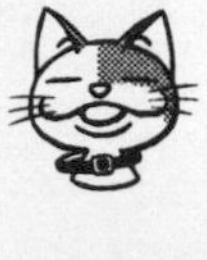

WORLD TRIGGER

Bonus Character Pages

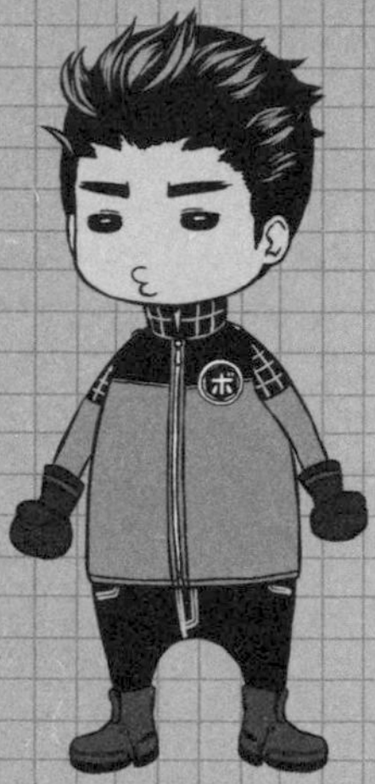

IKO

Eggplant Curry Straight from Naniwa

It says Naniwa, but he's actually from Kyoto. He learned *iaido* from his grandfather and somehow became a master of doing victory poses while looking at the camera. His expression doesn't change often but he's quite a sensationalist who is thrilled by all sorts of random things. He recently started playing guitar to get popular with girls but has no idea where or when he should show off his skills. Because of this, he's started to wonder if he should switch his hobby to cooking.

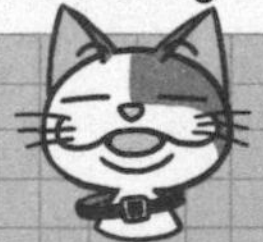

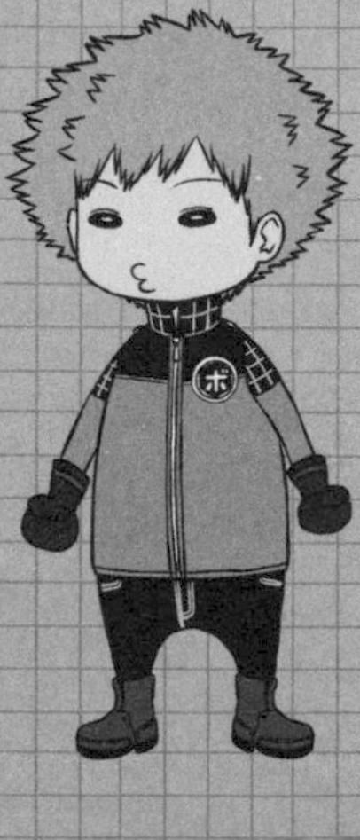

MIZUKAMI

Liar Broccoli

A yellow vegetable and the best shogi player at Border, and was on track to become a professional shogi player until middle school. He can perform a high-level but plain technique where he shouts out an attack name different from the one he's actually doing. But he's said that this pretty much means nothing to anyone outside of Border. His hobby is rakugo, and he's even memorized 20 to 30 classics. He may go to an average school, but he's got excellent grades. He's from Osaka.

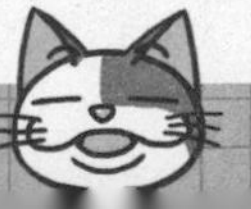